The Invention of Party Politics

STUDIES IN LEGAL HISTORY

Published by the University
of North Carolina Press in
association with the American
Society for Legal History

Thomas A. Green and
Hendrik Hartog, editors

GERALD LEONARD

The Invention of Party Politics

Federalism, Popular Sovereignty,
and Constitutional Development
in Jacksonian Illinois

The
University
of North
Carolina
Press

Chapel Hill
and London

Designed by April Leidig-Higgins
Set in Sabon by Copperline Book Services, Inc.

The paper in this book meets the guidelines for
permanence and durability of the Committee on
Production Guidelines for Book Longevity of the
Council on Library Resources.

Some material in this book has been reprinted with
permission in revised form from "Party as a Political Safeguard of Federalism: Martin Van Buren and
the Constitutional Theory of Party Politics," *Rutgers Law Review* 54, no. 1 (2001), and "The Ironies
of Partyism and Antipartyism: Origins of Partisan
Political Culture in Jacksonian Illinois," *Illinois Historical Journal* 87, no. 1 (1994).

Library of Congress Cataloging-in-Publication Data
Leonard, Gerald, 1960–
The invention of party politics: federalism, popular
sovereignty, and constitutional development in Jacksonian Illinois / Gerald Leonard.
p. cm.—(Studies in legal history)
Includes bibliographical references and index.
ISBN 0-8078-2744-4 (cloth: alk. paper)
1. Political parties—Illinois—History—19th century. 2. Illinois—Politics and government—19th
century. I. Title. II. Series.
JK2295.I42 L46 2002   324.2773'09'034—dc21
2002006439

06 05 04 03 02   5 4 3 2 1

For Alissa

CONTENTS

ACKNOWLEDGMENTS

It is a happy tradition that allows me to publish along with this book my heartfelt thanks to a number of very important people. From my undergraduate days, I remain indebted to my co–history major Jonathan Levy as well as to a terrific trio of professors—Gary Kornblith, Heather Hogan, and the late Geoffrey Blodgett—who together implanted a passion for history that seems to be permanent.

The list of fellow graduate students who made my years at the University of Michigan a joy is too long to try to include here, but I certainly have to mention a few. John Quist and Ben Brown provided me with desperately needed intellectual community in my first semester of graduate school and for years thereafter. Ben and his generous, high-powered wife, Louise Rankin, also provided me with hospitality (and more) during several research trips to Illinois. And Paul Bernard, while never caring especially for Jacksonian America, has been an intellectual and personal fellow traveler with me for more than fifteen years now.

In the history department at Michigan, Lorna Alstetter, Connie Hamlin, Dorothy Marschke, and Janet Rose were ever helpful and kind to us needy and poverty-stricken graduate students. John Shy and Maris Vinovskis each did me important kindnesses that they probably do not remember but that were of vital importance to me. As for people who have had something to do with the substance of the work, directly or indirectly, it is a pleasure to thank Ron Formisano, Tom Green, Dirk Hartog, Chuck McCurdy, Terry McDonald, Mike Morrison, Bill Nelson, Amy Olson, Rick Pildes, David Seipp, Jim Turner, Sean Wilentz, and some other people who I'm sure I'm forgetting. But, as a historian, I owe by far my greatest thanks to Mills Thornton. Mills has been an intellectual inspiration for me from my first week of graduate school, and it gives me the willies to think of learning to be a historian without his personal and professional example.

In becoming a book, my one-time dissertation was transformed in rather important ways by my entrance into the world of legal scholarship, first at the University of Michigan Law School and now on the faculty at Boston University School of Law. I am deeply indebted to the faculties of both schools for providing the intellectual atmosphere in which I came more fully to recognize the legal and constitutional dimensions of my story.

And, finally, I thank the people who made the book worth writing. The list starts with my mother, Nancy Leonard, and my father, Ed Leonard; my brothers and sisters, Joe, Weeze, Eddie, Mary, Tom; and my wife's parents, Judith and Sol Elkin (whose nearly constant subsidies and devotion to family made it possible to have my dissertation and my family grow at the same time). My "pride and joy," who have revealed to me what that phrase means, are my daughters, Sarah, Talia, and Abigail, each a wonder to me in her own magnificent way. And, finally, Alissa. I have read a lot of acknowledgments that practically say the author's spouse walks on water, but Alissa is better than any of those people. After all, none of them made all my work worth doing; only Alissa did.

The Invention of Party Politics

This is a book about political parties and the American Constitution between the founding of the United States and the Second Party System of the 1840s and 1850s. In those years, and especially between 1820 and 1840, the idea and fact of party organization gained a preeminent place in the American constitutional order, even though the Constitution itself had been designed as a "Constitution against parties."[1] In all the massive literature on American political history in that period, however, there was little indication of what I have since come to understand: that the early history of party is best understood within the history of the Constitution, just as the history of the Constitution is best understood within the history of party development.

In the nineteenth century, the mass political party dominated American politics and, in fact, came to be the defining institution of modern "democracy," a status it still enjoys (perhaps in tandem with the market economy). Yet thousands of years of prior human history had yielded practically no efforts to justify party organization or institutionalized opposition. Virtually every political thinker before the nineteenth century condemned "formed opposition" as destructive of the public good and fatal to public peace. The freedom of individuals to express dissent might sometimes be celebrated, but the organization of a political club in continuing opposition to the policies of the government—perhaps even conceiving of itself as a potential replacement for those currently in power—smacked more of conspiracy and treason than of healthy political competition. In the early nineteenth century, however, all that changed. Americans embraced mass party organization, and politics and governance were altered forever. Eventually, this embrace of party became a commitment to a "party system"—an enduring competition between democratic parties within a basic constitutional consensus, expecting to exchange power and office in indefinitely long cycles[2]—as the sine qua non of democracy in America and much of the world.

This revolution in political structure lies at the foundation of modernity, but it was not America's present two-party system that I wanted to understand through this study. I thought I already knew what I cared to know about that. The necessity of a competitive system of mass parties in a democracy seemed obvious to me, as it did to the many political scientists who had studied the modern system. And the basic character of the major parties as broad coalitions rather than narrowly ideological formations seemed equally natural in a majoritarian system. What sparked my interest, then, was the question of how early Americans could ever have thought otherwise. What assumptions or values could have led them to think that institutionalized party competition might be avoidable in—even antithetical to—free government? Once I had begun to understand this alien worldview, moreover, I wondered how these early Americans had managed to blaze the trail from that strange world of the Founding, in which antipartyism was the unquestioned premise of all political thought, to the world of the 1840s in which party identification had become the organizing principle of democracy.

My investigation of this question soon indicated the prime importance of the Constitution and especially the question of federalism or states' rights: what powers exactly had the Constitution assigned to the new national government and what powers or rights had it reserved to the states and their people? The centrality of the Constitution to the thinking of the "partyists," as I will call the first advocates of party, had not been obvious to me at the outset. Like most Americans, I reflexively understood constitutional history as the history of constitutional litigation in the courts, much as John Marshall, the great chief justice, seems to have intended. The history of parties, on the other hand, seemed a matter of political history rather than the history of constitutional law. Neither the Founders nor many of their immediate heirs, however, understood the Constitution as modern Americans do. For the Founders, the Constitution was a blueprint of a government; they did not expect it to be a subject of litigation, except incidentally. Constitutional law, then, especially the all-important law of federalism, would lie much more in "politics," in the practice of legislatures and executives, in the daily initiatives of government, than in the relatively rare and reactive constitutional holdings of the courts. And this assumption was shared by those who otherwise differed radically on the meaning of the Constitution. Thus for the nationalist Alexander Hamilton, the limits of federalism would be defined more through the national government's brute exercise of specific powers—to charter a national bank, for example—than through any particular judicial rulings. Meanwhile, at the opposite end of the constitutional spectrum, localists expected states' rights to be vindicated by state legislatures' assertions of power—for example, the claimed power to tax the national bank—rather than through judicial review of federal statutes. Those who expected the Constitution to live in the "political" branches of government more than in the judiciary, moreover, were well vindicated in subsequent years, even if, committed to the doctrine of antipartyism, they failed to anticipate that political control of the Constitution would come to mean party control of the Constitution.

The history of the Constitution, then, which had once seemed to me synonymous with the history of judicial politics, now seemed largely the history of electoral politics. And the importance of the Constitution was not simply that it provided a starting point for the American experiment in electoral democracy, nor even that its majoritarian electoral structure encouraged presidential candidates to organize grand coalitions.[3] Rather, fundamental as these aspects were, it was the problem of federalism that preoccupied those who actually built the bridge from antipartyism to partyism. And intimately related to the meaning of federalism was the meaning of the Constitution's principle of popular sovereignty. Was this principle to reflect a merely nominal sovereignty in the people, with real power residing in the distant institutions of the national government? Or was it to reflect a genuine retention of effective power in the people, acting in their local communities? The nation's break from England had ultimately represented both a rejection of centralized, distant, imperial government—thus the importance of states' rights in the new order—and a removal of sovereignty from an elitist Parliament to the people themselves. It was only in defense of this localist, democratic model of the Constitution that a justification for party organization—as an organ of the Constitution itself—began to crystallize. It may or may not have been the case that the development of a party system was in some sense inevitable, but I discovered that those who created the first mass parties did so not by invoking modern explanations of the system's inevitability but by trying to figure out how to implement the Constitution's promise of democracy through federalism—even as that Constitution ostensibly rejected party.

The constitutional history offered here, then, is not primarily a history of constitutional litigation or judicial politics—the history that John Marshall and Joseph Story sought to give us and that Supreme Court interventions from *McCulloch v. Maryland* to *Dred Scott* to *Bush v. Gore* have made out as *the* history of the Constitution. Rather, it is a history of an alternative vision of constitutional development, rooted in the Framers' own understanding of the Constitution as a charter of governance rather than a subject of adjudication. The history of the legitimation of the political party turns out to be a history of the invention of party control of the Constitution (in uneasy negotiation with the courts). What once appeared obviously to be a problem of political history—how did antiparty Americans invent the mass political party?—ultimately revealed itself as hardly political history at all, but constitutional history played out in election campaigns. The partyists did not self-consciously design the mass political party as a way of building electoral coalitions; instead, they gradually found it implied in their ballot-box defense of a democratic, states'-rights Constitution against that Constitution's supposedly aristocratic enemies.

The historiography of party as an element of the American constitutional order has been surprisingly slight. Fifty years ago, in his pioneering "prospectus" for an American legal history as a history of governance,[4] James Willard Hurst wondered at the failure of the Framers of the Constitution to specify the place of parties in American governance. They had, of course, specified the places of most other governmental institutions: a national legislature, a national executive, and a federal judiciary. They had further divided lawmaking authority between the national government and republican state governments. To Hurst, however, it seemed obvious that political parties were lawmaking institutions as central as any of those provided for in the Constitution: "For most of the nineteenth century, the parties furnished legislative direction. They did this mainly outside the regular legislative machinery, through the inner circle of party leaders, the boss, and the caucus." They also controlled the legislatures through control of the legislature's own committee structure and other "machinery." And these facts highlighted for Hurst "one of the most puzzling features of our constitutional history"—that "no constitutional provision was made to fit the party into the structure of government."[5]

In observing the dominance of the political parties across the last two-thirds of the nineteenth century, Hurst has been joined by such scholars as the political scientist Stephen Skowronek, who has famously characterized that constitutional system as a "state of courts and parties." Skowronek's phrase suggests an underdeveloped American state, in which legislatures and executives were controlled by party organizations, with courts alone retaining significant lawmaking authority independent of party organization.[6] In narrating the history of party conflict, moreover, a multitude of political historians has detailed the mass political parties' domination of American governance between the 1830s and the 1890s.[7] In the twentieth century, public authority has in some measure migrated away from the weakening parties to other abodes, including new institutions like the modern administrative agency.[8] But for the last two-thirds of the nineteenth century—the "party period" in American history—institutionalized parties held effective control over much lawmaking.[9]

Having recognized the ascendancy of parties, however, neither the legal/political historians nor the political scientists have adequately addressed the larger question behind Hurst's concern: where did the parties come from and why were they embraced? If parties were not only absent from any formal frame of government but in fact one of the chief diseases against which the Framers of the American Constitution sought to inoculate republican governance, then how did they insinuate themselves into the Constitution's institutions? How did they come to control the lawmaking of the legislative and executive branches in both the states and the nation?

Part of the answer, of course, lies in the obvious electoral advantages that accrue to a politician who can command a large-scale organization. These advantages make it appear inevitable that politicians would build parties, and this apparent inevitability seems to underlie most accounts of Jacksonian politics, which tend to slight the developing theory of party. But the mass party did not appear inevitable at all to the antiparty Americans of the 1820s, as historians have often recognized.[10] Rather, its invention and ultimate legitimation were matters of protracted struggle in the political press and on the stump circuit. First and foremost, therefore, an adequate explanation for the rise of party must explain both the genesis and the subsequent history of partyist theory—the theory by which the partyists sold the idea of party organization and party authority to a largely antiparty electorate.

The central idea in partyist theory was that there existed a body called "the democracy" and that the Constitution made the democracy sovereign. Party came into the picture as the institutional device by which the democracy might exercise its sovereignty in practice. Even the partyists, however, rejected party division *within* the democracy; and so they reaffirmed a kind of antipartyism, by which they meant to connect themselves to the still dominant antiparty tradition. It is this idea—party as the embodiment of the undivided democracy—that has been largely missing from the historiography of party.

What exactly was *the* democracy? Like the idea of "the aristocracy," it denoted a constitutional stratum in society. Contrasted with an American aristocracy of commerce, the democracy was that "immense majority"[11] of the people characterized by a commitment to radical political equality, consequently to the Constitution's principle of majority rule, and, somewhat more tenuously, to the independence of agricultural life rather than to the dependencies of commerce. But that was not all. The democracy was also characterized by its localism and so, under the American Constitution, by its attachment to states' rights, because any unnecessary centralization of power threatened to distort democratic decisionmaking. To the modern mind, it is perhaps not obvious that majoritarianism and localism (and attachment to the land, for that matter) necessarily go together. Presumably, a majority of "the democracy" could choose to centralize power in the national government without losing its commitment to equality and majoritarianism. In partyist thinking, however, a genuine majoritarianism depended absolutely on localism. A decision to forsake states' rights could not be a truly democratic decision, even when made by an electoral majority, in the same sense that a majority decision to disfranchise the population generally or to sell the majority into chattel slavery could not really be thought democratic. Any evidence that a majority had abandoned the principle of states' rights, therefore, was only evidence that something—whether outright corruption or more subtle forms of influence—had "biased" the processes of democratic choice.

In the partyists' commitment to the idea of an indivisible constitutional unit—comprising the vast majority of the people and invested with a complete sovereignty—lay their paradoxical perpetuation of an antipartyist constitutional tradition. And in their commitment to the defining localism of the democracy lay their preeminent devotion to states' rights. Thus, for example, when the Democratic party of the 1830s made a party test of its proposal for an "independent treasury" to replace the national bank, it justified its position not simply as good economic policy but as the necessary position of "the democracy" as a whole, the only position consistent with continuing equality and states' rights, the policy of the Constitution itself. And, to the partyists, it was only this identification of the party with the entire democracy—itself sovereign and internally free from party—that could reconcile party organization to a still dominant antiparty tradition.

The partyist theory just sketched has largely escaped historians. Even those who have examined parties in great detail have been little concerned with antipartyism and its continuing connection to the Constitution after 1820 or so. The emergence of the party system, after all, has seemed so inevitable to modern eyes that any lingering antipartyism has seemed uninteresting, even though it was, in fact, a central preoccupation of the partyists themselves. And "the democracy" is so thoroughly lost as a constitutional category that its implications for antipartyism and for states' rights must be doubly lost to modern thinkers.

The main historiographical culprits here, Richard Hofstadter and Michael Wallace, must also be heroes to anyone working in this field.[12] Hofstadter and Wallace attended carefully to the antipartyism of the Founders and offered a fascinating and powerful account of the emergence of partyism. Writing in the wake of the "pluralist" political scientists of the mid-twentieth century, they had in mind a model in which the parties carry little in the way of ideology but manage competition among minority interest groups by building coalitions within the parties.[13] And they found this model almost perfectly anticipated in the writings of Martin Van Buren and his political club, the so-called Albany Regency of the 1820s. New York's leading Jacksonian politician and eighth president of the United States, Van Buren is rightly portrayed by Hofstadter and Wallace as the chief architect of the Democratic party and of partyist theory itself. But Van Buren and his comrades had much to say that Hofstadter and Wallace missed or misinterpreted. Van Buren's preoccupations with the democracy, antipartyism, and states' rights are largely absent from the Hofstadter-Wallace interpretation. Such omissions might make sense if one were seeking out precursors of pluralist political science,[14] but not if the object is to rediscover the bridge that Van Buren and the partyists actually built for the electorate between antipartyist tradition and partyist practice, a bridge built explicitly on the sovereignty of "the democracy" and the pervasive problem of states' rights.

In the years since Hofstadter and Wallace, Jacksonian historians have mostly abandoned the questions they addressed. Most of the historiography of Jacksonian politics has sought to explain the socioeconomic bases and ideologies of nineteenth-century politics, not its institutional or constitutional structure. The emergent consensus in this vein is that the births of the Democratic and Whig parties in the 1830s represented opposed responses to the explosion of the market economy amid broad suffrage and ethno-religious diversity. The Democrats were generally wary of the dependencies created by the market, while the Whigs embraced the market wholeheartedly. The Democrats thus opposed government promotion of banks, aid to internal improvements, and protective tariffs, and supported cheap and rapid sale of the public lands. Whigs generally took the opposite positions. The Whigs appealed to evangelical Protestants, while the Democrats appealed to "pietistic" Protestants and Catholics. This historiography does not directly address the origins of party itself as a mode of governance. Instead, it simply implies that the growth of democratic political conflict amid an emergent market and ethno-religious diversity made parties inevitable and that there is little more to say in explanation of their rise, legitimation, and evolution as institutions.[15]

To be fair, the problem of continuing antipartyism has been addressed creatively by a handful of historians. They have revised Hofstadter and Wallace by suggesting the persistence of a kind of country-party antipartyism even among Van Buren's Democrats.[16] Still, the general truth is that political historians have for a generation skimmed over the origins of partyism, both because the reigning interpretation has obscured the idea of "the democracy" and because the main concern of recent historians has not, in fact, been with governmental institutions—that is, constitutional development—but with social conflict. As Richard John has argued, not only social historians but the most recent generations of political and legal historians have tended to see the history of governmental institutions as merely epiphenomenal to the history of social cleavage.[17] Parties as institutions, therefore, have been of surprisingly little concern to political historians, while the substantive ideologies and social bases noted above have been front and center.

Legal historians may have a greater professional inclination than political historians to understand party development as an aspect of constitutional development. Since Hurst, legal historians have widely understood themselves as historians of governance and have occasionally joined in Hurst's recognition that parties were constituent parts of American governance, even if they were not part of the written Constitution itself. Still, the half-century since Hurst's prospectus has brought little sustained attention to how parties in fact infiltrated the constitutional system.

Thus, for example, Hurst moved beyond the courtroom to the legislature to paint a picture of American law in this period as relentlessly focused on the "release of energy," that is, on the promotion of economic growth.[18] More recently, William Novak has followed Hurst beyond the courtroom in order to revise the great man's conclusions, arguing that antebellum American law was actually governed by a more traditional model, the ideal of the "well-regulated society."[19] In both cases, much of the point is to debunk the myth of laissez-faire and reveal a system of active governance. Neither, however, attends much to the possibility that *both* these principles were important and in competition with each other,[20] nor that this competition came to be reflected in the divisions between the *parties* that actually controlled the legislatures. It is one thing to embrace legislatures as central actors in legal history and to acknowledge, as Hurst does, that "the parties furnished legislative direction." It is another thing, so far ignored by legal historians, to investigate why and how parties became the real legal actors, the real partners of the courts in Skowronek's "state of courts and parties." Without an understanding of how "the democracy" came to entrust social policy—whether the release of energy or its close regulation—to party mechanisms, the importantly constitutional dimension of the production of social policy will remain obscure.

Enough of the historiography; let me turn to the history itself. This study is an effort to recover the constitutional history that the partyists themselves, as well as their opponents, would have recognized. It is important to remember, though, that the history of party is only half of the larger constitutional history of "courts and parties." The precise scope of authority of courts and parties was far from a given at the Founding. With respect to the courts, questions regarding the scope of constitutional review in a federal system,[21] the authority of common law relative to statute law,[22] the appropriateness of elective judiciaries relative to appointive ones,[23] and other questions of institutional authority appeared quickly and remained important for much of the century. The question of party authority closely resembled these questions—that is, revealed its constitutional nature—in that the debates were ostensibly not about the substance of the law, not about the content of legal standards, but about the processes and institutional structures that might legitimately create or find law.[24]

Still, the historical problem of party authority was very different from the problem of judicial authority in its particulars. For one thing, unlike the judiciary, the political party was altogether anathema to the first generations of Americans. The Madisonian Constitution itself was centrally an effort to exclude parties or factions from the lawmaking process, as Federalist no. 10 most famously argued. This pervasive antipartyism, which the Constitution reflected, presented a formidable challenge to those who would later attempt to legitimate party organization. And so the mass political party did not become established as an institution of public authority until at least the 1830s, as the Madisonian vision of the Constitution was finally superseded by a theory and practice that embraced the mass party as an indispensable institution of American governance and of the Constitution itself.[25]

The process that would replace the "Constitution against parties" with a Constitution completely dependent on parties was necessarily set in motion by the politicians, especially the local political entrepreneurs who energized every hamlet. They built the parties and they sold them to the electorate, not so much in Washington, D.C., as in the states and localities. This book focuses, therefore, on the politicians and activists of a single American state, Jacksonian Illinois.

No more "typical" than Hofstadter's New York or any other state, Illinois in the 1820s and 1830s offers a fascinating, understudied site for the investigation of partyist reform. Entering the Union in 1818 and originally settled mostly by migrants from the southern states, Illinois was governed from the start by a constitution as democratic as any in its time—that is, it provided for white manhood suffrage and frequent elections—and a highly egalitarian culture to match. Its white population, probably less than 40,000 in 1818 but growing rapidly, was concentrated in the southern third of the state and mostly engaged in subsistence or otherwise small-scale agriculture. But there were also salt works of some economic significance, some lead mines, and a growing measure of economic ambition as manifested in campaigns for banks, canals, and divisions of counties. The ambitions of the white population were further reflected in their treatment of the nonwhite population. In these early years, the state had a temporary slave population of perhaps 1,000, and there were intermittent efforts to render slavery a permanent institution. In addition, Illinoisans in this period sought to clear the state of its large Indian population, a goal pursued through predictable violence and largely accomplished by the end of the Black Hawk War of 1832.

Although migration from the east was tiny at the start, it picked up rapidly. Chicago showed promise of becoming an important town by the mid-1830s, leading the growing northern region's fight for construction of a canal between Lake Michigan and the Illinois River. It was in this period that Stephen A. Douglas, Illinois's soon-to-be "little giant" of politics, arrived in Chicago from the East, stopping off only briefly before taking the gospel of partyism south to mid-state Jacksonville. As migration filled the northern part of the state, the agitation for internal improvements spread and intensified. The increasing balance in the population also made it plausible for mid-state interests to argue for removal of the state capital from the small southern town of Vandalia to centrally located Springfield. This feat was accomplished in 1839 by, among many others, Illinois's other giant of the future, the anti-Democrat Abraham Lincoln.[26]

The changing demographics of the state clearly played a role in the rise of party in the 1830s, since migrants from New York and other points east brought extensive experience—both positive and negative—with the theory and practice of party. But it is also true that the champions and opponents of party never adhered to any simple law of demography. If Illinois was among the slower states to embrace party organization, as pointed out by Richard P. McCormick's classic *The Second American Party System*, patterns of settlement undoubtedly had something to do with that. So did the national pattern of party development, identified by McCormick, that saw party competition emerge region by region, the western states generally developing party structures later than did others. Beyond such demographic and regional influences, however, McCormick rightly identified a diversity of local circumstances that greatly affected the timing of party formation in the several states, even as he suggested that the basic experience of party growth, centering on presidential elections, was substantially similar from state to state.

The sources of partyist revolution lay in the national collapse of the "First Party System" in the 1810s. At that point, neither regularized party competition nor open party organization generally characterized the politics of the states, and nowhere was the dominance of antiparty ideology broken, even amid broad suffrage and democratic values and even after the experience of a kind of sustained party competition between Federalists and Republicans. By the time Illinois gained statehood in 1818, the Federalist party was dead but for small pockets in the eastern states, and most of the nation was celebrating the obsolescence of party as a consequence of the obsolescence of the Federalists. Infant Illinois, too, embraced the general antipartyism of traditional, Anglo-American constitutionalism.

Within Illinois and many other states, however, a small cadre of partyist reformers, a Van Burenite avant-garde, stood ready with a theory of governance that would glorify party in, oddly enough, antipartyist terms. Abjuring any theory of party that rested merely on a substantive policy platform, these politicians developed both a series of reforms in political practice, especially the use of nominating conventions and the associated ethic of party loyalty, and a theory that justified those reforms as essential to the suprapartisan sovereignty of the democracy contemplated by the Constitution. I do not mean to deny that the reformers also had substantive interests—whether simple personal advancement or the promotion of a preferred economic policy—nor that those interests supplied much of the motivation for their institutional reforms. But they did not justify party to Illinoisans simply as a useful or even indispensable device for pursuit of substantive policy goals. Rather, they justified it in constitutional terms. They told the people of Illinois that it was the essential institution for interpretation, defense, and implementation of the intertwined constitutional principles of popular sovereignty and federalism. In Illinois, the theory that would justify party authority necessarily purported to be a conservative defense of traditional antiparty constitutionalism—the proposed party was to be a party of the whole sovereign democracy, not just a part of it—and of the states'-rights Constitution itself. In the name of such conservatism, however, it called on Illinois's voters to embrace the startling institutional innovations of regular nomination and strict party loyalty.

Given the centrality of the Constitution to political argument in Illinois, it might be useful to explain at the outset the many senses in which partyist theory was "constitutional." First, the theory represented an effort to control what is sometimes called the "unwritten constitution": the collection of sociopolitical customs within which politics must be conducted to be thought legitimate—or, as Bruce Ackerman describes it, "the constitutional regime, the matrix of institutional relationships and fundamental values that are usually taken as the constitutional baseline in normal political life."[27] Examples might include England's "mixed government" or, much later, the American two-party system, each of which has dominated the public life of its time and place without any firm basis in a written constitution. Thus, in the case of the partyists, an insistence on regular nomination and strict party loyalty was a direct attack on the entrenched institutions and customs of Illinois's antipartyist order. It was, therefore, an attempt to amend or reconstruct the unwritten constitution. (That said, it should also be noted that even such a clear case of "unwritten" constitutional reform could be recast as a reconstruction of the written Constitution itself, since the latter had been designed specifically to forestall governance by party.)

More important than the mere fact of the partyists' reformism, of course, were its purposes. Partyist theory reflected a concern with the unwritten constitution here, too. The grand purpose of party organization was to preserve the sovereignty of the majoritarian democracy, but the partyists had an acute sense that the democracy could be outmaneuvered by the possessors of concentrated wealth, at least once that wealthy few had succeeded in drawing power away from the states and localities and consolidating it in the national government. Here, partyist concerns link up with Hurst's notion of the "balance of power." To Hurst and others who have followed him, there is a way in which all substantive policy decisions are "constitutional" because they represent redistributions of power, whether through redistribution of wealth or otherwise.[28] This notion would have resonated for the partyists, but they went further, linking the problem of concentrated wealth to the equally fundamental problem of federalism. They would never have advocated frank wealth redistribution so as to equalize the "balance of power"; wealth redistribution by the government was one of their greatest nightmares. Rather, they insisted on local control—states' rights—for the very purpose of minimizing the capacity of the wealthy themselves to use government to redistribute wealth. In this sense, even the partyist reformers' substantive concerns with concentrated wealth can be and were seen as "constitutional." Concentrated wealth was a problem not because democrats were entitled to an equality of material condition but because concentrated wealth tended to be the product of centralized government in the first place, tended to produce social and therefore political dependency, and thus tended to deliver disproportionate influence over government to those who controlled that wealth in a worsening cycle of economic accumulation and constitutional consolidation.

Large corporations,[29] for example, especially those with special franchises,[30] thus presented "constitutional" problems of the sort the partyist reformers thought their new institution could solve. The great example for them was the excessively concentrated wealth and thus unconstitutional power of the Second Bank of the United States. For Democrats in Illinois and elsewhere, that institution not only distorted democratic process by its sheer size and financial power. It also stood as the great emblem of the implied-powers, consolidationist constitutionalism of its creator, Alexander Hamilton, and its protector, the Marshall Court. Partyist objections to the Bank, therefore, began in the realm of the unwritten constitution; the Bank's enormous wealth allowed it to create a grand network of dependencies that effectively bought it the votes of otherwise free democrats. But those objections quickly slipped into the realm of the written Constitution; such enormous wealth was predictably the product of a distant government out of the reach of the localist people, usurping power that the states'-rights Constitution had not granted.

Once the partyists were thus on the subject of federalism, the arguments from the written Constitution multiplied. The Constitution, they claimed, was an essentially democratic, majoritarian document. From that premise, they could not quite argue that a democratic party organization was mandated by the Constitution in the narrowly legal sense that the presidency, the Congress, the Supreme Court, and the states were. But they did contend that every argument against party organization amounted to an argument for illegitimately broad principles of constitutional construction and a subversion of the legally mandated relationship between the national government and the states. Thus, according to the partyists, in order to alter permanently the structure of American political power (the unwritten constitution, perhaps), self-interested minorities—"aristocrats"—sought to undermine the democratic interpretive principles of strict construction and states' rights. These were the most fundamental legal principles embodied in the federal Constitution, they thought, and they drew on a constitutional tradition going back through the Jeffersonians to the Anti-Federalists to legitimate their claims.[31] In their view, the absence of a mass democratic party organization would permit small knots of neo-Hamiltonian elitists to siphon power to the federal government, far from the people in their "primary assemblages," in defiance of the strict constitutional enumeration. They would offer seductive policy proposals, like the Bank or grand schemes of public works, that would both serve their material interests and, symbiotically, entrench their minoritarian, consolidationist, implied-powers constitutionalism. By such loose-constructionist governance, the vaunted sovereignty of Illinois and every other state would be drained of substance.

Finally, this general, consolidationist project would be assisted in a most fundamental way by one particular defect in the Constitution that only party could fix: the provision for presidential election by the House of Representatives whenever the electoral votes of the states failed to produce a president. Of course, the constitutional provisions for an electoral college and House election had been adopted as part of the Madisonian project of antiparty filtration of—rather than obeisance to—the popular will.[32] But that did not stop the radically egalitarian partyists from insisting that House election was actually out of place in an otherwise democratic Constitution. In the absence of a single democratic party organization, the reformers observed, no popular will could ever coalesce, and elections would routinely go into the House. There, intrigue, faction, and the consolidationist aristocracy, not the democracy, would prove sovereign. Such a result was predicted by partyists before 1824 and seemed confirmed by the reputedly "bargained" election of the ultra-nationalist John Quincy Adams in the House in 1825—a "bargain" that apparently encompassed even the vote of Illinois's lone congressman.

The Democratic party of the reformers' vision, then, was an essentially constitutional organization. The purpose of the new party was to replace lawmaking (and constitutional interpretation, for that matter) by a Madisonian deliberative Congress with lawmaking by expression of popular will through the party; to replace president-making by electoral college and House with president-making by popular will through party nomination; and to replace constitutional interpretation by the consolidationist Supreme Court (and Congress, for that matter) with constitutional interpretation by a localist people through their party-disciplined representatives in the regular course of policymaking.

Of course, for the reformers' opponents, political parties themselves presented constitutional problems as important as any that party was supposed to solve. Illinois's traditional antipartyists viewed parties as concentrations of influence in a handful of politicians and thus an illegitimate redistribution of governmental power to those few. And governance by such networks of interest and dependency was just the bogey that Madison and his like had in mind when they framed a Constitution against parties.[33] Moreover, while often less worried about national consolidation than were the partyists, the antipartyists also pointed out that glorification of party actually tended to concentrate power not just in the national government but in the president alone as leader of the party. While developing these arguments at length, the antipartyists also discovered the necessity of open party organization if they were to defend their own understanding of the Constitution against the offensives of the partyists. The origins of mass party competition thus lay in a battle not so much about the social and economic positions for which the Democratic and Whig parties are well known, but in a battle over the question of party itself and its relationship to the Constitution, neither party ever fully accepting the constitutional legitimacy of the other.

Pictured this way, the struggles between the partyists and their opponents illustrate the constant interpenetrations, and thus the tenuousness of the distinctions, among three modern categories: a "normal" politics of choice among substantive policies; a politics of "constitutional construction" in which the basic structures and customs of democratic governance—the unwritten constitution—are at stake; and a politics of constitutional interpretation in which the meaning of the constitutional text itself is at issue.[34] These three levels of politics and their interrelations can be illustrated by looking at the main policy initiative of the nation's preeminent partyist, Martin Van Buren. On taking office in 1837, Van Buren proposed the Independent Treasury, in effect, a cessation of the federal government's dealings with banks, as a response to the bank panic of that year. This measure was not simply an effort to address an economic crisis with an economic measure but also a climactic effort to establish a states'-rights interpretation of the Constitution. In 1819, the Supreme Court had announced the constitutionality of a national bank, a declaration contested by President Jackson in 1832. Now Van Buren's Democratic party pressed the Independent Treasury as a vindication of the states'-rights interpretation of the Constitution as against the consolidationist ambitions of the Supreme Court and its allies. In enacting this measure, the party would establish its own authority to make and enforce that interpretation and thus entrench the party itself—in place of the Court—as the Constitution's indispensable institution. As retailed by the Democratic parties of Illinois and the rest of the states, then, the Independent-Treasury campaign was not simply a struggle between economic interests or philosophies, nor just an effort to carve out a place for party, nor exclusively a contest of constitutional interpretation. Rather, it was all these things at once, and few Democrats thought these several purposes needed to be teased apart. For Van Burenites, the fusion of these three kinds of goals in the Independent Treasury campaign proved that these aims were all of a piece, that politics and constitutional development were essentially indistinguishable phenomena. Similarly, the Van Burenites' opponents tended to fuse three corresponding efforts: their campaign for flexible constitutional power in the federal Congress,[35] their defense of the unwritten constitution against the Democrats' shocking partyism, and their policy objective of shoring up a national credit system.

In pressing or resisting partyist reform, the politicians well understood this interpenetration of politics and constitutional development. They saw its persistence from 1787 to 1840, the Civil War, Reconstruction, and beyond, and they were probably much less inclined than we are today to see those levels of politics as meaningfully distinguishable, to see politics as *working within* a constitutional order rather than *working out* that constitutional order. They could not see themselves as working within a "party system" when the central issue between them was whether and how parties might legitimately exist in the American order at all. They knew, as historians and legal scholars have been rediscovering in recent years, that much of the most important constitutional interpretation in the American system—especially with respect to federalism—has been and must be done in the "political" branches of government, in the normal course of policymaking, rather than in the judiciary.[36]

Moreover, they knew that parties as such not only became the main interpreters of the Constitution in many situations but that the Democratic party
was in fact invented for and legitimated by that very purpose.

All of this emerges from a close analysis of the constitutionalized politics of
Jacksonian Illinois and its relationship to the politics of the other states and
the nation. Of course, in early Illinois, there were no grand theorists of politics
or constitutionalism. There was, however, a growing supply of ambitious stump
politicians, ready to transmit Van Burenite theory to Illinois and spark that
state's constitutional transformation along with their own political careers.
Armed with Van Buren's theory as well as their own independent access to the
traditions that made that theory resonate, the local stump-men could consti-
tutionalize abolitionism and economic policy for Jacksonian Illinois and in so
doing justify party organization, even as their opponents resisted them in similarly constitutional, but even more traditionally antipartyist, terms.

But no one, of course, was fully in control of this reconsideration of party
and the Constitution. The climax of the story is the election of 1840. By then,
the Van Burenites had largely succeeded in using the language of the Constitution and antipartyism itself to accomplish the partyist reform: they had vitiated the constitutional provisions regarding presidential election by forcing
elections permanently on to party grounds; and they had gone a long way toward substituting the constitutional interpretations of the Democratic party
for those of the Supreme Court. This success represents the great transformation—the integration of the political party into the constitutional system[37]—
that is related in the chapters that make up the heart of this book. But in important ways the Van Burenites' successes proved evanescent, as the anti-
Democratic coalition resisted every step. This opposition unified itself under
the Whig banner with a call to a traditional brand of antipartyism that featured a deliberative, Madisonian Congress of independent men. And, under
this banner, they actually won the presidential election of 1840—an eventu-
ality that partyist theory had declared impossible once the democracy was adequately organized. Thus the process of integrating the political party into
American governance included crucially a resistance to that very process, both
before and after 1840, that rendered the resulting constitutional reform—
a nascent two-party system—as different from the one planned by the Van Burenites as it was from the antipartyist model that Van Buren's opponents
sought to preserve.

As the concluding chapter will argue, the initial partyist successes of the Van
Burenites were themselves vitiated by resurgences of antipartyism both within
and without the Democratic party. Not even the apparently institutionalized
two-party competition after 1840 managed to fully legitimate the two-party

system. After all, the ultimate product of the "Second Party System" was the apocalyptic, sectional power struggle that culminated in the Civil War. The parties' performances in that crisis were hardly calculated to convince the people that competition between mass parties preserved popular sovereignty. Rather, nearly everyone came to see one or both mass parties as impotent at best and revolutionary at worst, until the dynamics of partyism and antipartyism within and between the parties left the system at the mercy of the constitutional vision of the Supreme Court in *Dred Scott*.[38] That was the very institution Van Buren's party had been meant largely to replace as constitutional interpreter after the Marshall Court's pro-Bank consolidationist decision of 1819, *McCulloch v. Maryland*.[39] But here was the Court returning to the political thicket.

Dred Scott might illustrate both the successes and the failures of the partyist reformers. The fact that the question fell to the Court as it did reflected the failure of the Democratic party to achieve the constitutional hegemony that Van Buren and his coadjutors had declared as its birthright. Rather, persistent antipartyism combined with the sectional crisis to undermine the partyist vision and open the door to a two-party constitution. In place of the Constitution of the sovereign, undivided democracy, there emerged the state of "courts and parties"—the two-party constitution that, lacking a hegemonic party of the democracy, came to depend on a resurgent Supreme Court to break its constitutional impasses. Out of the firm declarations in most antebellum political rhetoric that democrats could not divide into permanent parties and yet remain democrats, there eventually developed the firm conviction that two-party competition among democrats was virtually the defining institution of democracy. Well before the full ascendancy of that pluralist ideology,[40] however, the partyists had buried the Madisonian "Constitution against parties" and given birth to the shifting, contested, but, in that day, unparalleled constitutional authority of the mass political party.

CHAPTER ONE

The Antiparty Constitutional
Tradition from Bolingbroke
to Van Buren

I t is now familiar enough that James Madison and many of his
colleagues in the Convention of 1787 had aimed to exclude
party from the functioning of their new Constitution. They
had sought to implement a constitution of popular sovereignty
not by way of mass party competition but through an institutional design that would actually limit popular influence and neutralize
party.[1] In the words of Scott Gordon, these founders had tried to establish a
constitution of "countervailance," in which checks on governmental power
were achieved by replacing the idea of an active sovereign—here, the people—
with that of an interlocking set of institutions. No sovereign body would steer
the government; governmental action could result only from the concurrence
of multiple, nonsovereign governmental institutions.[2] Half a century later,
however, the partyist reformers sought to stand the elitist, antiparty Framers'
Constitution on its head. Rejecting the Framers' premise of an "absent People"—whose nominal "sovereignty" would be functionally supplanted by a self-
checking institutional design[3]—they drew on an alternative tradition from the
founding generation. This tradition did anticipate an active popular sovereign
within the constitutional framework.[4] But, where that populist, constitutional
tradition had continued to reject the device of party into the nineteenth century, the reformers of the 1820s finally concluded that a partyless Constitution
must always be an undemocratic Constitution. Since the written Constitution
did not actually say anything explicit about political parties, good or bad, the
partyists remained free to "construct"[5] a Constitution in which party was fundamental to popular sovereignty. And so they did.

As of the 1820s, the established constitutional order in America had not included a regular place for party organization. Even as a rising democracy marginalized advocates of rule-by-the-best-men, the Madisonian constitutional
commitment to a partyless lawmaking process had remained pervasive. Numerous episodes of economic and cultural dislocation had left unshaken the

popular antiparty consensus. But the battle to intrude party organization into that order was in the offing.

This battle was not the inevitable product of broad suffrage and a modernizing economy, although those features of American life were, in the event, important conditions of the development of mass parties. Instead, the war over party was produced by a constitutional reform movement that sought self-consciously to revise the entrenched antipartyism of American political and constitutional culture. In fact, quixotic as the ultimate goal may have been, the reformers sought to establish for the Democratic party, and only the Democratic party, a kind of lawmaking authority at least as important as that of any formal branch of government.

In order to make the arguments stick, however, the partyist reform movement necessarily seized on the concrete sufferings of the people. The reformers worked to prove that economic problems were not just economic in nature but constitutional.[6] Only Democratic party organization, therefore, could adequately address them. Thus did the social and economic battles of the 1820s and ultimately the great controversy over the Independent Treasury in the 1830s become episodes in the campaign to replace a designedly elitist Constitution with one in which the party of the popular sovereign was in command of the institutions of government.

But the story begins well before the Jacksonian period with the tradition of antiparty constitutionalism. The purpose of this opening chapter is to emphasize the genuinely revolutionary quality of the partyists' ambitions by recovering the deeply antiparty constitutional traditions of the early republic.

The Anglo-American Unwritten Constitution before the Revolution

The unwritten constitution of early modern England celebrated the political autonomy of the undivided locality. Each locality was connected politically to others by little other than the common necessity of maintaining a central authority (such as Parliament) whose main function was to sanction and protect local autonomy. Within these communities the central constitutional value was unity through hierarchy. All politics and governance had as its fundamental purpose to sustain the structure of the local hierarchy of families, to make clear the sources of ultimate authority in the community, and thus to preempt any possible cause of division among the people as a whole.[7]

Division of the community would ultimately arrive by way of the central authority's extension of its power into local affairs,[8] but experience had shown that division was not only expensive, dishonorable, and subversive but pregnant with violence as well. Especially after the persistent civil unrest of England's seventeenth century, according to Richard Hofstadter, "party was associated with painfully deep and unbridgeable differences in national politics, with religious bigotry and clerical animus, with treason and the threat of foreign invasion, with instability and dangers to liberty. Even in 1715, the Tories, the opposition party, could still be seen as quasi-treasonable."[9] Society simply lacked regular mechanisms for resolving large-scale clashes of interest. All assumed that the roots of division were in private interests, which were further assumed to be inconsistent with the public interest of a naturally harmonious community. Such divisions within the ruling class were expected to be worked out quietly, lest division be extended to the electorate as a whole and the ruling structure of the community itself be challenged. There was little or no challenge to the model of localist, paternalist aristocracy and little doubt that the symbiotic relationship between hierarchical authority and communal peace lay at the core of the unwritten constitution.[10]

This model of the British constitution was not merely an abstract ideal. Although membership in the House of Commons was elective, these elections had traditionally featured only a single candidate, presented by the local elite for mere ratification by the restricted electorate. Most of the way through the eighteenth century, a large majority of elections to Parliament remained uncontested. The mutual obligations of aristocracy and people continued to reinforce the unity of the local polity against the potentially divisive exercise of authority by the central government.[11]

At the same time, British emigrants carried these constitutional convictions to the New World. The great majority of colonists remained fully within the British culture of monarchy. They believed in unity, dependency, and deference, not in popular initiative or popular politics. Depending ultimately on the king for protection, they forthrightly avowed their allegiance to him. And they understood the hierarchy that descended from royal authority to the local elite as the legitimate political structure of royal protection and popular allegiance. In this picture, division of a community necessarily reflected a factious dissatisfaction with the status quo and thus a constitutional challenge to the royal structure of authority.[12]

The clearest examples of the passion for unity through hierarchy appear in the Puritan colonies. There the theory of covenanted communities and the unitary nature of God's will impelled the people to political unity.[13] And this imperative to unity was manifested in election procedures. In many Massachusetts towns, for example, if an election was contested, it was common practice to announce only the winners. Names of the losers and their vote totals were withheld on the premise that such information would only encourage resentment when the community should be uniting under the legitimate authority of the winners. The purpose of the town meeting, where decisions were made by consensus, not by majority, was less to make policy decisions than to reaffirm the unity of the town.[14]

If the commitment to unity was most easily seen in the land of covenants and Christian mission, it was present elsewhere too. The attempts to create stable political and social structures in all of the colonies drew on the assumptions of the monarchical culture of dependence. Nothing was more important to stable government in this vision than the existence of an elite that bore the standard marks of authority: wealth, education, family, aristocratic bearing, and the rest. Such an elite could manage society without having its authority questioned and thus without risking political division. Unfortunately, the absence of such an indigenous elite in the New World was the central political characteristic of the colonies.[15] Bacon's Rebellion, for example, has been explained as the product of the Virginia political elite's weak claims to its status and power by seventeenth-century standards. Challenges to authority in New York and North Carolina had very different histories but again can be explained not as efforts to escape the constitution but to rescue it from false elites. In fact, Bernard Bailyn's survey of the colonies attributes their general political instability to the colonists' desire to see a closer match than was possible between constitutional ideals and political reality. The New World's greater equality of condition, combined with the imperial establishment's patent inability to reproduce the British constitution of hierarchy and unity in the colonies, opened the door to the colonies' frequent challenges to authority and consequent factionalism. Factionalism—or party contention—was the *prima facie* evidence that the constitution had been corrupted. And political competitiveness remained a source of unease as the colonists clung to constitutional tradition.[16]

Origins of the Discourse of Party

Before the eighteenth century, then, there hardly existed a discourse of party, unless routine, blanket condemnation counts as a discourse. Party, or faction, was any group organized to further its private interests at the expense of the public good. Party had virtually no defenders, and its opponents, therefore, had virtually no reason to refine the theory of antipartyism. But the eighteenth century would bring refinements that would prove crucial in the later, American invention of permanent, legitimate party organization. The key idea here is that society and polity were constituted by estates. The monarchy, the aristocracy, and the democracy were distinct strata of both society and polity, and each might, in rare times of crisis, embody itself temporarily as a kind of "antiparty party"—a special sort of party that might defend the constitution against the attacks of the more conventional sort of party, the self-interested cabal.

In England, the constitution to be defended was the "balanced constitution" or "mixed government." Looked to as the guarantee of England's unrivaled freedom, the constitution was "mixed" or "balanced" in the sense that it incorporated the three distinct estates or constitutional orders into a single governing structure. The crown, the nobility, and the commoners were not just constitutional abstractions but easily recognized, discrete elements of both society and polity. By institutionalizing the three constitutional orders in the monarch, the House of Lords, and the House of Commons, each limiting the others' ability to engross power, history had presented eighteenth-century England with a constitution that offered the hope of eternal liberty. This far, nearly all the English polity was in agreement.[17]

The development of English society and politics after the Glorious Revolution, however, prompted fundamental disagreement over the actual functioning of that constitution and its relationship to the greater society, especially in light of the eighteenth-century financial revolution.[18] Thus, on the Whig side, the secretary of the treasury, Sir Robert Walpole, set out to settle the essentials of the English constitution by establishing a permanent interdependence among the branches, by which the dominance of any one of them would be forever forestalled. To this end the Whig oligarchy refined government by "influence," a regularized connection between the ministry and the House of Commons. "Influence" was achieved by the ministry's appointing members of Parliament to executive offices or "places" and by the ministry's reliance on this influenced Commons for its effectiveness. It made for efficient government by a fairly coherent ruling group. It excluded Tories from affecting policy or otherwise wielding influence. And it prevented either King or Commons from dominating the other, since they were mutually dependent. In all these ways, influence put into operation the Whig view of mixed government as rule by a single constitutional party—although most Whigs would have rejected the term party—embodying the entire legitimate political nation and acting through the interdependent branches and estates of the balanced constitution.[19]

To the Tory opposition, of course, the Whig oligarchy was nothing more than the worst kind of faction. It was a ministerial party, armed with the new resources of the financial revolution—the national debt as well as the government-chartered corporations that held that debt. And the oligarchy's "influence" did not ensure a healthy mutual dependence among branches but reduced the

Commons, the people's bulwark, to a mere tool of the paper-money ministry. Party government might bring efficient government, but efficiency in the service of faction and at the expense of the landed, locally rooted gentry was hardly to be applauded.[20]

Led by Lord Bolingbroke, the Tories envisioned, instead, a kind of party balance among the three branches, each estate being prone to pursue its own constitutional dominance at the expense of the balanced constitution.[21] That is, although all professed to worship the balanced constitution, the executive would inevitably seek a constitutional order of effectively unchecked monarchy, the nobles a constitution of unchecked aristocracy, and the commoners one of unchecked democracy. The balanced constitution, then, was a balance of hostile constitutional parties.[22] This notion of parties as embodiments of constitutions would, under a fully democratic rather than mixed government, become a key to the constitutional thought of Americans all the way into the Jacksonian era.

While the English of this period normally used the language of estates or orders rather than constitutional parties to describe the balance, Americans of the next century, lacking the clearly defined estates of England but sensing the presence of the same three constitutional orientations among their people, would use the language of party to distinguish individuals of different constitutional orientations. Their later concern, under an unmixed democratic Constitution, was to identify and legitimate the overwhelming democracy and delegitimate the small but resourceful aristocracy (and the lesser party of monarchists). But, while these later Americans used the notion of a constitutional party in a way only rarely used in Augustan England, they shared the English conviction, pioneered in this period, that the only justifiable party was a constitutional party. In particular, the only legitimate party would gather all adherents of the true constitution in a campaign to expose and defeat an anticonstitutional party's effort to replace constitutional rule with party rule.[23]

Given these views of party, contrasting views of spoils followed naturally. For Bolingbroke, as for the next century's American Whig party, independence was all. Only a governing class of independent gentry, rooted in and true to their local communities, could produce good government. The substitution of spoilsmen, as they would be called in the United States, or placemen, as they were called in England, enmeshed in the new networks of debt and paper money, was the substitution of dependents of the central executive for the independent men of the country. Places, so multiplied and enriched by the financial revolution over which Walpole presided, were the means by which the independence of the three branches was compromised and the independence of the country gentry made ineffective in parliamentary affairs.[24]

Such criticism from an anticonstitutional opposition had little effect on Walpole. Far from corruption, the rewarding of stout adherents to the Glorious Revolution was just, natural, and good policy. Was Walpole expected to reward the traitorous or entrust the administration of government functions to opponents of the fundamental rules of English governance?[25] Just such arguments justified the spoils system of the Van Burenites a century later in their own struggle with an anticonstitutional opposition.

The controversy over the Excise Bill of 1733 dramatizes these convictions. This tax bill was debated less as an economic measure than as a battle in the constitutional war. Like the Bank War of the American 1830s, the Excise Bill controversy had more to do with the abiding structure of power than with economic policy. Walpole introduced the Excise Bill as an economic measure, but the initiative in the debate was seized by his opponents. They insisted that the real purpose and effect of the bill was constitutional, to increase the government's patronage and thus its influence over elections and to further sap the resources of the landed relative to the new monied men.[26] Having succeeded in blocking the bill, Walpole's opponents followed with explicitly constitutional proposals, a place act and repeal of the Septennial Act. Had they succeeded, these measures would have reduced the ministry's "influence" in Parliament and, by making parliaments shorter, rendered MPs more dependent on their constituencies and less on the ministry. They did not pass these measures, but they did succeed in making Walpole's every policy throughout the 1730s a constitutional question.[27] Meanwhile, in the American colonies of the 1730s, constitutional assumptions were much the same as in England. The colonists shared the British devotion to mixed government and to the universal antipartyism of the time, and they joined in the developing recognition that there was a difference between party-as-faction and party as antiparty defender of the constitution itself.[28]

The conditions of society in the colonies encouraged their inhabitants to embrace the theory and practice of the constitutional party as an antidote to their own apparent instability. The absence of a fixed aristocracy or hierarchy, the wide availability of land, and the scarcity and high price of labor produced an unusual level of sociopolitical competition. The consequence was a broad unwillingness to defer to the social or political leadership of the moment. But democratization and division did not reflect a desire to do away with hierarchy and unity. Rather, instability prompted efforts to restore an order of unity and hierarchy in each colony.[29]

These efforts only produced further divisions in many colonies. Governors' efforts to establish a firm imperial presence and create a leadership cadre of officeholders met with assembly factions' efforts to nip executive corruption in the bud. When the colonists looked for someone to blame for constitutional instability, they turned to the same source that the English Tory opposition suggested: ministerial faction, exemplified in the mother country by Walpole's ruling group and embodied in the colonies by the royal governors and by the rest of the empire's ministry-dependent officeholders.[30]

Massachusetts can serve as an example. Shortly after the Glorious Revolution, the House of Representatives and the colonial executive began fifty years of constitutional struggle over the practical terms of the colony's new charter.[31] The resistance to the officeholders knew itself as the "popular party." Its unifying assumptions were that officeholding was just a species of avarice and that the king's first constitutional obligation was to protect his sworn subjects from his officers, especially in the colonies, where patronage went not to a local elite but instead to a transient class of ministerial favorites.[32]

Seeing little of the traditional, expected structure of authority,[33] therefore, the colonists resisted every exercise of power by these transient officeholders. Thus the colonial legislature insisted on the right to elect its own speaker, to adjourn on its own authority, to audit executive expenditures, and to control the governor's salary.[34] Each of these issues evoked the colonists' sense that their executive branch was an interest in itself, an appendage of the ministerial faction in England that Bolingbroke taught the colonists to see as corrupters of the English constitution. In contrast, the popular party claimed to be the party of the entire legitimate polity. And the near unanimity with which the House acted affirmed the popular party's sense of itself as the embodiment of the constitution against officeholder factionism.[35]

The "popular party" was not a party in any modern sense; it had no institutional life or organization, and it disappeared when crises passed.[36] But it reemerged when the crisis of ministerial faction that culminated in the Revolution began, climaxing only when George III himself sided with the structure of official faction and thus exposed monarchy itself as the very source of the colonies' endemic factionalism.[37] Revolution and the move from monarchy to republicanism were, then, a grand effort by a constitutional party to again eliminate party from the polity. As the Constitution would be a "Constitution against parties,"[38] so this revolution against monarchy was a revolution against party.

Studies of other colonies also reveal a politics suffused with constitutionalism at many times and places but especially in the imperial crisis. The revolutionaries increasingly sensed that the independence afforded them by the libertarian balanced constitution was endangered by the dominance of a ministerial faction both within Parliament and within the imperial bureaucracy.[39] Decades later, Martin Van Buren would look back on the Revolution just this way, as the creation of an American republican polity that had excised king and ministry, the structural source of party. But Van Buren would find that, even with hereditary aristocracy absent and monarchy eliminated, a republican polity nevertheless contained persons of aristocratic and even monarchical inclination. And, if unchecked, they would re-create the social structure of dependency necessary to the re-creation of mixed, and inevitably factional, government. Sensing faction at every turn, Van Buren would seek to re-create the party of the Revolution as the American sovereign.

Constitutions against Parties

Inherited from this colonial and English experience, the Founders' fear of and antipathy to parties is now well known to constitutional historians and scholars of all sorts.[40] The familiar story of the Constitution is that traditional antiparty commitments combined with the experience of party-ridden government in the states in the 1780s to inspire the Framers' "Constitution against parties." In the newly independent states, the pre-Revolutionary imperial crisis of government by faction had inspired the making of antiparty state constitutions, while the federal Constitution of 1787 was in large part a reaction to the failure of those constitutions.[41] The new states hardly produced harmonious politics,[42] but their internal factionalism, far from prompting new justifications for party organization, became one of the main catalysts of the movement to write a new, antipartyist, federal Constitution.[43] In the words of Richard Hofstadter,

> While most of the Fathers did assume that partisan oppositions would form from time to time, they did not expect that valuable permanent structures would arise from them. . . . The solution, then, lay in a nicely balanced constitutional system, a well-designed state which would hold in check a variety of evils, among which the divisive effects of parties ranked high. The Fathers hoped to create not a system of party government under a constitution but rather a constitutional government that would check and control parties. . . . Although Federalists and Anti-Federalists differed over many things, they do not seem to have differed over the proposition that an effective constitution is one that successfully counteracts the work of parties.[44]

To the Federalists of 1787, then, the 1780s had been a triumph of democracy and the faction-ridden misgovernment inherent in that system. Consequently, their Constitution attempted to create a gentleman's government within a near-democracy. Rooted necessarily in a party-ridden democracy, it would be operated by a suprapartisan governing elite, not subject to the self-interested whims and caprices of the democracy. To this end, Madison and his cohorts famously established a system of representation designed to ensure that only men of reputation and character could be elevated to the federal Congress, never men of mere partisan connection or conviction.[45]

Madison conceptualized matters this way both in his private writings before the Convention[46] and in his public advocacy after the Convention, most famously in Federalist no. 10. This latter document now stands as one of the sacred texts of the founding among constitutional theorists,[47] largely because of its affirmation that legitimate constitutional government must lie in suprapartisan deliberation. Freed from party, national policy would partake of a substantive rationality that guaranteed minority rights against majority rule or, as Madison put it, "majority faction."[48] Good government could never result from the mere clash of parties or from the coalition of private interests in a majority party.[49] The vices of the American constitution(s) after 1776 had lain fundamentally in majoritarian democracy's tendency to oppress minority interests in pursuit of short-term goals. This was party or faction at its worst, the short-term self-interest of a majority inspiring the coalescence of a ruling faction, freely disregarding the just rights of a minority and thus the "permanent and aggregate interests of the community" as a whole.[50]

The cure for the disease of party was to be a system of representation that would ensure actual governance by the purest, wisest, most far-seeing and well motivated leaders, even as the democracy retained a basic role in government as voters and through the reserved powers of the states.[51] Thus popular election of the House would vindicate popular sovereignty, but the provision for large districts would ensure that only gentlemen with established reputations for public service would be elected.[52] Senators would remain few in number, chosen by the state legislatures and given long terms to insulate them from popular pressures and encourage collegial deliberation in the public interest.[53] If these basic devices failed in any particular case to elevate the "permanent and aggregate interests of the community" over the desires of a "majority faction," then there remained backup devices like the executive veto and judicial review.[54] Establishing roles for the democracy and a kind of governing aristocracy, these devices did not render the Constitution a restoration of mixed government as such, but they did suggest that the Framers still had English constitutional categories in mind as they sought a restored polity of hierarchy and harmony.[55] The Constitution was an attempt to create a polity that incorporated both democracy and an aristocracy of independent men (and even elements of monarchy) into a system that would transcend party.[56]

Sharing the belief that the democratic state governments had shown themselves incompetent to the tasks of republican government, Alexander Hamilton joined with Madison in campaigning for ratification of the Constitution as a means of removing practical governance to an aristocracy. But Hamilton went further. Even the federal Constitution he found to be a "frail and worthless fabric" as long as the government it created lacked a neo-Walpolean "influence." The government, he thought, had to do more than rely on elite representation. It had to be able to make an aristocracy dependent on it and, by good policy, render the democracy deferential toward that aristocracy. He and Madison shared an abhorrence of parties and a longing for a peculiarly American brand of aristocratic leadership. Like Madison, he believed that, "We are attempting by this Constitution to abolish factions, and to unite all parties for the general welfare."[57] But where Madison hoped parties could be controlled by the carefully contrived aristocratic structure of a federal government presiding over a large republic, Hamilton apparently believed they could be controlled only by the hierarchical stability and uniformity of interest that could be created by influence. For Madison, in Richard Hofstadter's words, the Constitution was a "Constitution against parties." But for Hamilton, it would only become so if he were able to add to it an influence-based, aristocratic, unwritten constitution against parties as well.[58] This division between men who were otherwise the allied geniuses of the antiparty American founding was of vital importance, because it was Hamilton's effort to implement his own ideas of stable governance in the 1790s that inspired Madison's opposition and the first steps toward regularized party organization in the American system.

Origins of Constitutional Parties: The Jeffersonians

The written Constitution has never, of course, been the sum of American constitutionalism. Instead, it has been the object of conflicting constructions from even before its ratification. Intended, by Madison at least, to institutionalize the partyless rule of locally elected elites and to cure the disease of faction even within the states, the Constitution instead yielded fundamental conflict from the very start. The conflict centered on the interrelated—almost interchangeable—questions of loose versus strict construction, broad national power versus states' rights, and aristocracy versus democracy; and it necessarily renewed the debate about when, if ever, party might have a legitimate role under a constitution against parties.

For Hamilton, political localism—the dominance and independence of the state governments—and rule by party had in practice been the same thing. Hamilton's purpose on entering office as Washington's secretary of the treasury was to take Madison's Constitution and build upon it a constitution of practical federal power at the expense of states' rights. He would draw monied men to the support of an energetic federal government by having their immediate interests made uniform across state boundaries and tied to that government. The government itself must be operated by men of vision, ambitious for fame, and they must be sustained in their caretaking of society by the pro-government self-interest of the aristocracy. This was not, in Hamilton's view, government by party but the grand statesmanship that was the only alternative to feeble government and ultimate enslavement.[59]

To this end, Hamilton would fund the federal debt held by the monied elite. The federal government would assume the similar state debts. It would also create a national bank as a centerpiece of monied activities and of the economies of the states. These measures would stabilize and unify the interests of a national monied elite linked to a strong national government. These naturally influential men would, in turn, hold disproportionate influence within the states. With the ascendancy of the federal government and the eclipse of states' rights, a national polity might transcend and neutralize the factionalism of the state governments.[60]

If Hamilton thought of himself as invigorating the written Constitution with the virtues of a neo-Walpolean unwritten constitution, Jefferson and his coadjutors feared that Hamilton would destroy republican government altogether. The Constitution had been written to curb the epidemic of party in the states, not to substitute the ascendancy of party in a fully sovereign central government. Resisting Hamilton's conversion of the constitutional enumeration into a plenary grant of power to a financial aristocracy, antiparty men like Jefferson and Madison self-consciously resumed the position of a country opposition. Their party existed only to defend strict construction and states' rights[61] against an anticonstitutional party of the executive, threatening a revival of aristocratic or even monarchical[62] dependency.[63]

Fear of aristocrats and "monocrats," then, provided the impetus for Jeffersonian Republican party formation in the 1790s. But, of course, there was no such thing as a class of nobles or a royal line in the United States. "Aristocrat" connoted not a member of a distinct estate or even class but an advocate of the hierarchical dependency that was the essence of English society and constitutionalism. Thus the poorest and most uncultivated man might be an "aristocrat" if he sought special privilege or political ascendancy for a fixed minority. Such a minority might be Hamilton's monied interest, or the slave-owning class, or, later, for example, the incorporated moral reform organizations associated with the Whig party.

Similarly, Jefferson's term "monocrat" obviously meant not a person who was or would be king but one who advocated monarchical government and its structures of dependency. And the term democrat, correspondingly, referred to any adherent of democratic constitutionalism, regardless of that person's social position. "The democracy," then, was the great mass of Americans devoted to the constitutional principle of majority rule. The perceived conflict between democracy and aristocracy, as embodied in party conflict for decades after the Revolution, was an adaptation of the language of the balanced constitution in which the conflict was no longer between actual estates but between the advocates of the competing constitutional theories traditionally associated with such estates.[64]

Jeffersonians and, later, Van Burenites did not believe that the United States contained estates. But they also did not believe the nation had yet secured itself against the re-creation of a social order in which a commercialized and modernized but still fixed aristocratic estate might come to dominate.[65] Republican ideologist John Taylor spoke for many in fearing that Hamilton's loose-constructionist "combination" represented a calculated, realistic attempt to re-create in America the English sociopolitical order of rank and influence:

> If the public debt has been accumulated by every possible contrivance, buoyed up by means of the sinking fund, made in a great measure perpetual, and formed into a powerful monied machine dependent on the fiscal administration, to this combination it is due. If . . . a dangerous inequality of rank has been created . . . thereby laying the foundation for the subversion of the government itself by undermining its true principles, to this combination it is due. . . . If a practicable means of influence whereby the members of the legislature may be debauched from the duty they owe their constituents has been found, if by implication and construction the obvious sense of the Constitution has been perverted and its powers enlarged so as to pave the way for the conversion of the government from a limited to an unlimited one, to this combination they are due.[66]

The shadow of the balanced constitution thus remained. The truncation of mixed government that was the wholly democratic Constitution of the United States might yet be reversed. The same monied neo-aristocracy that had come to dominate the government of England under the guise of a dominant House of Commons might yet come to dominate American government in the name of confederated democracy.

Justifying themselves as defenders of the popular sovereign, then, the Jeffersonians of the 1790s became the nation's first self-consciously constitutional party and the greatest party organizers to date. Before perhaps the 1810s, however, virtually no one had ever theorized a positive role for a permanent party organization. Even early defenders of party in some of its aspects, like David Hume, thought every party would fall away from whatever legitimate purpose it might have begun with in the effort merely to perpetuate itself. Edmund Burke's famous defense of party in 1770 focused only on elite, parliamentary "connections" rather than on party structures, organizations, or constituencies. Burke's ideas, moreover, limited as they were, got no reception at all in the United States. And the handful of American public remarks in the eighteenth century observing that parties might serve some good purposes neither added up to a developed theory of party nor had any durable effect.[67] Once in power, however, the Jeffersonians' accomplishments turned out to include an unintended legitimation of permanent party organization for many of the next generation of leaders, a legitimation achieved by firmly identifying the Jeffersonian organization with unfiltered democracy, strict construction of the federal Constitution, and states' rights.

Jefferson himself was the idol of this new group of party leaders, and his constitutional thought underlay their own theory of party. In 1813, he wrote that the "same political parties which now agitate the U.S. have existed thro' all time . . . in fact the terms whig and tory belong to natural, as well as to civil, history."[68] And the essential question which divided those parties through all time was whether "the power of the people, or that of the aristoi should prevail." Later pronouncements made clear that the "tory" or Federalist party in the United States was the party not only of aristocracy but of monarchy. More generally, it was the party of those who would consolidate political power in the federal government and especially in the executive branch. In fact, the elective monarchy that was the presidency signified to Jefferson an acceptance and incorporation into the Constitution of the tory principle of irresponsible power, although only with substantial safeguards to prevent its invasion of the "representative branch" of the government.[69]

The "whig" or Republican party was the party of the people but more essentially the party of majoritarianism. Even a tory had to respect the principle of majoritarianism because it was enshrined in a Constitution that even the Federalists claimed allegiance to. Even a tory had to accept the constitutional limits on the tory branch of the government, the federal executive. Just as the tory party was embodied by the federal executive, so the whig party was embodied by the "representative branch" of the government. Each was legitimate within its constitutional abode. Each had its place under this not-very-English sort of balanced Constitution, which balanced not formal estates but the constitutional principles once associated with those estates. But only the Republican party, the current manifestation of the eternal whig party, was legitimate as a political organization, because only it embraced the core constitutional principle of majority rule, whereby both the whig and tory branches or aspects of constitutional government were preserved.[70]

Integral to this majoritarianism for Jefferson was a commitment to states' rights. In Jefferson's vision, no small, organic republic could long survive on its own but must instead come under the authority of a central government. That central government, however, need not be the sort of metropolitan center of a consolidated empire that dominated Europe. Starting in America, the integration of multiple republics into an empire could take the form of an "empire for liberty," an empire of equality rather than consolidation.[71]

The metaphor here was a pyramid, in which there existed a perfect political equality at each level, whether the individual or the county or the state, and a strictly limited delegation from those equal units to the governmental unit one step above. The purpose of that delegation, moreover, was to maintain peace and equality among the delegating units, not to give away power over each unit's internal affairs. Formally equal individuals could not be trusted to respect each other's equality over the long term, and the republics that they formed could not, in their turn, be trusted to respect the equality of other, neighboring republics. Thus the necessity of a union of republics under a central government, the task of which was only to preserve peace and equality among its constituent republics, as well as between the union and the rest of the world:

> We should thus marshal our government into, 1, the general federal republic, for all concerns foreign and federal; 2, that of the State, for what relates to our own citizens exclusively; 3, the county republics, for the duties and concerns of the county; and 4, the ward republics, for the small, and yet numerous and interesting concerns of the neighborhood; and in government, as well as in every other business in life, it is by division and subdivision of duties alone, that all matters, great and small, can be managed to perfection. And the whole is cemented by giving to every citizen, personally, a part in the administration of the public affairs.[72]

Every citizen must possess a personal role in governance or else the principle of perfect political equality is a sham. And the actual exercise of governing power must be divided and subdivided and limited to the lowest practical level on the same principle. Thus the central government, in particular, must be strictly limited in its powers lest it disrupt rather than protect the equality of its constituent parts, the states. In this scheme, bills of rights within the states were necessary to restrict the state governments clearly to their proper tasks, but a bill was equally necessary at the national level, not so much as a direct protection of individual rights as an explicit restriction of the national government to its place in the pyramid, that of preserving peace and commerce among its constituent republics without displacing any more than necessary the republican states' preeminent role in governing the people as such.[73] Jefferson's "natural" parties thus divided not on the question of democracy versus aristocracy simpliciter but on the question of confederated democracy versus consolidated aristocracy.

Once the Constitution had accepted and met the challenge of these natural parties in 1789, however, Jefferson believed that the parties should not have had to become manifest. As long as the constitutional arrangement was respected there was no need for parties among the people. Only in those presumably rare times when someone had the temerity to challenge an established constitutional order should party organization reemerge, and only in the shape of a constitutional party of majoritarianism.[74]

With this substantial and sophisticated refinement of the theory of party as rooted in nature, yet wholly destructive until neutralized by a majoritarian constitution, Jefferson only strengthened his fundamental antipartyism while justifying a Republican party of near-national unanimity in defense of the Constitution. And so Jefferson's presidency became an effort to eliminate party through party.[75]

The Jeffersonians had become convinced of the Federalists' anticonstitutional designs by a long series of events beginning in the 1790s. Funding, assumption, the chartering of a national bank, and the imposition of an excise tax exposed the neo-Walpolean character of Hamilton and his hostility to the constitutional enumeration of powers. All these measures seemed planned, as in a sense they were, to shift the balance of property in society and thus the balance of power in government away from the landed democracy to a consolidating, monied aristocracy.[76] They even had the effect of solidifying a debt-holding, bank-stock-holding faction in Congress, inevitably under Hamilton's sway.[77] The Jay Treaty, the foreign policy crises of the late 1790s, and the Alien and Sedition Acts only reaffirmed the Republican picture of the Federalists.[78] And the last of these was yet another example of Federalist exercise of powers beyond the constitutional enumeration.[79]

The Revolution of 1800, then, was indeed a revolution to Jeffersonians, to new Jeffersonians like Van Buren as much as to venerable Jeffersonians like Jefferson himself. That transformative presidential election was not, to them, the triumph of one set of policies over another but of one constitution over another. It was the restoration of a balance between the whig and tory aspects of the Constitution by the restoration of the majoritarian principle and its American corollary, strict construction. When Jefferson announced in his inaugural address that Americans were "all republicans; . . . all federalists," he anticipated the withering away of party organization before a constitutional settlement that elevated majority rule above all other principles.[80]

Party, of course, did not wither away immediately. The Federalists proved resilient, and Jefferson remained a chief manipulator of party throughout his two terms in office. But his party activities were always intended to bring nearer the death of party. In his distribution of patronage he avowed his nonpartisanship but found the offices of the federal government occupied generally by partisan Federalists. In that circumstance, only judicious removals could make way for an appropriate balance between Federalists and Republicans. Once the proper balance was achieved, Jefferson could appoint officers according to his preferred criteria: "Is he honest, is he capable? Is he faithful to the Constitution?" Once a proper balance was achieved, party patronage would be unnecessary, since party was only constitutionally useful to restore the balance of the Constitution, not as a permanent agency of government.[81]

Similarly, the simmering hostilities with England that dominated both the Jefferson and Madison administrations brought a stubborn Republican effort to avoid those measures that were thought to nourish aristocracy, executive government, and party. The Republican resistance to high taxes, to the creation of a military establishment, and to accommodation with a Britain that was the chief transgressor against American rights on the seas reflected an abiding fear of an aristocratic party in the central government. When war was declared in 1812, the United States was largely unprepared to fight, but Republican leaders had concluded that the years of feeble resistance to England were no longer protecting republican constitutionalism but threatening it. The electorate was increasingly receptive to Federalist charges of Republican weakness. If republican constitutionalism were to be saved, then the Republican party would have to be preserved in power first, and war had become the only way to do that. With war declared, the Republicans continued their string of lopsided election triumphs in 1812 and 1816, even after a military stalemate. The concluding non-events of the war—the abortive Hartford Convention of the Federalists and the post-peace Battle of New Orleans—only cemented the overwhelming dominance of the Republican party and the withering away of the opposition party, a condition that had seemed imminent to Republicans since 1800 but which was finally a reality.[82]

To Jefferson, Madison, and their generation, the War of 1812 was the culmination of a long struggle to overcome party and secure the republican revolution. But to the younger generation of Republicans, the conflict of constitutional parties was the only politics they had ever known. And if Federalism had been routed in the national government, many young Republicans in the states knew that there was a younger generation of Federalists as well, ready and eager to challenge Republican dominance.[83]

Martin Van Buren and a Positive Theory of Party

To the younger generation of Republicans, Jeffersonian constitutionalism was the political bible.[84] They knew that political warfare was constitutional and that, as the political embodiment of the landed democracy, the Republican party was itself the foundation of the Constitution. Far from being just one of many possible parties within the Constitution's structure of governance, the Republican party was the only legitimate party and its natural state was an "exclusive and towering supremacy"[85] over the small but resourceful monied classes.

In 1815, this natural dominance seemed largely realized and the constitutional order finally settled. To the older generation of Republicans and, in fact, to many of the younger generation, that settlement suggested that the need for party was over. America did not have a "Patriot King," but its patriot presidents had succeeded in uniting the people and eliminating party.[86] With the Federalist party all but defunct after the war, James Monroe looked forward to presiding over a partyless polity. But to some of the younger Republicans the threat of aristocracy remained, and organized, single-party ascendancy was a constitutional arrangement to be perpetuated under all circumstances, not to be tossed away just at the moment of its triumph.

That younger generation would come to revere Andrew Jackson as a kind of icon of democracy,[87] but their true leader, both intellectually and politically, was Martin Van Buren. Van Buren thought himself a thoroughly conservative defender of Jeffersonian constitutional orthodoxy. He was faithful to Jefferson's view that there were two eternal, constitutional parties, one a party of the people and of states'-rights, strict-constructionist majoritarianism, the other a party of the aristocracy and of consolidationist, anticonstitutional elitism. He moved beyond and even against Jefferson, however, in two ways. First, his Constitution did not balance a people's representative branch against an inherently aristocratic or monarchical executive branch but mandated a wholly and radically democratic structure. The entire federal government carried within it the danger of consolidation, but it was limited by an unqualifiedly democratic Constitution.

Second, he believed that that democratic Constitution had to be the ward of a permanently and highly organized democratic party, by which every aspect of government would be made directly responsible to the majority will of the people. This was the party that Van Buren thought he remembered from his apprenticeship in the Revolution of 1800.[88] The events of the First Party System had legitimated for men like Van Buren the permanent dominance of a sole legitimate constitutional party over the eternal efforts of the tory party. They would spend the rest of their political lives not trying to create a modern party system or "party government" in the modern sense[89] but working to perpetuate the constitutional order of democratic single-partyism they had experienced under Jeffersonian ascendancy.

Secondary work on Van Buren has generally related his story as a case study of the transition from a politics of "magnates and notables" to the modern politics of party competition within a democratic consensus.[90] In fact, Van Buren is widely given credit for inventing that politics, although not without the contributions of many others. Raised in upstate New York during the First Party System, the ambitious but principled Van Buren was an instinctive Jeffersonian. His town was dominated by a Federalist gentry, and he understood from an early day that advancement in life and especially in politics depended on the patronage of that gentry. But he also understood that such patronage could be withdrawn at any time and that dependence on an elite was not democracy. He took Jefferson and the Republicans, on the other hand, to announce that the days of arbitrary rule by fortuitous elites had passed with the Revolution.

Moreover, his own rise in the Jeffersonian Republican party showed him that there was a practical alternative to dependence on a political elite. The common people might take matters into their own hands through the mechanism of party organization. In this way, the dispersed might concentrate their power without regard to the opinions of an elite and elevate their own kind. Observing the family-centered factionalism of New York politics in the early 1800s, Van Buren aligned himself with the followers of George and DeWitt Clinton. The Clintonians claimed to be the true Republicans and to operate by the principle of party regularity—regular nomination by party majorities— rather than by servility to the Clinton family itself or any other family leadership. On both the state and national levels in this period, Van Buren saw what he took to be the triumphs of democrats over once unassailable elites. And in these triumphs of Clintonians and Republicans, Van Buren learned the democratic merits of party organization.

The lesson of undeviating adherence to party mechanisms and regularity was brought home even more deeply by the events of the 1810s. De Witt Clinton, Van Buren's early idol as the apostle of party regularity, proved himself a constitutional aristocrat when he challenged the congressional nominating caucus and flirted with Federalists in the years leading to the War of 1812. Maneuvering and scheming within the state Republican party throughout the

1810s left the resolutely regular and ambitious Van Buren in the shadows of the great Clinton by 1819. But then Van Buren went to work. Imposing caucus control on his "Bucktail" wing of the party, gaining control of the Erie Canal patronage, establishing a party press devoted to the principle of party regularity, creating corresponding committees, and deploying circuit-riding lawyers to deliver stump speeches, Van Buren and his allies created one of the most highly organized political machines to that date. The work paid off in the general Bucktail victories in the election of 1820. Van Buren went to the U.S. Senate, and only the governor's office eluded the Bucktails until 1822. All the while, the call for party regularity as the indispensable mechanism of democracy was not just a tactic but an increasingly fundamental principle of the party and plank of the platform.[91]

Van Buren went to Washington in Monroe's Era of Good Feelings with the goal of restoring the nation to a democratic era of openly constitutional conflict. Finding the Republican party so dominant that it was disintegrating into factionalism, he set out to restore its unity. By 1822 there were at least four nominally Republican presidential candidates in the field, each building a faction within the party, each disregarding the activities of the seemingly moribund Federalists or, worse, seeking to recruit Federalists to their candidacies. President Monroe, a traditional antiparty man of the Revolutionary generation, did nothing to unify the party but rather seemed quite content to let it dissolve.[92] The only hope for keeping the party undiluted by Federalism and true to its democratic principles was to restore its unity behind a single, authentically Republican, party candidate. And the only established mechanism for this purpose was the congressional caucus.

In the absence of an avowed Federalist candidate to contend with, however, no leading candidate would submit his name to the caucus, except William Crawford. Crawford was duly nominated by the minority of congressmen who attended, while John Quincy Adams, Henry Clay, and Andrew Jackson all ran against the legitimacy of caucus dictation. Crawford ran weakly, and the Bucktails botched the election in New York, but they and others of the nation's "radical" Republicans stood by Crawford throughout the House election in defense of the principle of party regularity.[93]

That principle had not proven resonant in the electorate in 1824, but the radicals received a godsend in the House election. The supposed "corrupt bargain" by which Adams leapfrogged over Jackson into the presidency, despite his trailing in the popular vote, was the great event that proved the elite's disregard of the popular will. It showed that the Constitution's mechanisms could be followed to the letter and yet leave the sovereign people without the power to choose their servants. The House election immediately made the anticaucus

Jackson the favorite for 1828. But it also gave new weight to the radicals' argument that party was the only mechanism by which the people could guarantee themselves the choice of their rulers, at least until the Constitution was formally amended to guarantee direct popular election of the president.

The Jackson movement of 1828 was not simply a partyist movement. It contained many firm opponents of party, including most of those who had supported Jackson in 1824 against partyist dictation by the congressional caucus. Jackson himself had been an old-fashioned antipartyist.[94] For this reason, Van Buren was wary of supporting Jackson, but the only alternative was Adams. Adams was not only the son of the arch-Federalist John Adams, bearing a congenital antipathy to the constitutional enumeration; he had also made clear from his first utterances as president that the will of the people was of little importance to him, the will of a party even less.[95] The result was that Van Buren supported Jackson but did all in his power to make his election a party rather than personal success and thereby resurrect party competition. In a now famous letter to Thomas Ritchie, Van Buren insisted that he sought to unify the anti-Adams vote behind Jackson but also to achieve "what is of still greater importance, the *substantial reorganization of the old Republican Party*," a goal that he acknowledged was contrary to the antiparty prejudices of the mass of the electorate.[96]

Had Jackson been elected in 1828 without the aid of party, perhaps even against the principle of party, as in fact would have been the case if he had succeeded in 1824, that result might have destroyed Van Buren's cause for a generation. Such an election of Jackson would have confirmed for the people that their will could and must be made effective without the mechanism of party. In the event, however, Jackson himself warmed to partyism during the campaign and throughout his two terms. Van Buren succeeded in placing the election of 1828 on an organized party basis in much of the Union and, over time, in turning Jackson into the nation's most important advocate of partyism.[97]

At this point in the story, one might want to conclude that Van Buren and the Bucktails had set the two-party system in motion and that modern democratic politics had arrived. There is a certain obvious truth to such a conclusion. Competition between two major parties, at least on the national level, has been a dominant and enduring feature of American politics since the election of 1828. Significant third-party challenges have sprouted at times, and many individual states have had long stretches of single-party domination. Nevertheless, the two-party system has been a resilient part of American political life since Jackson's election.[98]

Still, Van Buren's partyism was not modern two-partyism. Innovator though he was, Van Buren adhered firmly to much traditional doctrine. The supposed prophet of the party system was imbued with antipartyism's condemnation of parties as enemies to the general interest. He rejected the possibility that there could be a legitimate pluralism of parties under the Constitution; that a happy diversity of economic interests in the market economy might be healthily managed by the restrained, nonfundamental conflict of a party system; that the permanent dominance of an American democratic party could ever face a realistic challenge by any other party. In short, he rejected core assumptions cherished by modern adherents of two- or multi-partyism. Instead, his carefully worked out constitutional theory makes clear that he aspired only to perpetuate what he saw as the grandest of Jefferson's achievements: the structural dominance of the (generally landed) democracy—the Constitution's only genuinely sovereign body—over the small, anticonstitutional party of the monied aristocracy. An extended look at that theory, frequently articulated during his political career and later elaborated in his *Inquiry into the Origin and Course of Political Parties in the United States*, is the necessary introduction to any account of the partyist reformers of the 1820s and 1830s.[99]

To Van Buren, "the democracy" was a natural product of American soil: "The great principle first formally avowed by Rousseau, 'that the right to exercise sovereignty belongs inalienably to the people,' sprung up spontaneously in the hearts of the colonists, and silently influenced all their acts from the beginning."[100] Although one would not want to make too much of a single reference to Rousseau, Van Buren's concept of democracy was close to Rousseau's in at least one respect: he seems to have conceived of the democracy almost as a unified body with a single true will. Van Buren was less a philosopher than a politician and certainly knew that democrats constantly clashed with each other. But underneath the day-to-day difficulties of politics, which he blamed generally on the machinations of closet aristocrats, he seems genuinely to have believed that the great mass of small farmers, and even the nonfarming minority that depended on farmers for their sustenance, formed a body with a real collective interest best identified and expressed by majority vote. In political terms, this natural entity was the small-"d" democratic party that Van Buren sought to institutionalize as the Democratic party.

Before the Revolution, according to Van Buren, political parties did not manifest themselves in America, and the Revolution itself was not only a rising of the body of democrats but also of that brand of aristocrats who truly loved liberty. During the Revolution and the Confederation period, the natural party division between democrats and aristocrats became muddled. Democrats mingled with aristocrats in the Patriot cause, and many democrats resisted good measures lest they unknowingly fall into an aristocratic trap. Under the Confederation government, wrote Van Buren, party conflict between "Federalists" and "Anti-Federalists" arose "out of propositions to take from the State governments the rights of regulating commerce and of levying and collecting impost duties, and for the call of a Convention to revise the Articles of Confederation." To Van Buren, these Federalist measures were all healthy in themselves and correctly supported by many true democrats as well as by the aristocratic Whigs and Tories who formed the Federalist party. But most democrats objected to them on the grounds that "the views of the Federalists were rather political than financial,—that they were at least as solicitous to gratify their well-understood passion for power, through the adoption of these propositions, as they were to maintain public credit."[101] The party division, in the minds of these opposition democrats as recounted by Van Buren, was constitutional. It was a battle between localist democracy and centralized aristocracy, fought out on questions of the government's role in the economy. But, in the particular instance, the pro-Constitution Van Buren had to argue that the confusions of the Revolutionary period had led good democrats to misjudge the measures. Lacking organization, the democracy had yielded a great number who were excessively wary of the movement for competent national government.

This situation persisted through the ratification debates after the drafting of the new Constitution in 1787. The unorganized democracy was on both sides of the contest. The Anti-Federalists, according to Van Buren, again possessed the correct principle, localist democracy, but so did most supporters of the Constitution. Its opponents misread the Constitution as an elitist document when in fact it was, as subsequent decades showed, a fully democratic document when strictly construed.[102] This unfortunate struggle, however, fortuitously concluded with ratification. That result had been spearheaded by Federalists, of course, but Van Buren emphasized that the Constitution had taken its final character from Anti-Federalist insistence on democratic principles, including a bill of rights.[103]

Of course, there is no shortage of modern historians and constitutional theorists to dispute Van Buren's radically democratic characterization of the eighteenth-century Constitution. But, in the nineteenth century, Van Buren represented an important, even dominant, strain of constitutional interpretation, running back through the Republicans to the Anti-Federalists, that had consistently understood the Constitution not in Madisonian terms but in fundamentally democratic terms.[104]

Under a democratic Constitution, then, Van Buren's natural politics, the natural separation between democrats and aristocrats, could resume. The Anti-Federalists disappeared, and if all had then abided by the settled democratic Constitution—accepting the unlimited sovereignty of the people and the radically limited scope of federal power—parties would always have been mere passing factions: "Without any open question affecting permanently every interest . . . as is the case with such as relate to and embrace the sources of power and the foundations of the government, if the Constitution had been upheld in good faith on both sides partisan contests must of necessity have been limited to local or temporary and evanescent measures and to popular excitements and opposing organizations as shifting and short-lived as the subjects which gave rise to them. But Hamilton took especial care that such halcyon days should not even dawn on the country."[105]

In Hamilton's candid moments, according to Van Buren, he avowed his admiration for the British constitution, complete with corruption and unequal representation.[106] And he led the Federalist effort to construct an aristocratic, centralizing constitution by willful misconstruction of the democratic, localist Constitution. In so doing he necessitated the organization of the sovereign people into a national party of resistance. Van Buren wrote that Hamilton's plan had two aspects. Hamilton sought, first, to create a "MONEY POWER,"[107] joined to the power of the national government, which would overcome the influence of the landed democracy in America, "an immense majority of [the] people,"[108] just as it had sapped the independent landed aristocracy of eighteenth-century England.[109] Complementarily, Hamilton sought to enact a series of patently unconstitutional measures, by which the principle of loose construction of the Constitution would become established. The Hamiltonian program would sustain his cherished, commercial aristocracy, but, even more importantly, it would establish the central government's general power to do whatever it conceived to be in the national interest, regardless of constitutional restrictions.[110] Together these two aspects amounted to a constitutional revolution. A written, democratic Constitution, a strictly limited grant of power, was to be replaced, through a series of sophisticated measures, by an unwritten constitution of unlimited power, wielded by an interlocking aristocracy of public office and finance. The fundamentally democratic principle of states' rights, distinctly incorporated into the supreme law of the land, was similarly to be rendered nugatory by this aristocracy of loose construction and consolidation.

Hamilton's revolution was countered in the Revolution of 1800, according to Van Buren, but the anticonstitutional party of the monied elite, changing its name as often as its constitutional character was exposed, persisted in its efforts down to the date of Van Buren's writing. From 1789 to the 1850s, the Federalists, the National Republicans, the Whigs, and the sectional Republicans of the 1850s promoted any number of pernicious measures. But always the point of the measures was less the particular policy at issue than the constitutional project of centralized aristocracy through loose construction:[111]

The principle of construction contended for by Hamilton, and for a season to some extent made successful, was not designed for the promotion of a particular measure, for which the powers of Congress under the Constitution were to be unduly extended, on account of its assumed indispensable importance to the public safety, but intended as a sweeping rule by which those powers, instead of being confined to the constitutional enumeration, were to authorize the passage of all laws which Congress might deem conducive to the general welfare and which were not expressly prohibited; a power similar to that contained in the plan he proposed in the Convention.[112]

In Hamilton's day, the project had seemed all but achieved when, to the surprise of the Federalists, the people seized on the device of party to rise up in constitutional revolution. The many controversies under the elder Adams "sprung out of questions which arose after the two great parties of the country—which have been substantially kept on foot ever since—had been completely organized and had taken the field, the one to accomplish and the other to resist a great national reform which could only be constitutionally determined through the medium of a struggle for the succession."[113] The popular conviction that Hamilton and Adams were monarchists at heart, which Van Buren shared,[114] solidified a permanent union between the old Anti-Federalists and the newer Republicans in the Republican party.[115] That union was an almost spontaneous rising, yet tight organization was its most indispensable aspect: "Sustained by a great preponderance of the landed interest in every part of the country, the old Republican party attained a degree of vigor and efficiency superior to that of any partisan organization which had before or has since appeared on the political stage."[116]

The particular issue that settled the contest in 1800, according to Van Buren, was the Alien and Sedition Acts. The Sedition Act, especially, mocked that Bill of Rights by which the Anti-Federalists had finally ensured the democratic character of the Constitution. Thus the contest turned to a large degree on a particular measure, but only because that measure went to the heart of the constitutional conflict.[117] Since that time, contests had always depended on passing substantive issues, but rarely had the issues been treated as more important than the abiding constitutional principles that separated the permanent, natural parties: "Questions of public policy, disconnected from considerations of constitutional power, have arisen, been discussed, decided or abandoned and forgotten, whilst the political parties of the country have remained as they were."[118]

The Revolution of 1800, then, was a restoration of the Constitution by party organization. To Van Buren, that revolution was the origin of a permanent revolution, rewon in every quadrennial test of the American people's constitutionalism. And the permanent necessity of a kind of revolutionary popular politics implied as well the permanent necessity of 1800's agency of revolution: the organized political party, united by the principle of majority rule as mechanized by adherence to the regular nominations of convention or caucus.

The permanent and thorough organization of a political party comprehending every democratic citizen was a great step beyond what Jefferson had contemplated. More generally, of course, it was a step apparently at odds with all political tradition and with nearly universal antipartyist conviction. The Federalists and their successors through the generations, according to Van Buren, always made the most of this popular prejudice: "It is a striking fact in our political history that the sagacious leaders of the Federal party, as well under that name as under others by which it has at different times been known, have always been desirous to bring every usage or plan designed to secure party unity into disrepute with the people, and in proportion to their success in that has been their success in elections." In contrast, the Republican party, "whenever it ha[d] been wise enough to employ the caucus or convention system" in good faith, had always been successful.[119]

As should be abundantly clear by now, Van Buren did not conceive of this party organization that he celebrated as a mere electoral machine or as an agent of a particular set of social or economic measures or even ideologies. Such a party he would have regarded as factious. His party was the constitutional party of the sovereign people. An analogous brand of party had been conceived in an older, more aristocratic culture, its chief early theorist being Bolingbroke. Versions of the idea were later embraced in different contexts by Burke, Jefferson, and others.[120] But in Van Buren's hands the constitutional party became a mass party, organized down to the last democrat in the land. It anticipated no single millennial victory but permanent triumph through permanent constitutional struggle, every election a ratification election for Van Buren's partyist Constitution of pure majoritarianism and strict construction.[121]

Van Buren himself was a kind of antipartyist then. Not only was his party an attempt to defeat the permanent rule of a faction and to forestall any party division within the democratic polity, such as constitutes the essence of the modern party system. He was, as well, capable of yearning for the "halcyon days," the "real 'era of good feeling,'" which the nation might have enjoyed absent the Federalist attack on the Constitution itself. Arch-partyist that he was, Martin Van Buren rooted his partyism, in fact, in a traditional commitment to antipartyism within a settled constitutional order.

The contest with the Federalists and their successors, therefore, was always a kind of antipartyist one-upsmanship. Facing the constant challenge of Federalist antipartyism, Van Burenites endlessly insisted that that sort of "anti-partyism" was a ruse. It was not a determination to forgo party unity in favor of the constitutional imperative of individual independence. Rather, the Federalists were permanently and easily unified by the nature of their interests:

> A political party founded on such principles and looking to such sources for its support does not often stand in need of caucuses and conventions to preserve harmony in its ranks. Constructed principally of a network of special interests,—almost all of them looking to Government for encouragement of some sort,—the feelings and opinions of its members spontaneously point in the same direction, and when those interests are thought in danger, or new inducements are held out for their advancement, notice of the apprehended assault or promised encouragement is circulated through their ranks with a facility always supplied by the sharpened wit of cupidity. . . . Sensible of these facts, the policy of their leaders has been from the beginning to discountenance and explode all usages or plans designed to secure party unity, so essential to their opponents and substantially unnecessary to themselves.[122]

The permanent contest over the Constitution, therefore, resolved itself into a contest over the unwritten constitution's disposition of the question of party. At each election, the Democrats had to renew their call for constitutional party conflict as the best kind of antipartyism in the circumstance of anticonstitutional conspiracy. And at each election, according to Van Buren, the enemies of the Constitution would renew their call to put down party. If the naturally democratic public ratified Van Buren's partyist constitutionalism—that is, simply the forcing of all elections onto party grounds—then popular sovereignty itself was assured. If Federalist antipartyist constitutionalism predominated—that is, the running of elections among candidates not openly tied to parties—then the victory of Federalist anticonstitutional governance was equally certain.

The conclusive proof that constitutional governance depended directly on the question of party lay in Van Buren's own 1820s. During the four presidential terms of Jefferson and Madison, he insisted, popular adherence to party organization had translated automatically into mandates for constitutional democracy at the polls and into strictly construed, constitutional governance in the capital. Under the Monroe and Adams administrations, however, the negative of the proposition was proven. Without even the agitation of any "disturbing public questions," the ascendancy of republican constitutionalism was disrupted by the neglect of Republican constitutionalism:

The Republican party, so long in the ascendant, and apparently so omnipotent, was literally shattered into fragments, and we had no fewer than five Republican Presidential candidates in the field.

In the place of two great parties arrayed against each other in a fair and open contest for the establishment of principles in the administration of Government which they respectively believed most conducive to the public interest, the country was overrun with personal factions. . . .

The occurrence of scenes discreditable to all had for a long time been prevented by a steady adherence on the part of the Republican party to the caucus system; and if Mr. Monroe's views and feelings upon the subject had been the same as were those of Jefferson and Madison, the results to which I have alluded . . . might have been prevented by the same means. . . . Mr. Monroe and a majority of his cabinet were unfortunately influenced by different views, and pursued a course well designed to weaken the influence of the caucus system, and to cause its abandonment. Mr. Crawford was the only candidate who, it was believed, could be benefited by adhering to it, and the friends of all the others sustained the policy of the administration. Those of Jackson, Adams, Clay, and Calhoun, united in an address to the people condemning the practice of caucus nominations, and announcing their determination to disregard them. Already weakened through the adverse influence of the administration, the agency which had so long preserved the unity of the Republican party did not retain sufficient strength to resist the combined assault that was made upon it, and was overthrown.[123]

By the middle of Monroe's second term, moreover, the president had reversed his former stout adherence to the exclusion of Federalists from appointive office.[124] Increasingly this caucus-nominated president was "doing openly all that a man . . . could be expected to do to promote the amalgamation of parties and the overthrow of that exclusive and towering supremacy which the republican party had for many years maintained in our national councils."[125]

The result of such a revival of antipartyism was inevitably the revival of centralizing anticonstitutionalism, even among dyed-in-the-wool Republicans. Thus, when Monroe abandoned his once supreme adherence to Republican organizationalism, he also began to slip in the principles that governed his policies as president. Most dramatic was his reversal of his quarter-century commitment to strict construction by avowing the federal government's unlimited power to fund internal improvements projects: "A diminished zeal for the support of [the party's] pure and self-denying principles was the natural consequence of a diminished, might I not say an extinguished solicitude for its continued ascendency. It was almost inevitable that efforts to destroy the republican organization should lead to the gradual abandonment of the principles it sustained."[126]

For Van Buren, then, consistently partisan use of the patronage, as of caucus and convention, was not partisan but republican. Republican government itself was identified not with an intraconstitutional party system but with the "towering supremacy" of the constitutionally faithful partyists over the anticonstitutional antipartyists by means of party organization. And if the constitutional party was not merely partisan but an antiparty party of the Constitution, then its spoils and conventions and caucuses were not merely partisan devices but constitutional mechanisms.

The culmination of the antipartyist revival among much of the Republican leadership was, to Van Buren, the election of John Quincy Adams, "the latitudinarianism of whose constitutional views extended beyond those of any of his cotemporaries."[127] Adams, in short, was a Federalist enemy to the Constitution in all but name and could only have been elected in the absence of party organization. Such a man could never have received a Republican regular nomination. His bargained election alone was enough to restore many Republicans' commitment to organization, and his subsequent administration restored many more to their original faith. Not only did he pursue unconstitutional objects, such as federal construction of internal improvements; he even frankly urged Congress not "to be palsied by the will of their Constituents" but to boldly aid him in his splendid projects.[128] Such sentiments could not be tolerated by any true republican, according to Van Buren, and even those most wary of party, excluding Secretary of State Henry Clay's personal following, subsequently returned to the party fold.[129]

The most important among these prodigal sons was Andrew Jackson himself. Jackson's famous amalgamationist letter to Monroe in 1816[130] and his opposition to the congressional caucus had made him suspect to "old republicans." But his mistreatment in the House election of 1825 boosted his already impressive popularity and made him the only alternative to Adams's Federalism. Van Buren hoped "that by adding the General's personal popularity to the strength of the old Republican party which still acted together . . . we might . . . be able to compete successfully with the power and patronage of the Administration . . . ; that we had abundant evidence that the general was at an earlier period well grounded in the principles of our party, and that we must trust to good fortune and to the effects of favorable associations for the removal of the rust they had contracted."[131]

The measures and principles of the younger Adams, supposedly perpetuated by the anti-Jacksonian, Bank-led opposition of the 1830s, proved to all who would listen that party organization, popular sovereignty, and the Constitution were inseparable. Through two Jackson administrations, Van Burenites hammered the partyist argument home. And if Jackson's election was not entirely the doing of a party organization, as Van Buren had wished above all else for it to be, Van Buren's own election, eight years later, was exactly that, as was every Democratic success to follow.

Anti–Van Burenite Republicanism

Van Buren idolized Jefferson and believed himself a mere carrier of Jefferson's own constitutionalism. But so did everybody else. As Van Buren could cite Jefferson as a party leader, so the "amalgamators" of the 1820s could cite him as an opponent of party. In fact, it has been argued that all presidents before Jackson were, in their own minds, something like republicanized "patriot kings." If nothing else was consistently true among the first six presidents, they all sought the deliverance of American government from party in a way akin to that outlined by Bolingbroke.[132] As Jefferson and Madison conducted their frequently partisan presidencies in pursuit of that happy day when constitutional stability would render parties unnecessary, so James Monroe and John Quincy Adams believed that day had arrived during their administrations.

When Monroe took office in 1817, he, like his predecessors, felt it necessary to take party into account in appointments because there remained a postwar residue of Federalist leaders who "entertained principles unfriendly to our system." At the same time, however, he made the famous tour through the northeastern states during which the term "era of good feeling" was coined and by which he sought to accelerate the developing political unanimity of the people.[133] He made the promotion of unity a chief purpose of his tenure from the outset: "Equally gratifying is it to witness the increased harmony of opinion which pervades our Union. Discord does not belong to our system. . . . [The American people] constitute one great family with a common interest. . . . To promote this harmony in accord with the principles of our republican Government and in a manner to give them the most complete effect . . . will be the object of my constant and zealous exertions."[134]

On being reelected virtually unanimously in 1820, Monroe could indulge the belief that party really had become obsolete. He detected, as he thought, powerful forces for unanimity as the Union strengthened and stabilized itself: "That these powerful causes exist, and that they are permanent, is my fixed opinion; that they may produce a like accord in all questions touching, however remotely, the liberty, prosperity, and happiness of our country will always be the object of my most fervent prayers."[135] In particular, the absence of the contending social orders of nobility and people as well as the absence of the tumult of direct democracy made an enduringly harmonious politics possible for the first time in history.[136]

With such language Monroe evidenced an utter blindness to what Van Buren saw as covert aristocratic efforts to re-create a rigidly stratified socio-constitutional order and, consequently, an utter disregard for the organizational integrity of the Republicans. But Monroe's antipartyism was the natural and traditional conviction of most Americans to that date. The Van Burenite support for the 1824 congressional caucus in the absence of a Federalist party candidate was not at all popular. The resulting factionalism might have been regrettable to most voters, but handing over the choice of the president to a centralized party caucus hardly seemed an appropriate cure. Rather, in the presumed absence of a challenge to Monroe's new constitutional stability, traditional antipartyism and constitutional democracy seemed to mandate a choice of president only by constitutional election among independent republicans, without the intervention of party.

John Quincy Adams, of course, took his elevation to be just such an election, partyless and constitutional. He was, obviously, aware of the electoral factionalism in which he and other honest republicans had taken part. Such passing factionalism, however, was easily tolerated in comparison to either the great competition of constitutional parties that he believed obsolete or the recurring competition of organized interests he meant to transcend in his presidency. His inaugural address celebrated the absence of parties and looked forward to an aggressive engineering of a grand, national public good without the obstructions of parties.[137]

Pointing to the foreign policy crises that were resolved by 1815 and to the supposed constitutional consensus of the 1820s, he made clear his differences with Van Buren regarding the sources and history of parties:

[Between 1789 and 1815] the policy of the Union in its relations with Europe constituted the principal basis of our political divisions and the most arduous part of the action of our Federal Government. With the catastrophe in which the wars of the French Revolution terminated, and our own subsequent peace with Great Britain, this baneful weed of party strife was uprooted. From that time no difference of principle, connected either with the theory of government or with our intercourse with foreign nations, has existed or been called forth in force sufficient to sustain a continued combination of parties or to give more than wholesome animation to public sentiment or legislative debate. Our political creed is, without a dissenting voice that can be heard, that the will of the people is the source[,] and the happiness of the people the end[,] of all legitimate government upon earth. . . . If there have been those who have doubted whether a confederated representative democracy were a government competent to the wise and orderly management of the common concerns of a mighty nation, those doubts have been dispelled. . . . Ten years of peace, at home and abroad, have assuaged the animosities of political contention and blended into harmony the most discordant elements of public opinion.[138]

Adams shared Van Buren's understanding of the word "principle" as denoting constitutional principle, but disputed Van Buren's notion that parties of principle still battled in America, if they ever had.

The problem of party, to Adams, was now reduced to the small parties to be transcended by the federal government: "The collisions of party spirit which originate in speculative opinions or in different views of administrative policy are in their nature transitory. Those which are founded on geographical divisions . . . are more permanent, and therefore, perhaps, more dangerous."[139] A central benefit of the federal government, then, had to be a reconciling of the different sectional interests of the nation. Through such federal action, the last source of durable parties in the American system would recede. Adams concluded his address with a call for the national internal improvement system that would so often be held out as just such a party-transcending, section-joining agent of national conciliation.[140]

Henry Clay, as well, saw in the 1820s the glorious day when anxiety for the Constitution might finally recede and the national potential be fearlessly pursued. For Republicans of his stripe, Adams's presidency was the first opportunity for America to spread its wings without the worry that there were aristocrats behind every positive measure of public improvement. They foresaw American grandeur and unity arising from a great democratic network of commerce and self-improvement. To such men the partyist "radicals" of 1824 were mere opportunists, trying to keep obsolete fears alive in order to sustain political careers that offered the people nothing but pointless conflict and consequently pathetic government.

The Supreme Court, meanwhile, under the leadership of the Federalist John Marshall and the nationalist Republican Joseph Story, began openly to champion the sort of loose construction of the Constitution that Van Buren identified with the Federalist anticonstitutional project. In *McCulloch v. Maryland*[141] and other cases, the Court affirmed Congress's power to exercise its enumerated powers quite broadly.[142] And in *Martin v. Hunter's Lessee*[143] the Court affirmed its own power to police the state courts in their interpretations of the Constitution and other federal law.[144]

With the Supreme Court opening the door, Adams, Clay, and their ilk confidently proposed ambitious exercises of federal power like Clay's American System. The American System was a plan for the federal government's development and encouragement of American commerce of all kinds, but its economic effects were intended centrally to bind together a union that seemed forever on the verge of dissolution. Clay himself was not the antiparty purist that Adams was. Nor was he a party-builder like Van Buren, although he was more than willing to use party when it was the best available option. His grand vision was an essentially suprapartisan one, resting on the anti–Van Burenite assumption that there existed no principled grounds on which to rest permanent political division in the American republic. The American System's goal was to transcend all sources of division, partisan or sectional, in the pursuit of progress and union, the indispensable characteristics of American republicanism. In such expansive federal power, Van Buren may only have seen aristocracy, but Clay and his like saw an ever grander democracy.[145]

Conclusion

The politicians of the 1820s were the heirs of the antipartyist theory of the British balanced constitution. Removed now from any society afflicted with authentic nobles or monarch, they continued to wonder how mixed government's truncation, a representative democracy, might be constituted, how "the democracy" might practice and sustain its constitutional sovereignty over the long term. They clung to the category of aristocracy and sought out its American variant, whether monied men or party politicians, in order to isolate the enemy but also to define the Constitution's "popular sovereignty" by its constitutional antithesis.

For the Clay and Adams men of the 1820s, the democracy had to be unafflicted with party, the device by which neo-Walpolean knots of politicians might obstruct the essential democratic pursuit of self-improvement through popular government. For the Van Burenites, the democracy had to prevent the government's reversion to elite control. By self-denying commitment to party organization, the democracy might sustain the Constitution as written. Anything less would open the door to subversion of the constitutional enumeration, sap the authority of the states, and surrender the government to that central principle of aristocracy, unchecked power. In a world dominated by aristocracies, post-aristocratic America struggled for the means to give the Constitution life and thus to keep the partyless democracy's hands on the lever of government.

CHAPTER TWO

The Antiparty Consensus
of the Illinois Democracy

Explaining the "market revolution" of early national America, Charles Sellers has recently observed that "democracy was born in tension with capitalism, and not as its natural and legitimizing political expression."[1] Sellers made this point because capitalism and democracy appear to have become irrevocably fused over time in the public mind, even though many early democrats thought corporate capitalism incompatible with popular sovereignty and even, in a sense, "unconstitutional."[2] In the same way, democracy and multipartyism are today widely assumed to be inseparable. But the early national democracy's skepticism of capitalist economics was matched by its hostility to party organization. The modern fusion of democracy, market capitalism, and the party system is a distinctly artificial development, one that required both the full-scale cultural revolution launched by the democratic partyists in every state and the unpredictable circumstances that turned that revolution far from its original goals. In the terminology of Keith Whittington,[3] the partyist revision of popular sovereignty represented an aggressive, disturbing, and utterly novel "constitutional construction." What, then, did American democrats think popular sovereignty meant before the ascendancy of the party system and the market? A look at early Illinois will suggest an answer.

When Illinois entered the Union in 1818, it entered with a written constitution, but also with the unwritten, antipartyist constitution common to all states at that time. Its non-Indian population in 1818 came mostly from the southern states, a region largely untouched by partyist political theory. But settlers from all regions believed themselves the pioneers of democracy in the post-aristocratic world, and they brought with them antipartyist constitutional assumptions derived from those outlined in the previous chapter.[4]

Illinois's constitution provided for universal white manhood suffrage and frequent, popular elections.[5] Although these arrangements remained well shy of the racially pluralist and gender-inclusive structures now thought essential to democracy, Illinois's constitution was a democratic document by almost any standard of the time and fairly represented the dramatic democratization of American constitutional culture since the writing of the Madisonian Constitution.[6] But such formal provisions did not exhaust the meaning of popular sovereignty. Just as important was the state's universal rejection of party organization and partisan behavior. Democratic suffrage provisions, Illinoisans thought, granted the vote to be exercised according to individual conscience, not the needs of a political organization. The electorate expected candidates to be public-spirited and independent, not regular nominees of parties. In these latter respects, Illinois's unwritten constitution shared the spirit of Madison's written Constitution. But it broke with Madison by placing an active popular sovereignty at the center, not the margins, of Illinois's constitutional culture.

Antipartyism at the Birth of the Polity

Illinois had no "First Party System." Federalists were unknown in the territory, and the label of Jeffersonian Republican was usually superfluous. There had, however, been factional divisions when Illinois was part of Indiana Territory. Grounds of conflict included Governor William Henry Harrison's appointments, methods for getting around the Northwest Ordinance's ban on slavery, the actions of the territory's land commissioners, and finally the creation of Illinois Territory out of Indiana in 1809. Certain personal alliances also seem to have been stable over several years. But, as the national parties proved superfluous to territorial politics, so the territorial factions failed to entrench themselves.

When Ninian Edwards was named the first governor of Illinois in 1809, some attempted to perpetuate old divisions. Edwards, however, was studiedly neutral, and many former comrades could soon be found on opposite sides of political questions. Little, if any, factional coherence survived. In the years before statehood in 1818, there did develop some degree of factional division around Edwards. This division, however, was as evanescent as its predecessors.[7]

As the territory began to approach the population necessary for statehood, then, factional divisions within a small elite were familiar enough. These divisions were neither stable nor deep, however, and they had not begun to shake the polity's antipartisan convictions. If anything they seem to have reinforced them.

Typical was the *Western Intelligencer*'s endorsement of Nathaniel Pope for delegate to Congress in 1816. Central to Pope's qualifications was his freedom from "those party disputes which have so frequently disturbed the reposed of the Territory."[8] Pope's competition was Russell L. Heacock, who advertised himself as a common man sharing in "the common interest" and lacking the wealth that inclined men to serve a separate interest or a "particular class of citizens." Heacock lamented that elections sometimes turned on "warmth of party spirit, and influential favoritism" rather than on "good sense and judgment."[9]

This routine exchange between two candidates illustrates three things. First, it reflects the antipartyist consensus that suffused Illinois's political culture before the 1830s. This outlook not only condemned party but mandated that the voter be guided by his independent judgment of the public good rather than his own individual or group interest.

Second, Heacock's statement introduces the most common early definition of party: a set of men motivated in their political behavior by private rather than public interest—a faction. At this time, few would have argued that pursuit of one's private interest through politics was compatible with the polity's pursuit of the indivisible general good. And the political manifestation of private interest was party.

Finally, this exchange suggests an identification of authentic antipartyism with the democracy rather than with an educated or monied elite. In contrast to Pope, Heacock argued that the common man was the best judge of the homogeneous interests of a society made up overwhelmingly of farmers. His man of wealth was attached to the separate interests of a monied minority of the polity. Thus partisanship was to be expected from this self-interested minority, whereas party was alien to anyone attached by one's daily labor to the general democratic interest, to the legitimate democracy itself.

In these days, there was little dissent from the Madisonian notion that a coherent general interest did exist and that party division was destructive of it. Even in the 1830s, party would be justified not as a practical mechanism for compromising a variety of interests but as the very embodiment of a still undivided general interest, defined by majority vote. Candidate Heacock's campaign statement concisely introduces the fundamentals of Illinois's original unwritten constitution, its commitment to a democratic order free from party and the identification of party with faction.

As the campaign for statehood began in late 1817, one writer articulated an understanding of party that was apparently distinct from faction. "A Republican" described a kind of party division that reflected differences in constitutional principles, not just policy goals. Such constitutional parties were defined by their abiding attachment to republican, aristocratic, or monarchical government. Responding to the antistatehood argument that "the population of the territory, was in too great a state of ignorance and too much lacerated by party contentions to become independent," the pseudonymous "Republican" insisted that the bulk of the population was familiar with republican government and that even the monarchist remnant (the French population which had originally settled Illinois) had shown itself attached to "true republican principles."[10] In making this argument, he apparently took "ignorance" to mean ignorance of republican government and took "party contentions" to mean conflicts between republicanism and monarchism, not just differences over particular policies.

This understanding of party would prove to be of great salience as partyism waxed in the 1830s. In 1817, however, the author rejected the idea that parties did or should exist in Illinois. He made the routine assumption that the absence of party was fundamental to good government. The editor of the *Intelligencer* quickly reinforced this assumption when he argued that the necessity of Illinois's remaining in colonial status was over, since "no territory has ever been admitted into the union where so little division of sentiment, (as well on great political questions, as on the present occasion) has prevailed as in this."[11] The implication was that a society which did contain substantial division might not be fit for republican self-government.

The First State Elections: Nomination and Campaign without Party

Antipartyist assumptions persisted in the era of statehood even though there did exist two parties of sorts in earliest Illinois. The "Edwards party" took its cues from the former territorial governor, now senator. Another collection of politicians gathered around the new governor, Shadrach Bond, the other senator, Jesse B. Thomas, and the secretary of state, Elias Kent Kane—the "Bond party," for short. However, these parties did not acknowledge themselves as parties, much less adopt party names or platforms or organizations. If they were parties, it was only in the loosest sense of the word—sets of men informally acting together from time to time. Politicians on both sides, in fact, continued in time-honored fashion to disparage party behavior as the worst evil in a republic. And these parties had no formal presence whatsoever in elections.

In 1818, Bond was elected governor without opposition. In 1819 and 1822, Daniel Pope Cook and John McLean ran against each other twice for Congress, with Cook winning both times. In the intervening election in 1820, Cook defeated Kane. Cook was said to be of the Edwards party and McLean and Kane of the Bond party, but no man ran as the nominee of a party or acknowledged any connection with any party. Each was nominated by means of a simple announcement of candidacy in the newspapers and ran without any public connection to other concurrent elections.

Brief accounts of these elections and others even less partisan will confirm the persistence of antiparty constitutionalism in the new polity and introduce the age's characteristic modes of nomination. In preparation for the August election of 1819, Cook announced his candidacy in April. He noted the presence of two parties in the state, attached to men, not measures, and disavowed subservience to either.[12] In 1820 Cook was again "self-nominated" for Congress when the *Illinois Gazette* ran the standard notice that it was "authorized to announce" him as a candidate. The *Gazette* ran a similar announcement for Kane in the same issue.[13] During the months leading to the August election, candidates for both county and statewide office would be similarly self-nominated — nominated in the newspapers by self-declaration or by the action of "friends."[14] Henry Eddy's self-nomination for state representative presents a sharp contrast to the practice of regular nominations that would arrive in later years: "The subscriber availing himself of the right, which he in common with his Fellow Citizens has of obtruding himself upon the publick for their suffrage, respectfully informs them that he is a Candidate for the House of Representatives, in the next General Assembly."[15] In the next generation, in contrast, the partyists would deny the right of any person to run for office without a regular nomination.

The sole example of partyism in these elections was the assertion made by Kane, reputed to be one of the most partisan politicians in the state, that he was positively attached to the "great republican party of the union." As suggested above, however, Kane's adherence to this constitutional party was not the attack on the antipartyist consensus that it may appear to be. Kane's statement, in fact, was a defense to the charge that he was a party man. "Under no obligations to consult the desires of any party of men — I owe allegiance to none, and feel prepared to come before the people, promising, if elected, to represent the public interests and wishes. . . . For myself I shall take no pride in an election, unless on grounds independent of particular questions, men or parties — with the *single exception*, that I am attached to the great republican party of the union. I detest the attempt to detach Illinois from the republican family, to serve the purposes of aspiring, unprincipled men."[16]

Kane implicitly distinguished between two kinds of party: the first was party as faction, which Kane condemned as vigorously as anyone; the second was constitutional party, the aggregation of all who believed in a particular form of government, in this case republican. Kane's statement was the first hint in Illinois of Van Buren's theory of party. In 1820, however, this hint was only the slightest twist on the usual antipartyist assurances of candidates to voters. Moreover, if Kane sought to modify prevailing prejudices against partyism and to justify an active "republican party" by painting Cook and his cohorts as the advance guard of an aristocratic "federal party" in Illinois,[17] he failed. Cook won the election in a landslide.[18] Insofar as the question of party was salient in the election, Cook's supporters appear to have been successful in making Kane out to be a "factionist" of the "slave party," exactly the sort of illegitimate party that Kane contrasted with the great republican party. They also made him out to be an opponent of the Monroe administration and, therefore, hardly republican.[19]

In 1822, the major election was a four-way gubernatorial race won by Edward Coles, an antislavery immigrant from Virginia. This race typified state politics at the time because the unattached candidates campaigned as much on their personal characters as on their positions on issues. Historians' efforts to determine one particular question on which this race turned or to locate a party alignment beneath the candidacies have failed because politics at the time lacked the firm alignments that parties would later give it.[20]

Joseph Phillips's self-nomination for governor appeared in the *Intelligencer* a year and a half before the election.[21] Three more candidates' names were announced during the campaign.[22] None of these candidates avowed any party affiliation. All ran as independents, and at least two explicitly declared that their nominations were their own and not authorized by parties.[23] All evidence suggests that these declarations were accurate, that, while individuals naturally communicated with their friends about the propriety of running and about the logistics of a campaign, the candidates were self-chosen and supported by no organizations worthy of the name. Although historians have sometimes tried to make this campaign turn on a conflict between a proslavery party and an antislavery party, neither the rhetoric of the campaign nor the voting patterns support the notion that slavery, much less parties organized on that question, played the major part in the campaign.[24]

The inclination to see slavery eclipsing all other issues comes from reading the rhetoric of the campaign of 1824 back into 1822. And the inclination to see the election organized by parties comes from reading back the modern sense of their inevitability. The election of 1822 was a contest among true independents on issues that included state banking, internal improvements, and public land policy as well as slavery[25]—a range of issues that had not in the 1820s been assimilated to party platforms or ideologies but that left each candidate free to form his own individual constellation of positions.

The most local levels of politics in this period have left behind little evidence. An 1822 letter from a candidate for sheriff to his distant brother, however, describes Illinois's thoroughly democratic electoral culture in gratifyingly concrete terms that complement the evidence drawn from gubernatorial and congressional campaigns:

The general Election for governor, members of congress, and the State Legislature, is near at hand, and the whole state is overwhelmed by the sea of politics: All are deeply engaged from the hoary headed grandsire, to the youthfull stripling. . . . Whenever a man is announced as a candidate . . . he becomes a target at which every scribbler, who can wield a pen, shoots his squibs and crackers, with impunity. The candidate wheather he aspires to the high office of governor, or that of Representative of the people; he is obliged to ride over the whole state or district as the case may be attending every log rolling petty muster or barbecue; where he is expected to make what is called a stump speech wheather he possesses a talent for that sublime species of eloquence or not—he must relate his political experience, and recapitulate his political creed, which he takes care shall always coincide with that of his hearers. If he has not been in the wars and has no [scars?] to show, he must purpose some plan of relief. . . . And whilest he speakes of the pecuniary distress which pervades the country, a frequent application of the kerchief, to his eye is not amiss because it serves to show that he really feels for the miseries of his fellow man. This together with the right of instruction will bare out the candidate. I am a candidate for the Sheriffality of the county. This office is elective. I have five able opponents but it is thought I have nothing to fear.[26]

This letter makes the routine assumption that candidates from sheriff to governor were to be announced, not nominated, with the result that there were six candidates for sheriff in the writer's own county and, ultimately, four candidates for governor. And parties are completely absent from the description, even as the letter conveys a radically democratic culture amid hard economic times.

Since this new and untested democratic culture rested on a pointed antipartyism, even local questions like county division were readily inflated to touch the health of the unwritten constitution itself. George Churchill's legislative campaign address in 1820 emphasized his opposition to the division of his county in two. The problem with division was not only that it would sacrifice the interests of the "*many*" for those of the "few," although that was bad enough. The greater significance of the sacrifice was that it would advance the subordination of the legislature to faction, specifically to the "townmakers and speculators" who often were the prime movers in county division. "Ignorance and imbecility will become the sole passports to the legislative hall" since better men would not consent to be the tools of speculators. "In this manner, the people will become divided into petty factions . . . and the general harmony of the state will be destroyed. This is not chimerical" where "the spirit of speculation" has taken root.[27]

As of 1822, Illinois remained very much in the infancy of its effort to establish the norms of democratic practice. The constitution directed that all white male inhabitants of six months' residence and twenty-one years of age could vote. The constitution and statutes established a wide range of offices that would be filled by popular election. But constitution and statute said nothing about how candidates should be chosen to run for those offices. In the earliest days, self-nomination through newspaper announcement was almost the exclusive mode of nomination. But some believed that a genuine popular sovereignty required a new, more democratic way of nominating candidates.

One meeting in Harrisonville labeled self-nomination an "aristocratic practice" and proposed instead that townships and counties hold nominating meetings. The nomination list should include more than one man for each office, and no man should be nominated who was a delegate to the nominating meeting. All voters should then be encouraged to vote for men on these lists to the exclusion of anyone nominating or electioneering for himself.[28]

Elsewhere, "The Hustings" offered a similar plan, identifying self-nomination and electioneering as relics of English aristocracy. The virtuous did not thrust themselves forward for nomination nor electioneer for themselves. They could be placed in the public service only if the people nominated them first and then chose from among them on election day.[29] None of these advocates of nominating meetings, however, publicly advocated partisan conventions, even though such conventions were no longer unprecedented in American politics by 1819.[30]

Opponents of organized nominations, however, emphasized the equivalence of organization and partisanship. "A Republican" responded to "The Hustings" by asserting that "nomination by delegates, is a party measure" and that such a "caucus nomination" would substitute "the will of the *few*, for the will of the *many*." Thus the legally prescribed mode of choosing officers—popular election—would be made "subservient to an illegal . . . caucus." Almost as an aside, this writer then made the interesting concession that in places where parties existed, such as in former times in the eastern states, party nominations were sometimes necessary. In Illinois, however, parties did not exist.[31] "A Republican" again distinguished between two core meanings for "party": party as faction—"the few"—for whom organized nomination was a means to seduce the electorate; and party as constitutional party—as in the constitutional clashes of the First Party System in the East—for which party nominations were regrettable necessities until a constitutional consensus became firm, as in Illinois.

"Zero" reinforced the argument of "A Republican" by describing some of the history of nomination. He acknowledged that self-nomination in England had traditionally indicated one's intent to buy an election, but he thought the alternative of nomination by delegates had proven itself far worse. Delegate nominations of the supposedly unambitious had been tried in the eastern states:

> Whoever has seen, as we have, how regularly drilled and organized, is the system of elective nomination, in the eastern states, where *modest* men, and till of late modest *anglo-federalists*, and modest *Hartford Conventionists*, have been returned to Congress, would see how specious, how plausable, and yet how pernicious, is this course. Instead of the direct individual influence of the candidate, on the community at large, arising from the open declarations of his pen; his public demonstrations of the interests of his country at *the Hustings* . . . instead of all this, he is enshrined as the Juggernaut of his party.

Zero went on to describe the "little private caucuses" that "cut and dried" the nomination before the actual nominating meeting. That meeting was then attended by "*all* of the partizans of the intended candidate" while the mass of the people went about their business, intending only to do their part on election day, but finding themselves inevitably influenced by the nomination. Even in the best case, Zero foresaw that "designation of candidates by any portion of [the community], however correct that designation might be, is an assumption of anti-republican power and influence, which would lead, by practise, to a prescriptive aristocracy . . . more to be dreaded than the mistaken exercise of our own judgment, which the next Hustings might *correct*." Zero's fear of a prescriptive aristocracy, of course, would be realized in the age of party, as continuing party leaderships came to have great influence over their public's choice of candidates.

In contrast to this gloomy picture, Zero painted a glorious portrait of self-nomination. Under that system, men forthrightly offered themselves and campaigned for themselves before a discerning people. Self-nomination was the only way that the community could elevate those talented men who lacked the intriguer's "knack of soothing the turbulent, courting the rich, or imposing on the weak or ignorant" in pursuit of a caucus nomination.

> Every citizen who appreciates his consequence, as an *equal* member of this sole and august nation of freemen, will independently judge and act for him-

self, . . . uninfluenced by caucuses, nominations, or delegations. Experience has shewn, that they are political machines in the hands of the designing, the wealthy, and the vicious, by which they essay to influence, guide, and govern popular opinion. It is beneath the dignity of an American citizen to suffer any man or set of men to think or act for him in estimating in the *first* instance his qualifications for office, or in the exercise of his elective franchise.[32]

At this time, the preponderance of public opinion and the whole weight of tradition were on Zero's side. Before 1824, virtually all candidates for public office were self-nominated. Party was pervasively stigmatized, and organized nominations of any description were likely to be labeled as party intrigue. The deficiencies of self-nomination did lead to a couple of proposals for reform. But the electorate overwhelmingly rejected such proposals, if only by inaction, and rested secure in the faith that theirs was as democratic a polity as existed, sensitive to every hint of party or organized nomination.

The Elections of 1824

The usual assumption among historians is that partyism arose because the government engaged increasingly in certain kinds of social policy. Most prominently, the growing presence of the market economy in the daily lives of Americans and in the policy dilemmas of the government has emerged as a central source of the party ideologies of the Second Party System.[33] The story of the parties' emanating from the preexisting economic orientations of the people leaves the reader to assume, however, that any powerful, politically divisive phenomenon occurring within the context of broad suffrage would inevitably breed a party system. But the case of Illinois suggests that much more than the mere presence of political controversy was necessary to turn an antiparty democracy into a two-party democracy. Similarly, much more than the mere presence of broad suffrage was necessary to induce politicians to invent permanent structures for recruiting voters to their causes.[34]

Elections through 1822 offered plenty of political controversy. Especially divisive issues through 1822 included the movement to build a canal between Lake Michigan and the Illinois River and the chartering of a state bank, the latter event triggering "a series of county meetings and petitions that continued throughout the [1822 gubernatorial] campaign."[35] Still there was no semblance of party organization in the elections.

The most divisive political moment in pre-partyist Illinois, however, was the convention campaign of 1823–24, which centered on slavery. At the same time, the presidential campaign was heating up, and all the regular state elections were held. Taken together, the elections of 1824 were the most dramatic and divisive episode in Illinois politics perhaps until 1840. But the central fact is that the various elections did not merge into a single statewide party competition. Confronted with the entrenched doctrine that popular sovereignty could not survive sustained party division, none of the divisions of 1824 sparked the formation of a party system, although a small coterie of partyists took what advantage they could.

In the winter of 1823 the General Assembly called a popular election to determine whether a state constitutional convention should be held. In the campaign that followed, "non-conventionists" asserted that the proposed convention would try to smuggle slavery into the state and that a vote for the convention was a vote to ratify the party-bred schemes[36] by which the resolution passed the legislature. "Conventionists," on the other hand, presented a variety of reasons for calling a constitutional convention. Some of them frankly avowed their support for slavery, but most claimed that other defects in the Constitution needed fixing. In any case, the campaign employed far less organization and discipline, ideological or otherwise, than one might expect given the emotional intensity of the issue. And the rhetoric of the campaign remained overwhelmingly antipartyist, both among the ultimately victorious opponents of the convention and among its supporters.

Following the lead of the legislative minority's public protest against the resolution,[37] pamphleteer Morris Birkbeck established the basic themes of the anticonvention campaign. He argued that both the party tactics in the legislature and the proslavery intentions of the conventionists made the proposed convention dangerous. These arguments merged in the assertion that the underlying principle of the conventionists was not just economic self-interest but an anticonstitutional pursuit of arbitrary power in opposition to republicanism.

Birkbeck described the underhanded tactics by which a "faction" turned the legislature against its better judgment[38] and then urged rejection of the convention to cure "the disease in the legislature."[39] The alternative, he warned, was a government of factions succeeding factions, "a tyranny of knaves, without honour or principle, or public spirit!"[40]

Birkbeck's objection to slavery, which he believed was the immediate object of the conventionists, was essentially the same as his objection to party and faction: it granted irresponsible power to select individuals. It was, therefore, incompatible with the idea of a republican polity as an undifferentiated mass before the law. Just as the precedent of faction would end in a "tyranny of knaves," so slavery would end in a "confederacy of tyrants, pure aristocratical despotism" by slaveholders, not only over their slaves but over the nonslaveholding class.[41] Here, Birkbeck anticipated the increasingly nuanced arguments of antebellum, antislavery northerners, who considered slaveholders aristocrats by definition. Appropriating the fruits of others' labor, they not only reduced their workers to open slavery but radically and unnaturally skewed the distribution of labor-created wealth in the South generally. The nonslaveholding white majority was left so far behind by the "slavocracy's" illegitimate accumulation of wealth and power as to mock any idea of a republican South.[42] Bringing the two parts of the anticonvention argument together, Birkbeck asked, "To what motives, then, can [the conventionists'] zeal be imputed, except the love of arbitrary power, and aversion to industry—and . . . political rivalship?"[43]

Thus did opposition to slavery come to dominate the anticonvention argument, but resistance to the infusion of party and political organization into Illinois politics remained an important theme on both sides.[44] The conventionists did not justify the party tactics in the assembly in themselves but as necessities for defending the true majority will. The real factionists, they suggested, were those legislators who had disregarded instructions from their constituents in opposing the convention.[45]

Although the convention campaign failed to legitimate party, it did witness a temporary introduction of organized nomination into Illinois politics, linked always with disavowals of partyism. The Monroe County antislavery organization, for example, formed to disseminate antislavery political information, but it spent as much effort acknowledging the dangers of political organization as it did justifying itself. Political groups, the members wrote, always risked becoming tools of faction, "little dark scenes of political intrigue, for the purpose of promoting men, and not measures." They therefore opposed fanaticism in the antislavery cause almost as much as they opposed slavery itself. From their own near transgressions against constitutional propriety, they moved on to indict the legislature, whose "log-rolling" was "nothing less than perjury" and whose "nocturnal caucuses" and legislative "bribery" in creating offices for its own members constituted a corruption of representative government.[46]

Other meetings, too, acknowledged that special justification was necessary for their actions. In January 1824, St. Clair County anticonventionists resolved that "the present crisis of our state requires that the friends of freedom concentrate their votes at the next election" and, therefore, that a public meeting should devise a method of selecting candidates.[47] A month later, "A Voter" observed the nominating meeting and reported good news. Not only did the nominations improve the chances for defeating the convention, but an important step had been taken toward replacement of self-nominations with nominations by the people. He dismissed those who would call this meeting a "*caucus*." A caucus was the "unauthorized act of individuals," whereas a public nominating meeting would always be "the act of the people"—not a party—

as long as the citizenry elected to the nominating committee only those who had "an eye single to the common weal." Such men would nominate not from among themselves but from the population at large. Of course, this qualification pointed out exactly the problem that opponents of convention nominations traditionally raised. Organized nominations would always require an unrealistic degree of attentiveness from the people. In the absence of popular vigilance, small cliques would make selfish nominations while plausibly claiming to act in the name of the people.

"A Voter" went on to insist that the meeting's nonpartisan character was unaffected by the fact that conventionists were excluded from it. The conventionists were "so directly opposed to the great interests of the community" that their exclusion made the meeting no less genuinely "of the people" than if they had been allowed to stay.[48] A modern observer might brush aside this argument and join the excluded conventionists to label this meeting a party convention. But the writer's justification for organized nomination, whether he believed it himself or only felt that an antipartyist electorate required it of him, was distinctly pre-partyist.

Other anticonventionists also called for nominating meetings because of the need to concentrate votes when issues were of such unusual moment.[49] This argument invoked the antipartyist tradition that approved extraordinary, temporary political organization when no other means remained to head off a faction's attempt to impose party rule on the polity.[50] As Governor Coles put it, paraphrasing Edmund Burke, the proconvention organization was strong and "should as far as possible be counteracted. When bad men conspire, good men should be watchful."[51]

Meanwhile, some conventionists organized as well. A "central committee" at the state capital announced itself and declared the slavery question an anticonventionist ruse. Opposition to the convention was, in fact, "a mere struggle for power."[52] The Monroe County Convention Society emerged about the same time and called on other counties to form similar organizations.[53] At the beginning of March, Randolph County joined in with a proconvention meeting,[54] but none of these had taken the important step of nominating candidates. Nevertheless, an anticonvention writer blasted the conventionist central committee and the developing conventionist organization: "Can public good be the primary object of that party, whose measures are born in silence and concealed in darkness? Which finds it necessary for its support, to establish and sustain an internal police, more vigilant and vigorous, than was ever established by the emperor of France?"[55] And "Speak Out" found in the convention party's hierarchy of committees "five hundred and twenty men secretly at work . . . to undermine the constitution."[56] This frightening hierarchy, this secret police, was the writer's characterization of a political committee system that was very ordinary when compared to the next generation but which in 1824 was unprecedented in much of the Union.[57]

Amid this novel degree of organization, an occasional writer did seem to slip over into partyism. The *Spectator*, for example, once approximated the party-system ethic: "We have not the slightest objection to the conventionists holding meetings. . . . We have no wish to interfere with their nominations; nor have they any right to meddle with ours."[58] And "Junius" argued that the republican maxim of "Measures, and not Men" was being challenged by a conventionist party whose motto was "divide and conquer," the slogan of the factionist. In this crisis, one set of nominees or the other would be elected; so anticonventionists must "discard all our prejudices or antipathies" and support "the candidates of our own party" lest conventionists' inferior numbers triumph by superior "*management*."[59] These quotations do reveal a potential for partyism within the antipartyist polity. But they were very uncommon. And, in fact, they were all but unutterable except with the excuse that faction was on the march and had to be met with its own weapons, weapons to be discarded at the end of the battle.

For all the innovation in the campaign, it is impossible to confirm that organized nominations were made in more than a handful of Illinois's thirty counties. Moreover, the ones that were made revealed less party discipline and less of the ethic of party loyalty than one might expect. If a handful of meetings explicitly tied themselves to a position on the convention question, another handful apparently had no discernibly partisan character at all.

A nominating meeting of the "inhabitants" of Edwards County, which identified itself with no party in any way, did nothing except ballot for General Assembly candidates. The most extraordinary part of the meeting, however, was the unanimous resolution, before the balloting, that "the candidates, nominated on this day, shall be the only ones to be supported at the election."[60] Here was a statement of the Van Burenite ethic of loyalty to the will of the convention but without any other statement of political principles. Was this a conventionist meeting or anticonventionist, or was it perhaps motivated by some local question? Neither this statement of proceedings nor a communication two weeks later explained any of the reasons for the organization of the meeting in the first place. The later communication did, however, refute the apparently easy acceptance of the convention ethic. Theodore C. Cone, one of the candidates for the Senate defeated in the meeting, wrote to deny that the resolution of binding support for the nominees had ever been presented. He claimed that many members of the meeting continued to feel free to vote on election day for the "best qualified" candidates regardless of the nominations.

Moreover, such a resolution could hardly claim to bind the electorate as a whole. Finally, he declared that he was "in common with the great body of the people of this county . . . opposed to the *Caucus system*."[61] Politics was certainly competitive in Edwards County, but were there party affiliations of any sort at work in this controversy? Even amid an attempt to introduce the ethic of binding nominations, no presence of party was apparent.

Finally, a Clark County nominating meeting apparently came off without the least reference to the convention or any other issue or party. An observer of the meeting guessed that William B. Archer would be elected to the legislature as the representative from Clark and Edgar Counties, but the only controversy in the meeting had concerned which county would supply the representative for the coming term.[62] The disregard of any issues that might cut across county lines (like the convention question) suggests that the participants understood themselves as a "primary assembly" of the people of the county, not a party convention. The pre-party nature of this meeting is also suggested by the use of words like "meeting" instead of "convention" and "People" instead of "party." And all of this appears not in political propaganda but in a rather casually written private letter.

Collectively, these small controversies suggest that antipartyism remained as central as ever to the popular understanding of popular sovereignty. Wariness of political organization remained extremely strong even as public, organized nomination made its first strides. Meanwhile, self-nominations steadily appeared in the newspapers and remained the dominant mode of nomination.

When the convention had been easily defeated, "Spartacus," writing in the *Intelligencer*, expressed well the ideals of the polity. He encouraged his fellow anticonventionists to be magnanimous toward the mass of misguided but well intentioned conventionists and implied that the campaign had indeed been aimed against party rule as much as anything else: "By [a magnanimous] course, you will promote social happiness, allay the virulence of party spirit, and contribute to the public weal. . . . Endeavor to quell, and not to increase, that rancorous spirit of party, which now distracts the state. And when the standard of faction shall again be raised in our land, may you boldly take the field."[63]

The organized nominations of the convention campaign stand as something of an aberration in the years before 1834. However, the congressional and presidential campaigns of the same year offer some evidence that a small, mostly ineffective, but persistent cell of partyists was busy in the state. Its futile efforts in 1824 mostly illustrate the continuing power of the antipartyist construction of popular sovereignty, but they also represent an early elaboration of constitutional-partyist ideology.

In the congressional race, traditional antipartyism easily withstood an attempt to link the candidates to the convention-election alignments. The proconvention editor of the *Gazette* attacked another proconvention editor for trying to defeat Daniel P. Cook by implying party links between the concurrent elections.[64] According to the *Gazette*, Cook had not taken a position regarding the convention, and half the conventionists in the area were determined to vote for Cook as the best man. Similarly, a conventionist in the *Intelligencer* argued for Cook's reelection despite opposition to him by "the devotees of a party."[65] When Cook beat Shadrach Bond in a landslide, substantially outdistancing even the 57 percent majority against the convention,[66] the *Gazette* lamented that the convention was lost "from the effort made by Governor Bond's friends to force him upon its supporters, against their declared preference for Mr. Cook."[67] Although evidence from Bond's side of the question is sparse, it seems clear that there was an effort, probably linked with William Crawford's presidential campaign the same year, to make the August elections of 1824 into party-organized elections with informal party tickets. It seems equally clear, however, that the effort failed.[68]

The pro-party efforts and the reasoning behind them were a little clearer in the presidential campaign. Most of the rhetoric was strongly antipartyist. As early as February 1823, "A Citizen of the West" tried to prevent the injection of party into the contest. He noted the partyist assertion in the *Star of the West* that John Quincy Adams's endorsement by Federalist papers made him the Federalist candidate. He refuted this assertion by pointing to a wide agreement on politics among many Federalist and Republican papers that proved the happy obsolescence of the old party divisions. Moreover, he blamed the effort to perpetuate those divisions artificially on "a certain *faction*, formed of the most violent of one [party], and the weakest of the other . . . justly denominated the *radical faction*. Upon this faction rest all the hopes and expectations of Mr. Crawford."[69]

Crawford's status as partyist bogeyman became a major theme of the campaign. For example, the editor of the *Spectator* supported Adams but also avowed a willingness to accept any other candidate except Crawford.[70] The *Gazette* attacked Crawford for seeking the presidency by means "in derogation of the rights of the people, by *caucusses*, and by management." All other candidates had rejected such methods, especially the use of the congressional caucus. Moreover, the republican claims of Crawford and his party were belied by Crawford's opposition to the administration of Monroe, a republican of impeccable credentials.[71] Months later, during the congressional election, the *Gazette* went further. Claiming that Illinois was unanimously pro-tariff, it asserted that Crawford stood as an anti-tariff candidate. It then linked the tariff to the congressional election and to partyism: "Is it unfair to presume that Gov. Bond is governed by [his opposition to a tariff], in his preference for Mr. Crawford? Or does he support him on the still more exceptionable grounds of his devotion to a party" which has attempted to force Crawford on the people "by perverting their forms, and trampling upon their principles?"[72]

If the opposition to Crawford emphasized his partyist determination to separate the sovereign people from control of their government, support for other candidates also routinely featured such warnings against the danger of partyism. "Constantius," for example, attacked the eagerness of southern and western state legislatures to nominate favorite sons. Such behavior would divide the nation and produce "an immediate coalescence . . . among all the Northern hive of politicians" to the detriment of non-northern interests.[73] "Party intrigue" had already begun, he warned, twenty months before the election. "This spirit should be carefully avoided . . . for . . . it must be evident that unity of sentiment and interest should be the leading trait in the character of a Republick, as indispensably essential to its long standing, prosperity, and firmness."[74]

A writer in the *Spectator* adopted the same antipartyist outlook in the service of John Quincy Adams just after the state elections of 1824. Now that the convention election was over, "A Republican" wrote, "the first object of every good citizen should be . . . to promote harmony and concord amongst all parties." He then suggested that a ticket of Adams for president and Andrew Jackson for vice-president would be the "most likely to unite the people." He concluded, "*We are*, and ought to feel that we are, but one people; and in choosing our rulers we should only inquire, who will best promote the harmony and prosperity of the nation?"[75] As did Constantius, he used the rhetoric of antipartyism to promote his own candidate. But he was also correctly noting that Adams and Jackson were the two strongest candidates in Illinois. To join them on a single antipartyist ticket seemed an eminently sensible way to harmonize the polity after the discord of the convention election.

In addition to the usual newspaper wars, public meetings regarding the presidential election began by early 1824, with Alexander P. Field, soon to be Illinois's secretary of state and later a prominent Whig, organizing meetings in several counties that endorsed Jackson for president.[76] In a Gallatin County meeting, Jackson won a straw poll over Clay and Adams, and his supporters agreed unanimously to support Henry Eddy, editor of the *Gazette*, for presidential elector. This was the closest thing to a nomination yet in the campaign. Even in this circumstance, however, Eddy did not consider himself regularly nominated but felt constrained to print a self-nomination in the newspaper. And he came under some attack for his nomination as well. Joseph M. Street followed Eddy's public nomination with his own self-nomination. He justified himself on the grounds that he was a supporter of western rights and, more importantly, that he was "the candidate of no Caucus, nor have I been put in nomination by any meeting, or company of individuals."[77]

A defender of Eddy sustained the candidate's traditionalism by claiming that Eddy would be willing to withdraw in favor of a previously self-nominated candidate, Daniel Boatright. Eddy would do so even though he had been nominated by a "respectable portion of the people"—not by a caucus and not with the expectation of caucus or party support. He would not, however, withdraw in favor of Street,[78] who was portrayed by several of Eddy's defenders as a tool of the Crawfordites.

Field, Eddy, and others may have been trying to get up something of a Jackson organization, but the meetings they raised did little more than rouse the electorate a bit and inspire some of the more zealous to do a little campaigning. They created no committees and contemplated no general convention. They presented themselves simply as outlets for the opinions of the people gathered at court. When Jackson won overwhelming support at these meetings, the implication, in theory, was not that these were Jackson meetings from the start but that Jackson had simply won the straw poll in each gathering.

A few similar meetings were held for Adams, again arguing his qualifications for the presidency but making hardly a move toward organization.[79] Meanwhile, candidates for presidential elector were being self-nominated in all the newspapers while other candidates were withdrawing in the name of unity. None of these nominations or withdrawals was done under the auspices of any avowed organization.

Crawford, meanwhile, was absent from this antipartyist campaign except in the suspicions of anticaucus editors who sniffed a subterranean effort to smuggle one of Illinois's three electoral votes to him. Those suspicions took concrete form when a Jackson-Clay meeting in Madison County spoke the slogans of constitutional partyism. It professed "to be actuated and governed by the principles and doctrines of the *Republican Democratic* party" that had produced the Revolution of 1800. The principles of that revolution still counseled resistance to any merger of "[Democratic] doctrines and principles, in the cry of the era of good feelings, and an amalgamation of party, for the purpose of" restoring Federalist aristocrats to power. The resolutions concluded with a call for a district convention to nominate an elector.[80] The pro-Clay editor of the *Intelligencer* responded to this meeting by reporting that the Jackson-Clay fusion effort was rumored to be a Crawford scheme.[81] It is unclear at first glance how a Jackson-Clay meeting could have aided Crawford, but the unmistakably partyist rhetoric of the meeting sustains the editor's suspicions.

The partyist district convention met in October and nominated James Turney to vote for the presidential candidate "most likely to succeed against Mr. Adams."[82] Crawford's name again was not mentioned as either friend or foe of the cause. The point of the conventions was less to elect anyone in particular than to provide a vehicle for a rudimentary statement of partyist political theory. By demonizing Adams, the partyists sought to unify the democracy behind a particular vision of American politics: the persisting constitutional division between a few ex-Federalist, consolidationist aristocrats now backing Adams and the overwhelming majority of states'-rights democrats presently divided among a multiplicity of candidates (including the two-faced Adams).

Partyist challenges to the established construction of popular sovereignty in 1824 were both rare and less than forthright. The partyists never presented themselves openly as an organization with a slate of candidates, but in retrospect their presence and their faithfully Van Burenite ideology is apparent. Ex–New Yorker Elias Kent Kane had formed a local branch of Van Buren's "old republicans" and, at least in private, parroted Van Buren's theory of party. Here is Kane in a letter to Senator Jesse B. Thomas in early 1824:

> The determination . . . to support the regularly nominated *democratic* candidate was formed . . . under the full [expectation?] that Crawford would be that man. If we fail in realizing this pleasing expectation we are committed to the devil where the democrats must all go without a nomination—What singular operation of nature has turned republicans into partisans? Is the fruit of twenty five years hard labour to wither before a miserable spirit of division? . . . Political freedom was once the boast of France when the division of parties marked [?] a difference of principles. When principles gave way to the less rigid dispositions of personal partialities the Gerondites Robersperians +c. divided and ruined the most beautiful and intelligent country in the world. Shall the Calhounites Adamsites +c. do the same for republican America? I suspect the great cause for the present divisions may be traced to the [fact?] that the republican party is now so numerous that expectants cannot all be provided for. What will be their situation if the sleeping monster who has for eight years been [hidden?] by the tapestry of "amalgamation" and "good feelings" should rise in the majesty of his strength and [rushing?] through the openings formed by these divisions seize upon the sovereignty of the country?[83]

Kane and the partyists believed that only a single, dominant party organization could sustain democratic sovereignty. The alternative was partisanship within the democracy and aristocratic exploitation of that partisanship to control the government. Kane, like Van Buren, envisioned a party encompassing all democrats and eliminating intra-democratic partisanship by making the democracy's regular nominations sacrosanct. This arch-partyist sought to perpetuate the essence of democratic antipartyism—unity of the entire democratic polity—through the indispensable expedient of permanent, anti-aristocratic, party organization.

Illinois continued overwhelmingly, however, to rely on self-nomination and to reject party organization. In particular, Illinoisans saw Crawford behind whatever partyist movements occurred, and they buried him in the election.[84] Supporters of all other candidates disavowed partyism of any kind, especially the use of caucuses whether in Congress or in the locality, and attempted to attach the stigma of party exclusively to Crawford.[85]

When the elections of 1824 were over, the convention had been defeated, Cook had been returned to Congress, and Jackson had won two of Illinois's electoral votes to Adams's one. In the legislative elections the results were not conclusive, but the consensus at the time was that the anticonventionists had failed to control the new legislature even though they had rolled up a 57 percent majority on the most prominent question on the ballot.[86] Despite the presence of a clique that "call[ed] themselves (*the party*)," according to Illinois senator John McLean, it seems clear that the electorate had not placed men in the legislature who avowed adherence to party or to any particular party. The polity had just endured a campaign that some observers thought verged on civil war,[87] but the crisis did not create durable parties or a party system. All tradition, after all, held that times of crisis were times for rooting out parties, not perpetuating them, and the constitutional tradition held fast.

The Elections of 1826: The "Corrupt Bargain" and Other Signs of Aristocracy

Daniel P. Cook ran for reelection to Congress in 1826 but lost to a relatively obscure state legislator named Joseph Duncan. Duncan was destined to be Illinois's great champion of antipartyism. But his dramatic upset of Cook in 1826 seems to have derived from Cook's part in the famous "corrupt bargain,"[88] an event that partyists soon appropriated as the enduring proof that aristocracy persisted in American politics, especially in professors of antipartyism.

In the 1825 presidential election in the House, Cook had given Illinois's vote to Adams despite Jackson's having won two of Illinois's three electoral votes.

In so doing, Cook unwittingly convinced many Illinoisans that self-interested politicians were busily rendering the democratic institution of popular election an empty exercise. Cook's vote seemed part of a pattern: Missouri's lone representative had also voted for Adams against the apparent will of the electorate,[89] and Kentucky's delegation, supposedly under Henry Clay's corrupt influence, had violated instructions from home in voting for Adams.[90]

In the campaign, Cook futilely justified his exercise of discretion by noting that no candidate had won a majority of Illinois's popular vote. In August, he lost almost twenty percentage points from his 1824 showing in falling to a political unknown.[91] It is crucial to note, however, that the charge against Cook was not that he belonged to the wrong presidential party but that he had allowed himself to be influenced by party at all in derogation of the people's will. Thus was the antipartyist Duncan the immediate beneficiary of Cook's miscalculation, even as the partyists prepared to exploit the "corrupt bargain" for their own purposes.

Despite the intrusion of national politics into the congressional race, the campaigns of 1826 for governor and for legislative seats represented a return to the partyless campaigns to which Illinoisans were accustomed before the temporary organizational innovations of 1824. Efforts to produce organized nominations were extremely rare and wholly abortive, while warnings against any voter's sacrificing his independence were routine.[92]

The sentiment remained nearly universal that men should be elected on their personal merits rather than on their affiliations. This position directly contradicted the Van Burenite tenet that elections should turn not on talents but on the candidates' willingness to subordinate themselves to the democratic party will. This partyist response to personal politics had so far failed to muster noticeable support in Illinois, in part because the antipartyist Duncan had momentarily preempted any partyist exploitation of the "corrupt bargain." Democracy and party, nearly everyone agreed, remained incompatible.

Conclusion

The politics of earliest Illinois undeniably addressed important social questions—slavery, banking, and internal improvements, among others. Just as undeniably, however, Illinois's infant politics constituted an ongoing construction of popular sovereignty itself. If Madison and his co-Framers rested the Constitution on a kind of marginalized, attenuated popular sovereignty, theirs was not the only understanding of that document or of American governance. The Anti-Federalists, the Republicans, and others had understood the Constitution from the start as the warrant of a genuine, vibrant popular sovereign—

"the people" in their respective states.[93] This survey of early Illinois's public life reveals a politics centered not just on social policy but self-consciously on the preservation of that sovereign's control of its agents. The steady drumbeat of arguments against party's intrusions on "the people" reveals the stability of the antipartyist construction of democracy. Yet the potential for constitutional reconstruction through politics was revealed in the occasional movements to create new nominating devices that might refine the people's capacity to speak, to elect, and to govern.

None of these movements managed to upset the status quo, however. Nor did Kane's halting attempts to reorganize the "great republican party." In fact, the partyists' first thrusts would hardly be worth notice but for the significance partyism would assume in later years. Not only did partyism suffer crushing defeats, but partyism itself was fundamentally antipartyist. The only party Kane approved in the republican United States was the old Jeffersonian republican party. Any other was, by definition, an attempt to undermine the Constitution, and any internal division of the party—any conversion of "republicans" into "partisans"—was equally illegitimate. Kane's innovation, then, was not advocacy of party division among democrats. Rather, it was importation of the Van Burenite idea that the only way to *avoid* division of the democratic polity into parties was to organize the entire democratic polity as a unit. By such organization, the minority of anti-democrats would be kept effectively outside the American polity.

Antipartyism was so pervasive that even the partyists and the advocates of organization managed to be essentially antipartyist. It was common ground that democratic governance required the exclusion of faction from the lawmaking process. The slowness of partyism's growth, then, should not be surprising. In fact, the only way the antipartyist tradition could die would be at its own hands. The partyism that would emerge from antipartyist culture was a partyism justified on antipartyist, constitutional grounds.

CHAPTER THREE

State Sovereignty and the "Proscriptive Party," 1828–1830

The antipartyist construction of popular sovereignty remained almost completely intact through 1834, even though movement toward partyist reconstruction is discernible in retrospect. It is true that Andrew Jackson's election in 1828 turned out to be a founding moment of the so-called Second Party System. In that and the next three presidential elections, as the story generally goes, a broadened suffrage equipped politicians to crystallize the social divisions of the growing market economy and ethno-religious loyalties in the form of two great parties and the modern party system;[1] that is, a system in which two democratic parties alternate in power and present opposing platforms but share basic constitutional tenets.[2] In America those tenets have included the sovereignty of the people, majority rule, and the indispensability of mass party competition itself.[3]

The previous chapter has shown, however, that Illinoisans in the 1820s did not think party division among democrats was necessary to or even compatible with democracy. Later chapters will show, accordingly, that the party system emerged in spite of, not according to, the wills of all concerned. However powerfully the parties were ultimately shaped by economic and ethno-religious divisions, a partyist reconstruction of popular sovereignty in Illinois depended first on the development of new constitutional theories of party organization itself.

In Jacksonian Illinois, the new democratic, egalitarian orthodoxy demanded that any reconstruction of popular sovereignty rest not on the Madisonian premise of an "absent People"[4] but on the alternative premise of an actively sovereign people. Emergent theories of party, therefore, sought to show that all democratic politics could—and must—be constitutional politics. To date, however, party remained almost universally identified with the obstruction of such popular action, not its facilitation.

As Jackson's 1828 triumph approached, then, there was little expectation that a competition of two durable, organized parties would soon monopolize the state's political system. The election seemed a culmination of the discrete constitutional crisis sparked by the "corrupt bargain" of 1825, not the founding moment of a new constitution. When the partyists used that election to tie Jackson to partyism and then gained control of significant amounts of the administration's patronage, however, alarm bells rang for antipartyists. By 1829, party had lodged itself in the executive branch. Antipartyist politicians responded immediately by turning the gubernatorial election of 1830 into a referendum on the acts and theory of the "proscriptive party." In that referendum, they sought to expose the destructive consequences of allowing party a role in lawmaking and executive action, consequences that would include the reduction of Illinois from a sovereign state to a mere unit of a consolidated national government.

The Elections of 1828

In retrospect Jackson's presidency proved vital to the creation of the two-party system as it developed, but his first election, at least in Illinois, did little in itself to upset the antipartyist consensus. The partyists did attach partyism to Jackson's triumph in some degree, but they were unable to extend partyism into state politics. Outside the presidential race, self-nominated candidates contested virtually all elections. Antipartyist rhetoric remained pervasive. Presidential politics proved only intermittently relevant and was fiercely resisted as an influence on state politics. Even the presidential race itself appeared to be no great threat as long as its party division was assumed to be temporary. The organization of these presidential movements was innovative but rudimentary, and only the little caucus of Van Burenite politicians might have expected any organization to outlive the campaign.

Illinois's 1828 Jackson movement actually began in 1825 after Daniel Pope Cook voted for Adams. That is not to say that there was an active campaign underway from that time, but there was little doubt that Jackson would run and win in Illinois. The combination of his own 1824 following and the anti-Adams vote, solidified by Cook's supposed betrayal, made him a formidable candidate. The first proof of Jackson's strength came in the election of the unknown Joseph Duncan over Cook in 1826. But before 1828 the Jackson movement had no truck with party. Not until the former Crawfordites jumped on the bandwagon would there be an organized Jackson party in Illinois.

On the national level, the Crawfordite "old republicans" became Jacksonian in order to legitimate partyism. Led by Martin Van Buren, these men had had no special love for Jackson in 1824. Jackson, after all, had opposed the caucus nominee in 1824 and thus hardly seemed a reliable party man. In the meantime, however, he had cemented his status as national democratic hero by virtue of the "corrupt bargain." When he also proved willing to work with Van Buren and the partyists, they adopted him as the best vehicle for legitimating partyism. When Van Buren decided to support Jackson so as to advance "the *substantial reorganization of the old Republican Party*,"[5] he articulated the rationale of the Illinois partyists as well.

Organization in Illinois began with a public meeting in Fayette County, the home of the state capital. The meeting proposed that each county in the northern electoral district should send three delegates to a Jackson convention in Springfield. The convention would nominate a presidential elector. The delegates should then recommend to the Jackson voters a unified support of the nominee. The meeting also urged the eastern and southern districts to adopt similar plans.

The Fayette gathering, however, was very modest in its manner. It explicitly declared its unwillingness "to dictate to the friends of General Jackson in other parts of the state" and merely hoped that this plan would meet with approval. It did not take for granted that this sort of organization was acceptable in 1828. The meeting well knew that advocating such organization would inevitably provoke the charge of "dictation." So it suggested convention nomination only for the office of presidential elector and did not try to extend party organization into state politics.[6]

A gathering several weeks later at Belleville joined the Fayette meeting in attaching partyism and conventionism to the Jacksonian juggernaut of democratic reform. Apparently led by William Kinney, an 1824 Crawfordite and one of the arch-organizers in the state, it concurred in the convention plan, called a convention at Kaskaskia for the southern district, and offered the justification that if we allow "division among ourselves *a minority may again rule*," a reference to Adams's election by the House. The meeting went on to call for amendment of the Constitution to allow direct popular election of the president, lest the popular sovereign again be defied.[7]

Numerous county meetings ratified the convention plan, and at least two of the three[8] district conventions came off in May and June. Each convention nominated an elector who succeeded in unifying the Jackson vote in November.[9] And each referred back to the "corrupt bargain" by resolving that "we believe [Jackson's] elevation to the Presidency by the votes of the people, would prove highly useful in sustaining the purity, principles, and practice, of free and unbiassed elections." The fundamental issue for the Jacksonian conventionists was restoration of the people's right to elect their own rulers, a right without which all others were empty. And their tool was the popular convention, a supralegal device of "higher lawmaking"[10] by which the people themselves might insist on de facto, direct popular election of the president in the face of aristocratic efforts to exploit popular divisions.[11]

The absence of any significant self-nominee for Jackson elector in 1828 testifies to the control of the Jackson movement achieved by these organizers. Candidates who had been self-nominated before the conventions either withdrew or were buried in the election. Representative of the 1824 Jackson movement's fate in 1828 was that of Stephen Kimmel, one of many men who had been floated for the office of Jackson elector. As the organizers got going, Kimmel and the rest of the "original" Jackson men joined up. Kimmel wrote in the *Gazette* that he would not consider dividing the Jackson vote by running on his own hook. He declared, "I should conceive myself unworthy the trust reposed in [an elector], were I to insist on being run, or even to thrust my name before the public uncalled for"; but he would "lend my feeble aid in support of any set of individuals, who may be PUT IN NOMINATION, by a convention of delegates properly appointed to do so."[12]

In reaction to Kimmel's withdrawal, "An Original Jacksonian" wrote that he regretted that a politically consistent man like Kimmel would be replaced by an "*eleventh hour man*" who had converted from Crawford or Clay just to be on the winning side. "I wish unanimity in the Jackson lines, but not at the expense of discarding *merit* and rewarding *treachery*."[13] Later in the campaign, "Senex Jackson" urged true Jackson men to reject the nominees of those "mercenary" men who joined the Jackson campaign only when Jackson's strength was clear. He named Bond, Kane, Kinney, and other Crawfordites as the new "rulers of the Jackson party" who would usurp the spoils. They represented "Crawfordism in masquerade," and their success in controlling the Jackson movement in 1828 augured nothing better than replacement of Adamsite minority rule with Crawfordite minority rule.[14]

The body of the original Jackson movement had accepted the leadership of the organizers because it seemed the only guarantee of Jackson's receiving electoral votes commensurate with his popular support. Jackson had been anti-caucus in 1824 and vigorously opposed Adams's supposed use of the federal patronage to influence elections. He was the hero of the Battle of New Orleans. There seemed little danger that he could be party-ized by such men as the Crawfordite rejects of 1824 who now came to Jackson late in the game. Moreover, the office of elector was largely a ceremonial one. There seemed little that an elector could do to undermine the popular will short of baldly violating his pledge to vote for Jackson. Distasteful as it may have been for some to cooperate with old Crawfordites, the end justified the means.

While the Jacksonians organized conventions, the Adams men campaigned more conventionally. But they too sought to unify their movement behind a single set of electors. Disdaining the pseudo-democratic organizational loyalty sought by the partyists, these men believed that the best way to unify the Adams vote was to have community leaders consult the people of their counties and then communicate among themselves to determine an unobjectionable slate of electors.

The *Intelligencer* announced a ticket of three candidates for elector in February 1828. It reported that two of them had been agreed on by administration men at the supreme court session in December as requested by the people of their several localities. The third candidate had been selected by a similar process of consultation in the eastern district since few men of that district had been at the court session. In making the announcement, the editor wrote: "As it is extremely desirous that the vote of all in favor of the election of Mr. Adams, should be concentrated upon one ticket, it is to be hoped that no attempts will be made to bring out any other candidates, and that the above will give general satisfaction."[15]

A small number of men thus attempted to impart unity to the Adams cause through an informal sort of organization. But the theory of this method contrasted sharply with partyist theory. The nominators assumed that formal organization increased rather than decreased the danger that the popular will would be manipulated. The request for popular ratification took a deferential tone rather than suggesting that the nominations bound anyone. This was not an attempt to establish a continuing formal organization. Rather, even assuming the normal mix of ambition and virtue among the activists, it seems fairly described as simply an ad hoc effort to deal with the realities of the 1828 presidential contest. The election was going to be a simple two-sided affair, but it was complicated by the necessity of voting for electors rather than directly for presidential candidates. An uncoerced unity in the Adams camp was indispensable, they thought; permanent organization and the ethic of party loyalty remained anathema.

To Jacksonians, of course, such nominations constituted elitist dictation, and the Adams men knew it. One of those consulting during the sitting of the court wrote privately that he had thought an address to the people would be a good accompaniment to the nominations. However, the meeting rejected the idea out of fear that it would be attacked "as a *self constituted caucus dictating to the high minded honorable and independent yeomanry of Illinois*: And as this sort of slang is so potent, and so familiar to the mouths of ignorant demagogues, it is perhaps best not to provoke too frequent a use of it in this *here kingdom of theirs*."[16] The Adams men were caught between the perceived necessity of electoral unity and the cultural reality of antipartyism. In this situation, they took the minimal step of offering candidates without issuing an address.

Partisanship on both sides reached heights that were distressing for an antiparty polity. The *Gazette* apologized for its own participation in party warfare during the campaign but blamed it on the Jacksonians. The power of party originated in Washington where the people's representatives went to get corrupted: "The leaders at Washington seem to be drilling the small fry very effectually . . . [who] vote throughout as *partisans*, and not as public agents, who ought to have minds of their own, and know that the measures of a party are not always the measures most beneficial to their constituents. This is particularly applicable to our representative. We do not blame him for preferring Jackson, but we blame him for preferring every act of his party to every interest of the state which he represents."

In particular, neatly foreshadowing the antisouthern politics of the 1840s and 1850s, the pro-tariff editor thought the Jackson party had become a southern anti-tariff party and that western Jacksonians like Joseph Duncan had become slaves of the South through the mechanism of a presidential party.[17] The unfortunate consequence was that such parties of the selfish forced party behavior on the virtuous: "We know that party spirit, and party rancor, has been carried to too great extremes on both sides: But self-defence is the first law of nature—the opposition were the aggressors . . . who wish to break down the present administration, for the purpose of enjoying the offices themselves." He did not wish to attack Jackson himself nor Jackson's "*real* friends," but only "the *interested* leaders of the opposition"; that is, the southern partyists.[18] And he did not wish to involve himself in party conflict. "But the party rancor which exists now did not, in the first place, originate with the people at large—It commenced with their representatives and a few other disappointed demagogues about Washington, at the close of the last presidential election. . . . We still look upon party strife with disgust, at the same time that we have to take a part in it, in self-defence."[19]

On the local scene, party was every bit as corrupting as it was in Washington. Alexander P. Field, for example, repeated his circuit-riding campaign of 1824. But this time his meetings were designed to send delegates to the district conventions, not just rouse the locals. And, in the *Gazette*'s recounting, his methods turned out to be exactly what one would expect from a partisan rabble-rouser in a country of virtuous common folk. Field would round up at most twelve to fifteen loiterers around court, buy them a round of drinks, and transform them into a "large and respectable meeting" choosing delegates in the name of the county for the district convention. The editor never made the contrast explicit, but the Adamsite nominations certainly began to look comparatively democratic to anyone who believed the *Gazette*'s version of the Jackson meetings.[20]

When the election was over, the *Gazette* lamented the prevalence of party and faction and argued that limiting the president to a single term would be the surest cure. It would prevent "on the one hand, a corrupt exercise of power, and dispensation of patronage [by the President], and, on the other hand, an unprincipled opposition to the measures of an administration" by those ambitious men who feared that a popular incumbent would be in their way at the next election.[21] Both kinds of behavior were causes and symptoms of party.

The polity's antipartyism survived the contest of 1828 largely intact. In a two-sided contest turning on the purity of the electoral system itself, there was far more willingness to embrace devices that would unify the cause than there had been in the 1824 election. However, enduring commitment to political organization in principle or to any particular organization was confined to a few partyists who never even attempted a full public statement of the partyist case. They were content to take credit for Jackson's election in Illinois and thereby control the federal patronage necessary to build a party in the state.

The general absence of a commitment to partyism is even clearer in the state and local elections, although there is relatively little evidence about them. In the congressional election of 1828, the Jacksonian incumbent, Duncan, was opposed by George Forquer, an Adams man who denied that presidential politics had any relevance to the congressional race. Of course, this was easy for him to say since he would lose if he ran as an Adams man. Still, that position remained widely accepted in Illinois in the 1820s, whereas it would have been absurd in later years. Reporting Forquer's campaign speech, the *Gazette* wrote that he avowed his support for Adams but claimed "he was not the partizan of Mr. Adams or any other political man. . . . No person had a higher opinion of General Jackson as a military man, than he had, but he would not ride into office on his back or the back of J Q Adams." And, once elected, he would vote with or against the administration issue by issue as his conscience, not a party, dictated.[22] Forquer thus implied that Duncan illegitimately sought election on Jackson's merits and not his own, as a partisan rather than as a public servant. The charge was no doubt true to a degree, but Duncan himself had become a renowned antipartyist and, like Forquer, self-nominated.

In county elections, the newspapers were peppered with self-nominations in the traditional style, although I have discovered one 1828 effort to make organized nominations at the county level in Belleville, St. Clair County. Even this Belleville meeting, however, was vigorously antipartisan and reminiscent of earlier proposals for nonpartisan county nominations. It outlined some of the failings of recent General Assemblies that resulted in oppressive taxation and then urged the sovereign people to take the initiative, to nominate good men rather than waiting for the ambitious to thrust themselves forward. The meeting disclaimed "any intention of arraying our fellow-citizens on opposite and hostile sides" in the election. Instead, it asserted both the right of the people "to meet, consult upon, and recommend measures for the public good" and the necessity of "a concentrated effort" if good legislators were to replace bad. "To do that, we do not invoke this or that Party, the friends of this or that man, but a union without reference to party. The common good should know, no party, but ought to unite the whole for the common benefit."[23] Despite such efforts to activate the sovereign people, however, the overwhelming practice remained self-nomination, not organized nomination.

Apparently typical was a legislative election in the extreme northwest, where a close contest among five self-nominees produced a victory by mere plurality. This kind of result was just what partyists sought to avoid, election by a minority under a supposedly democratic Constitution. But "Admirer," writing just after the election, saw it another way. He understood that when many candidates ran for the same office, the majority's ultimate preference could not be known and thus was likely to be beaten. He even thought that had probably been the case in this particular election. Yet "when men vote without being biased by any party question . . . they certainly are better able to make a just choice than if they supported men for office because they are found supporting a particular party to which they may belong."[24] Candidates who had nothing to offer but a servile, partisan disposition could not hope to succeed; but the winner's attraction of a plurality of votes among a partyless electorate was adequate proof of his character and qualifications, even if it did not prove that he was necessarily the ultimate preference of the majority. Here were shades of Federalist no. 10 in Jacksonian Illinois.

In 1828, the partyists had succeeded in one small but crucial matter. They had used delegate nominating conventions to control the presidential election. In so doing they improved political organization's democratic credentials since it had aided the elevation of the unimpeachably democratic Andrew Jackson. They had not, however, institutionalized permanent organization yet at any level. That would take time and spoils, both of which they gained in Jackson's election.

"Influence" and "Proscription": Patronage in the 1820s

Even in the age of partyism, the polity never fully accepted the "spoils system," as is easily shown by the vitality of the civil service reform movement after the Civil War.[25] Traditionalists saw spoils as a device by which, as Henry Adams later complained, the parties "twisted their roots around and among the organs of the Constitution itself."[26] But partisan use of the patronage was a central element of the partyist understanding of democracy. After Jackson's election, disposition of patronage became an important tool of party but also the main source of antipartyist criticism.

To Van Burenites, government offices had to be reserved for members of the "great republican party" because only party members could be relied on to carry out the will of the majority in their official capacities. Van Burenites also sought spoils to reward faithful workers in the party cause. But this use of spoils to reinforce partisan loyalty was not inconsistent, theoretically, with an honest devotion to the democratic principle and to the party as its embodiment.

The pre-partyist construction of the appointing power was, however, very different. The orthodox test of a man's fitness for public office was Jefferson's: "Is he honest, Is he capable? Is he faithful to the Constitution?" One did not openly ask, "Is he a good party man?"[27] As late as the Jackson administration itself, dismissal of a public officer simply on party grounds was so widely thought unconstitutional that Jackson might have risked impeachment if he had frankly admitted the nature of many of his administration's removals.[28] Of course, the constitutional partyists claimed that they too relied only on Jefferson's criteria, but they openly identified real faithfulness to the Constitution with fidelity to the Democratic party.

In the decade before Jackson's election, opposition to spoils in Illinois took two forms: first, an opposition to Walpolean control of the legislature by appointment of legislators to executive offices; second, resistance to the creation of an electioneering corps of officeholders paid to manipulate the people's will at election time. Robert Walpole's management of Parliament in early-eighteenth-century England had become for Americans a standard lesson in the corrupting of a free polity by party. By distributing places in the House of Commons, Walpole had purchased the people's bulwark against arbitrary rule and made it his party-controlled tool, or so the story went. The story ended with the irretrievable corruption of the English polity across the eighteenth century, which ultimately necessitated the American Revolution.[29]

Consequently, American constitutions commonly contained place clauses. These prohibited legislators' holding other government offices while they served in a legislature.[30] In Illinois, I have found only one attempt to enforce this provision in these early years. A resolution was offered in the state senate in 1823 to discontinue as a director of the state bank anyone who was also a current member of the General Assembly, lest the blending of financial and legislative power "create a monied aristocracy."[31] The resolution was tabled by a vote of twelve to four, perhaps on the argument that the bank was not actually a state agency. The legislature then went on to elect several of its own members bank directors.[32] Some time later, "L." called for the purging of the General Assembly of all state bank officers because they were constitutionally ineligible,[33] but nothing came of the suggestion.

A similar case arose regarding the partyist senator Jesse B. Thomas. Secretary of the Treasury William Crawford, the 1824 presidential candidate of the partyists, appointed Senator Thomas to examine land offices in the West in 1822. As Thomas began to look to reelection, Ninian Edwards privately complained of Thomas's character in allowing himself to become "the hireling and dependant of a head of department" when his position in the Senate required him to scrutinize executive departments independently. When this dependence on Crawford was combined with Thomas's promising offices to legislators in Illinois, Edwards began to see "a species of Walpole management, that it is to be hoped our country is not yet ripe for."[34] Publicly, a writer in the *Intelligencer* objected that Thomas resembled a member of a Walpolean parliament, "consisting of men holding *places* and pensions under the crown, where the people's money was squandered to corrupt the people's representatives."[35] The notorious conventionist legislature reelected Thomas in spite of these objections.

Worries about Walpolean uses of "influence" in Illinois were complemented by a concern that federal patronage might be used proscriptively to create and discipline electoral parties. Thus Senator Edwards in 1820 appealed to the Monroe administration to distribute Illinois patronage more equitably, since it all seemed to be going to Thomas's allies. He was careful to deny that he had partisan motives and, in fact, assured Monroe that he was only trying to prevent partisanship from arising in the state.[36] Nevertheless, even Edwards's closest friend in the administration, Attorney General William Wirt, took Edwards to be playing too partisan a role. Wirt urged him to fight partisanship by rising above it instead of sinking to the partisan's level.[37]

William Brown's memoir of Daniel Cook reinforces the sense that Illinois's Crawfordites were the least scrupulous managers of patronage. Brown recalled that Crawford's appointments as treasury secretary all indicated that his election to the presidency would divert Illinois's share of the patronage to the "Bond party channel."[38] Still, even the Crawfordites did not yet openly advocate partisan patronage. Only during the Jackson administration would they attempt a reconstruction of the appointing power as an element of the partyist reconstruction of popular sovereignty itself.[39]

In the wake of Jackson's election, hope for a quieting of party spirit and a return to a politics of individual merit was widespread, but controversies over patronage took center stage instead. For a short time, Adams men and original Jackson men nourished the belief that Jackson would live up to his antipartyist past and resist partyist pressure for removals.[40] But in a matter of months, the alleged "proscription" practiced by the Jackson administration had become the chief issue in politics for antipartyists.

Before Jackson's inauguration, the antiparty *Gazette* acknowledged the threat of partyist politicians while noting that the state legislature, at least, had resisted their influence so far. The General Assembly had shown that political differences need not be party differences when it elected an 1828 Adams man attorney general and unanimously made an 1828 Jackson man a U.S. senator. Turning to the national scene, the editor cited a Jackson letter of 1825 in which the candidate argued for a constitutional amendment to prevent the appointment of congressmen to positions in the executive branch, lest corruption and party feelings intrude into Congress. Jackson's place-clause letter and the General Assembly's nonpartisan patronage encouraged the editor to hope that party would remain at bay in the new administration and that Jeffersonian constitutional orthodoxy would be respected.[41]

In his inaugural address, Jackson himself emphasized that federal patronage had been misused in the past and would not be under his administration.[42] Such declarations hardly ended the suspense regarding the administration's patronage policy, but antipartyists on both sides of the presidential question allowed themselves some hope. Even Adams men could hope that their defeat was only a momentary loss on the policy front rather than a revolutionizing of the government.

They were soon disappointed. To antipartyists the Jackson administration proved itself the most ruthlessly partisan administration to date. In the first months of Jacksonian patronage, antipartyists who had made temporary concessions to organization in 1828 reasserted their fundamental antipartyism. For Adams men, this came easily. Original Jacksonians, however, faced a good deal of tension between their long-held commitment to Jackson and the current misdoings of his administration. Their solution was to put the blame on Secretary of State Martin Van Buren as a modern Walpole, manipulating the patronage to build a controlling executive party in the national legislature. Adamsites might have noted that that made Jackson a modern King George, but original Jacksonians could not afford to.

The experience of Pascal P. Enos, the pro-Adams Receiver of Public Moneys at the Springfield Land Office, illustrates the process of disillusionment that antipartyist politicians went through. Enos knew his job was in jeopardy after the election, but he had some hope that Jackson would adhere to the tenets of the antipartyist faith that had found a place in Jackson's own writings. His first word from the administration came through original-Jacksonian senator John McLean. McLean said that Jackson had laid out three nonpartyist rules to govern removals. The first was that inefficient officers must "go out." The second and third were that "all those who had fairly and honestly exercised the rights of freemen, and thought another person was more suitable for the office of President than himself he should not molest. . . . But all those who had been a writing for the public papers and had been about the country a making speeches with a view to inflame the public mind, and had lyed like the *Devil* about him must go out." Enos was temporarily relieved, but two months later he wrote that "the work of proscription has taken a different turn from what was expected by [McLean] at the time he had the interview with the President [and] I now think as I did previous that in all probability that many of us must go out."[43]

Enos was removed on September 7, 1829, but he did not stop fighting for his office. Partisan removals were still commonly thought illegitimate—even unconstitutional[44]—and Enos seems to have attributed them to Van Buren's power. He thought that if only Jackson and his true friends would recognize the wrongs being done to officers under Van Buren's partyist influence, then he and his like might be reinstated. Writing to John P. Van Ness, an old acquaintance and "the principal" of the Jacksonian central committee in Washington, he complained that "all the removals in this part of the country have been made with an eye to the next Presidential election, as I find every one of the men appointed as far as my knowledge extends are advocates for the same individual tho many of them to my knowledge [were] hostile to him before." These new appointees, of course, were members of the Van Burenite band of Jacksonians, men who had opposed Jackson in 1824 but who had since come to his support for partyist purposes. Enos concluded that Kane, Kinney, and Emanuel J. West, Illinois's leading Van Burenites, had all preferred men of no talents for offices, even when men of great talent were available, simply because the latter were of the opposition. Van Buren and his Illinois puppets corrupted the political process by using patronage to buy men's convictions and build a party at the expense of competent administration.[45]

Like Enos, Ninian Edwards too thought Jackson needed only to have the facts presented to him in order to put down Van Buren, Kane, and partyism. Edwards wrote to Enos urging him to fight "those who have caused you to be proscribed." And he also sent Enos a copy of a letter that he had written to Jackson in an attempt to lessen Van Buren's sway. He argued to Jackson that as long as McLean was excluded from patronage discussions "any individual appointed, like Mr. Kane himself, would prefer Mr. Van Buren to either Mr. Calhoun or yourself—They are all of that breed of Jackson men, to whom, as you will eventually be convinced, a decided majority of your supporters at the last two elections, are more opposed than to any other politicians of the state."[46] Kane and Kinney, like Van Buren himself, were engaged in a partyist plot to elevate Van Buren and enrich his partisans with Jacksonian patronage. Edwards and his like believed that Jackson's native principles were antiparty-ist, but disillusionment with the president was setting in.

Meanwhile, Enos accurately predicted to McLean the coming of a great contest. It would be fought between the partyists on one side and a combina-tion of the "old administration party" and McLean's antipartyist brand of Jacksonians on the other.[47]

This portrayal of Jacksonian patronage from an Adamsite perspective was largely congruent with the "original Jacksonian" reaction to the events of 1829. McLean's position is implied in Enos's letters. The state's other leading original Jacksonian was Joseph Duncan, whose Washington diary chronicles a rapid disillusionment as he observed the ascendancy of the partyists and the consequent marginalizing of antipartyist Jacksonians like himself:

Feby 23 [1829]. From the persons who surround the Genl. I fear he is to be improperly influenced in his first appointments. . . .

Called to see the President[-Elect] he says he will remove no officer on ac-count of his political opinions, unless he has used his office for the purpose of electioneering. . . . I agree perfectly with his views. . . .

March, 1829. Governor Kinney & E. J. W[est] wish me to request the re-moval of certain officers from office which I decline as i am opposed to remov-ing competent and worthey men on account of a mere difference of opinion. They appear to be dissatisfyed but that will make no difference in my con-duct as such a course would be averse to all my notions of propriety. . . .

March, 1829. Kane McLeane & Myself met in McLeans room to consult about appointments in the event of any removals or vacancies. McLeane and myself opposed removals except for some good cause other than polit-ical. . . . K. rather differed in opinion about removals. . . .

March, 1829. . . . Got a letter from [my brother, James;] he wants to be appointed Indian agent . . . [and] he requests me to use my influence[;] this I cannot consistently do as I am unwilling to ask or receive a favour which would place me under obligations to the executive power of the government while I am a representative of the people . . . and I think every person applying for an office should have the recommendation of the people with whom he resides, or with whom he is to serve. . . .

April, [1829]. . . . Went with K[inney] to see the president. . . . K. urges the necessity of removals[,] says the republicans had fought hard and had gained a great victory but if the old Federalists were left in office the same battle will have to be fought over again. he said if it was left to him he would drive them all out as he would a parcle of dogs out of a meat house.

The P[resident] laughs hartily at this remark but made no reply. . . .

20th March 1830. . . . E. K. K[ane] senator told [me] that he had dined twice & had the 3rd invitation to dine with the president 18th of March. This is to my mind another conclusive proof that the President does not rely upon the propriety of his acts or appointments for the support of the senate as I have heard of no member of the H of R being invited more than once but this is only one of many instances that I have observed of an effort to conciliate the senate to use no worse term.[48]

Duncan thought that all appointments should have been in accordance with the will of the locality to be served, that officeholding should have been a matter of merit more than partisan service, that Jackson's partisan removals and appointments were attributable to Jackson's Van Burenite cronies as much as to Jackson himself, and that the recent behavior of the administration threatened the very safety of American political institutions.

The points made by Duncan and Enos in these private forums were the same ones being made in the newspapers. In the middle of 1829, the *Gazette* echoed Duncan and offered examples of Jacksonian violations of the popular will (although none from Illinois). It then claimed that citizens were responding appropriately to these abuses of the appointing power,

rejecting with scorn the officers tried to be forced upon them, and cherishing and promoting those upon whom party is wreaking its vengeance. . . . Men lately removed are *elected*—not appointed by a few individuals, but *elected* by the people among whom they live, and who know their merits— to the legislative halls; while those preferred to responsible stations, are unable to give the securities required by law even from among their own political party, or are discountenanced, and official communication with them avoided by their neighbors.

The presidency of Andrew Jackson revealed its anti-democratic character in a patronage policy that ignored the popular will. But this anti-Jacksonian writer reached out to Jacksonians by putting the blame for patronage abuses on others. Thus, "we would much rather ascribe the vindictiveness of the course now pursued to too easy an acquiescence in the advice of his counsellors—counsellors who are plotting their own future aggrandizement . . .—counsellors too, we believe, out of the pale of the cabinet."[49]

As the transformation of Jackson from mythic democratic hero to chief magistrate began in 1829, politicians on both sides of the division of 1828 began to identify Jackson's administration with Van Burenite partyism. The conventions of 1828 and the spoils of 1829 had begun to make concrete in Illinois the threat of organized partyism, and many men who had joined in the former revolted from the latter as they began to see where Jacksonism was headed. The gubernatorial election of 1830 would present the first opportunity for antipartyist politicians to take their response before the electorate.

Antipartyism, State Autonomy, and Economic Policy

Central to Illinoisans' anxieties regarding partyism and proscription was their fear that the state's existence as an independent polity was in danger. Antipartyism was not the only political abstraction to which American democrats clung in the 1820s. They also believed that democracy depended on the states' protecting their constitutional spheres of independence from the national government. Richard Ellis has rightly observed that, from the ratification period to the Civil War, distribution of power between the federal and state governments was "the central constitutional and political issue in American history."[50] Naturally enough, then, alarmed antipartyist politicians fused antipartyism, states' rights, and specific policy issues in their 1830 counterattack against the "proscriptive party" of the imperial federal executive.

The federal government, as Americans never tired of saying, was a government of limited, expressly delegated powers. Each state thus held jealously to its right to regulate its own internal affairs while, in theory, looking to the federal government only for regulation of its dealings with other states and nations. And, in this period, the general opinion was that the great body of public affairs were, in fact, internal, state affairs. Almost any manifestation of federal power within the boundaries of the state, therefore, could be a source of anxiety.[51] And when that power seemed to come in the form of party, the anxiety was multiplied.

In the 1824 convention campaign, for example, one of the most powerful arguments available to proslavery politicians had been that the federal ban on slavery in the Northwest Territory was inapplicable once Illinois entered the Union. After all, everyone acknowledged that slavery was a wholly internal matter for every state outside the northwest. To admit the continuing applicability of the Ordinance would be to admit that Illinois was somehow less equal than other states.[52]

In the late 1820s and early 1830s, the disposition of the public lands within the state was the issue that most prominently raised questions of federal-state relations and, in the event, questions of partyism as well. Most of Illinois was still federally owned, and Governor Ninian Edwards was shrewd enough to see the significance of that fact. Federal ownership posed both a threat to Illinois's independence from federal politics and a sensational electioneering opportunity. Consequently, Edwards began a crusade to gain cession of all federal public lands to the appropriate states. He argued that the Constitution gave western states the same right to own their own territory that the eastern states had. But he also showed how federal ownership of the public lands was helping to create an organized party in Illinois and advancing partyism. This organized party, moreover, caused the manifest interest of the states in owning their own lands to be thwarted by the state's own party-bound representatives. Here was contemporary evidence for the traditional assumption that party interfered concretely with the people's pursuit of their manifest interest.

Edwards first advocated federal cession of the lands at the tail end of his inaugural address of 1826, noting that thousands of miners there leased their land from the federal government and thus constituted a large class of voters dependent on Washington. Such a bloc was big enough to impair the interests and "the independence of the state."[53] The proposal did not get much attention from the legislature at first amid a noisy investigation of the state bank.

In the campaign of 1828, it again received limited attention. Running for Congress, George Forquer did argue for cession but only in passing.[54] The general question of federal control of the state's politics, however, was salient. Forquer, for example, was very concerned not to let the congressional election turn on the presidential question lest the state's interests be lost in national party interests.[55] Meanwhile, Edwards wrote to Senator-to-be John McLean and urged him, as a principled Jackson man, to support Forquer. By doing so, McLean would reprove the partyists' insistence

> upon making the Presidential question control every other election in the State, which is, in effect, to proscribe and disfranchise every man who happens to differ in opinion with them. . . . Consolidation [of power in the gen-

eral government] has hitherto been the terror of the great Republican party of the Union. Why? Because of the danger of submitting the local affairs of the States to the control and influence of the General Government. But if the Presidential election is to be made to control the State elections, it must have its influence on State affairs, and will eventuate in the most dangerous species of consolidation in fact, by strengthening the Executive Department of the Federal Government the most powerful and most to be dreaded.[56]

If Edwards was not yet single-mindedly pushing his land proposal, he was ever alert to the relationship between partyism and consolidation.

After the election, Governor Edwards returned to the public lands question. The bulk of his annual message pushed for state ownership of the lands as an alternative to the federal government's domination of Illinois's politics; that is, land cession would eliminate the national government's siding with the "*particular* interests" of the eastern states or the interests of any "*particular class*" therein, against the interests of any other part of the nation. "The surrender of the lands to the states in which they lie, is the only means of effectually quieting the public mind, and terminating forever dangers now formidable, and whose constantly augmenting force is more alarming to the peace and welfare of the Union, than any others which it is likely to encounter."[57] A letter from Duff Green in Washington encouraged Edwards to build his national ambitions on this platform, and in August of 1829 Edwards let candidate-to-be John Reynolds know that he would support no man for governor who failed to adopt his own position on the public lands.[58]

In this same period, of course, the state's original Jackson men were learning that the new Jackson party meant to impose national, presidential party divisions on the states. This intent seemed clear from Kinney's ability to channel Illinois's federal patronage only to those who worked with his party on the state level. And one original Jacksonian, Stephen H. Kimmel, learned the lesson directly from Secretary of the Treasury Samuel D. Ingham. Ingham responded to patronage concerns by saying that "some of our friends in your state have suffered by yielding to a combination with the coalition party for local purposes, one object of which may have been among the coalitionists to divide the Jackson interest, & retain all the Adams & Clay men in office. It is impossible for the administration here to recognize such movements, & maintain its character for consistincy."[59] Ingham thus served notice that the national Jackson leadership intended to impose Jackson parties on each of the individual state polities as well as on the national.

To Ingham and Kinney, this policy seemed necessary to maintain "consistincy" and perhaps even to protect state sovereignty against the supposed loose constructionism of the anti-Jacksonians. To antipartyist Jackson men like Kimmel, however, this policy was an abandonment of original Jacksonism in order to feed such partisans as the "Wolfy Kinney gang," with whom he had cooperated in the 1828 election. The price of this kind of consistency was subordination of state government to the national executive by means of party organization. Yet Kimmel and others clung to Jackson because they still could not believe that Jackson himself had become a Van Burenite.[60]

By 1830, then, Edwards and the original Jacksonians looked for a way to thwart the partyists' erosion of state autonomy, even as the partyists would insist that partyism was the only reliable guardian of states' rights. For Edwards, the public lands question was the vehicle. The genius of Edwards's proposal was that it helped Illinoisans merge their fondest economic visions, which hinged on access to land and improved immigration, with their desires to sustain state autonomy and to keep their state free from party. In Edwards's scenario, the federal government seemed to have two natural and complementary tendencies: the breeding of party and encroachment on states' rights. Edwards confronted these tendencies of the federal government through the public lands question even as the partyists tried to convince the people that national party organization could mean political and economic equality, not faction and consolidation.

The 1830 gubernatorial candidacy of the original Jacksonian John Reynolds was launched by the spoils question, but Reynolds also adopted Edwards's position on the public lands. In so doing, he and Edwards joined a concrete interest of most of the electorate with a defense of ancient political principles as the centerpiece of the 1830 electoral season. The fact that Reynolds's opponent was the spoils-wielding William Kinney only made it easier for the antipartyists to insist that consolidationist, anti-states'-rights partyism was the main issue. The campaign thus converted the abstract antipartyism of Illinois's original Jacksonians into an issue-specific, antipartyist exposé of the federal partyist ascendancy of 1829.

Reynolds's memoir of the campaign claimed that he was pushed into his candidacy by leading men from across the state who feared rule by Kinney and his "furious *ultra* Jackson party, that would govern the State with a rod of Iron, as to party rage and proscription." The election was a contest for control of the principles of Jacksonism between the "proscribing" element and the "calm and conservative" element.

Reynolds was not strictly opposed to the idea of party, though; he was a proud adherent of the Jackson party. But he was a violent opponent of party organization. Parties-as-popular-movements, dividing in a principled way over a great public question, he applauded as manifestations of freedom and popular initiative. But when he wrote his memoirs in 1855 he had to conclude that "party conventions and party discipline decide the elections, without giving the masses that power and strength in elections which a free government, and the constitution, requires." He wrote that the 1830 gubernatorial election had been a contest between these two notions of party. He was proudly elected without "party discipline, or corrupt conventions." And, although he would remain a Democrat as party organization gained ascendancy, he resisted to the last the transformation of the popular movement of 1824 into the hierarchical organization that was the Democratic party by the 1850s.[61]

The anti-Kinney newspapers of 1829 and 1830 largely confirm Reynolds's interpretation of the campaign. In endorsing Reynolds, the *Galena Advertiser* reaffirmed that Jacksonism was consistent with refusal to become "the slave of a party."[62] The *Crisis* lectured the electorate that "no matter what [a voter's] predilections may be—no matter what his duty to a party may be thought," he has a higher obligation to "the prosperity of the whole State." Consequently, Reynolds should be supported as the "true candidate of the Jackson democratic party of this state for governor."[63] Note the editor's ability to use the word "party" positively and negatively in the same breath. He took for granted that one should never serve a party organization but that one might adhere to a "party" in the sense of sharing principles with a segment of the community and voting with that segment for the true candidate of those principles.

The *Gazette*'s correspondents easily and naturally joined the questions of partyism and excessive federal influence on state politics. One ridiculed the notion that Kinney should be supported on the basis of his firm support for Jackson. Anyone running for governor "upon the ground that he has had more zeal, and been more clamorous, in some party contest, ought to be viewed by the people as unfit. . . . I would ask the candid and impartial republicans of Illinois what Jackson has to do with the position of Governor of this state?"[64]

Similarly, one editor condemned Kinney for trying to make a virtue out of his prevailing "by some means, upon the executive of our government, at Washington, to remove certain officers in this state, in violation of pledges given." If Kinney's patronage successes signified that he was a federally approved Jacksonian leader in Illinois, that hardly constituted an "eminent qualification" for the governorship. Reynolds, in contrast, having supported Jackson long before Kinney, "manifested a confidence in General Jackson's ability to manage [the federal patronage] without his dictation" and preferred to be elected by the people rather than by "*official influence.*"[65]

Both gubernatorial candidates were originally self-nominated and subsequently ratified or renominated at a few local meetings. But organization in the campaign was minimal. There were no nominating conventions beyond these isolated meetings. Self-nominations, appearing regularly in the press throughout the campaign, were the order of the day from the governor's race down through the list of county offices.

The one public attempt to form a party ticket occurred when Kinney declared the fusion of his cause and that of self-nominated Zadok Casey, candidate for lieutenant governor. Not many years later, the forming of such tickets would, of course, become routine. But in 1830, the *Gazette* had hoped "that the election for Lieutenant Governor could be accomplished without any extrinsic considerations affecting it. If a different determination has been made by the gentlemen themselves, they must abide the consequences" of "the singular, and it seems to us, momentous, relation which Mr. Kinney has proclaimed between himself and Mr. Casey." "We are opposed to party tickets," he announced.[66]

While Reynolds and his allies hammered away, Kinney's campaign suppressed the candidate's partyism even as it trumpeted his connection to Jackson. Kinney rejected all partisanship except, implicitly, constitutional partisanship. In a long campaign address he defended himself against a number of charges, including that of being "a violent and intolerant party man. This is not true any further than that I belong to the Republican party, and advocate reform [i.e., removals] only when the public good requires it."[67] Rejection of party was an absolute necessity to a candidate in Illinois in 1830, but affirming one's adherence specifically to the "Republican party" was, for Kinney, a declaration of one's belief in the right of the people to govern, a right secured by the Jeffersonian Republicans in the elections of 1800 and after. It was not a declaration of membership in a formal political organization—even Kinney could not yet publicly endorse such a thing—but in an informal union of the democratic. Kinney's partyism, therefore, insofar as he affirmed any at all, was implicitly constitutional partyism. To preserve, faction-free, the union of all democrats founded by Jefferson was not to be a "violent and intolerant party man" but, in fact, to be the best kind of antipartyist.

If the campaign rested mainly on the question of party and proscription itself, it also made the public lands the chief policy question. The link between policy questions and constitutional questions during the campaign was often only implicit.[68] Governor Edwards, however, thrust himself forward in the middle of the contest to provide the campaign's clearest linking of partyism to subordination of state interests. Ostensibly, Edwards published his statement only as a response to partyist slanders in the campaign, but it was apparent that the document was also meant to aid Reynolds and perhaps even suggest an Edwards candidacy for the U.S. Senate.

Edwards painted himself as a man entirely independent of other politicians' influence and devoted to cession. In contrast, Kane, Kinney, and friends were "a club of politicians," enslaved by party and opposing cession. Edwards explicitly refused to impugn Kane's motives for opposing cession, but the inescapable implication was that Kane's policy positions derived from the necessity of keeping his "club" together and keeping himself in his superiors' good graces, not from the needs of his constituency.[69]

Edwards described the power of Kane's organization, and, in so doing, connected proscriptive partyism to the public lands. He said that Kane's merest "hint" set his allies, their "minor agents," and their "grocery agents" to work to besmirch Edwards's name: "Hence you have seen . . . ridiculous effusions . . . spread over the State . . . not forgetting, occasionally, to leave large heaps of them in certain land offices, the incumbents of which have *no particular partiality for my views concerning the public lands*."[70] To this point, Edwards had let the association between the politicians' partyism and their position on the public lands speak for itself. But no longer. A party that disciplined and sustained its members by means of the federal patronage could hardly favor a reduction of that patronage, even when manifestly in the state's interest. The exigencies of party thus compelled Kane and his ilk to sacrifice the state's autonomy on the altar of consolidation in the federal executive.

Reynolds won the election in August by a wide margin, and the antipartyists did not hesitate to interpret the result. The magnitude of the victory was attributable, according to the *Gazette*, to Kinney's political character. Not only had he proven his vacillating nature in his eleventh-hour conversion to Jacksonism, but in "true keeping with the spirit that has characterized the 'eleventh hour Jacksonians,' every where Mr. Kinney's next push was for offices under the new Administration—and to his intrigues are we indebted for the proscription in this state. . . . The original Jacksonmen, almost to a man, disapproved of the proscription as much as the friends of Mr. Clay; and heartily joined in putting down its author."[71]

And in the wake of this test of Jacksonism, writers continued to develop accounts of manifestly beneficial measures' being sacrificed by party's distortion of legislators' judgments. "Lowndes," for example, began with constitutional principle but soon brought the argument down to economic policy. He found that "proscription" was the chief political issue across the nation because it undermined the fundamental freedom of political opinion. "The most prominent measure of Gen. Jackson's administration is the one which that portion of his friends who 'suck the swill' term 'reform,' but which by the tolerably [unanimous?] consent of all others, is termed 'rewards and punishments.' " Who, the writer wondered, would be willing to risk his family's subsistence by speaking his mind politically when the penalty for disagreeing with the administration was unemployment? "I see no authority [in the Constitution] for the President to remove officers, merely because they voted for his opponent, or to provide for his minions, or his minions' minions, merely because they voted for himself, or belong to the self-styled 'democratic party.' " To grant the power of removal for political reasons as well as for official misconduct would reduce America to the level of Great Britain, oppressed not by force but by "the insinuating and sapping influence of public patronage corruptly bestowed." Jackson himself, Lowndes wrote, had railed against such uses of patronage in his first message. Everyone agreed that neo-Walpolean corruption was wrong. Yet, between removals and grants of public printing, the executive had spent hundreds of thousands of dollars to control the opinions of influential office-holders and editors and thus public opinion itself. Referring to the *Louisville Advertiser* and the veto of the Maysville Road appropriation, Lowndes asked, "Does any man suppose [a] certain 'Advertiser' a little way up the Ohio, would have *blinked* the *question*, and approved the *veto* if the 'sternness' of its Editor's patriotism had not been previously assuaged by a *sop*, which fortunately was out of reach of the Senate?"[72]

This conviction that party had the concrete effect of tying the public's servants to the will of the president, rather than to the will of the people of the states, remained salient as the General Assembly turned to Kane's bid for re-election to the Senate. "A Citizen" noted that Illinois had supported Jackson in 1828 on the grounds of his support for internal improvements and a protective tariff. Jackson had since changed his mind on these matters, perhaps justly, but "is that any reason why Illinois, and the West generally, should alter their views? . . . Is he not the veriest slave to party, who, for party sake, will desert the interests of his own constituents, and vote for the conflicting interests of other sections of the Union?" Now, Citizen went on, the attempt is made "to rally the friends of General Jackson upon Mr. Kane, and to make his election a party question. How futile the attempt, when the days of party rage have closed, and our citizens have met upon mutual ground, as evidenced by the election of Judge Reynolds over the most decided party man in the State—excepting Mr. Kane." On questions touching no interest of Illinois, Kane might be free to indulge his partyism. "But I object, in the name of thousands, against his claim to cover, with the mantle of party, such votes as that upon the Indian Bill, the Salt Bill, and the Internal Improvement Bills." No party could justify "a principle so depraved" as to subordinate Illinois's own clear interests to those of the president or other states. "Neither do we want a party Senator whose party is that of Mr. Van Buren. . . . But the Senator we do want, would come sufficiently recommended, if he was of the true Illinois party, let him side as he might with Jackson or Clay, Van Buren or Calhoun."[73]

The only kinds of parties this writer recognized were those in Washington, D.C., and these were of two kinds: "the true Illinois party," corresponding implicitly with the "true party" of every other state, each representing its undivided political interests in the national arena; and the presidential parties, parties with which Citizen was relatively unconcerned just so long as the interests of Illinois did not become their victims.

Just before Kane's reelection, the editor of the *Gazette* hammered home the point, specifying the Maysville Road and the Bank of the United States as two measures opposed by Kane as a party man that were transparently in the interests of Illinois. The clinching fact was that Kane had supported Maysville before Jackson's veto but then voted against the bill after the veto. Here was incontrovertible evidence of his anxiety "to gratify an administration of which he was a zealous partisan. . . . As to the honesty of Mr. Kane's motives, we do not question them—but as to the absolute, and we do think peculiarly unfortunate, control of party feelings over his understanding and firmness; and as to the error of his political principles, there can be, it would seem to us, but one opinion."[74] When word of Kane's reelection came, the editor appended to this article the reflection that the event only proved "how completely the judgment may be perverted by party feelings." In other words, Kane had successfully transmitted the influence of party from the national administration down the hierarchy to the legislature that reelected him.

Governor Edwards had predicted such a result in the midst of the legislative campaign. Organized party activity had already secured pledges of support for Kane by numerous legislative candidates when, according to Edwards, no other senatorial candidate pursued such pledges. The power of organization to influence even antipartisan candidates when the only other presence in the campaign was the disconnected candidacies of traditional antipartyists was clear. For that reason, Edwards had thought "*very humbly* of any chance" he might have had of being elected senator.[75]

Nevertheless, Governor Edwards appeared to resume his campaign for the Senate when he opened the General Assembly with a manifesto of antipartyist, pro-cession politics. Devoting the entirety of his gubernatorial message to the public lands, he argued that federal ownership threatened economic stagnation from weak immigration and from the drain of land-purchase money out of the state. Moreover, it threatened a federal "*imperium in imperio*" by which the federal government might exercise political influence "over our general elections" by its control of its lessees. To secure cession, an object of such paramount importance, Edwards concluded, "Union . . . among ourselves, is, at present, more important than anything else."[76]

Edwards sensed that the pro-cession position could transcend the party divisions in Illinois. Not only did it serve the interests of almost everyone in the state. It addressed as well the very source of parties in the American federal system: the presence of federal power and patronage within the states. Cession of the public lands would remove substantial federal patronage from the state; it would remove federal economic leverage from the local electorate; and it would remove a vital interest of the whole state polity from the corrupt, national sphere of president-making where the people's real interests became mere bargaining chips among the parties. The cession proposal redefined a politics of the general interest in opposition to a politics of party interests. By identifying that general interest in concrete terms, Edwards hoped that parties would be exposed for what they were: embodiments of private interests from outside the state, addressable only by the polity's reasserting itself as an undivided entity, independent of the other state polities and the general government.

Conclusion

The presidential election of 1828 represented the real, but meager, beginning of partyist reconstruction in Illinois. In the years just before and after the "corrupt bargain" of 1825, numerous constitutional amendments had been offered in Congress to bring election of the president more closely under control of the people.[77] Amid the failure of these amendments, though, the partyists aggressively followed an alternative track of "higher lawmaking,"[78] in which de facto direct election would be accomplished without recourse to the cumbersome procedures of Article V of the Constitution. The partyist alteration of constitutional practice did not get far in Illinois in 1828 and would not until the 1836 election. But the reformers did manage to produce organized nominations for presidential elector and unify the Jackson vote behind those electors. Perhaps even more importantly they succeeded in controlling federal patronage in Illinois, including appointment of land officers.

The use of politics to construct and reconstruct constitutional arrangements, however, soon redounded to the benefit of the antipartyists. Governor Edwards and Governor-to-be Reynolds responded to the limited partyist successes by painting a compelling picture of an imperial federal executive, headed by Van Buren more than by Jackson, determined to use the device of party to vitiate Illinois's constitutionally guaranteed autonomy. Requiring resources with which to consolidate their national party, the Van Burenites seized on such public wealth as the federal lands, denying the state any independent use of the vast federal tracts within its borders and using them further to deny the state any independent use of its increasingly party-bound federal representatives. The Jackson administration might claim the states'-rights mantle on the basis of its reining in such constitutionally questionable federal powers as the funding of internal improvements. Edwards and Reynolds, however, insisted that the real question in federal-state relations was whether manifest state interests would be subverted by Illinois's own representatives, under the pressure and seduction of a federal, consolidationist party in the national executive.

Reynolds's election seemed to show that Illinois's citizenry saw the threat of party and national consolidation for what it was, but the extraordinary power of Jackson's personality would eventually prove too strong. The day after Edwards's valedictory, newly inaugurated Governor Reynolds endorsed Edwards's land-cession proposal, but he also expressed his wariness of disrupting national harmony by insisting on the measure too strongly.[79] Later in the session, the House unanimously resolved that the federal government "ought not" to hold public lands within the states.[80] This resolution retreated from a proposed declaration that the federal government had "no right" to hold the lands.[81] Moreover, the connection between Jackson and the partyists on the national level presented a formidable obstacle to Edwards and his followers. Cession, in fact, lost all force in Illinois as its extreme states'-rights orientation came under the shadow of the nullification controversy.[82] Meanwhile, Kane's reelection and the electorate's continuing enthusiasm for Jackson both evidenced some Illinoisans' ongoing willingness to ignore signs of partyism in men of otherwise democratic credentials. The power of partyism in the state could never be discounted as long as Jackson remained both overwhelmingly popular in Illinois and devoted to Martin Van Buren and the partyists.

Governor Reynolds himself was the best illustration of this point. He was elected on the strength of his antipartyism, but he would never have gone anywhere without credible status as a Jacksonian. Thus, in his inaugural address, he launched a vigorous attack on spoils: "Proscription, 'for opinion's sake,' is, in my opinion, the worst enemy to a republic." And he followed this attack with a call for Illinoisans to unite "to promote the welfare of our common country; and to banish forever that monster, party spirit." But his next thought was to praise Jackson and call for a second term for the president.[83]

Understandably, a frustrated anti-Jacksonian wrote that he approved the entire speech "except the little Jackson clause, which seems rather misplaced at the heels of the very manly dissent expressed against the late course of proscription adopted by the administration."[84] How could one be against Jacksonian proscription and in favor of Jackson's reelection at the same time, many wondered? For Reynolds, the answer was easy. There was a difference between Jacksonism, which stood for equal rights for all, and Van Burenism, which Reynolds believed Jackson must ultimately reject as a cover for political privilege. To anti-Jacksonians, Reynolds's distinction was rationalization at best, and they were not surprised when Reynolds and others allowed their devotion to Jackson to make them into Van Buren men and partyists in a few short years. The state remained antipartyist at base, but it had become equally committed to Jackson as the personification of democracy. It could respond enthusiastically to Edwards's antipartyist, states'-rights arguments for cession of the public lands and yet shed little of its devotion to the increasingly partyist Jackson.

In this connection, one might go on to speculate that had Jackson been elected in 1824—in opposition to the partyists and preempting any "corrupt bargain"—there might have been no significant tension between the embrace of democracy and the traditional force of antipartyism in this generation. But Jackson was, in fact, denied election in 1824; the partyists did seize that event as proof of the necessity of partyism in a democracy; Jackson did then tie himself to the partyists; and a tension did thereby develop that would ultimately force a choice between traditional antipartyism without Jackson and the neo-antipartyism of the constitutional partyists with Jackson. That choice, however, was not forced on most Jacksonians until Van Buren's emergence as Jackson's successor after 1834.

In 1830, the original Jacksonians could still pretend they were true disciples of the president even as they joined with anti-Jacksonians in an ad hoc coalition to rid the state of partyism and consolidationism once and for all. Engaging in an explicitly constitutional politics in response to the partyists' constitutional thrusts of 1828–30, this coalition elected an antipartyist governor and believed that it had won a referendum on partyism, a kind of ratification election for what it understood to be the true, inherited Constitution. The antipartyists would soon learn that partyism had many more lives, but they had accomplished important things in the campaign of 1830: they had made the Jackson administration's partyism the chief issue in Illinois politics; they had shown how partyism in the federal government eroded state sovereignty and autonomy; and they had worked out an argument that blamed the federal government's frustration of the most compelling interests of the state on the organizational needs of the "proscriptive party." They had fused the polity's reflexive antipartyism and constitutional localism to a very plausible version of its policy interests in a way that partyist constitutional reformers were unable to rebut until Van Buren assumed effective control of Democratic party rhetoric with his presidential nomination in 1835.

National Politics, the Constitution, and the Price of Party in Illinois, 1831–1834

After the elections of 1830, some years yet remained before the organization of state and local elections would change noticeably. Party extended itself first to presidential elections and national issues. This separation between the structures of state and national politics suggests that Illinoisans expected little in the way of political purity from the distant, artificial national government or from the quadrennial exercise in president-making. They resented challenges to partyless democracy, whether in the shape of the party politician or the monied aristocrat, but they seemed relieved to see such challenges largely confined to federal politics and diverted from the home-grown, organically democratic institutions of the states. They would soon learn that the partyists had no intention of leaving state structures untouched, but at least through 1834 the focus of partyist reconstruction remained federal.

This chapter will explore the boundary between a partyless state politics and a national politics that Illinoisans increasingly saw as the arena of constitutional and party struggle. As the partyists went about the business of "reform"—manipulating the spoils to build a presidential party—their opponents used the presidential campaign of 1832 and the subsequent "Bank War" of 1834 to make clear that *the* issue in national politics was constitutional: partyist reconstruction, they argued, was already eroding state autonomy and must systematically marginalize the public good in favor of private interests. And they reinforced these arguments by explaining at length the real economic price to be paid by Illinoisans for the partyists' constitutional "reforms."

Local Elections: The Partyless Democracy in a Presidential Election Year

By 1832, the convention nominations of presidential electors in 1828 were a distant memory, and the antipartyist cry against "proscription" was a proven vote-getter. Open party organization, never a very powerful force to begin with in Illinois, was in retreat during the elections of 1830 and 1831. The democracy's right to unmediated choice of its representatives remained firmly in place.

The local elections of 1832, therefore, remained free of party and organization despite the powerful presence of the presidential question. Although there was heated debate on questions of organization for the presidential campaign, next to none of that spilled over into congressional or county elections. Candidates sometimes avowed their presidential preferences, but they just as often coupled such avowals with declarations of antipartisanship. Convention nominations were virtually nonexistent, and organization of almost any kind was absent. Party names attached themselves to no candidates but those running for presidential elector. Self-nominations appeared steadily throughout the campaign in partyist and antipartyist newspapers alike.

The only organized nominations that appear in the available sources were entirely free from party and thus echoed occasional earlier attempts to substitute public, nonpartisan nominations for self-nomination. A meeting "of the citizens" of Lick Creek in Sangamon County, for example, nominated one man each for the offices of state representative and county commissioner but issued no statement or address.[1] In the same county, a Sugar Creek meeting sought more aggressively to reform a decaying electoral system. It observed, without referring to party, that the last legislature had disappointed the people on a number of fronts: increasing the state's indebtedness, passing an unfair road bill, and mishandling the state's school lands. The meeting therefore sought a way to elect men of ability to the legislature. The current system of "electioneering"—traveling the county to buy drinks for the voters—was "in the highest degree fraught with corruption and dangerous to our liberties . . . and prevents in a great degree our ablest citizens from suffering their names to be entered on the list of competitors for office." The consequences of electioneering were manifest in the destructive legislation previously described. If the state wished to be better governed, then it had to have better men in the legislature. And the only way to get better men was to preempt the influence of electioneering and treating with that of nomination by the people at large. To that end Sugar Creek invited every precinct in the county to join them in sending delegates to Springfield to make nominations for county offices.[2] Policy gripes, it seems, required constitutional solutions.

The Sugar Creek delegation showed up at the appointed time some weeks later, but no one else did. Disappointed, but determined to obey their instructions from home, the delegation nominated Zechariah Peter for representative and declared: "If he is elected he will not be indebted for his election to a combination, or to his own personal exertions; and will be the Representative of the people."[3] Peter finished eleventh in a thirteen-man race to fill four positions. His counterpart from the Lick Creek meeting, however, finished third and was elected.[4] Here, then, was a fairly typical election of the antipartyist consensus: thirteen candidates contending for four seats; all candidates but two self-nominated; party affiliations of any kind nonexistent; efforts at constitutional reform largely unheeded and ineffective.

Presumably, most elections were still contested by self-nominees. Some of these, no doubt, dragged presidential politics into the campaign, but some did not. And it is impossible to tell what the proportions were. In Madison County, for example, William Starr relied on his antipartyism fused with his Jacksonism: "Believing, under existing circumstances, [Jackson] is the only man that can administer the government, during such boisterous and violent times; being able to guard and protect against the designing and ambitious politicians of the day; and at the expiration of his term of service, I hope some Jefferson may be found to fill his place—to settle party strife—to unite men on measures—do away party distinctions—quiet the disaffected, and perpetuate our Union by the strongest bonds."[5] But his two opponents hardly mentioned party or national politics at all. Each mounted a separate hobby, one of them the mishandling of the state bank, the other the desirability of getting the federal government to pay the expenses of Illinois's Indian wars.

If local elections were free from anything resembling party even in a presidential year, one might at least expect something like party-organized elections for the three congressional seats available that year. One would, however, be disappointed. The year before, Duncan had trounced four competitors in a statewide campaign in which no candidate had anything nice to say about party. Now in the newly created northern district of the state, Duncan was again triumphantly reelected with no apparent effort and with 77 percent of the vote.[6] Duncan maintained his status as a Jacksonian despite his many differences with the administration in its first term; his opposition to the spoils system apparently did not hurt him. In the southeastern district of the state, Lieutenant Governor Zadok Casey, soon to be a leading anti-organization Democrat, began a ten-year domination of the district.[7] Of the three candidates in the race, only two appeared on the nominations list in the *Advocate*, and none had a party affiliation attached to his name.[8]

In the southwest, five candidates nominated themselves. Each claimed to be a Jackson man, but none claimed to be the candidate of the Jackson party, and each offered a different constellation of positions on the issues.[9] Henry Webb, whom one might interpret as the most Jacksonian on the issues, said nothing about party in his address. He was running as an admirer of Jackson and as an opponent of an excessive tariff but not as the candidate of a party. Sidney Breese also made no mention of party. Charles Slade began his address by avowing loyalty to Jackson and adherence to his administration but only as long as it followed its current course, "always reserving, to myself, the right to judge of the propriety of the measures it may recommend." This standard articulation of Jacksonian antipartyism was matched in Slade's conclusion by his declaration that "if party strife shall continue to increase, this fair fabric of our republic must fall." Finally, Ninian Edwards used similar antiparty flourishes: he claimed that he was induced to run only when numerous solicitations without respect to party overcame his reluctance; and he declared his opposition to proscription even as he asserted his support for Jackson. No one attempted to justify removals from office.

Judged both by these few antiparty remarks and the general absence of reference to party otherwise, the antipartyist consensus was well and coexisting with a Jacksonian hegemony in Illinois despite the Jackson administration's partyism. This coexistence could persist for two related reasons. First, Illinoisans continued to attribute the administration's partyism not to Jackson but to Van Buren. But second, and more fundamentally, membership in the "Jackson party" in Illinois, unlike membership in a Van Burenite party, did not in these days signify allegiance to an organization. By declaring allegiance to Jackson or even to the Jackson party, as these diverse congressional candidates all did, one did not declare one's political opinions or organizational affiliation, and most certainly not one's abandonment of antipartyism. One only affirmed one's constitutional soundness, one's commitment to popular government, without subordinating state politics and interests to national.

The determination that state politics should remain free of party organization even amid the increasing partyism of national politics was reflected as well in the failure of anyone to call for a nominating convention in this last congressional race. The race was very competitive and had at least two candidates whose Jacksonian credentials were highly suspect. Edwards had battled the leaders of the partyists publicly for years and had sat on the fence in the presidential election of 1828. Breese had, in fact, been for Adams in 1828 and was rumored to have been a distributor of the infamous, anti-Jackson "coffin handbills." Clearly, this was a case in which, by the standards of the later party era, a convention was necessary. But holding a convention to unite the genuinely Jacksonian vote was inconceivable at this time and place. The editor of the *Advocate* was busily promoting the national Democratic convention as well as local conventions to choose delegates to it, but any attempt to extend the rationale for a presidential convention down to the state level would have been too advanced.

The polity was not yet willing to accept organization in state politics the way it grudgingly did in national, presumably because it would have meant conversion of state politics into a mere tributary of federal politics. Accepting conventions and organization in state politics would also have meant that the federal government was not alone as a sink-hole of party corruption. It was one thing, and not altogether surprising, to see that the distant national government had become infected with such party scheming that popular organization might be necessary to remedy the situation. But to admit that the state governments, the local, organic creations of the people, had reached that point seemed too much like an admission of defeat for the American experiment in popular sovereignty. Moreover, if such national party organizations were allowed to structure the state's politics, the resulting parties would not even be the indigenous factions that came and went in every state. Instead, they would be the creatures of political forces external to the state and thus perhaps tameable only by those foreign forces. So much for the idea of a self-governing state.

The Convention Controversy:
The Vice-Presidential Nomination of 1832

The only significant political organization in 1832 happened at the vice-presidential level. Jacksonians that year divided between the candidacies of Van Buren and Senator Richard M. Johnson of Kentucky. Or perhaps it would be more accurate to say they divided between those who supported and those who opposed the authority of a national Democratic convention, since each candidate stood for a constitutional position more than for a personal following. In important respects, this division perpetuated that of 1830. Johnson was the candidate of Reynolds and the original Jacksonians, Van Buren the candidate of Kinney and the organizers. And the heart of the conflict was the original-Jacksonian fear that conversion of a popular political movement into a national party organization would merge an organic state politics into the mechanized world of national politics. The federal nature of the Union would fall before the consolidating force of party. In 1830, Reynolds had been able to manage the tension between his antipartyism and his Jacksonism, but in 1832 things were not so easy. Jackson had endorsed the leader and the principal institutional device of partyist reconstruction. If many of Illinois's "original Jacksonians" wished to cling to the old doctrine, they would have to defy Jackson more directly than they had before.

Organization began with a meeting of Jacksonians at the Supreme Court in Vandalia in December 1831. This meeting designated the state's congressional delegation and T. W. Smith, a justice of the Illinois Supreme Court, to represent Illinois at the national Jackson convention in Baltimore. It also recommended that county conventions choose delegates to three district conventions to nominate presidential electors. After surveying the unparalleled achievements of the Jackson administration, the meeting noted incredulously that Jackson was nevertheless faced with the most "malignant" opposition known to all history. Defeat of this opposition required unity, and that could be achieved only by organized nomination of electors.[10] In ratifying the doings of this meeting, a Madison County Jackson meeting recalled the successful district conventions of four years earlier. If they were called for in that crisis, then certainly they were called for now.[11]

These justifications for organization did not involve any vision of permanent party competition. Instead, they asserted that a particular crisis in national affairs now required certain tactics to secure unity on the presidential question, the test question of the nation's constitutional character. Such calls for organization, moreover, routinely included antipartyist elements. The Vandalia meeting, for example, endorsed the single-term limitation for presidents. That limitation was an old antipartyist proposal intended to discourage a president from using executive patronage to build a party for his own perpetuation in office. While openly avowing their adherence to a national party during a crisis, these Jacksonians continued to speak much of the language of antipartyism and betrayed no sense that party competition had become the permanent means of organizing national politics, let alone state politics.

Original Jacksonians, meanwhile, determined to resist partyist hijacking of the Jackson movement this time around. After 1828, the original Jacksonians had learned that acquiescence in partyist control of a campaign meant loss of influence once in power. Jackson administration patronage policies had quickly reopened the breach between partyists and antipartyists. In 1832, the antipartyists were no longer prepared to sit back and tolerate the partyists' tying the Jacksonian electorate to Van Buren by means of organization.

Following hard on the Vandalia and Madison meetings, Johnson supporters met in Vandalia to voice their preference for the vice-presidency. Their proceedings do not survive, but the commentary of the pro-Clay *Sangamon Journal* does. While refraining from supporting Johnson, the paper seized the opportunity to clarify the nature of the division in the Jackson party. Sarcastically, the editor announced that the Johnson nomination "must go for nothing" since his supporters failed to consult "the eleventh hour oracles of the party." The Johnson men had failed to understand "Martin Van Buren's system of caucussing" by which some "regency" assisted by its "county managers" and "runners and whippers" determined proper measures for all to support. Such measures, of course, were to serve only the interests of Van Buren, who was able to maintain control of this network of underlings through "office or the hope of office." The difference between Johnson men and Van Buren men, then, was the difference between principled support of one's favorite, however misconceived, and unprincipled acquiescence in the will of a party leadership out for its own ends.[12]

Van Burenites, though, did not yet actually come out for Van Buren. Rather, they advocated the national convention and hoped all Jacksonians would abide by its decision. Thus the differences between Van Buren men and Johnson men ostensibly had less to do with the particular men than with the means of nomination. Where one camp sought a national convention whose decisions should bind all Jacksonians, the other advocated strictly state-level, popular efforts to support the champion of one's principles. A national, binding convention, the latter thought, compromised one's conscience and one's right to free expression on the intolerable grounds that free expression might cause fatal division in the ranks. To convention men, however, public expression of a preference for Johnson was an attempt to preempt the unifying work of the national convention and create divisions in the party.

One Johnsonian protested the efforts of "little squads of Van Buren men," servants of a "pure party man—of the most unchastened ambition," who were attempting to quash public expression of Illinois's preference for Johnson. Passing by the argument that unity required a certain amount of deference to the mechanisms of the party and prudence in public expression, he rejected the idea that there was "danger to the republican party in this State from the free expression of their opinion on the subject of the Vice Presidency."[13] Similarly, members of the Johnson meeting attacked the *Illinois Intelligencer* for refusing to publish the meeting's address and thereby revealing a devotion to Van Buren greater than its devotion to free expression. Must freemen, they asked, "HIDE THEMSELVES, LIKE SNAKES IN THE GRASS, UNTIL THE GREAT POLITICAL JUGGLER BIDS THEM SHED THEIR SKINS?" They did not object to others' attempts to organize Illinois's Jacksonians just so long as that did not interfere with any man's right to express himself and act for himself. As for themselves, they would "NOT VOTE FOR VAN BUREN ON ANY TERMS WHATEVER" even if he were "juggled into a nomination at the Baltimore Convention."[14] In short, getting the like-minded mobilized for a campaign was not wrong, but an ethic of party obligation that limited individual expression in the service of party was unacceptable.

So far the conflict had a familiar ring, and the original Jacksonians might well have felt confident, led as they were by a governor who had rolled up a large majority with similar kinds of anti-organizational rhetoric two years before. But then the bomb dropped. In 1828 partyists had drawn strength from Jackson's victimization in 1825, arguing that electoral triumph over the national political aristocracy justified whatever means proved necessary. Now in 1832 the still unscrupulous manipulators in Washington—supposed elitists like Clay, Calhoun, and Webster—rejected Jackson's nomination of Van Buren as Minister to England.

At least one Illinois Jacksonian had anticipated that a rejection would "ease Vanburen here" and pave his way to the vice-presidential nomination.[15] And so it did. One of Senator Kane's correspondents wrote, "Much excitement and indignation is felt by the real friends of Gen¹ Jackson throughout the State at the rejection of the nomination of Mr. Van Buren as minister to England"; and "I have no hesitation in saying that it is the general wish of the party that *Martin Van Buren* should receive the nomination of the Convention for the Vice Presidency."[16] Publicly, "A Friend" reported that the new Calhoun-Clay-Webster party had martyred Van Buren and inspired gatherings of the people "in their primary assemblies . . . in the incredibly short space of four weeks; brought together by spontaneous action without pre-concert or design, or the usual arts and efforts of party machinery."[17] And, in fact, the weeks after Van Buren's rejection did witness a series of county meetings disapproving the Senate's action and approving the district and national Jackson conventions. Some of the local meetings and one of the district conventions preferred Johnson but announced their willingness to abide by the decision of the national convention. Others deprecated the idea of bringing out vice-presidential candidates independently of the Baltimore convention. Together, they evidenced the authority of Jackson as the democracy's tribune, the willingness of all Jacksonians to interpret direct defiance of Jackson as an inherently aristocratic act, and the readiness of even antiparty Jacksonians to embrace a national convention and a Van Buren nomination when presented as the Jacksonian response to a specific act of the national political aristocracy.[18]

The Johnson men did go through with their state convention, but the movement petered out rapidly. They nominated Johnson and a slate of five electors but left the electors free to vote for another man if it appeared that Johnson could not be elected. They went on to disclaim any intention to divide the Jackson vote. They were, after all, simply promoting the candidacy of a great republican in Richard M. Johnson. And they hoped no one else would endanger Jacksonian unity by, for example, forcing "upon the people an obnoxious individual for the Vice Presidency."[19] One county meeting later resolved, "That we do not recognize the right of the Baltimore convention, to dictate to the people who they shall support for the office of V. President; and that the Jackson party in Illinois are not bound by the nomination of a Convention, to which they sent no delegates."[20]

By this time, however, Van Buren's nomination was a foregone conclusion. The rejection of his appointment had guaranteed his nomination and, for Jacksonians, obscured his former reputation as a pure party man. The Johnson movement was not heard from again after April and had no candidates in the field in November. The partyists had again succeeded in controlling the Jackson movement at the presidential level.

The partyists were, of course, right that two tickets of Johnson and Van Buren electors could have divided the Jacksonian vote and resulted in the minority election of Clay electors, but the anticonvention argument should not be dismissed as hopelessly naive. Rather, it sought a sensible balance in the circumstances. Although it was absolutely necessary to ensure that the Jackson vote would go as a bloc to a single slate of electors, it was not at all necessary that those electors be tested for their adherence to a national convention's vice-presidential nomination. Any single slate of Jackson electors determined at the state level, whether Johnson men or Van Buren men or a mixture, would have saved the state for Jackson while causing no greater harm than sending the vice-presidential election into the Senate. That danger might have been significant, although it was never mentioned in the campaign, but it would have been balanced by the extremely desirable result that Illinois would have retained its ability to speak its political preferences independently of national party organization and independently of the East. Thus, even as they embraced some degree of organization at the presidential level, they nevertheless defended the integrity of the state as an autonomous polity, free from national party organization and from the convention ethic.

The Presidential Election of 1832:
The Policy Consequences of Party Rule

The internal Jackson division, however, was not the only division in the state. Weak as he was, Clay had enough support to give him almost a third of the vote in November and make the *Sangamon Journal* the mouthpiece of a significant segment of the polity. Before the August elections, the *Journal* confined itself to exposés of the partyist character of the federal administration and descriptions of the price Illinois had already paid for tolerating party rule. The paper pursued several themes: that Van Burenism had consumed Jacksonism after 1828 and made the administration partyist against Jackson's own instincts; that the immediate effect of party was to replace men's principles with mere obedience to every whim of their party superiors; that the spoils system was incompatible with competent administration; and that the consequence of all this was the replacement of good public policy with the selfish interests of party leaders. Disastrous policy, in short, was readily traceable to corruption of the constitutional structures of popular sovereignty.

In late 1831, the *Journal* expressed pity for a certain editor who was an "original Jackson man" and thus might "wait upon the political table," but, with spoils reserved for the partyist crowd, "must never taste of the banquet."[21] The following week, readers were treated to an account of a grizzled old yeoman's visit to the *Journal* office. This emblem of democracy was moved to deliver a short address to the editor on Jackson's fall from grace. He had voted for Jackson in 1828 because the general seemed honest, free from party, pledged against partisan patronage or appointments for congressmen, and in favor of internal improvements and the tariff. Since then, however, the president had violated every pledge and founded a party based on devotion to his person. He was now violating his last pledge in seeking a second term and seeking it by the purchase of political allies through the patronage.[22]

The *Journal* persistently elaborated on the anti-libertarian mechanics of party organization and the bad policy produced by party obedience. On receiving the rebellious report of the secretary of the treasury that favored rechartering the Bank of the United States, despite the president's opposition, the *Journal* praised the report but feared Van Buren's continuing influence. Van Buren had populated the Jackson administration with the heterogeneous adherents of "*the* party": pro-Bank and anti-Bank men; pro-tariff and anti-tariff men; pro-improvement and anti-improvement men; even a few principled men, but mostly party men, who would never take a public position until instructions from Washington informed them of their principles. Thus Illinois now saw party-induced opposition to the Bank, to the tariff, and to federally funded internal improvements, even though the state had been unanimously for these measures in the 1828 campaign. Even defenders of partisan patronage and executive appointments for congressmen now appeared for the first time.

The editor was not without hope for Jackson, however. The recent cabinet reorganization, ordered by the instinctually antipartisan but apparently naive Jackson, had produced a cabinet far better than the degraded one that preceded it. The Treasury report itself was the product of a competent cabinet's replacement of a partisan one. It only remained to be seen whether this trend would overcome the inertia of three years of partisan administration, providing Jacksonians finally with "some fixed principles" and auguring the day when "the asperity of party will cease."[23]

The *Journal*'s optimism grew with Congress's passage of the recharter bill, but great disappointment followed when Jackson vetoed it. The veto must now constitute the party line: "We shall now witness the effect of the magician's art upon sundry characters who have heretofore stood uncommitted on the Bank question—Had he signed the bill for its re-charter, they would have approved of the measure as most wise and patriotic; but he has vetoed the bill, and they will throw up their caps and shout—hurrah!"[24] The editor also described at some length the economic hardships for Illinois that would follow on the loss of the Bank, a loss made possible only by partyist politicians' willingness to place their consciences at the service of their leaders' interests.

But what mechanism caused politicians to follow others' dictates? Spoils, of course. And another event of 1832 proved the point. During the Senate debate on Van Buren's nomination as minister to England, Senator William Marcy scandalously avowed that New York politicians did indeed expect to enjoy the spoils of political war when campaigns were over. To the *Journal*, this was an open admission that the partyists sought to supplant republican constitutional mechanisms with those of party sovereignty: "Such is the system which Martin Van Buren seeks to establish in this republic. Any man who shall dare to think differently from himself of the qualifications of men for office, is to be put under the ban of his displeasure and practically disfranchised. Every office of government is to be bestowed upon political partizans, who are to employ all the additional influence which these offices give them, in managing the affairs of the party."[25] The material consequences of such a policy included paying off Van Buren with the mission to England even after he had, as secretary of state, allegedly undermined American relations with England in relation to the West Indies trade. On the local level, consequences could include the Black Hawk War that had devastated much of northern Illinois in 1832. A Major Forsyth, who had been agent to the Sac Indians, had been uniquely able to control the Indians in his agency according to the *Journal*. "But the day of proscription came," and no talents or character "could save him from the vindictive wrath of the party in power." The consequence was a million dollars in damage, distress on the frontier, murder, a check on immigration to the state, and the spreading of disease. "Take all these facts into view, and we may then learn what calamities this State has, and is still likely to experience, from a single 'REFORM!!' "[26]

In sum, the *Journal* described party as hierarchical and sustainable only by the temperamental servility and greed of a rank and file for whom office was a higher ambition than public service. These party hacks exploited both the money and the prestige of public office for the electoral good of the party and thus for perpetuation of their own officeholding. In pursuing office, members of the party necessarily sacrificed their consciences to the interests of their superiors from whom office came. Thus an artificial uniformity of opinion, serving the interests of the very top of the hierarchy, was imposed on the entire party rank and file through the incentive of office. This uniform opinion was then purveyed to the masses with all the force that money, desperate ingenuity, and the prestige of government office could give it. Only the most extraordinarily vigilant electorate could resist such force. While systematically interfering with the sovereign people's governing capacity, party produced strained foreign relations, Indian war, and economic backwardness.

After months of working out these arguments, the *Journal* still had said virtually nothing directly about the presidential campaign. A Clay movement appeared only after the August election, and for the first time, anti-Jacksonians made some use of conventions. A National Republican convention in Baltimore had nominated Clay in December of 1831, although the *Journal* took only the barest notice of the event.[27] The *Advocate*, on the other hand, leaped at the chance to condemn the hypocrites "who, a few years back, made such an outcry about *caucusses*" but now made their own caucus nominations. "What a solemn farce!!" the *Advocate* concluded.[28]

Nominations for elector began with the *Journal*'s report that citizens of several counties had recommended a full slate of five nominees and that these five men were unobjectionable.[29] Concurrent county meetings, however, resisted such nomination by newspaper and advocated other methods of nomination. One called for district conventions, and another called a state convention.[30] The state convention did eventually nominate five electors, two of whom had been on the *Journal*'s list. Real organization was scarce, however. No one seemed to know whether the convention would actually come off until it did,[31] and it seems to have drawn delegations from no more than a few counties. Nevertheless, its nominees received the concentrated vote of Clay supporters in November.[32]

Of course, the *Advocate* made it its business to label the Clay meetings "caucuses."[33] But the Clay meetings' only explicit acknowledgment that such organization, feeble as it was, might be inconsistent with antipartyist principles came in the Adams county meeting. It resolved that "whilst we deprecate caucussing in the common acceptation of that term, and disapprobate all unfair means of bringing candidates for public office before the people, we hold the practice of making their selection, the result of a free and deliberate consultation, among good citizens of the same politics, to be altogether commendable and republican."[34] This convention, then, was deemed no different in principle from previous, less organized nominations of electors, such as

1828's nominations by an informal Adams gathering after "extensive consultation" in the localities.

In coming years, proto-Whigs and Whigs would hold many more conventions, but they consistently and resolutely distinguished the theory of antiparty organization from that of partyist organization. Far more than Democrats, they would claim to hold conventions only when compelled by the threat of partyist organization. And they would reliably insist that their conventions lacked the partyist ethic of enforced obedience. A proto-Whig convention like the Adams county meeting was thought just one of many means of extensive consultation, whereas a Democratic convention was the exclusively approved way for a Democratic elite to enforce conformity among the rank and file.

As the election approached, each side reiterated its main claims. In the *Journal*, the state convention's address suggested that the election was not really between Clay and Jackson but between Clay and Van Buren. A vote for Jackson was, in effect, a vote for the national ambitions of "a corrupt party in New York" whose strength came from that state's banking aristocracy, which had been the prime mover in the defeat of the Bank of the United States. The result of that party's domination in the last four years had been corruption of the political process and consequent economic stagnation in the states.[35]

The *Advocate*, on the other hand, praised Jackson's defense of the common man on a number of economic issues before finishing with a justification of Jackson's patronage. Jackson, the paper said, "removes from office all who are not faithful to the trust reposed in them . . . but Mr. Clay calls this, '*proscription for opinion's sake*,' and boldly proclaims . . . that monstrous aristocratic doctrine that a public office is private property." Where the Clayites saw a spoils system effectively negating the public will, the Jacksonians saw just removals preserving the democratic character of the government against permanent occupation of offices by an old elite.[36]

As of 1832, overt political organization remained virtually nonexistent in Illinois below the presidential level. If some concessions had been made for presidential politics, the conviction remained unshaken that one's immediate political community—one's county or state—had to remain free of party. And even at the presidential level there remained significant resistance. The original Jackson movement in 1824 had been, in part, an antiparty response to the "dictation" of the congressional caucus. The Jackson campaign of 1828 had had much of the same spirit, and, in 1832, a states'-rights resistance to the authority of party organization, with its conventions and spoils, blossomed as a

Johnson movement in some states and as a vice-presidential movement for Philip Pendleton Barbour in others.[37]

In both 1828 and 1832 the partyists used particular political bombshells as ad hoc justifications for organization at the presidential level. But these organizations were only ad hoc and only presidential—so many Illinoisans still believed—because no one doubted the bedrock antiparty convictions of the people. The electorate's faith in Jackson overcame its disgust for partyism in 1832, largely because much of that faith in Jackson was faith in his ultimate transcendence of parties. So the 1832 election did not represent a popular embrace of partyism or permanent two-party competition. If most of the electorate compromised its antipartyism for tactical reasons in 1832, it was because voters remained convinced that the state polity must be kept partyless by keeping the federal government in its place; and if the latter could be done only by means of temporary organization at the presidential level, many Illinoisans continued to hope that Jackson would be no party man and continued to believe that state politics would resist the infection of partyism.

The Meaning of the Bank War, 1834

Jackson opened the Bank War when he vetoed the recharter of the Second Bank of the United States in the middle of the 1832 presidential campaign, but the veto had little political effect in Illinois before 1834. Jackson's landslide in Illinois had been expected before the veto and was realized after. In 1834, Jackson's decision to remove the government deposits from the Bank finally brought the issue to the fore. But the Bank question did not simply divide the electorate into Democrats and Whigs according to economic ideologies. Rather the substance of the issue was more constitutional than economic. That is, the debates emphasized questions about the proper location of political power more than questions of economic justice or propriety. And the party division it fostered in the electorate was not understood as a democratic "party system," as a recognizably democratic constitutional structure in itself. Rather, that division reflected profound disagreement on the very question of party's place in a democratic constitutional order.

Before the campaigns of 1834 had begun, Alexander F. Grant, an anti-Jackson politician and editor, wrote a series of letters to Illinois's junior senator, John M. Robinson, explaining the centrality of the Bank issue to the constitutional, not economic, character of the nation. He warned Robinson that to place himself too squarely in the Van Buren camp, especially regarding the Bank, would end in Robinson's complete "political fealty" and his political suicide in Illinois.[38] But Grant pushed his worries aside and declared Robinson "impregnable to the assaults of party."[39] Robinson's reply, however, was not encouraging: "I fear you over rate my avertion to partyism[,] at least what you deem such[,] I mean as to the deposite question." Robinson meant to support Jackson's removal of the deposits because, much as he favored the recharter, he thought it impossible to achieve. It made sense, therefore, to remove the deposits gradually from a bank that was going out of business.[40]

Grant's sharp response to Robinson brings home the constitutional nature of the Bank issue. To Grant, deposit-removal and the veto represented not mistaken efforts to pursue the popular interest but a self-conscious, partisan disregard of the popular will in the pursuit of executive power, sustainable only by the unhallowed power of party over such legislators as Senators Kane and Robinson.

You misapprehend me in supposing me to charge you with any *devotion to partyism*, although the opinions you hold in regard to the deposite question, I think, go to confirm a party despotism, as irresponsible and absolute, as its practical operation has been & will be oppressive and ruinous to the enterprising people of the country. I would never acknowledge as a principle of action as a legislator that a measure called for by the interests of the People, and urged by a majority of the people and their representatives, should fail because of executive opposition. The presumption should be that the executive would either change his opinions upon more mature reflection, or yield to the might of enlightened public sentiment. To act upon the principle that the *veto* is uncontrolable, or rather insurmountable, appears to me to be yielding still another prerogative to the mass of powers lately claimed to belong to the executive. Indeed the President of these United States, at the rate at which we are now going on, in my humble opinion will soon be out of sight in advance of Louis Phillippe or William 4th. The question is which is most likely to yield, laying personal characteristics out of view, the legislative department of the government, sustained in the constitutionality of its position by the judicial, or the executive. The legislative speaks more directly the popular will, and it is to be presumed that the Executive will ultimately arrive at different conclusions from those adverse to the vox populi. At all events, the people are those really concerned, and is it a proper presumption that they will give up their interests, and abandon their positions, merely because their executive differs with them. It is idle to talk of the *people* being opposed to the Bank. The brokers, and little bankers are, the partisans of the President are, and a few on high constitutional grounds are, opposed to it—but the *people*, as is obvious, are in favor of it, and demand [it] so that to act upon the presumption that the institu[tion] will not be re-chartered is to yield the popular [will] and the interests of the community as its members under[stan]d them, to the veto of a mere agent.[41]

As much as Grant desired the economic services the Bank could offer—and adverted to the economic ruin that awaited their withdrawal—his argument here is strictly constitutional and foreshadows precisely the future Whig party's theory of democratic government. Not only had the president acted illegitimately in vetoing a measure desired by the people, but he had managed to neutralize the people's check on him by the extra-constitutional device of party. The extraordinary power of party lay in the executive's need to control only one-third of one house of Congress, enough to sustain a veto, before otherwise independent men like Robinson would simply acquiesce in the executive's "party despotism." For Grant such acquiescence meant the supplanting of popular sovereignty by party sovereignty. As in Walpole's time, so in the present day, the executive branch was the ultimate source of party through its control of patronage. If the legislative branch regularly yielded its powers to the executive branch under such circumstances, the result would be a reproduction of Walpole's England, rule by a party utterly distinct from the people.

The *Sangamon Journal*, the main pro-Bank paper in the state, had remarkably little to say about the Bank during the campaign, perhaps because it so thoroughly despaired of a congressional override of Jackson's actions.[42] The *Journal* had made its position clear in 1832, seeing in opposition to the Bank both the rise of party tyranny and economic disaster. In 1834, it confined itself to little more than congressional summaries as it focused its editorial energies elsewhere.

On the Jacksonian side, however, the Bank was central, and the concern was constitutional. One congressional candidate after another declared the Bank's economic functions to be somewhere between "indispensable" and tolerable as long as proper safeguards were placed on its political actions. Adam Snyder, who noted the indispensability of the Bank, also noted the "baneful tendency towards controling political power" of any "monied aristocracy."[43] Snyder's main opponent, Governor John Reynolds, did not mention the Bank in his election address, but in campaign correspondence he took the common position approving the Bank but not its interference in elections.[44] A Morgan County meeting, at which the young Stephen Douglas was the moving spirit, noted the Bank's power to manipulate the economy but laid far more emphasis on the Bank's political actions. The resolutions declared that "the perpetuity of our truly Republican Government" was at stake when the Bank placed its considerable funds "at the disposal of its President for electioneering purposes" and when the Bank was found "interfering with the free exercise of the elective franchise, and attempting to control public opinion through the medium of the press." The resolutions concluded by approving the idea of a Bank with "such restrictions that it cannot interfere with the politics of the country."[45] This was no expression of opposition to banks in general—or even a national bank—but to the kind of bank that was so powerful and so partisan as to vitiate the sovereignty of the people.

Congressman Charles Slade's circular to his constituents declared his increasing wariness of the Bank but also his willingness to support "a new Bank, which shall furnish the same financial and commercial advantages afforded by the present institution, and not possess its dangerous political power."[46] A Hillsboro meeting of Jackson loyalists attacked the Bank for its "opposition to the government" and its "interference in elections," especially by buying up newspapers, thereby threatening rule by a "heartless *monied aristocracy*."[47] And Acting Governor William Ewing told the legislature that the Bank was the author of "all the partizan strife and excitement which now convulse the country."[48]

In short, the campaign of 1834 provided little evidence that Illinoisans feared the Bank as the agent of illegitimate or misconceived economic practice as such. Rather, anti-Bank Illinoisans feared aristocratic manipulation of their fragile constitutional right to govern themselves. For pro-Bank Illinoisans, meanwhile, the attack on the Bank was a mere by-product of partyism. And if they perhaps exaggerated the slavishness to Jackson of the anti-Bank men, they were nevertheless correct that the Jacksonian attack was a constitutional attack that put the immediate economic welfare of the nation on the back burner. For these Jacksonians, the economic price was a small one for the defense of popular sovereignty; for anti-Jacksonians, it was a disastrous example of the material consequences of partyist constitutionalism.[49]

Conclusion

In Illinois in these years, national politics was constitutional politics. Really, it was about nothing but construction and reconstruction of the popular sovereignty and state autonomy said to be guaranteed by the Constitution. The Bank debate was only the most important policy question in the constitutional struggle among anti-Jacksonian antipartyists, Jacksonian antipartyists, and Jacksonian partyists. It supplied the partyists with the latest national crisis they needed to succeed the controversies over the congressional caucus in 1824, the corrupt bargain in 1825, the proscription of 1829, and the Senate's rejection of Van Buren in 1832, each of which had suggested that national politics was an arena of persistent constitutional attack and counterattack. Only in the states had the familiar mechanisms of partyless democracy continued to structure politics. Only in the states, ironically enough, had Madison's original constitutional goal of party-free lawmaking been approximated. The most that could be hoped from national politics—which the Framers had designed as the sanctuary of partyless, deliberative lawmaking in the American system— was that it would prevent the national government from encroaching on the autonomy of the states.

The split between the Jacksonians and the Van Burenites in 1832 rested on dueling accusations that either a partyism emanating from the federal executive or a loose-constructionist antipartyism was the greatest threat to a Constitution of limited national authority and firm state autonomy. The advocates of Clay added to the accusations against the federal partyists by tallying the specific price paid by Illinois for the misgovernment entailed in partyist reconstruction. And the 1834 consensus in Illinois on the economic utility of the national bank made clear that the Bank War was about the Constitution, about whether the Bank or a party of the federal executive was the greater threat to popular sovereignty and states' rights.

Still, while each side had exposed and explicated its opponent's constitutionalism, neither partyists nor antipartyists had gone far yet in embracing and developing their own constitutional theories publicly. Antipartyists had begun to collect an impressive array of examples of destructive policy that would not have been implemented without the exertion of party discipline. But they had not refined a theory of how partyless democracy might sustain itself in the face of increasing tendencies to organization in the political system. And partyists in Illinois had still made only the smallest inroads on the antipartyist consensus, too prudent to make the full pro-party argument openly yet. They had offered ad hoc justifications for party organization at the national level, particularly in the presidential election. But no one in Illinois advocated permanent party organization as a positive constitutional reform before 1835. And no one on either side openly advocated consolidation of state and national political systems, even though such consolidation seemed imminent to many, whether in the broad national policymaking favored by proto-Whigs or in the national party organization favored by proto-Democrats.

CHAPTER FIVE

Partyism Unchained, 1834–1836

The overt partyist effort to amend the unwritten constitution and, in fact, informally amend the Madisonian Constitution itself began in 1835. What had been apparently ad hoc and subterranean efforts of a "radical" faction, confined to the national sphere of president-making, were now made out by the partyists as permanent reforms indispensable to maintenance of the Constitution. To modern eyes, ratification of these "amendments" appears to have been complete by 1840, when the two-party system seems to have been entrenched in almost every state.[1] But to contemporaries, 1840 was merely the year that partyists began digging in for the long haul. At the beginning of 1835, Illinoisans still had not experienced party conventions for any office below vice-president nor witnessed an overtly partyist campaign. They had no idea what a mass two-party system might look like, and they certainly did not understand it as a possible, much less as a necessary, construction of popular sovereignty or states' rights. The creation of such a beast over the next five years was in no way their desire. It was not even the design of the politicians whose hands were actually on the levers. It was, instead, the unintended and unimagined product of a struggle between constitutional reformers and their opponents.

By emphasizing constitutional conflict, I do not mean to dismiss the importance of struggles over social policy. Illinois politics in the late 1830s was, of course, fed by important social and economic issues. Foremost among them would be the national financial panic that followed hard on the state's undertaking to build an enormous internal improvements system. Construction was financed in part by a new and controversial state bank, and the system was built mostly by an Irish Catholic population brought to Protestant Illinois just for the purpose. Financial panic and alien immigration were among the issues that made politics and constitutionalism matter in this period. They did not, however, create the party system between 1835 and 1840. The partyist movement and its opponents did. While necessarily addressing the state's economic and social problems as such, they rarely failed to emphasize the constitutional implications inherent in the handling of each issue. The party system thus emerged amid policy disputes, but its more proximate cause was a constitutional dispute: whatever the social issues of the day might be, how could the process of resolving them be reliably democratized?

More particularly, the constitutional dispute concerned the place of the convention system and partisan patronage within an antipartisan polity. Where constitutional partyism, with its reliance on regular nominations and spoils, had been only a shadowy presence in Illinois through 1834, it would become an overt and aggressive movement in the second half of the decade. Where condemnation of conventions and spoils had been pervasive among the partyists' opponents through 1834, the increasing organization of the antipartyist resistance led to finer distinctions between legitimate and illegitimate conventions and patronage. Both sides took themselves to be defending the fundamentals of antipartyism even while altering its traditional mechanisms.

Underlying this debate about the evolving mechanisms of popular sovereignty were two other constitutional debates. Both sides sought to prove themselves the true defenders of state autonomy within an antipartisan, democratic Constitution. And the partyists raised further controversy by insisting that party organization was necessary to effect an informal amendment of the Constitution, to take presidential elections permanently out of the House and put them reliably in the hands of the people.

The partyist campaign, therefore, had at least three goals, each thoroughly bound up with the others and each constitutional in a slightly different sense. The first, a reconstruction of the mechanics of popular sovereignty, involved little in the way of textual interpretation of the Constitution, even as it involved interpretation of arguably the Constitution's most fundamental principle. The second goal, protection of states' rights, involved a somewhat more explicit focus on constitutional text, as the partyists insisted that only a strict construction of the Constitution's enumeration of federal powers could adequately protect states' rights. The third object, vitiation of the presidential election procedures in Article II of the Constitution and in the Twelfth Amendment, was probably the most text-focused of the partyists' efforts; it sought explicitly to reconstruct, if it could not formally amend, the provisions for election by electoral college and House of Representatives. In the end, however, these three goals were of a piece for the reformers. Each was an important element of the effort to reconstruct the Constitution. And resort to explicitly textual interpretation, as opposed to interpretation of the Constitution's general principles, usually seemed superfluous. These were the concerns that created the party system, and it was in these terms that social and economic issues were so often discussed in Illinois.

This chapter introduces the partyists' first major offensive in Illinois, which centered on the use of party conventions in both national and local elections in 1835–36. But it begins with a look at some local elections of 1834 to show how firmly the constitutional debates of the party years were rooted in the antiparty assumptions of previous years. For partyists, local conventions and the national convention were the bottom and top of a pyramid of conventions that could restore popular sovereignty to a system often usurped by cliques and cabals. Ultimately, if each locality were fully mobilized in its "primary assemblages," then its choice of delegates to county, district, state, and national conventions would be authentically popular, and each level of government would be closely tied to the popular will. The securing of such a constitution of democratic politics was a central goal of the Democratic campaigns of 1835 and 1836.

In contrast, the anti-Democrats of these years understood conventions as mere caricatures of primary assemblages, arenas of manipulation fraudulently labeled as meetings of "the people" so as to preempt by extra-constitutional "regular nomination" the legitimate political action of the sovereign at the polls. The antipartyist resistance, too, founded its argument on an interpretation of the Constitution's popular sovereignty. Thus did some of the elections of 1835 and 1836 become the first undisguised tests of constitutional partyism. Other issues, including the Bank of the United States, the public lands, and internal improvements, played important enough roles to suggest that the elections were more than simply referenda on partyism. But the relationship between partyism and the Constitution was the chief source of debate in every campaign where the partyists made themselves felt.

The "Primary Assemblage" as Pre-Partyist Convention, 1834

Before the emergence of overt partyism and amid the still dominant practice of partyless self-nomination, 1834 witnessed the rise of the nonpartisan convention of the people as a way of restoring democracy to politics and governance. In the course of a very few years after 1834, conventions would become so common a tool of party, even at the state and local levels, that it is a great surprise to see this flowering of political conventionism utterly divorced from partyism. Previous years had seen intermittent, mostly unheeded calls for nonpartisan, organized nominations. Suddenly, in 1834, these calls were heard. It also seems clear, however, that much of the movement, at least in the northern part of the state, was the work of partyist politicians, who were disposed to favor organization even if they could not yet safely advocate party.

These meetings were universally free from party labels, but they implicitly shared the conviction of the constitutional partyists that the mass of the people were democrats who required organization to produce a majority will in defiance of economic or political elites. In the future, nearly all such nominating meetings would gather under party auspices, but these local conventions suggest that what Illinoisans originally sought in organization was not a two-party system but a way to reclaim the Constitution from faction, a way to give voice to the harmonious will of the democracy itself.

There is little to say about the three congressional races but that they went off in traditional, pre-partyist fashion. In the governor's race, however, nonpartisan organization far surpassed anything seen before in the state, except perhaps during the slavery controversy of 1824, although the main beneficiary of the organized nominations, one James Henry, died four months before the election. In the end, the traditionally self-nominated Joseph Duncan won the election with a large majority over two remaining opponents and with no overt organization. This election was the last clear-cut triumph of the traditional, Jacksonian, antipartyist core of the electorate.

In addition to Duncan, two others nominated themselves for governor in the usual way.[2] Meanwhile, partyist leader William Kinney received his first and only organized nomination of the campaign when a nonpartisan meeting of the citizens of his home county, St. Clair, put his name forward. It was the arguments used to justify Kinney's organized nomination and a similar movement behind James Henry that made the campaign noteworthy.

Just before receiving word of Kinney's nomination, the *Advocate* had meditated briefly on the question of convention nominations:

> By many, it is supposed that the *bringing out* of candidates, is the especial business of the people, and can only be done in convention; by others, it is thought that the mode practiced in the southern and western States of candidates *offering* their services and soliciting the patronage of the public, is the more eligible way, as it gives the voters a better opportunity of learning the views and judging the qualifications of the various candidates for office, whereas by the other mode they are obliged to take much upon hearsay. Each mode has its advantages and its disadvantages and it belongs to the people to decide which is the preferable way.[3]

These opinions represented a new openness to conventions but not to party.

Accordingly, the meeting that nominated Kinney was not called as a party gathering. Rather, the participants understood themselves simply as the active citizens of the county without reference to party. No party names were mentioned, and no partyist buzzwords snuck their way into the call or the address.

The meeting's address defended the gathering not on partisan grounds but as an example of the "frequent recurrence of primary assemblages" of the body of the people that was necessary to the maintenance of constitutional government. As firm an element of the constitutional culture as antipartyism was, just as firm was the claim that popular government could not stand if the people's right to assemble publicly was abridged. The very reference to a "primary assemblage" was an attempt to identify the meeting with the central means for the people collectively to overwhelm party schemes.[4]

Thus, the meeting went on to deprecate the excessive factionism of recent times and to promote Kinney primarily by the argument that he had stood aloof from party spirit. Such a declaration must have dropped the jaws of Kinney's recent opponents, who ranked him second only to Kane as a practitioner of Illinois partyism. But it would have been consistent with the views of his constitutional partyist followers. They understood Kinney's partyism as an effort to eliminate partisanship within the democratic polity so as to isolate more clearly the ever present aristocratic party: "In his whole political life he has been found upon the side of the democracy of the American People—. . . opposed to ARISTOCRACY."[5]

This meeting, then, represented an effort to maintain antipartyist politics through the uncomfortable expedient of organized nomination, justified by the unexceptionable doctrine of the people's right to meet to consult for the public good. That this doctrine was distinctly not applicable, by tradition, to the nomination of candidates for office went unremarked by these activists, although it was noted by other meetings.[6] In the future, such nominating conventions would bear explicit party labels and argue the necessity of adhering to the conventions' regular nominations lest the aristocracy sneak through the cracks opened by democratic factionalism. In December 1833, however, promotion of a true democrat by a "primary assemblage" was still reconcilable with the antipartyist consensus. In fact, the ultimate evolution of Democratic party conventions out of such antipartisan conventions lends further credence to the notion that Democratic party organization was born of an antipartyist impulse.

The story of this gubernatorial campaign recapitulated that of 1830: the decisive triumph[7] of an antipartyist Jacksonian, now Duncan, over a constitutional partyist Jacksonian, within a pervasively antipartyist constitutional context. However, the abortive movement to elect James D. Henry, a recent hero of the Black Hawk War, gave another lift to organized nomination. Henry himself expired only a few weeks into the campaign, but by then he had been nominated by several public meetings, which stressed only two things, his freedom from party and his freedom from ambition.

Henry's various nominators endorsed him as "a man whose strong hold upon the confidence and affections of the people make him independent of party leaders, and party management,"[8] "a man entirely free from the corrupting influences of political ambition," opposed to any "monied or *mental* aristocracy,"[9] "free from and above party and sectarian influence."[10] "The great end designed by [Kinney's] election," on the other hand, was "to advance the views of party."[11] The *Journal* soon defended such meetings: "We shall at all times advocate the democratic doctrine that the people have the right, and that it is their duty, to present candidates for office."[12] The editor did not acknowledge that such organized nominations were still a novelty in Illinois. Instead, he relied on the same sort of "primary assemblage" argument used by the Kinney meeting. Madison County chimed in with an endorsement of the right and duty of the people to meet to select their own candidates and in so doing to "soar above party views and sectarian prejudices" and nominate the sort of republican "who will neither seek for office nor refuse it when called thereto by his fellow-citizens." A meeting of northern Sangamon County also endorsed Henry and went on to nominate a full slate of county officers without comment, thus extending the practice of nonpartisan, organized nominations down to the county level.[13] Finally, another pro-Henry, Sangamon meeting nominated an entire ticket from governor down to coroner and justified its action simply by saying that the nominees were good men and that the meeting sought to put down "party spirit," without enlarging on how the nominations would do that.[14] In short, all this organization existed to attack party, not to establish it.

The nominations of Henry obviously shared much with the nomination of Kinney. All were made by gatherings that claimed to be nonpartisan meetings of the citizenry and that justified organized nomination as being within the democratic tradition of defending popular government by spontaneous popular movement. There was, however, a small but important difference between the Kinney meeting and the Henry meetings. The former identified aristocracy as its nemesis, whereas the latter emphasized party-bound politicians as the continuing threat to good public policy. In so doing, the two avowedly antiparty movements foreshadowed the coming difference in political orientation between the two major parties. The Democrats would adopt an ethic of submission to party authority in order to avoid submission to aristocratic authority. And the Whigs would adopt the tactics of party organization in order to resist government by party politicians. The movements of 1834 had not yet identified themselves with parties, and, it must be stressed, there is no reason to think that they expected two-party competition to be a permanent feature of their politics. But the fear of aristocracy and the fear of partisan politics already served as central elements in the actual division of the polity. Both were aspects of the fear that men in office would effectively appropriate the law-making power of the newly and insecurely sovereign people for selfish and destructive ends.

Meanwhile, one set of organized nominations in the north of the state hinted at the coming revolution, even as the great mass of candidates in 1834 was still self-nominated. Sangamon County exemplified both the persistence of self-nomination and the bubbling of organized nomination, as four slots for state representative brought out twelve self-nominees plus four candidates nominated by two separate, local, nonpartisan meetings. Only one of these latter candidates lasted out the race.[15] Similarly, as self-nominations multiplied, citizens of Tazewell and McLean Counties held a nonpartisan meeting to nominate a state representative,[16] and the *Chicago Democrat*, by February, reported the nominations of a number of meetings in the North. But arguments about the use of conventions materialized most fully in response to a convention at Ottawa, which made nominations for state representative and state senator for a six-county district stretching from Chicago to the Mississippi River.

The Ottawa convention adopted an address urging the state to build a canal between Lake Michigan and the Illinois River, and nominated James Campbell for senator and Edmund S. Kimberly for representative. The gathering had failed to attract delegates from half of the district's counties, yet the convention pressed ahead with an attempt at constitutional reform. It resolved that "in the system of nominating public officers through the medium of conventions composed of delegates representing the various parts of the district, we recognise the only mode by which equal rights and privileges can be respected."[17] The delegates' mission was not merely to nominate pro-canal candidates but to establish convention nomination as the exclusive democratic means of nomination. To be opposed to convention nomination was to be opposed to "equal rights," the principle that logically implied majoritarian popular sovereignty.

The convention did not, however, claim any party identification in its deliberations. Rather it specifically declared its distaste for partyism: "In the selection of the candidates above mentioned, [the delegates] have been governed by no party distinctions, but solely by a desire to present to you two of our fellow citizens, highly distinguished for patriotism, talent and integrity, and who are considered by the convention to be eminently qualified . . . to represent the district . . . with credit to themselves and benefit to their constituents, as to the state generally, and in the support of whom all can cordially unite." This early advocacy of the binding authority of the nominating convention and the implicit argument for thus vitiating the general election was completely free from advocacy of partyism. Conventions like this one, claiming to speak for the whole people, would be challenged by others claiming the same ability. But such conventions would not begin to use party labels in Illinois until the following year.

Almost as soon as it had gotten word from Ottawa, the *Chicago Democrat* endorsed the convention's acts and began to attack the legitimacy of political division once a popular convention had spoken. Spying a movement to make another set of nominations, the *Democrat* asked rhetorically, "Is it a struggle for men? It can be nothing else."[18] Any opposition to good nominations made by a popular convention could only be factious and self-interested. There was no room for political pluralism. Soon enough the necessity of isolating self-nominees who might flout the majority will would justify the further step of applying the Democratic party name to conventions. As yet, however, popular conventions seemed to need no party name, because they were "primary assemblages" of "the people," not party gatherings.

Needless to say, the *Democrat*'s arguments did not go unchallenged. A correspondent known to the editor as "Captain David" objected to the "new school of politics" in which free expression was suppressed and the voice of a convention "as implicitly obeyed as the 'order of an autocrat' to his subjects." In response, the *Democrat* ridiculed this opposition as a factious one-twentieth of the polity attempting to distract the nineteen-twentieths who would happily harmonize with the convention nominations.[19] The editor's position was consistent, at least in its own terms, with both the theory of nonpartisan nominating meetings and the constitutional partyist theory of regular nominations. That is, both theories supposed that organized nominations could and should be the acts of the people as a whole, excluding only the numerically negligible "aristocracy," defined as those disloyal to the majority will. The editor did not accept the possibility of a legitimate, organized, competitive opposition any more than his correspondent accepted convention domination of elections.

Debate about the legitimacy of conventions in general and of the Ottawa convention in particular continued until election day. "Many Voters" of Peoria County wrote to advance the claims of Dr. Augustus Langworthy for senator. A meeting had been held at Peoria at which Langworthy had not done well, but Many Voters asserted that his poor showing there was simply the result of his supporters' staying away. They were opposed "in principle to *caucusses*, and to all meetings held for the purpose of *anticipating* regular elections by nominations."[20] The constitutionally authorized election, not a pre-election meeting, was assumed to be the only legitimate device for gauging the popular will. In response, the *Democrat* accused Langworthy himself of having been present at the Ottawa convention and therefore of acting underhandedly in allowing his name to be used against the Ottawa nominee.[21]

But why was it underhanded for a participant in a public meeting to oppose the nominee of that meeting? The *Democrat*'s condemnation of such behavior made sense only if one embraced the startling new ethic of loyalty to regular nominations, the hallmark of party authority, even before party organization existed openly in Illinois. This was, in the event, a step toward party organization, but it is crucial to recognize that the theory of such nonpartisan organization was that it would not divide but unify all genuine democrats, all who embraced the majority as the ultimate source of authority. Opponents of the ethic and its theory, with just as little attention to party, saw such regular nominations as illegitimate preemptions of popular election.

Opponents of the Ottawa nominations in Cook County finally met to make a counternomination in May.[22] By the very fact of their meeting as well as by their nominations, they signalled that they were not so much opposed to nominating meetings as they were to the convention ethic of binding nomination. In naming a candidate for representative, the new meeting attacked the "foreign and artful scheme of conventions" by which the Ottawa meeting attempted to impose a "gag-law spirit" on the district, expecting "slavish obedience" from the people. In contrast, the anti-Ottawa meeting was "spontaneous" and merely publicized the virtues of its candidates without making any claims as to the people's obligation to vote one way or another.[23] The *Democrat*'s replies to this address emphasized that the sole point of the Ottawa meeting had been, in fact, to do away with divisiveness and "party feeling" in the interests of a united effort to elect a pro-canal legislative delegation.[24]

In the Senate race, the anti-Ottawa nominee was James W. Stephenson. Stephenson had originally been nominated by a meeting in Jo Daviess County before the Ottawa convention. The original meeting had been called to promote the canal but had gone on to nominate Stephenson, while expressing a willingness to compromise on the choice with the other counties.[25] When the anti-Ottawa meeting back in Chicago also nominated Stephenson, it joined the Jo Daviess meeting in the uncommon but no longer unprecedented practice of nonpartisan organized nomination, presenting candidates for public consideration without the convention ethic.

There were, then, three nominees for senator in the field: Campbell, the nominee of the proto-partyist Ottawa convention; Stephenson, the anti-Ottawa nominee but also, surprisingly enough, a member of the Ottawa movement;[26]

and Langworthy. Each of these three candidacies represented a different means of nomination—although the candidates did not all seem to share the scruples of their supporters regarding means of nomination. Campbell's candidacy was an attempt to organize the entire partyless district behind a nomination that was plausibly the act of the whole democratic polity and thus, in theory, ethically binding on all those who accepted majority rule. Stephenson's nomination was a somewhat more traditional act by meetings that represented themselves less as embodiments of the people than as attempts simply to present endorsements of good candidates for the consideration of the electorate. Finally, Langworthy's candidacy represented the traditional identification of any kind of nominating meetings at all with "caucussing." When Campbell declined the Ottawa nomination in favor of Stephenson in late May, the *Democrat* endorsed Stephenson as a good pro-canal man even as it sustained its attack on the Chicago faction that had nominated him.[27]

In the end Stephenson was elected, almost unanimously if the surviving returns are any indication.[28] And, in fact, the *Democrat* took early returns, in which the Ottawa nominees dominated the Cook County vote, as vindications of the Ottawa convention's claim to be the true voice of the polity as a whole.[29] The final results were far from a clear endorsement of organized nomination, however. The Ottawa nominee for representative was ultimately beaten by a self-nominee, who, judging by his election address,[30] was an entirely unaffiliated candidate and a supporter of the canal. When this self-nominee defeated both the Ottawa and anti-Ottawa nominees for representative while Ottawa's Stephenson swept the district in the Senate race, the electorate could hardly have been said to have sent a clear message regarding methods of nomination.[31]

The north of Illinois witnessed in 1834 a new degree of electoral organization, but conventions of various kinds continued to coexist with self-nomination while party remained anathema in local elections for all involved. In central Illinois, the ill-fated Henry movement produced a number of local, nonpartisan nominating meetings, but nothing like the Ottawa movement's attempt to preempt all other nominations by democratic right. In the end, these innovations represented only the smallest of inroads on the traditional, antipartyist, anti-organizational construction of popular sovereignty. And, at least in their public pronouncements, they represented not only a failure to undermine antipartyism but, in fact, an effort to democratize it with antipartyist organization. Only in the approach to the 1836 elections, under the shadow of Martin Van Buren's aggressively partyist campaign for the presidency, would nomination by party convention begin to appear in state and county level politics. And, judging by the events of 1834, the rise of the party convention at all levels of politics would result not just from the theories of men like Van Buren and Kane but also from the local efforts to overcome an increasingly partisan politics by means of organized, public, nonpartisan nomination.

The Democratic National Convention

In March 1835, the Illinois partyists began their campaign to legitimate the national Democratic party convention as the only democratic means for choosing a president. They asserted that only a national convention could adequately represent the will of the entire people. Naturally, therefore, the Democratic national convention was the "ancient usage" of the Democratic-Republican party, the party which had snatched republican government from the jaws of the Federalist "monocrats" in 1800 and defended it ever since. Or so the partyists claimed. In fact, the Democrats had had only one previous national convention, in 1832. They had nominated candidates by congressional caucus many times before that, but the mass of Republicans had repudiated the caucus in 1824 as corrupt and unrepresentative of the will of the people. Nevertheless, Democratic activists in 1835 began to insist that the convention system was the long-established usage of the party and that only popular ratification of this informal amendment to the Constitution, this vindication of the authority of the Democratic nominating convention, could genuinely root faction out of the American lawmaking process.

In endorsing the national convention, a St. Clair County meeting resolved that "the Democratic Republicans of this State . . . are in favor of the established usages of the Democratic party in selecting candidates for the offices of President and Vice President, by a regular nomination." The meeting noted that shortness of time made selecting and sending a state delegation to Baltimore impractical but that local meetings should be held around the state to approve whatever the national convention might do.[32] Of course, it would be better for Illinois to send a delegation, but the main goal was to establish the democratic legitimacy, not of this particular convention's acts, but of the principle of a national convention's speaking for the people. Should the people ratify the convention ahead of time, it would become more than just one of many bodies recommending candidates to the people; it would become the legitimated voice of the people themselves.

While other meetings revealed a similar degree of confidence in the Baltimore convention, there was also some anxiety that this convention be tied as closely as possible to the actions of the people themselves in order to approximate the ideal of a national pyramid of popular conventions. The editor of the *Advocate* regretted that pro-convention county meetings were not drawing full attendance, a circumstance that would reinforce the opposition's claim that the partyists' pyramid of conventions had no base in the people.[33] Meanwhile, meetings in several counties[34] assumed there would be a state convention to choose a delegation to Baltimore. And in the north of the state, meetings placed heavy emphasis on tying all nominations to thorough organization at the local level. The "Great Democratic Meeting" in Chicago announced that since "it is not consistent with the usages of the Democratic party, nor the rights of the citizen, to require its members to support candidates for office when they have had no voice in their selection," minute organization was necessary in all localities; and "we will not recognize the pretended claims of any aspirant to any office . . . unless he shall be nominated by a convention fairly called at which every member of the party has an opportunity of being heard either in person or by his delegate." The meeting concluded with a declaration of support for the national convention and for Van Buren or any other nomination "fairly made."[35]

Suddenly, some Illinoisans were calling for party organization in every hamlet for every election in a land where party organization of almost any kind had always been universally condemned. But the populist language of this and other meetings, such as the Shelbyville meeting that preemptively defended itself as a "primary assembl[y]" of the people, confirms that for these activists the Democratic party's purpose was not to divide the people but to unify the democrats through the anti-aristocratic "usage and custom of the democratic party to meet in Convention."[36]

At the end of April, a Democratic state convention did come off in Vandalia. It seems to have drawn delegates from only seven of the state's sixty-two counties, although some indeterminately greater number of counties had endorsed the convention system. Conceding its disappointment in the number of delegations present but refusing to concede its unrepresentativeness, the gathering named five delegates to the Baltimore convention. It resolved that, while Van Buren was the preference of Illinois, it would support whoever was nominated at Baltimore, since "the usages and well established principles of the democratic party have for a long term of years settled upon conventions" as the correct means for expressing the party's wishes on the presidential question.

The convention's address justified organization not only by this standard appeal to tradition (a tradition that did not really exist in Illinois) but by a constitutional appeal as well. Thus, first of all, Van Buren's chief opponent at this time, Hugh L. White of Tennessee, could not be considered a "democratic" candidate because of "his determination not to submit his pretensions to the decision of the democratic party, represented in the Baltimore Convention." Moreover, the object of such a candidacy could only be to throw the election into the House of Representatives, the sole arena in which a "federal" man might be elected. Witness the election of Adams in 1825, the only Federalist success since the dawn of the democratic era in 1800. Experience had shown that appeals to self-interest could easily sway a small body of representatives against the will of the people, as had been done in 1825. And it was well known that the Bank of the United States, the font of Federalist resources, had prominent legislators on the payroll. Since 1832 the Bank had been the chief nemesis of the people, according to the address, less for its role in the economy than for its power to control elections by the leverage of its enormous economic resources.[37]

With the arrival of the national convention's proceedings and Van Buren's letter accepting the nomination, the constitutional thrust of the campaign was confirmed. Andrew Stevenson's presidential address to the delegates asserted that the convention was an effort, in effect, to replace the Constitution's provisions for presidential elections with more democratic means. Constitutional amendments for direct popular election of the president having failed, Stevenson argued, "the democracy of the Union have been forced to look to a National Convention as the best means of concentrating the popular will and giving it effect in the approaching election."[38] The danger was not that another candidate might win the popular election but only that there might, in effect, be no popular election at all if the 1836 vote merely enabled the House, guided by champions of "monarchical systems," to elevate some minority candidate.[39] In sum, democratic party organization had become indispensable to the preservation of the Constitution's popular sovereignty against the threat of the Constitution's own defective electoral provision. The Constitution, therefore, had to be amended de facto, if not de jure, and democratic party organization was the only way to do it.

The opposition to the national convention movement, meanwhile, emphasized two main points: that the supposedly popular character and doings of the convention system were a farce played out by the officeholding elite; and that the current campaign climaxed the effort to merge true, conservative Jacksonism into the new-fangled Van Burenism of party organization. By this merger, exactly to the contrary of Van Burenite claims, the right of election would be effectively removed from the people and transferred to officeholders. To the anti–Van Buren activists, Jackson's two-term embrace of Van Buren had nearly delivered the mass of honest Jacksonians into the hands of men whose pro-party principles would otherwise have been dismissed as utterly alien to American constitutional values.

At the approach of the Democratic National Convention, the *Sangamo Journal* declared that local Democratic meetings in Illinois were not meant to give voice to the people but only "to commit Jackson men against HUGH LAW-

SON WHITE, of *Tennessee*,—a long tried friend of Gen. Jackson, who has been called before the people by his fellow citizens as a candidate for President."[40] But how, Illinoisans might have wondered, would Jacksonians become committed to Van Buren just by attending primary assemblages, those bulwarks of popular independence? "*A true and steadfast friend* of GENERAL Jackson" answered the question by outlining the partyist ethic of the Democrats' usages. He wrote that all "may be assured this meeting [in Springfield] is for the purpose of getting them committed to Van Buren, for if they vote in the meeting, if they do at all, it will then be urged against them that they have sanctioned the pretensions of Van Buren."[41] The Van Burenite convention ethic, by which any participation in a convention bound one to support the actions of the convention's majority, was far from taken for granted in 1835. It remained necessary to warn innocent Jacksonians that Van Burenite meetings were not like other meetings, not like the "primary assemblages" to which party conventions often likened themselves but which left participants free to act by their consciences. To attend, especially if one voted, was to sacrifice one's future independence on any question decided by the meeting or else to bring accusations of aristocracy down on one's head.

The standard antiparty refrain was that such party meetings were "got[ten] up and conducted by *Office Holders*," who sought effectively to replace the constitutional mode of election with the extra-constitutional device of regular nomination. Combining officeholder control with the partyist ethic, conventions became "nothing more nor less than an effort of the *few* to govern the *many*, and to relieve the people of the troublesome task of choosing a President for themselves" so that "an aristocracy of *Office Holders*" might do it for them.[42] "One Who Knows" chimed in to claim that should the electorate accept such officeholder dictation, the real election would no longer happen at the polls but at the Baltimore convention.[43] To this writer's horror, presumably, partyists would have actually agreed that the extra-constitutional convention should reduce the constitutionally contemplated election to a formality. As suggested by Stevenson's speech above, they conceived of the Democratic National Convention as a more democratic institution than the nominally popular election which, through a constitutional anomaly, would in fact produce an election by the House rather than by the people.

To the more traditional, however, the notion of elevating a convention, reputedly populated largely by officeholders, above the constitutional mode of election was not only absurd on its face but had been directly repudiated by the Jacksonians of 1824. In that year, argued a *Journal* correspondent, Van Buren had brought Crawford out by means of a caucus hardly different from the convention of 1835, and the people "*did denounce it from Maine to Geor-*

gia, as a measure wholly at variance with Democratic principles." Jackson had been supported as the "candidate of the People, not of a caucus. . . . Did we not say, let all become candidates for the Presidency who please? that the people would settle the dispute at the ballot box."[44] Finally, a Shawneetown paper noted that the series of Van Buren meetings had only begun in earnest since the return of Illinois's congressmen from Washington, where they had gotten their orders "to establish a branch of the Albany Regency" in Illinois.[45]

Summing up the anticipated nature of this presidential election, the *Journal* announced that "the great question to be decided in the coming Presidential election is,—shall government officers, with the teats of the Treasury in their mouths, by the aid of caucuses and corruption, control our elections; or shall our elections be controlled by the People."[46] The *Chicago American* agreed that this election was, first and foremost, about the constitution of democratic self-governance itself and in particular, about the place of party in the American unwritten constitution: "There is a *party*, of which Mr. Van Buren is the head . . . whose principles are indefinable, and whose object is the security of patronage and power in its own hands. . . . Since it is founded only on the abstract idea of '*party*,' the leading doctrine of its creed inculcates uncompromising submission to the will of its leaders, and excommunicates" anyone who fails to support "the 'caucus candidates.'. . . Such we understand to be the 'usages of the party,' which are spoken of with so much reverence, as if an infringement upon them indicated a want of all political virtue. We ardently hope, that the usages of the *party*, will not be found to be the usages of the *country*."[47]

The Connection to Local Elections, 1835

With the national Democratic convention, Illinois Democrats finally avowed that party was all, even in some of the most local of elections. In northern Illinois a handful of city and county elections became the first vehicles in the partyists' open attempt to legitimate party organization at the polls. Before 1835, the limited degree of party organization that had characterized presidential politics in Illinois had conspicuously failed to filter down to state and local contests, but in 1835 some of these local contests became virtual referenda on the question of party. Partyists intended to fuse the most local and the most national elections by elevating conventions, for the first time in Illinois, from a matter of mere expediency to a matter of grand principle.

In the summer of 1835, the Cook County elections focused entirely on questions of democratic electoral practice. When announcing the convention nomination of a Democratic ticket, the *Democrat* did not emphasize the candidates' positions on substantive issues but simply observed that "this is the first instance in which the people of this State have adopted this mode of *selecting* their candidates. Believing as we do that this is the only proper way of bringing candidates before the people, we feel a deep interest in their success."[48] Consequently, the editor declined even to announce the self-nominations of other candidates, even those who claimed to be democratic. Nonconvention nominations were inherently anti-democratic because "when the aristocracy are making every effort to crush the principles of Democracy, by sowing dissension in the party," unity among democrats must be paramount. And unity could only be had by way of convention.

Finally, the editor added, "For ourselves we are ready to be advised and instructed by the party—the people themselves—we will always *obey the voice of the majority.* . . . But never will we admit the principle that a *few* individuals have a right to dictate to the people."[49] The editor was so confident that the Democrats were the democrats—the people themselves—that he declared that the "opposition here know that they are too weak to maintain even a show of strength when parties shall be *organized,* and yet there are many of our political friends *professedly* who are opposed to any party organization. They join the aristocracy in decrying meetings of the people, Conventions, &c."[50] Anticonvention democrats were not democrats at all once democracy and aristocracy were distinguished by attitude toward the convention system itself. Embrace of the convention system meant merging oneself in the majority of the people. Rejection of the convention system indicated one's stubborn insistence on one's own preferences. In short, one's adherence to the convention system (or not) was a fundamental test of one's commitment to the majoritarian Constitution itself.

The *Democrat*'s glorification of the convention system's ability to give body to the majority of the people, however, appeared laughable to "A Jacksonman." He claimed the convention at Flag Creek comprised all of six men, five of them from Chicago, all of them seeking to pad the convention's numbers with spectators. Yet even within this sorry clique democratic practice did not prevail. The convention, such as it was, had concluded to nominate one man for county recorder when the local strong man of the party arrived to dictate the nomination of a different man, one Peter Pruyne.[51]

Condemnations of the Flag Creek Convention in particular and of the convention system in general—"the atrocious New York drill system of politics"—were the nearly exclusive campaign weapons of the anti-Democrats in this election. A typical correspondent in the *American* attacked the rule of "King Caucus" and rejected the authority of the county convention, populated, in this version, by only four men, including the dictator who all by himself constituted "the 'Democratic Party.'"[52] In a bit of hopeful exaggeration, the editor even suggested that the convention system was so absurd that the people might eliminate it permanently by electing the anticonvention candidate for county recorder: "Before another paper is issued from this office the fate of the caucus system will have been decided; . . . The people now have the choice either to be free, independent, and masters of their own suffrage, or to wear the bonds and shackles of *party*!"[53]

Even when promoting their own candidate, the incumbent Richard Hamilton, the antipartyists were concerned almost exclusively to represent him as free from caucus nomination. Few other attributes of the candidate mattered. He was requested to run in a letter signed by twenty-six men. Making no claims that such a nomination should obligate anyone, the editor simply asserted that Hamilton had proven himself competent and that the "enlightened people of this county" would not be "cajoled out of their rights by a nomination made by a few partizans."[54] At the same time, "Truth" ridiculed the rumor that Hamilton was opposed to the canal. Even then, the author's preoccupation was the constitutional question, mentioning the rumor only long enough to condemn it as one of "the desperate shifts [Hamilton's] enemies resort to, to effect their double purpose of imposing their system of dictation upon the country and defeating him."[55]

The anti-Democratic conviction that all the caucus men were after was the legitimation of convention nominations was true. As the *Democrat* advanced Pruyne's candidacy solely on the basis of his having received a Democratic convention nomination, so it supported a nominee for state senator solely because he was nominated by a district convention at Ottawa. The candidates were hardly mentioned again in the campaign, but long defenses of the convention system filled the *Democrat*'s columns.

These defenses emphasized that the system offered every democrat equal influence in the creation of a majority and required only a willingness to remain true to that process and merge oneself in that majority as it solidified. What was wrong, the editor wanted to know,

in those who have a common stake in the same principles, meeting together to decide what measures they will take to ensure the prevalence of their principles in the government; Is it not on the contrary the only true republican course? . . . How can any member of the party be heard except in caucus or convention? No way can be devised, he comes to the polls and must vote for measures and candidates, which he may not prefer and in the adoption of which he had no voice, or desert his principles. But the convention system provides a way in which every man can have his just influence in the doings of his party.

In convention, great diversity might reign as to policy and candidate preferences. But a Democratic convention was premised on unanimous, prior endorsement of the democratic principle of majority rule. And that principle guaranteed that the convention participant would always have the clear choice on election day of "sustaining his principles"—democratic majoritarianism—or abandoning them.[56] The convention might have rejected one's personal preferences, but, by virtue of participation in a convention of majoritarians, one had necessarily adopted new preferences, those of the majority. To be a good democrat was to presume the superiority of the majority's judgment—the people's judgment—over one's own. A genuine convention nominee could not be incompatible with a democrat's "principles," as long as "principle" meant constitutional principle. Policy questions, however important, were not questions of "principle" in partyist theory. And a loss in convention on a policy or a candidacy could not change a democrat's obligation to adhere to "principle" on election day.

If the *Democrat* believed conventions indispensable to party unity, it also argued the absurdity of the anti-Democratic position that parties need not exist at all. There were two parties, whether the opposition admitted it or not. The opposition liked to rail against "'*the tyranny of party*,' '*proscription system*,' &c.," but "in doing this they act *together, as a party*. . . . They are desirous not of extirpating party, but of effecting such a change or modification of party as will bring them into favor." And, if there must be a party of democracy and a party of aristocracy, then the so-called proscription system merely reflected the right of "the people, or what is the same thing, a *majority* of them" to see that the government was carried on according to majoritarian principle, while the convention system was the only way the majority could reliably infuse elections with that same principle.[57] Had the "aristocrats" sought openly to limit the suffrage to the monied, the partyist argument suggested, they would have done little more than they already sought to do in their opposition to party organization, the *only* tool by which "the people, or what is the same thing, a *majority* of them" could discover and implement its collective will.

When the summer campaigns were over, the anticonvention Hamilton had been elected over Pruyne, but a number of convention-nominated candidates had also succeeded. The *Democrat* chose to interpret the results as a legitimation of conventions, while dismissing Hamilton's win as the last gasp of old-fashioned politics.[58] It did not, however, waste much time on the question, since the partyist offensive had many battles still in its future. The next step was to return to the national level and organize a state convention to nominate presidential electors and advance full organization at all levels.

The Democratic National Address: Party Organization as Constitutional Amendment

Some months after publication of the proceedings of the national Democratic convention, the national address of the Baltimore convention finally arrived in Illinois.[59] Following the summer elections, the partyists were eager to maintain the connection between the local ideological war and developments in the national struggle. For that purpose, the national address was a vital tool, as it elaborated the constitutional nature of partyist reformism.

The burden of the national convention's address was to justify party organization and, in particular, the national convention. The startling premise from which the argument proceeded was that among the greatest threats to "public liberty and our happy system, next to revolution and disunion, *is an election of President by the House of Representatives.*"[60] In a House election, authorized by the Constitution though it was, the fundamental constitutional principle of rule by popular majority would be replaced—as it had been in 1825— by minority selection of the president. Presuming that the anti-democratic usurpation of 1825 was the controlling political memory of the nation in 1835, the address argued that election by a distant, elitist House in a nation wedded to the ethic of localist democracy provided too many means by which "ambition and Party might successfully triumph over the People's will."[61]

Also startling, at least on the surface, was this use of "Party" as the antithesis of "the People's will" in an address whose central purpose was to show that party was in fact a tool of the popular will. The authors still had at least one foot stuck in traditional antipartyism, in which party was by definition the tool of a minority, even as they invented a new kind of party to transcend older categories. This new kind of party would encompass all adherents of majority rule and neutralize such inevitably anti-democratic parties as had suffused aristocratic societies. A democratic constitutional party would be united not by policy goals or by the compatibility of a collection of ethnic or religious groups, but by universal deference to the will of the majority.

Complementarily, an aristocratic constitutional party, whether such a party would so avow itself or not, was a collection of groups grudgingly united by the constitutional principle of elite rule, grudgingly because each group wanted to be the elite that ruled. These groups were self-interested adherents of substantive principles like abolitionism and "bankism," regardless of the will of the people. They could justify any use or misuse of government power to that substantive end because only the substantive goal was fundamental—or constitutional—to each of these disparate groups. Outside the borders of the democratic polity, all the groups of substantive rather than procedural principle constituted a single polity in themselves. In partyist theory, this polity recreated an old-fashioned aristocracy complete with endemic factionalism, its only unity coming from a common fear of democratic constitutional reform. Each group pursued substantive self-interest rather than a principled elitism, but self-interest could not triumph over the general interest without an implicit constitutional elitism. Thus Democratic constitutional partyism implied a kind of interconstitutional party system—a contest of constitutions and the organizations that championed them—very different from the modern understanding of the party system as an intraconstitutional institution.[62]

Given this understanding of American politics, the Democrats concluded that, even if their national convention had not been perfectly representative, its defects must be minor when measured against the dangers of the only alternative, "the calamities of an election by the House of Representatives, the Pandora Box of" the Constitution. Here, the address went so far as to accept that conventions were merely a second-best alternative to the formal amendment process:

> Until some amendment of the Constitution shall be adopted to cut off the possibility of an election by the House of Representatives, and cause the will of the People to be respected in the choice of their Chief Magistrate, it should be the duty of the Republican party, either through National Conventions, or some other efficient mode, to concentrate their power, and produce harmony and union among their friends. . . . [Should such an amendment succeed], then will our argument in favor of nominating candidates for . . . President and Vice President, through the medium of a National Convention, be obviated, because then the sovereign right to choose these offices will be secured to the People themselves in that contingency.[63]

In the meantime, however, imperfect as it may be, the convention system stood as an indispensable, de facto, direct-election amendment to the Constitution, speaking the will of the whole people—or, as the *Democrat* had put it, "what is the same thing, a *majority* of them"—better than any other institution the written Constitution or the unwritten constitution had to offer.

Confirmation that a "principled" party had to be a constitutional party recurred in the Convention's rebuke to those who reflexively condemned all parties alike. In Great Britain, party had defended the balance of the constitution against "the great and overweening power of the monarchical and aristocratical branches of the government," while in this country, the two great parties would, respectively, "secure the Constitution on a firm basis" or "overturn that Constitution."[64]

The address perorated, "We sincerely believe, that upon the preservation of the old Democratic Republican party the prosperity and happiness of our country greatly depend."[65] It did not say that the state of the nation depended on Democratic victory; victory was taken for granted if only the party of the democracy were preserved. Once the party was organized on a purely constitutional basis, any opposing party must necessarily oppose the Constitution itself and its foundational majoritarianism, and no danger could come from a party that openly avowed such principles. Danger lurked only in the otherwise laudable antiparty sentiment that anti-democrats regularly exploited in campaigns.

The Democratic State Convention

In September, county meetings began to convene, generally endorsing the national convention and naming delegates to the state convention, which would nominate presidential electors. But these meetings revealed a notable variability in their support for the convention system's fusing of local and national politics. State conventions to name presidential electors had been held twice before but had gone no further than that single function. They had respected the wall between state and national politics. Now, however, a number of the county meetings urged the state convention to effect an immediate and thorough organization of the state or, as the editor of the *Democrat* put it, to promote the convention system in general as "a system of politics . . . that will give the humblest citizen of Illinois a voice in selecting candidates."[66] Others expressed continuing concern that all conventions be as accessible as possible to the people in order to sustain the claim that they were, in effect, primary assemblages. Many meetings, however, made no such gestures to promote organization. They apparently expected the state convention to behave as conservatively as the conventions of 1828 and 1832 had.[67] In the event, the state convention produced a dramatic showdown that imposed limits on the partyists' attempt at a full-scale reconstruction of popular sovereignty.

Initially, at least, the more conservative expectations were met. As usual, only a minority of the state's counties were represented, and the published resolutions of the meeting, while justifying party more sharply than previous state conventions had, nominated only presidential electors and discussed only national politics. Conventions were sanctioned as old usages of the party only for nominating presidential candidates and presidential electors, far short of the comprehensive endorsement the organizers sought.[68] After passage of the resolutions, divisions regarding conventionism resulted in the addition of four new men to the address-drafting committee. Two of these were the rabid partyists, Ebeneezer Peck and Stephen Douglas.[69] In the end, the address did not urge the convention system at the local level as aggressively as it might have. Conservative forces remained strong even within the Jacksonian camp. But the committee's statement was the most explicit and vigorous defense of constitutional party organization yet to emanate from Illinois.

The statement vindicated conventions by reference to the people's right, guaranteed in the Illinois Constitution, "to assemble . . . to consult for their common good." In principle, they were not different from the previous year's nonparty conventions or from the tradition of popular actions that had punctuated the Revolutionary Era and that had helped define the popular sovereignty on which and by which the Constitution was constructed. While obliquely conceding that the state convention had not attracted a full representation of the people, the address characterized the convention as essentially popular and defended the use of party conventions in constitutional terms: "Our only object is to induce the friends of democracy to act together; to embody and give effect to the popular will." The address therefore urged that "care be taken that these conventions emanate directly from the people, be held at some central point, and at a time of which all shall be aware." Defining the "republican party" as "friends to the administration, and to the adoption of conventions," the convention desired "that our republican friends should not participate in caucuses; but, when advisable, to act in concert by use of primary meetings, and consultations, publicly notified, and regulated in a manner, which every citizen in the state, may exercise his legitimate influence in the control of the party and its candidates."[70] This declaration offered Illinois a party that was less a party than a means of organizing the entire democratic polity. The address concluded with a short list of the concrete accomplishments of the Jackson administration, but the only real aim of the paper had been to vindicate the convention system as a defining institution of popular sovereignty, as indispensable as the institution of representation itself.

Even this argument for party organization, however, did not go as far as the radical organizers of the north had hoped. They tried to push the convention to full implementation of the convention system but could not budge most of the members. The *Democrat*'s correspondent admitted that some debate over the convention system divided the convention,[71] but the particulars of the debate appeared only in the anti-Democratic *Sangamo Journal*, conspicuously unrebutted by the Democratic papers.

The *Journal*'s correspondent reported that Ebeneezer Peck introduced a resolution that "this convention would nominate candidates for state officers." To this correspondent, it was unsurprising that a resolution so alien to the Illinois democracy should have come from a man lately arrived from a British province, reputedly a member of the crown-dependent Canadian legislature only months before, now disguising himself as a Jacksonian.

> Peck . . . avowed it as his object and determination to introduce and make general throughout the State what he called "the wholesome system of Conventions." At this I saw many heretofore faithful faces turn pale. Each countenance seemed in mournful silence to say, "And has it come to this, that we, in our devotion to one [Andrew Jackson], who long since defended our shores from British aggression, have so degraded ourselves, as to be here submissively receiving lessons on republicanism from a British subject; and quietly . . . hear him express his determination to lord his caucus system over this once land of the free and home of the brave?" Peck was finally prevailed with by those of his collar brethren who knew better than he, the maximum size of a [nut?] that could be got down the throat of a western backwoodsman, to withdraw his resolution for the present; and then the Convention adjourned to some time tomorrow. Williamson, senator and delegate from Shelby, came out of the House swearing he would never be caught in another "YANKEE TRAP" while he lived.[72]

On the following evening[73] the debate on the convention question resumed, with Peck again taking the lead. Peck's object, according to the reporter, was to "introduce into this State, the convention system, for the purpose of nominating candidates for all state and county officers, and so prevent the appointment and election of all persons for office who will not submit to the dictation, or the decision, as Mr. Peck called it, of these systematic conventions." Peck went on to acknowledge southern Illinois's "prejudices" against the system but also to insist that it was the wave of the future, that it was the system that had elevated Van Buren at every step of his career, that through its use the party could control all offices "forever," and that the party had an obligation to disabuse the southerners of their biases. In the meantime, however, he was willing to settle for the system's being used only in the third congressional district, which covered the northern half of the state.

Rising to support Peck, the young Stephen Douglas argued that the system was the democracy's only effective weapon against the elitism of traditional politics:

> Mr. Douglass of Morgan, said he had lived all his life in New York, was well acquainted with the convention system; and knew that it was the only

way to manage elections with success. When well adhered to it was omnipotent. . . . It elected every officer, from the Governor down, and could
not be beaten. Gentlemen, he said, were mistaken, when they supposed that
the people of the West had too long enjoyed their own opinions to quietly
submit to the regulations of a convention. He knew better. He claimed the
honor of having introduced it into the county of Morgan; and there, it had
already prostrated one distinguished individual, holding a high office heretofore. He said he told the party that, this individual was making every exertion to defeat the democrats. That he was continually holding midnight caucuses, plotting and forming schemes against the friends of the people; and,
that conventions alone, could put him and all the enemies of Mr. Van Buren
down; and thereby secure all office, power, honor, forever to the democrats.[74]

This anti-Democratic reporter assumed that the convention men were simply
after office. Perhaps they were. But constitutional partyist principle is easily
discernible in the report. Douglas promised that in a democratic country, democratic organization would secure political control to the people as a whole
forever, whereas failure to adhere to party organization would yield political
power to "distinguished individuals" only. He acknowledged the traditional
antipartyism of the public but insisted that experience showed that the convention system could work even in that circumstance.

Bursts of opposition to the convention system were also reported. Early in
the evening, the chairman, who had been appointed by Peck, stepped down.
He acknowledged that the system would be the best thing for the party, but on
the other hand he "believed the whole system to be anti republican." Ultimately, "he was afraid it would not go down with the old fashioned democrats, who always like to see those who profess to be their public servants, face
to face, and to give their votes upon their own judgment."[75] Active politicians
may have had few scruples about political behavior, but they felt strongly that
their every action had to be justifiable to a scrupulously traditional electorate.

Regardless of what was in the politicians' hearts, it seems clear that they
thought most of the electorate still required them to oppose conventions below
the presidential level, and the convention closed on an anticonvention note.
William J. Gatewood, an anti-Democratic senator from Gallatin, crashed the
convention and delivered what was, in effect, the opening speech in his campaign for Congress. Gatewood responded to a challenge to his democracy by
avowing himself "a democrat of the old Jeffersonian school; . . . one of those
who believed it not only right, but practicable, for the people to govern themselves." He then attacked "the claims of the Van Buren party to the exclusive
democracy of the country. . . . Mr. Gatewood said, he did not wish to be un-

derstood as assailing the right of the people to hold conventions if they chose. . . . But, said he, what I do oppose is, the practice of a land officer, a post master, and a mail contractor getting together, and trumpeting forth their doings under the caption of 'A large and respectable meeting.'. . . It is the cursed hypocricy, that [conventions] enable party managers, to play off upon an honest and unsuspecting community that I oppose." He went on to use the just concluded state convention as an example. Small though it had been, it was larger than all the "primary meetings" together which had supposedly generated it.[76] And it was typical in that respect. Primary meetings were regularly gotten up by order of politicians outside the county and adopted resolutions sent down from the higher reaches of the party hierarchy, with negligible participation of the people at any stage. So much for party and convention as the very embodiment of the sovereign people.

Finally, Gatewood congratulated the convention on having ultimately rejected Peck's resolutions but castigated them for nevertheless failing to resist the partyist subversion of popular sovereignty and state independence by going ahead with an endorsement of Van Buren: "You cannot doubt but he is the author of that very system—rising into office solely by those very principles which you have so lately condemned—once permit this system to prevail in this state and the freedom of elections is gone. Elect Mr. Van Buren and the system, the odious system of conventions is established—riveted upon you."[77]

The Anti-Democratic Nominations

The anti-Democrats reveled in such divisions among the Jacksonians but also had some answering to do for their own suspect means of nominating candidates. If not by conventions, how was popular sovereignty to be implemented and institutionalized? On January 2, 1836, the *Journal* unveiled a "White Electoral Ticket" that was free of any convention taint. But it was not hard to anticipate the reaction of the *Democrat*: "How was this ticket got up—fairly and openly by a convention, held with the knowledge of the people, at which they were fully represented, or was it by a midnight caucus, held in some garret at Vandalia."[78] "Let the democracy of the country be warned . . . and observe how sincere are they, who now denounce party organization."[79]

The *Democrat*'s attack was ignored, even though anti-Democrats could have responded as they had in the past, that this ticket was simply presented to the public for its consideration, unlike convention nominations, for which Van Burenites claimed absolute authority among all democrats. More threatening to anti-organizational leaders were the rumblings within the anti-Democratic movement itself. In the north, meetings in Cook and Lasalle Counties matched the *Journal* in their condemnations of partisan patronage but hesitated to condemn the convention system or to endorse Hugh White, the anticonvention hero. Instead, they vaguely advocated local "organization" and supported William Henry Harrison for president. The Chicago meeting even used the name "whig," apparently its first use in Illinois. Still, neither of these meetings advocated convention nominations.[80]

In other counties, however, a movement to hold a White state convention for nominating electors did develop. The Democratic *Jacksonville News*, eager to foment divisions, reported a St. Clair County meeting called for this purpose and then added its own commentary, suggesting that most White supporters would prefer a convention as a democratic substitute for the "self-nominations" engineered by a "junto" at the capital.[81] In Tazewell County as well, anti–Van Burenites met and named delegates to a White convention in Springfield. The convention, however, never came off.[82]

The closest the convention movement got to a response from the *Journal* or any other anti-Democratic authority was the removal of one member of the *Journal*'s ticket in favor of a new candidate from the north of the state. This transaction was accomplished by a public letter from the candidate announcing his withdrawal, followed three weeks later by the editor's announcement of the replacement agreed on in the north.[83] Predictably, the *Advocate* met this maneuver with a sarcastic blast: "This appointment was made, we suppose, by the People, spontaneously, without the intervention of a convention or any such a thing."[84] In the end, however, the *Journal*'s nominees went effectively unchallenged from within the anti-Democratic ranks, receiving virtually all the anti–Van Buren votes in the November election.

The Connection to Congressional Elections, 1836

The election year's preoccupation with party continued as congressional and local campaigns took center stage in the summer. Both the federal and the state constitutions, of course, contemplated that representatives would be chosen by election, not by convention nomination. Wherever partyists dared to take their campaigns, however, they sought to legitimate conventions as, in effect, replacements for elections, and these efforts became the overwhelming issue of the elections. Even where they did not, moreover, anti-Democrats often used accusations of party leanings as their chief campaign weapon. Many localities, however, adhered without dissent to the traditional construction of democracy—a partyless system in which all were free to take their chances on election day.

When William Gatewood launched his anticonvention congressional campaign in the southwestern district, he did not meet with a partyist response but with the same pre-partyist justification of primary assemblages that had recently foreshadowed partyism in the north. The downstate *Alton Spectator* reviewed the speech by noting first that Gatewood "acknowledge[d] conventions to be correct in principle" but feared their abuse and so thought they should be "proscribed." The *Spectator* then objected to the stigmatizing of the fundamental right of public assembly just because it could be abused in some instances. "We are not particularly partial to conventions, though we believe them republican, and sometimes necessary to protect the people from the arts of designing men; we are satisfied with any mode that the people may choose to select their candidates; provided, the people do it."[85] Suggesting that the only "abuse" Gatewood really feared from a convention was rejection of his personal claims to a congressional seat, the *Spectator* ignored party here and only argued that nominations rightfully belonged to the people in their primary (not partisan) assemblages. Here was the same pre-partyist prelude to Democratic constitutional partyist campaigning that had occurred in the north in 1834. Late in the campaign, the Vandalia *Advocate* did circumspectly suggest that a convention be held to unify supporters of the Jackson administration behind one of Gatewood's opponents.[86] But in a southern district there never was any real hope for the plan.

Gatewood's initial focus on the convention system eventually broadened to the many evils of party, probably because his opponents, John Reynolds and Adam Snyder, ignored the convention system. So the pro-Gatewood *Alton Telegraph* argued that the current congressional delegation, including Reynolds, had subordinated specific state interests to "subserve the interests of a party." Thankfully, new candidates were out in each district with talents "untrammeled by party" and characters immune to the "displeasure of 'the party.' "[87] But, in the end, all of the anti-Democrats' best efforts were of little use in a district of the state so solidly Jacksonian as this one, at least as long as Van Buren's chief followers steered clear of the convention system.

In the other southern district, Alexander P. Field and the incumbent Zadok Casey had both been leading antiparty Jacksonians for years. Field was destined to join the Whigs while Casey would remain an irregular Democrat, insisting always on his good faith but consistently resisting the convention system. Casey probably supported Van Buren in 1836 while Field supported White, but neither man would have anything to do with conventions or party organization.[88] Casey won the election with roughly two-thirds of the vote.[89] Through 1836, then, the south of the state remained what the entire state had been in the previous decade—pervasively antipartisan in conviction and entirely free of explicit party organization.

The north was a different matter. In the Democratic state convention, the organizing activists of the party had determined to press the convention system in the northern congressional district, and the incumbent Democrat, William L. May, wrote a letter endorsing whatever action the congressional convention at Peoria might take, promising his willingness "at all times and under all circumstances . . . to act with the party and for the party."[90] Despite the usual sarcasm from the anti-Democratic papers,[91] the Peoria convention did meet and unanimously nominate May, who went on to win the general election in August in the name of partyist conventionism.[92] The brief proceedings of the convention resulted in four resolutions: they approved of Jackson's administration, of Van Buren as Jackson's proper successor, and of May's course in Congress, all without elaboration; but the fourth, longer resolution made the delegates' main point: "That conventions composed of the people, or their authorized delegates, for the purpose of nominating suitable candidates for office, now are, and ever have been, in accordance with the usages and customs of the democratic party, and that if we wish to preserve inviolate those principles for which we have so long struggled, it is essentially necessary that we sustain such candidates as are brought before the people by means of these well established republican principles."[93]

The constitutional partyist theory—that genuine popular sovereignty in a large republic depended inescapably on a pyramid of conventions resting on the primary assemblages of the people—had a beautiful, abstract logic. But articulations of this theory were never long published before the opposition would expose the realities of the "primary assemblages."[94] Accordingly, the *Journal* claimed that only five of the twenty-three northern counties were represented at Peoria and that the nomination of May was just the elitist humbug that all convention nominations were.[95]

At the same time, the anti-Democrats of the north inched their way toward an open party organization of their own. May's opponent, John T. Stuart, was the first candidate ever to be posted on the masthead of the *American*, and the editor recommended him to all who sought the best interests of the district and "who are also opposed to Van Buren."[96] This last comment hinted that this northern editor was less averse than most anti-Democrats to attaching local elections to national ones. His editorials did toe the antiparty line in boosting Stuart: "He is a true friend of the people, the *real* people,—and utterly opposed to those vile 'usages of the party,' which steal power from the many to confer it upon the few—the system of caucus and dictation, meet with no support from John T. Stuart." Yet he also advocated organization at times: "As the day of election is near at hand, and little or no arrangement has been made for the contest by the opponents of the convention system in this county, we would suggest the propriety of immediately calling public meetings in the different precincts, appointing committees, &c., &c. All that is necessary to carry the day in favor of JOHN T. STUART is unity of action."[97]

Here was the chief anticonvention spokesman of northern Illinois, identifying his side as "the opponents of the convention system," yet exhorting the faithful to organization in the service of a candidate who simply appeared on the masthead one week, with no explanation of how he came to be the exclusive antiparty candidate. It is easy to see why Democrats were skeptical of the antipartyist professions of such men. But if one can adopt the thinking of an antiparty, democratic traditionalist, then the nomination and organization seem more consistent with the rhetoric. For these antipartyists, organization was an expedient to save the Constitution from party. And their organization, unlike the Democrats', imposed no policy tests and no convention ethic. It embodied only the voluntary cooperation of the independent. Northern Illinois was the first part of the state where traditional antipartyists had to forsake some measure of their traditionalism in order to combat organized partyism. Consequently, it was also the area in which antipartyists first had to work out an ideological reconciliation between antipartyism and the necessity of organizing against an ideology of organization. At this stage, this reconciliation, as well as ideas about party generally, were more thoroughly elaborated in the local campaigns than in the congressional campaigns.

The Connection to Local Elections, 1836

Most newspaper attention in the north was, in fact, concentrated on the county elections, and the north was where the fierce battles over partyism and conventionism were fought. Democratic newspapers pressed the convention system down to the lowest offices as they increasingly insisted that party conventions were always and everywhere the one and only way to guarantee the democratic character of any government. At the same time, the fledgling theory almost died aborning when its foremost champion, the editor of the *Democrat*, chose incredibly to bolt the convention's nominee for state senator. Needless to say, this bolt played into the hands of the opposition. But the anti-Democrats too were beginning to move toward overt organization and so faced their own internal tension, a tension that impelled incremental refinements in their own theories of party and organization. Meanwhile, it must not be forgotten, the vast majority of elections in Illinois still went off in a wholly traditional, pre-partisan manner.

In June, the *Democrat* published a call for a Democratic convention of Cook and Will Counties, which would ultimately produce party nominations not only for the state legislature but for sheriff, coroner, and county commissioner as well. It then endorsed the convention as "one of the most important to the party and to the interests of the people, which has ever been held in this county," presumably because the movement to legitimate party conventionism, especially for such local offices, was still so young.[98] When the convention met, however, the proceedings did not turn out as the *Democrat* had hoped.

This convention at Flag Creek was only the Democratic party's second Cook county nominating convention, and the *Democrat* expected it to help entrench a still novel convention system. But the *Democrat* shocked the district by bolting the senatorial nomination as soon as it was made. Aware of the antiparty-ist ridicule that would come, the editor launched into a preemptive defense. He rejected the nominee, Peter Pruyne, because he lacked "*political integrity!*" In particular, Pruyne was said to spend his time hanging around the legislature seeking "monopolies" or office. He had "been for Conventions and against them, as it might suit his interests. In Vandalia last winter he was most violent in denouncing the *course of the party here!!* and in all things sided with the opponents of Conventions, and party usages." In his constant quest for office, he had even worked for the election of an irregular candidate for United States senator in opposition to "the regularly nominated Democratic candidate."

A nominee's history of irregularity was as close to a good justification of a bolt as a partyist could contrive, but the fact remained that Pruyne was now the regular nominee, and the editor's bolt must inevitably provoke charges of irregularity from Pruyne's corner. He could respond only by insisting that Pruyne had been "nominated by *unfair means* and against the remonstrances and entreaty of a majority of [the Chicago] delegation." He complained that the convention had let itself be swayed by charges "that there were certain individuals in Chicago determined to *dictate* to and control the party, and that a majority of the delegation from Chicago were their *tools*." If "the only object of a Convention is to harmonize public sentiment," it was the delegates' "duty to present some one on whom the party could . . . unite! When a convention does this . . . then it is the duty of every member of the party to submit."[99] It may well be that everything the editor said of the convention was true—anti-Democrats said such charges of manipulation accurately described every convention—but there was no easy way to avoid the conclusion that this chief advocate of the convention system was now bending the rules in a way his previously articulated theories could not accommodate.

It was true that, in partyist theory, conventions had to be properly constituted and fairly carried out. It was also true, however, that the right to bolt on the basis of improprieties in the convention—like an eighteenth-century Whig's right of revolution—was a theoretical right, virtually never to be exercised, lest every majoritarian convention be bolted by the minority on the basis of unavoidable, minor inequities. In this particular case, the editor implicitly approved the convention itself by ratifying all its doings and nominees except one. To bolt only one nomination of a properly constituted convention was conclusive evidence of one's elevation of self-interest over party principle. Moreover, the editor's claim that a convention's sole purpose was to harmonize public sentiment was odd. Certainly, harmony was valued, but the partyist mechanism for harmony was absolute individual deference to the will of any properly constituted majority. Maybe every majority ought to be generous to its minority, but to resist a majority decision was the one inexcusable sin in partyist theory.

When done justifying himself, the editor printed a letter signed by thirty-six men, nominating James H. Woodworth in Pruyne's place and claiming to defend the convention system by opposing its present nominee. These men identified themselves as "Democratic Republicans, and friends of the Baltimore nominations" and asserted that Pruyne's nomination was done by "corrupt means and that it is due to the convention system, to the usages of our party to resist such barefaced proversions of one or the other."[100] Woodworth then accepted his irregular nomination in the name of regularity. Endorsing fairly conducted, majoritarian conventions, Woodworth nevertheless insisted that "the majority" may at any time, "without violating the rules upon which conventions are advocated, withhold their support from any nominee brought forward under circumstances different from those above mentioned, and unite it upon any person they may choose."

In short, Woodworth thought his irregular nomination regular because it emanated from the only legitimate agent of nomination—the majority of the people. But the usual difficulty in determining what the majority willed was supposed to be solved by the convention system's providing the majority with an institutional voice. On what basis, then, did Woodworth judge his own nomination the work of the true "majority"? His evidence was the "number"—thirty-six men—and the "respectability"—not usually a central Democratic criterion—of those signing his nomination letter.[101] In the face of an apparent abuse of the great constitutional reform that was the party convention, these men reflexively turned to pre-partyist assumptions about nomination.

Meanwhile, Pruyne himself distributed a handbill attacking the bolt of the *Democrat*, a paper that the year before had made it an "unbending principle of democracy . . . that the party cannot and will not recognize the claims of any candidate for any office within its gift, unless called out by the voice of the democracy." The handbill further noted that when the convention nominee for representative had proven ineligible, a Chicago convention had nominated in his place a nonbolting Flag Creek delegate known "for his adherence to the strict usages of the party." But the *Democrat* revealed its hypocrisy again when it used a subscription letter to name a different replacement instead of honoring "the voice of the people."[102]

Perhaps everyone in this controversy was an opportunist and a hypocrite. Or maybe each was a genuine democrat trying to save a theory of the Constitution that was inevitably harder to apply than to articulate. In either case, the issue that overshadowed all others in this election was the question of party organization. Both sides agreed that the purpose of such organization was to give voice to the sole constitutional sovereign—the majority of the people. They and the electorate learned, however, how difficult it might be to perfect any theory of democracy in practice.

The anti-Democrats might relish such difficulties in the Democratic ranks, but they were hardly free of their own internal tensions. The centrality of party in the local elections was confirmed by the *American* and its contributors. Even before the Flag Creek convention, the editor warned that this period was "the *forming* time of our political . . . character." It was, therefore, crucial that, in place of the "*patent* candidates" sure to be nominated at the convention, the "Whigs" should support men of ability, free from "party sycophancy and intrigue."[103]

In the middle of July, candidates for the General Assembly spontaneously appeared on the masthead. Instead of an explanation for these nominations, the *American* launched into a long condemnation of the Democratic Flag Creek convention. If Cook and Will counties were to count for anything in the assembly, the editor concluded, "the people must select their candidates—not their keepers, but their servants—for themselves, and not confide in such wise acres as the self-nominated *Flag Creek Convention!!*"[104]

The intra-Democratic controversy over Pruyne's nomination gave substance to the *American*'s attacks on the convention system, but it did not help the editor clarify what a properly partyless nomination might look like when antipartyists needed to concentrate votes at the election. He necessarily called for a firm support of the anticonvention "ticket." But how might such a ticket be legitimated? The editor did not confront the question directly, but he distinguished his mere advocacy of candidates on their merits, including the merit of being opposed to and free from convention nomination, from Democratic insistence on the authority of "regular" nomination.

When two anticonvention candidates reluctantly accepted the public call of their "friends" to run for office—one apparently proper method of nomination—the *American* rejoiced that good men could still be found to make the sacrifice: "When the 'Doctors' of *the* party are 'disagreeing,' and the sacred and venerated mother of their political interests, the *humbug Convention*, has given birth to *political abortions*, . . . it is fortunate for our county and state, that men can be found among the people, uncontaminated by the intrigue of caucuses."[105] Presumably, such candidates became the exclusive antiparty candidates only by the virtuous forbearance of all other potential candidates and their "friends."

The theory was made more explicit by a LaSalle county meeting that named an "ANTI-CONVENTION TICKET" for the summer elections. It distinguished its nominations from convention nominations thus: "It is hoped that you will diligently enquire as to the character and qualifications of each individual candidate. . . . The candidates now presented *invite* your scrutiny, and their friends only ask that you try them by that genuine Jeffersonian test 'Is he honest, is he capable.' " These men were opposed to conventions "because they know that what are falsely called the primary meetings of the people, are in *fact* but private caucuses of personal friends, got up by the *candidates themselves*, . . . and you are called upon to endorse the falsehood under the *penalty* of being excomunicated from the fold of the faithful."[106] There was no claim here that the nominating meeting comprised the entire people or bore any special authority, only that the ticket was one free of conventionism and worthy of scrutiny.

These elections thus turned entirely on the question of the convention system as an essential institution of a partyist Constitution. But there was yet another twist. In its last exhortation to "the Independent Electors" of the county and district, the antipartyist *American* concluded a long discussion of the moral fiber necessary to defeat the convention system with a plea for its audience not to fear party excitement: "Party, in its legitimate sphere, is the true element of national prosperity; it is its *abuse*, and not its *use*, which is to be deprecated by the lover of his country. . . . Let party organization be the instrument, in your hands, of appointing able and faithful public servants."[107]

What can one make of this? In order to understand this anomalous endorsement of party as well as the occasional, casual reference to "our party" in the middle of an antiparty polemic, one needs to remember the distinction between party as permanent organization—the Van Burenite model—and party as ad hoc cooperation of the like-minded. This editor believed that Democratic organization could only be overcome on election day by organized co-operation among the "Independent Electors." For him, the "Independent Electors" constituted a "party" only because they were unified, in this particular election, by their very independence from and opposition to party control. Paradoxically, they required some kind of party organization to defeat the principle of party organization, but it would be an organization that emerged from their prior organic unity, not one that built an artificial unity out of selfish impulses. Their organization would not, therefore, require any change in political ethics comparable to the Democrats' elevation of convention authority over individual judgment. They did, however, require a degree of concert and activity to make their strength fully felt, something that could only be had by means of a voluntary organization of the "party" of the independent that in no way impaired the independence of any participant.

This sort of reasoning was not difficult to sustain one election at a time in the 1830s. Over the course of the Second Party System, however, the developing Whig party would struggle to maintain the differentiation between its brand of organization and the Democrats'.

The election results could be taken to ratify the convention system in this northern region of the state. Many convention nominees received between 70 and 100 percent of the votes; even Pruyne racked up a 68 percent majority.[108] So Democrats could readily believe that conventionism would deliver the nineteen-twentieths of the vote that partyist orators regularly claimed as the party's constitutional birthright.

The rest of the state, however, was a different world. Partyism was a factor in a number of other counties, but nowhere else was it embraced so thoroughly as in the north. And it appears that the system had no presence whatsoever in most county elections.

In Morgan, the home of Stephen Douglas, partyism had real but limited success. The county's Democratic convention nominees won most of the legislative seats. But a Pruyne-esque controversy erupted when, mid-campaign, one of the nominees bowed out, only to be replaced, mysteriously, by Douglas himself.[109] The antipartyists made great sport of the flexibility of Douglas's partyist principles and methods but failed to prevent his election.[110]

In Sangamon County, there was no attempt to hold a convention, but two parties, or perhaps more accurately, two editors, effectively controlled the election, yielding two candidates for senator and fourteen significant candidates for seven House seats. Even in the absence of a convention, the issue of "free elections" was at the forefront of the editorial war. The *Journal*, for example, reported that the local Van Burenite leaders had decided that "it would be unpopular to introduce the *convention system* into Sangamon County."[111] When candidates began quickly to appear on the masthead of the Democratic paper in Springfield, with seven of the ten announced candidates separated out as the "republican ticket," the *Journal* wondered "by what authority the editors have selected seven of them, put their names in large type, and proclaimed them the republican ticket?"[112] Meanwhile, self-announced candidates proliferated without party labels in the *Journal*'s columns.

Until its penultimate pre-election edition, the paper simply trumpeted its anticaucus convictions while displaying as many as thirteen self-nominated candidates for the House without party labels. Now, purportedly in response to the *Republican*'s forcing the election "ON PARTY GROUNDS," the *Journal* announced a ticket: "The Van Buren party have given us no choice but to stand by our ticket—for we must have one—or suffer a defeat when victory is within our reach." Regardless of personal feelings for or against men on either ticket, the editor argued, now was the time for "the anti–Van Buren party of this county" to vindicate its principles by voting a straight ticket;[113] that is, to resist partyism by voting with a party.

No overt party organization yet existed even in a county as attentive to the national party division as Sangamon. In most other counties, it appears that the infiltration of party was generally even weaker. In general, according to the *Journal*, party and the presidential question were salient in few areas: "One circumstance, neglected in most other counties, greatly contributed to [our victory here]: the full and fearless examination by our candidates of Martin Van Buren's claims to the Presidency."[114] The convention system, then, had its champions and made important inroads in Morgan, Cook, and other mostly northern counties, but even in this presidential election year, in which party organization was itself the chief national issue, the antipartyist construction of popular sovereignty remained unchallenged in most counties.

The Presidential Election

The presidential campaign reflected Illinois's persistent three-way division on the constitutional questions of Jacksonism and partyism much more than a division on policy questions, the candidates being Van Buren, original-Jacksonian Hugh White of Tennessee, and Ohio's proto-Whig William Henry Harrison. The *Advocate* renewed the long dormant presidential debate in June with an attack on White for his irregularity. Once a firm friend of Jackson, White's sole purpose in running now was to send the election into the House and thus to take "from a free People the choice of their future President."[115] For partyist

Democrats, the *Advocate* indicated, the presidential campaign would follow the predictions of the national party's address, pitting aristocratic efforts to exploit a constitutional loophole against the sovereign people's determination to retain the choice of president in its own hands.

White, the paper claimed, was now the purchased tool of Henry Clay, who had orchestrated his nomination by the Tennessee congressional delegation. While White continued to express regard for Jackson, he now voted with his one-time bitter enemies, Webster and Clay: "We think we have shown . . . that he has made himself a party to the scheme of Mr. Clay to throw the election of President into the House of Representatives; which last act makes him as thorough a Federalist in principle as his present associates of the Clay and Webster school."[116]

Of course, the partyists were right that the developing alliance between some original Jacksonians and the anti-Jacksonians was uneasy, to say the least. Thus the partyist claims that the anti-Jacksonian coalition lacked any unifying principle but aristocracy. But these charges were met by antipartyist claims of unity in democratic constitutional principle if not always in policy matters. As early as January, the pro-Clay *Journal* had justified its reluctant hoisting of a White ticket not by claiming that it shared that old Jacksonian's politics generally but by locating common constitutional ground: White endorsed the curtailing of executive power and patronage, nominations by the people rather than by "packed conventions and Presidential dictation," the granting of public office for public service rather than for partisan reward, and removal from office only for cause, not for political reasons.[117] In April, the same paper welcomed another Harrison editor's commitment to the White ticket as a proper sacrifice when "free elections" were at stake.[118] Differences over other questions might be worked out within a salvaged system of free elections. Let free elections slip away, however, and the Constitution itself was lost.

In the fall, after many fits and starts, the White movement officially became a White-Harrison fusion movement.[119] A Union ticket appeared in the anti–Van Buren newspapers, and the *American* assured the voters that the entire ticket would vote together for the stronger of either White or Harrison. "Thanks to the freedom of conscience and *no collars*, the party opposed to Van Buren are not bound down or pledged to any man" but only to principle. Such "independence of action," the editor feared, might cause practical problems against the highly organized opposition, but "a defeat under the free banner of the Constitution is more glorious than the victory of a pensioned band of political vassals."[120]

As the antipartyists identified their movement with the Constitution itself, the partyist *Advocate* responded in kind. Having anticipated the fusion movement, it now observed that no clearer vindication of the partyist theory of popular sovereignty could have appeared. That theory predicted endless maneuvers by "antipartyist" aristocrats to deliver the real power of elections into the hands of minority special interests, while leaving only an empty right to vote in the people. The Union ticket was a particularly clever device. Thanks to the constitutional provision for election by the electoral college and House of Representatives, it could turn any Jacksonian vote intended for White into a vote for the manifestly anti-Jacksonian Harrison.[121] The Whig insistence on "Principles, not Men" as justification for taking the stronger of either White or Harrison was ridiculous, the *Advocate* argued, when the supposedly Jacksonian principles of White were in fact diametrically opposed to the loose-constructionist American System principles of Harrison.[122] The White candidacy was only a ruse, by which honest Jacksonian votes would be transferred to Harrison as the strongest opposition candidate. But the scam did not end there. Even Harrison was not Federalist enough; so the final step would be the election of Daniel Webster by the House once the election was forced into that body. "If you vote for the Van Buren and Johnson electoral ticket, you know who you are voting for," the *Advocate* advised, but if, in trying to vote Jacksonian, a citizen voted for White, then he was only giving anti-Jacksonians license to use his vote as they liked.[123] Thus would fusion seize the vote of a constitutional democrat and turn it to the purposes of constitutional elitism and aristocracy.

One editor's aristocracy, however, was another's democracy. The *Advocate* was correct that White and Harrison had different principles regarding economic policy, but, as it so often pointed out, the election was only secondarily about policy and primarily about the nature of the constitutional order: "The main question to be decided by the people is, whether they will elect their own Chief magistrate, or whether they are content that the House of Representatives shall elect him?"[124] The *Journal* disagreed only on the proper statement of the constitutional questions at issue:

> The questions are now to be settled, whether a trained band of office holders, whose watchword, boldly proclaimed, is, that "the spoils belong to the victors," shall control the votes of the people, and thus "bring the patronage of the government into conflict with the freedom of elections"; whether the president shall nominate his successor; whether a Convention of office holders, self-elected and irresponsible, shall dictate to a free people;—whether the "public money" shall be used or employed to advance the interests of a few bantlings of power, and to elect a President of their choice, without re-

gard to the interests of the People;—in a word, whether Martin Van Buren shall be forced upon the American People, whether they will or not.[125]

On such constitutional grounds the unity of Harrison and White supporters against Van Buren was easily justified.

On election day, Van Buren received 54.8 percent of Illinois's vote, a substantial majority but a decline of thirteen percentage points from Jackson's 1832 victory.[126] The Democrats were acutely aware that that majority was much too small to vindicate their theory of party organization as constitutional amendment. The decline in the Democratic vote was a source of great hope for anti-Democrats: "The people may not have been able to meet successfully the organized party opposed to them; but they have at least shown that Van Burenism is not Jacksonism. . . . On one side were arrayed the People, contending for a reform in our Government—such as was promised by Gen. Jackson when he went into power. On the other were all that class of men who could be influenced by office, by the hopes of reward from a party who avowed 'that to the victors belong the spoils.' " To the *Journal* it was clear that Van Burenism was waning and that a revival of the true democratic Constitution was on the horizon.[127]

Conclusion

Well before the partyist offensive of 1835–36, the question of popular sovereignty's meaning was a live one. The Constitution rested its authority only on the authority of "the people"[128] and guaranteed a republican government to each state. But, of course, the federal Constitution and even the state constitutions went only so far in defining the institutions or practices of the people's sovereignty. The federal Constitution was designed to neutralize parties because parties were assumed to interfere with rather than facilitate the discovery of the sovereign will. But the Constitution did not actually say anything about parties and said little about the conduct of elections—its mechanism for presidential elections being a notable exception, and one marked for destruction by the partyists. Inevitably, then, the construction and reconstruction of the people's sovereignty in the context of elections—the only context in which an active people might routinely speak its will—was on the table, even to the point of reconsidering party's relationship to the Constitution and the legitimacy of the Constitution's own presidential-election provisions.

On the local level, most Illinois counties stuck to traditional practices of self-nomination for many years, but a few in 1834 began to produce nonpartisan nominations by "primary assemblages," one of which insisted on the new doctrine that such a nomination bound all honest democrats. And only in 1835 was there a significant movement for a general reconstruction of popular sovereignty in partyist terms. Starting that year, nominating meetings began to adopt party labels, yet continued to insist on their status as primary assemblages of the people, now more frequently claiming that their nominations bound all supporters of the democratic Constitution because such assemblages were the *only* possible incarnations of popular sovereignty and because they were based on no principle but majority rule.

It is important to remember, however, that, even by 1836, only a handful of Illinois counties were affected by this movement in the August state elections. Many more were touched by the partyists' efforts in the presidential election, as Democrats invoked the memory of the "corrupt bargain" to justify their explicit attack on the Constitution's provisions for House election. But neither the partyists' nor any other construction of popular sovereignty commanded clear popular support in these turbulent years. The *Democrat*'s bolt of the Pruyne nomination and the regular antipartyist exposés of the true character of nominating conventions showed that they were hardly yet the meetings of "the people" that their advocates insisted were indispensable to the Constitution. There were many alternative methods in play as well: traditional self-nomination; nomination by subscription letter; nomination by nonpartisan meeting (without any pretense to general attendance or binding authority); nomination by editorial consultation. Where self-nomination had dominated, suddenly the partyist claim that the Constitution was in danger had created new ferment in the construction of popular sovereignty. As the partyists introduced these questions into each locality, they quickly became virtually the only issues on the table, and all politics became overtly constitutional politics.

CHAPTER SIX

The Spoils Aristocracy and the Paper Aristocracy, 1837–1838

In a series of three cases between 1976 and 1990, the U.S. Supreme Court made clear that the spoils system is and always has been inconsistent with the First Amendment.[1] Disregarding one dissenter's assertion that the spoils system was a matter of "open, widespread, and [constitutionally] unchallenged use that dates back to the beginning of the Republic,"[2] the Court created a cause of action for those who had suffered public employment consequences on the basis of their politics, what the Whigs habitually called "proscription for opinion's sake." And it is clear that the Whigs shared the modern Court's reading of the Constitution. They did not, however, resort to the courts to vindicate the Constitution. Instead, they built a mass movement and justified it largely by their condemnation of the partyists' "proscriptive policy." Their movement rested on the antispoils constitutional position that truly did date back to the beginning of the Republic.[3]

If the Whigs naturally turned to popular politics rather than courts to vindicate the Constitution, that instinct was even stronger among the Democrats. The first Democratic appointee to the office of Illinois's secretary of state, John McClernand, did necessarily resort to the courts when the stubborn Whig incumbent, Alexander P. Field, refused to hand over the state seal and other appurtenances of office, but that only gave the state's highest court the chance to opine on the dangers of executive government while vindicating Field.[4] More generally, it was an article of faith for Democrats, reinforced by the Field case, that ultimate constitutional authority lay not in the courts, least of all the federal Supreme Court, but in the majority of the people at the polls.[5] Where Whigs demonized the spoilsmen as the chief threat to the Constitution, Democrats identified the "paper aristocracy" of corporate wealth. This faction would use class legislation to reestablish the socio-political structure of dependency on which Old World aristocracy rested. Against such a structure, the merely formal guarantees of popular sovereignty were, of course, useless. Instead, recourse must be had only to the court of the fully organized democracy, assembled at the polls.

Before 1838, however, Illinois's parties were insufficiently organized to reduce a statewide election to a clean contest of parties. Through 1836, Illinois politics had comprised three large groupings. Divisions between antiparty Jacksonians and partyist Jacksonians had been as salient as the division between Jacksonians and anti-Jacksonians. With Van Buren's nomination for the presidency on constitutional grounds, many original Jacksonians moved wholeheartedly into the Whig camp. And more would come over during the Independent Treasury controversy between 1837 and 1840. Other original Jacksonians opted to stay with the Democratic party, even as it became a Van Burenite organization rather than the popular movement it had seemed to be under Jackson.[6]

This chapter relates the emergence in Illinois of a clear two-party structure in statewide elections, if not generally in local politics,[7] largely on the basis of Whig opposition to spoils and Democratic opposition to corporate "aristocracy." It was no coincidence, of course, that this development followed closely on Van Buren's election to the office of chief spoilsman. More surprising at the time was the acute economic crisis that greeted Van Buren in early 1837, which would force each party to incorporate economic issues more systematically and explicitly into their constitutional arguments. The state's transition from a rough, three-way division of the electorate toward a durable two-party alignment was shaped by both of these factors, which fit neatly with the emerging parties' dueling claims that the Constitution was being perverted by either a "monied aristocracy" or a party of "office men."

Two Governors under Van Burenite
Ascendancy: Prelude to 1840

The memoir of an antipartyist Jacksonian, recounting his break with the Democrats, recalled that when "New York regency" politics was introduced into the state "the western people knew very little about the system; they felt that the field was open to every honest man who wished to be a candidate for office. . . . A great many of what was termed the old Jackson party were opposed to introducing this system into the western country. The same branch of the party was opposed to proscribing from office for opinion sake." And the leader of this stream of defecting original Jacksonians was Joseph Duncan.[8]

In the wake of Van Buren's election, Governor Duncan's address to the Illinois legislature focused on the constitutional abuses of the Democratic party. Preeminent among these was the partisan use of patronage: "The claim set up of late by a political party in this country, that the appointment of public officers and patronage of the government is given to the President of the United States for the purpose of sustaining his authority and extending his power and influence, is unjust and fallacious[;] to sanction the power of the President to remove men from office for an independent expression of opinion, or an honorable opposition to his measures is a species of opposition and proscription wholly incompatible with the spirit of our Government."[9] More specifically, he complained of the "grievous" growth of federal patronage by which officers of the "general government" were enabled to overawe those of the states. Finally, the unconstitutional but now customary power of removal enabled the government both to command officers' services at elections and to dictate their official conduct. Duncan condemned especially the multiplying appointments of editors—by which freedom of the press was threatened—and of congressmen—by which Congress became the servant of, rather than a check on, the executive.

With the Constitution under siege, Duncan prayed for relief from two sources: the legislatures of the several states, as opposed to the branches of the national government; and the people themselves in "their primary assemblies."[10] Echoing Governor Edwards's address to the legislature of six years before, Duncan emphasized that the natural source of party was the federal government, especially the executive. The people could resist party only by keeping their naturally partyless state polities independent of the artificial central power.

Duncan's call for reform was given a new context when a run on the nation's banks in early 1837 signaled the beginning of a major economic downturn.[11] Duncan's response to the Panic of 1837, however, was not to debate economics but to seek purification of an autonomous state polity. At a special summer session of the legislature, Duncan called for a halt to the internal improvement system about to be built by the state. He did so not because the panic had made construction impractical but because "such undertakings belong rather to arbitrary and despotic Governments, than to the republican institutions of a free people, as by the power and patronage of official influence, they tend to corrupt the many and exalt the few."[12] The Democratic defense of the project, however, insisted that the Governor had exaggerated the danger while overlooking the power of the "moneyed interests of other States and countries," which would dominate Illinois if Duncan's preference for private construction were adopted.[13] Where Duncan had seen a great constitutional crisis in the expansion of governmental patronage, the Democrats saw one in the prospect of a corporate aristocracy.

When the assembly next convened in December 1838, the state had a clear two-party division for the first time, and the Panic of 1837 had turned into a long-term depression with obvious consequences for the internal improvement system. Across the country, as well, the elections of 1838 crystallized the party system.[14] Duncan's final address, then, and the inaugural message of his successor, Democrat Thomas Carlin, came at a highly charged moment. And the two governors seized the moment to define the alternative views of the two parties. In addressing an economic crisis, they defined the terms of constitutional debate.

Paying no explicit attention to the developing depression but referring generally to the sorry condition of the improvements, Duncan reminded the legislature that "my chief objections to the passage of this bill . . . were the effects I anticipated it would have on the purity of elections, and the action of the Legislature." Experience now confirmed that "the want of economy, and the deleterious effect of such a system, owned, controlled and carried on by the State, are great and insurmountable objections to it; but, in my opinion, not so great, because not of such duration, as the power it confers on the State Government, through its numerous officers and dependants, to influence elections and legislation." Waste on a huge scale had plagued the system, and this waste was implicitly the product of political corruption, the use of state money "on objects of little or no general utility" for political purposes. In place of such large projects' being carried on by the government, he advocated a general incorporation law, which in addition to encouraging the investment of idle capital would "by limiting the number of appointments . . . prove an antidote to the schemes of those designing politicians who are making war upon every corporation for the purpose of concentrating all power in the hands of Government."[15]

Moving from the state level to the national, Duncan indicted the "United States Executive" for multiplying the patronage to such an extent that "it has now become exceedingly doubtful whether [the administration] are not able to sustain themselves in authority, in defiance of the people." The federal executive "notoriously" used that patronage "to influence state elections." Formerly, officers relied on their conduct to keep them in office, but "now their subservience to 'the party' is the most important requisite." Even seats in Congress had become mere stepping stones to executive appointment. Duncan concluded that only complete separation of patronage from the legislative and electoral processes could eliminate "the great lever with which the Executive is now controlling the politics and elections of the whole country. Correct [the abuse of patronage], and all other abuses, great as they are, will become comparatively harmless."[16]

As Duncan described patronage—the tool by which an elite might vitiate popular power—so Carlin described banks. The Van Buren administration had responded to the panic chiefly by proposing that the federal government "divorce" itself entirely from the nation's banks, conducting its business exclusively in specie and by means of its own "Independent Treasury." Adhering to the national Democrats' antibank line, Carlin's message emphasized "the impossibility of preventing [banks] from using their power and influence to affect and control the politics of the country." In his view, the collapse of the state banks across the nation made clear that the central political division was "between a National Bank and an Independent Treasury; and under these opposing measures, the two great political parties of the country have ranged themselves." It was hard for him to believe that anyone still favored a national bank, which inevitably created a "moneyed aristocracy," or a government bank, which would so consolidate power in the federal government as to "entirely defeat the objects for which that Government was instituted."[17]

Experience with the Bank of the United States had shown enough: "We have seen it violating the provisions of its charter, defying the authorities of the Government, interfering with the politics of the country, corrupting the public press, bribing the members of Congress, waging war upon the National Executive, and, by wanton panics and pressures, attempting to subdue the republican spirit of the people and coerce them into a submission to its recharter." In contrast, the Independent Treasury would concentrate power nowhere but would "dissolve the connexion between the Government and Banks—a connexion as unnatural and dangerous as the union of church and state—and . . . give to the General Government that degree of freedom and independence which was contemplated by the constitution" as well as having the salutary economic effect of creating a demand for specie.[18] The line of division between the parties, according to Carlin, while drawn between two economic institutions, was fundamentally constitutional and only secondarily economic.

This resistance to the Bank, moreover, reflected not just the peculiar evils of the one institution but a broader questioning of capitalist structures by constitutional democrats in this period. Just as Charles Sellers has remarked on the tensions between capitalism and democracy from their birth,[19] so Tony Freyer has observed that some strains of constitutional interpretation before the Civil War attempted to resist "unrestrained capitalism": "The periodic political party struggles that gradually determined the boundary between state and federal power involved a fundamental constitutional ideal: all public and private power should be checked by power external to itself. Throughout the antebellum period various social groups also appealed to this constitutional ideal in order to contain emergent capitalism. . . . Larger political party confrontations were symptomatic of underlying constitutional values of legitimacy and accountability that many smaller and weaker market interests could and did turn against mercantile and corporate capitalists."[20]

Economic problems in 1838 were acute, yet, as the speeches above suggest, they would fuel the party division more in their capacity to raise constitutional questions—what were the real structures of power under the ostensibly democratic Constitution?—than in their relation to the economic theories of the partisans. Constitutional democracy was deemed prerequisite to prosperity.[21] Economic and other social questions were necessary raw material, but the party system that subsumed them grew from a debate about democracy itself, a debate about party's place in the constitutional order.

Whig Organization and the Democratic Party Test: The Independent Treasury and the Elections of 1837–1838

Between 1837 and 1840, the decisive transition to the two-party system occurred, but not as straightforwardly or completely as is sometimes supposed. By 1840, the Democrats and Whigs dominated the electoral process, but their analyses of what was happening had very little to do with modern conceptions of a legitimated two-party system. In these years the Whigs became a party but resisted the implications of that fact every step of the way. The Democratic partyists, meanwhile, subordinated the anti-organizational wing of their party but failed to purge it. Battles over the convention system's legitimacy raged both between and within the parties. But it was the spoils question, linked with the economic crisis by way of the Independent Treasury question, that came to the fore. As the ascendant Van Burenites pressed partyist theory on the party and the nation, the opposition feared nothing less than a revolution in American governance.

In the spring of 1837, word arrived of Representative William May's "secession" from the Democrats by way of a deviating vote in the ongoing Bank War in Washington. In the coming months May fully withdrew from the party, citing the fusion of constitutional questions and economic policy that would crystallize the party system. Stephen Douglas's subsequent nomination for May's seat by the Peoria congressional convention[22] thus became an important step in the Democratic effort to legitimate conventions.

The convention justified its rejection of May by asserting that he had broken his pledges to the people and party who had elevated him. It portrayed conventionism as the necessary response to "a desperate struggle . . . now being made to reduce the people and their Government to a state of dependence on . . . a United States Bank, or a combination of moneyed institutions, that would be alike destructive to our happiness and prosperity, and subversive of the principles of our Republican system of Government." The delegates concluded that corporate bodies constituted, in effect, an "Aristocracy of wealth" in contrast to the "Democracy of numbers."[23] The Democrats' complaint was not that they were poor but that they would become increasingly dependent if corporate wealth, protected by the special privilege of government charter, were allowed to usurp the constitutional place of the democracy in determining the future character of the society.[24]

The *Washington Globe* printed the Peoria proceedings, presumably as an example to those who might resist the party test of the Independent Treasury. But May fired back. His response condemned the Democratic party's subservience to the linked measures of conventionism and the Independent Treasury. Just as the Democrats had indicted May and his political cohorts for using economic policy as a means to anticonstitutional ends, so May made the same charge against the party-bound Democrats.

Support of the Independent Treasury, also known as the "Subtreasury," was a position that almost no one adopted from principle, May claimed, unless the principle was party. The manipulator of the Peoria convention, one Josiah Lamborn, was the most salient example, since he had converted from Whig Bankism to wire-pulling bullionism in pursuit of the spoils that partyist conventionism showered on its functionaries. May, in contrast, like virtually every member of the Jackson party only two years before, had opposed the Subtreasury "as revolutionary and disorganizing, and tending more than anything that had ever been proposed, to consolidation. There needs but the union of the moneyed power of this government, with the power of the Executive, already too overgrown, by reason of the immense patronage attached to the office, to render the President more potent than any sovereign of Europe." May vowed obedience to popular desires, but he could regard neither executive will nor the convention system as reliable guides to public opinion or the Constitution's meaning.

The real purpose of the convention, he concluded, appeared in a resolution that requested the removal of the newly appointed register of the Galena land office. This man was not only honest and capable, with no charges brought against him and no evidence of unpopularity in the district; he was even a faithful supporter of Van Buren, not to mention Jackson. The convention's real object, like that of the partyists as a whole, was simply to appropriate the name of "Democratic party" to the office-seeking purposes of the conventioneers.[25] May's charges were well founded too, as Lamborn could soon be found soliciting the office.[26]

It is not necessary to embrace May's pretensions to spotless patriotism in order to suppose that many voters were prepared to believe his message. In May's and the Whigs' version of politics, the Independent Treasury was not an attempt to restore economic order after the panic but to consolidate power in the central government by equipping the executive with the funds and patronage necessary to pay the local operators of the convention system. The convention system, in turn, sustained the Independent Treasury itself by determining the party line for Democratic activists and electorate. Its spoilsmen operators used it to separate those who were true to party conventions and measures, and thus deserving of the patronage those measures created, from those who were not.

On the Whig side, John T. Stuart, whom May had narrowly beaten in 1836, was renominated without a convention but by consultation, newspaper leadership, and general consent. In December, David Davis told Stuart that all his friends in Davis's area assumed he would be the candidate and were working for him.[27] In January, Orville Hickman Browning congratulated fellow Whig John Hardin on getting a new paper started but wanted to know why he did not yet have Stuart on the masthead: "Are you opposed to his running? or are you waiting for a caucus nomination?" Browning urged him to lose no time in hoisting Stuart and calling on other sympathetic editors to do likewise, since there was no doubt he would be the candidate: "Some whig paper must suggest a candidate and why not you? I can't stand a convention."[28] A correspondent of the *Journal* also advocated Stuart but stood "ready to unite on any [Whig] who may be chosen by the public will."[29]

Such efforts as these resulted in Stuart's nomination by general editorial consent early in 1838 despite an attempt, predictably originating in Cook County, to call a congressional convention. It was suggested by a Cook Whig meeting on purely expediential grounds and reluctantly ratified by at least one other local meeting, but it never gained substantial support. These meetings, however, took the same grounds as other Whigs on campaign questions; that is, they asserted the existence of a depression caused by Jackson's and Van Buren's toying with the currency, and they attributed the Democratic experiments with the economy to a wholly political desire to consolidate power in the executive branch of the federal government by means of control over a great and growing patronage.[30]

It is unclear precisely what the terms of the stump debate were between Douglas and Stuart. Newspaper reports suggest they concentrated on national issues, especially the question of the Independent Treasury,[31] but Whig attacks on the Peoria convention and the Whigs' general linking of the Independent Treasury to illegitimate partyism suggest that party organization itself must also have been a central question. Stuart reportedly opposed the Subtreasury on the stump for placing the nation's money "within the control of party," while John Henry recalled that "I was with [Douglas] politically until the Jackson party made the issue upon the convention system which I opposed[;] that compelled me to take sides with the Whig candidate, Hon. John T. Stuart, for Congress, and against Douglas."[32] In August, Stuart won the election by so narrow a margin that Douglas did not give up the idea of challenging the result for another year.

There were two other congressional elections as well in 1838. In the southern districts, the convention system remained beyond the pale even in this year of increasing party organization. The Independent Treasury was made a national party test in 1838 for the very purpose of imposing permanent and pervasive organization on the party and ridding it of all who would not submit.[33] All three Illinois congressmen, however, resisted the new standards.

In the northern district, William May paid for his resistance with his political career, but in the southern districts resistance to party tests was not only possible but probably necessary for a candidate. The opposition *Sangamo Journal* was not too far off the mark when it presented what it believed to be these congressmen's perspective on recent events. Under the heading "Condition of the Party," the editor noted that Van Burenites had begun to confess the antidemocratic nature of a "party test":

> In the present instance, some of the Van Buren members of Congress do not hesitate to say that there has existed a power in this government, unknown to the constitution and laws, which has been able to direct its policy, and heretofore, to compel the members of Congress, belonging to the party, to support it, whatever that policy might be. They instance as illustrations of this fact, the veto of the U. States Bank; the "pocketing" of Clay's Land bill; the removal of the deposites; the specie circular; the policy of all these measures having been opposed to the wishes of the people as expressed by their proper Representatives.

The *Journal* continued with a description of the executive resources—the officeholders and the executive-funded party presses in the states—that together could destroy any man's political career. With this threat hanging over them, Democratic representatives went unconsulted on policy positions but, as they now freely admitted, were "required to stand up and defend them, or subject themselves to all the vengeance which the land officers, the press controlled by them, and the greedy and hungry aspirants for office, could inflict upon such as dared to avow themselves for their country, in opposition to the dictum of party."[34]

Zadok Casey, running for reelection in the southeast, was a model of resistance to Van Burenism for the *Journal*. After all three congressmen had voted against Van Buren in the fall, it remained a matter of some controversy whether Casey and Adam Snyder, the representative from the southwest, would continue to vote that way or come into line as the test character of the Independent Treasury was made clear.[35] To bring Casey within the discipline of the party, the *State Register*, formerly the *Advocate*, suggested to Casey's constituents that they might want to hold a nominating convention for Congress. But the editor, knowing that the only congressional conventions ever held in the state were the barely defensible and bitterly attacked gatherings of 1836 and 1837 in the northern district, did not press the issue: "We merely throw out the suggestion."[36]

Soon afterward, Casey's self-nomination appeared in the papers with no challenge to his candidacy appearing until late spring. Finally, a Democratic meeting in Paris pronounced a blanket condemnation of all those Democrats who had betrayed "that party of whom they had received all their power and greatness." Attacking Casey without mercy and declaring support for Van Buren and the Subtreasury, it called for a congressional convention and offered the name of Samuel McRoberts as a candidate. The *Register*, while finding the attack on Casey too harsh (probably because the editor knew he might yet have to support him), endorsed the call for a convention.[37] Backtracking the following week, the paper endorsed Casey, despite the uncertainty of his course, because he appeared to be the choice of a majority of the district's Democrats and because it was "inexpedient" to hold a convention.[38] No doubt the inexpediency came from the fact that Casey was both highly popular and, like his constituents, opposed to the convention system. There was risk, however, in supporting a man whose course was uncertain when one's party defined itself by a test question.

The *Register* lost the gamble when word finally came that Casey had voted unambiguously against the Independent Treasury in Congress. Dropping Casey's name from the masthead, the editor futilely called on McRoberts again.[39] But Casey rested his candidacy on a record of constituent service as well as opposition to spoils and partyist interference with manifestly public-interested legislation,[40] and he sailed to victory, virtually unopposed.[41]

In the southwestern district, original Jacksonism was again dominant, although the politicians were privately tempted by partyism. Snyder, the incumbent, was in the same position as Casey. Having voted to table the Subtreasury in the fall, he was on the brink of being read out of the party but for three facts: he was popular in his district; party discipline and test questions were not yet sanctioned in southern Illinois; and the final vote on the Subtreasury was still to be had. Unable to produce Peoria-style "impositions" in the south, the partyists tentatively embraced Snyder, even though he had shown himself opposed to " 'the party.' "[42]

Luckily for Snyder, southern Illinois swarmed with original Jacksonians. But Snyder, himself, like most practicing politicians, was more open to party, at least in private, than were the voters. For example, when John Reynolds, former governor, erstwhile antiparty Jacksonian, and persistent nemesis of Snyder, returned from Congress shortly after Van Buren's inauguration, Snyder described him privately as insufficiently committed to Van Buren and to party.[43] Contrasting himself with Reynolds, Snyder was firmly opposed to banks and convinced, like Van Buren, that the pro-bank opposition always turned out as a unit at even the most local elections, while the scattered yeomanry would only make themselves felt at general elections. Party organization, he implied, was a necessity.[44] Still, Snyder's partyism fell short of full-bore Van Burenism. Deviating from the administration on the Independent Treasury, he reaffirmed to a supporter his general adherence to the party but insisted that "there is a time that we should pause before we take hold of party extremes."[45]

Snyder's moderate partyism was matched by his moderate conventionism: "I do not believe that a [congressional nominating] convention can be got up at Kaskaskia," he wrote to an ally. "The truth is that the people composing my congressional district have never been used to that mode of bringing out candidates, it will not take[;] none but northern and eastern politicians pursue that course[;] for myself I have no doubt of its correctness, it is indeed the only mode by which you can test party strength."[46] His theoretical endorsement of conventions was moderated by other practical considerations as well. Discovering in his hometown newspaper an intimation that he would cooperate with a congressional convention, he fired off a correction to a close friend, Gustave Koerner. Enclosing a letter for publication to be used as Koerner saw fit, Snyder confided that "I know too well how these things are got up; were I on the ground travelling amongst the people I would willingly submit my claims [to a convention], but there is evidently a settled design to run me off the track."

In public, Snyder concealed his ambivalent embrace of partyism and conventionism and stoutly reaffirmed the tenets of original Jacksonism:

> In order that my views in relation to [a convention] may not be misunderstood, and knowing of no exigency, demanding a departure from the heretofore usages in selecting candidates, believing as I do, that the independent voters of the district I have the honour to represent, can at this election, as

they have in all former, decide upon the person who should represent them, without the aid of a caucus or the convention of a few designing men, besides considering myself the representative of the *whole* district, my claims for reelection will be submitted to the *whole* people and to no other tribunal.[47]

Two months later, he withdrew from the race on account of chronic illness. Through the rest of the spring he appeared to be back in the party fold as it became increasingly clear that Van Burenite orthodoxy was gaining firm control of his increasingly institutionalized party. His correspondence emphasized the importance of party unity in the approaching state elections, and he reluctantly accepted the party position on the Subtreasury bill as it became clearer that there was no middle ground between loyalty and opposition.[48] Snyder's relations with the party, as it sought in 1838 to unambiguously define people in or out, were summarized fairly enough by an orthodox "Democrat of Old St. Clair" in the *Register*:

Tho' he did give his best friends occasion to believe that he had left the party at the special session, by voting against Blair & Rives for public printers, against the issue of Treasury notes, . . . against the postponement of the fourth instalment of the surplus revenue . . . and against the great measure of the Democracy—the Independent Treasury bill; yet he has at this session . . . taken his stand again in the Democratic ranks. . . .

The Sub-Treasury must become the *test question*, and he who is not for it, cannot be considered a democrat;—on that, we must rally—by that, parties must be known and distinguished.[49]

Snyder would never again stray far from party regularity, but the commitment to party he made in the spring of 1838 had a cost of which he was well aware. In early 1839, he again reflected privately on partyism: "What you say in regard to independence of opinion + conscience I have been long since convinced of by experience. a perfect tyranny exists; god help the victim that dare express an opinion in opposition to the orthodoxy of party. it has only appeared since converted federalists, and newborn Democrats have seized the direction and control of the Democratic party. it must be purged of the self constituted leaders and then it will resume its wonted purity."[50] Snyder echoed the lament of many old Jacksonians who remembered when the party had been a movement much more than a party, when it had lacked organization and party tests but was unquestionably the embodiment of the democracy. These old Jacksonians still appeared to dominate southern Illinois, but those like Snyder, who had seen the machine at work and felt its fatal attraction, knew where the future lay. He could never go with the Whigs, who were nothing but neo-

Federalists, but neither could he put his whole heart into the party that had now overwhelmed the movement.

With Snyder out of the contest, a self-nominated Reynolds had an easy time in regaining his seat. He too disdained organization, but he did base his candidacy explicitly on party grounds, adapting a Van Buren campaign text in which America's democrats were constantly stalked by aristocratic seekers of special privilege and special constitutional status.[51] The gist of that text was not particularly novel. More novel was the notion that party organization—the convention system, partisan patronage, and test questions as means of disciplining political behavior—was the legitimate corollary of that political history.

In the gubernatorial race, the partyists announced their intention to press the convention system onto new ground. In the past, state politics had remained largely free of the national party divisions, and gubernatorial candidates in Illinois had practically always been self-nominated.[52] In 1837, however, the *Register* refused to publish the usual stream of private nominations in the hope that the Democracy might come to an understanding on one candidate. "A State Convention of the Republican party . . . seems to us to be the only plan which can ensure the success of a Democratic candidate; for the Opposition are so well drilled, they will be sure to run but one of their own."[53] The Whigs responded in kind, settling on a single candidate early in the day, and guaranteeing that nomination methods, patronage, and the relation of both to the Subtreasury would dominate the campaign. Both sides, however, still believed in the necessity of making arguments from expediency if their nomination methods were to be accepted. In a polity highly skeptical of any form of party organization, arguing for organized nomination as a positive good rather than as a necessity under trying circumstances was dangerous.

Rather than insisting that democratic theory absolutely required conventions, then, the Democrats at the General Assembly session in July resolved simply that a state convention would be "in accordance with the usages of the democratic party of the state and nation" as long as it rested on "interchange of opinion between brethren of the same principles in the primary meetings of the people."[54] In invoking the "usages" of the party, of course, these Democrats followed standard, partyist rhetorical practice and theory, but they were also false to the history of Illinois. They sought pragmatically to portray party conventions as conservative institutions rather than as innovations, when, in fact, such conventions were not only not well established but had never once been used to nominate Illinois state officers.

The *Register*, nevertheless, seized the opportunity to contrast this open meeting and its call for further open meetings of the people with the Whigs' "secret caucus," which had nominated Cyrus Edwards for governor without involving or even informing the people.[55] A Democratic convention in this circumstance was not an attempt to revolutionize constitutional practice but, in fact, a traditional tactic to defend democracy against covert aristocratic drill. The *Illinois Republican* identified the issue at stake: "The question is now presented *caucus* against conventions of the people. The people will decide on the first Monday in August next which they prefer."[56]

To help them decide, the July Democratic meeting named a committee to draft an address. The burden of the address was to prove the practical necessity of party organization among Democrats if they were to keep aristocracy at bay, but it began with a full-blown articulation of the constitutional-partyist history of American politics as a battle between "the rights of the People" and "the privileges of Property."[57] During the administration of George Washington, according to the address, this eternal contest lay dormant amid a partyless celebration of the "abstract" triumph of democracy. But, from the Adams administration to the present, "there has been an unceasing warfare between them; and an untiring effort on the part of the Federalists . . . to supplant the constitutional supremacy of the 'many.' "[58] Proof of their anti-democracy lay in the Alien and Sedition Acts, their opposition to the War of 1812, their devotion to the Bank, and their support of "the chimeras of the American system." In every case these positions represented an attempt to bring down democracy: "Let it be remembered by the Republicans of Illinois, that the principles of the Constitution are the principles of the Democratic Party—that the success of the latter is the safety of the former—that the principles of the whigs, as they are self-styled, as being friendly to strong government, distinctions in society, and exclusive privileges, are in subversion of both."[59]

Having established that political conflict reflected competing understandings of the Constitution and little else, the address now came to its justification of a state party convention. Soon enough, conventions would be justified as, in principle, the necessary institutions of popular sovereignty. But even those Illinoisans who accepted the partyist portrayal of the Whigs were not generally ready to accept partyist organization. To get the voters to embrace convention nomination required that the convention be presented not as a good in itself—a proposition few outside of Chicago would hazard—but as a necessary evil. They proved its necessity, then, by blaming the "aristocrats" for the first introduction of conventionism, asserting that "the Whigs [had] been organizing the force of their party, for some time past, by means of State Conventions."[60] Of course, the truth was that the Whigs had never held a state convention in

Illinois and, before 1838, had only rarely held conventions elsewhere. So pressed were the Democrats in anticonvention Illinois to legitimate their convention that, rather than rely on conventionist theory, they invented a nefarious Whig tradition of conventionism.

The main practical consequence of a failure by democrats to use conventions, according to the authors, would be a revival of the Bank, the great electioneering machine that the people had rejected in the last two presidential elections. Consequently, this preeminently anti-democratic institution's struggle against the Independent Treasury was inseparable from the contest over conventionism: "If we would preserve and perpetuate the principles of Washington, Jefferson, Madison, Monroe, Jackson and Van Buren, we must follow their advice and conform to their usages."[61]

Finally, quibbles about conventionism were rendered insignificant when one observed that the only alternative in 1838 was the Whigs' "midnight caucus," "a system of organization much more objectionable than Conventions" and one hardly consistent with the Whigs' unequivocal "condemn[ation of] all manner of party concert and unanimity."[62] In contrast, the Democrats "propose[d] to bring [their candidate] forward by the free and consentaneous voice of every member of their political association."[63]

The convention subsequently met in December at the opening of the General Assembly in Vandalia. Just as in 1835, however, it drew Democrats from only about one-third of the state's counties, falling a bit short of "every member of their political association."[64] Still, its nominee, James W. Stephenson of the northwestern county of Jo Daviess, provoked no significant intraparty objections.

Meanwhile, the Whigs slowly got their conventionless nominations off the ground. Reporting a suggestion by the Vandalia *Free Press* that Cyrus Edwards and William Davidson be the Whig ticket, the editor of the *Journal* happily concurred.[65] The Democratic *Register* had long since reported this nomination by the Whig members of the legislature in secret caucus, suggesting that Whig editors just waited until the proper moment to go through the motions of an extensive consultation. Of course, honest Whigs might yet have thought a legislative caucus, informally ratified by five subsequent months of conversation in the districts, to be a quite good example of extensive, democratic consultation. Even granting this much, however, the Whig editors were obviously less than forthcoming in their accounts of the nomination process.

Democrats were no more forthright, however, as they claimed that their meagerly attended conventions spoke the voice of the people. Both parties produced nominations by essentially similar consultations among elites who were conversant with the sentiments of their communities. The processes were presented to the public, however, in wildly different ways that reflected the difference between two idealized versions of free, democratic politics, the Democratic version in which the convention embodied the authority of the majority over all democrats and the Whig version in which the individual voter's judgment must never be compromised.

Thus, to return to the Whig nominating process, the editor of the *Free Press* reported the arrival of letters from all over the state, all "designating the same persons" for the Whig ticket, and he was therefore willing to take "the 'responsibility' " of floating their names. He did not theorize about how such unanimity might have come about. It may well be that he expected his readers to assume that there was a certain amount of elite cooperation in the original suggestion of the ticket but also to believe that these recent letters represented an authentic, popular movement. Significantly, though, he did not expect the automatic acquiescence in the nomination that the Democrats expected for their convention nominees. He merely asked for a response and for a good faith effort for unity: "If . . . those gentlemen, or either of them, shall decline a contest . . . or if a majority of our Whig brethren can present others who can unite greater strength, we will most cheerfully surrender all personal preferences."[66]

A Cook County meeting's previous call for a Whig state gubernatorial convention received little, if any, response.[67] The Edwards nomination, however, picked up enough steam through the spring to guarantee that he would be the only anti-Democratic candidate for governor. In February, a Bond County correspondent reported that the nomination was fully sanctioned there and that Edwards evoked admiration even from regular Democrats who, having been separated from their consciences, "say *they must support the party*.' "[68] A Pike County Whig meeting likewise ratified Edwards while confirming that the issue of the August elections was whether the people would be "faithfully represented" without interference from the executive or from officeholders.[69] Finally, on March 24, the *Journal* published Edwards's acceptance of the nomination.

This was all an elitist, party-organized farce to the Democrats. The *Register* ridiculed the Whig papers for hoisting state nominees in December without saying who nominated them or how, while they guiltily denied the *Register*'s July report of their secret caucus.[70] And "Fiat Justitia" hammered home the point by reemphasizing the need for Democrats to follow the Whig precedent of organization: "Constantly charging us with our devotion to party, the fact is we are far behind them in that particular." In particular, he divined a Whig party scheme to get John Reynolds out as a candidate for governor to divide the Democratic vote. This plot could only be nipped for sure by the self-sacrificing spirit of conventionist party loyalty.[71] The supposedly antipartyist Whigs were the real source of party and the reason that Democratic organization had become necessary.

The Democrats had far bigger problems, however, than the unpredictable maneuverings of Reynolds. Their nominee, Stephenson, turned out to be a defaulter to the federal government to the tune of tens of thousands of dollars in Land Office receipts. While Stephenson denied it and the various newspapers tiptoed through the issue, the Democratic leadership quickly confirmed the truth of the charge.[72] By early spring, newspapers began to drop the convention nominee, and the party was in trouble.[73]

Adam Snyder, who had seen the question of the Independent Treasury reduce the national Democratic party's numbers but imbue the remainder with a firm regularity,[74] urged that the Stephenson crisis should prompt a renewed emphasis on first principles. As on the national scene, so in Illinois party unity on the sole question of "democracy + Federalists" had to rule the election.[75] Questions of mere policy would kill the Democrats. After all, the main Democratic policy, emphasized in state convention, was the Independent Treasury. And the Whig attack on the Independent Treasury centered exactly on the kind of behavior that Stephenson presented: government by spoilsmen who were appointed only for the cupidity that made them zealous in the service of Van Burenite partyism. When new meetings in the northern counties began naming new candidates for governor, Snyder could hardly believe their stupidity in nominating none but Land Office appointees.[76]

The *Journal*, meanwhile, drew Stephenson exactly as Snyder feared. "Mr. Sub-Treasurer Stephenson" was made to embody "Loco Focoism" as Edwards was made the hero of "Conservatism" amid Van Burenite experiments on the politics and economy of the nation.[77] And as the scandal thickened, the *Journal* supplemented its indictment of the Subtreasury's spoils-based seduction of congressional consciences, discussed above, with a description of how Illinois was "LAND-OFFICE-RIDDEN." Not only had the Democratic convention nominee been a Receiver and a defaulter, but most of the floated replacements were Registers or Receivers, as were the congressional nominee of the Peoria convention (Douglas) and the favorite of the *Register* in its attempts to challenge Casey in the southeast (McRoberts). Everywhere one looked, the central qualification for Democratic nomination appeared to be control of a land office, the base from which one was expected to do the dirty work of the party. "The only just reason that can be given for this system of policy is—that the occupants of Land Offices have the money necessary, as we suppose, to electioneer among the people." If passage of the Subtreasury would facilitate executive control of state elections, the Land Office already served that purpose under the Subtreasury administration.[78]

Stephenson finally withdrew in May, and the party reconvened to name Thomas Carlin of Quincy, also a land officer, as the new candidate. The *Journal* ridiculed the convention as "THE LATE LAND OFFICE CONVENTION," managed by McRoberts, packed with land office men, not even pretending to represent more than one-third of the counties of the state, and scheming Carlin into a nomination over the candidate of the anti-Land-Office majority among the delegates.[79] The *Journal* summed up its position in a late editorial that pointed out that three-fourths of the states had rejected the Subtreasury, judging by recent elections. The sovereign had spoken. Still, the Van Buren administration sought to force the measure down the people's throats by means of patronage and regular nominations.[80]

The Democrats, as Snyder had hoped, responded with a case resting on first principles. They did not address Whig charges but readopted their resolutions of the previous December: they opposed the Bank as "naturally hostile to popular freedom" and to the Constitution; they defined the difference between the parties as the difference between devotion to the few and devotion to equal rights for the masses; and they stigmatized all seceders from the "republican" party in all eras as "enemies of equal rights."[81] Carlin's election circular addressed a number of issues: it advocated public schools as an obstacle to "aristocracy and despotism"; it supported state-owned internal improvements; it condemned banking as "irreconcileable with the constitution of the United States" and as a curse on the "producing classes"; it looked to a land policy of graduation and preemption to secure the independence of the settlers against speculators; finally, it avowed support for Van Buren and for the Subtreasury's separation of the government from banks as a measure "of the most vital importance to the perpetuity of our inimitable form of Government; and to the maintenance of our present glorious Constitution."[82]

In the end, Carlin eked out a win in an unprecedentedly party-controlled vote, with only one scattering vote reported out of over 60,000 cast.[83] On the basis of this election, one could say that the central element of the party system—competitive, two-party control of elections—had arrived at the state level. But many parts of the state were still, to say the least, immature in this regard, and virtually no one yet had a mature, modern conception of the democratic two-party system. Rather, party conflict continued to take its justification from the claim that the Constitution itself was under siege.

Conclusion

The elections of 1838 revealed the sort of reluctant evolution of political practice that activists only dared justify on pragmatic grounds. Publicly, everyone disdained party-as-faction and adhered to the principles of majority rule and individual independence. Thus Democrats considered their party the agent of "the majority of the people," and Whigs thought their party the defender of individual political judgment, while neither accepted that individual conscience and majoritarianism might be in tension with each other. Neither party admitted that any of the evolution of conventions and party behavior were positive innovations but only expedients for the conservation of traditional constitutional values.

In particular, each party justified its partyesque behavior by increasingly integrating policy questions into its theory of democratic practice. Democrats emphasized the power of banks and corporate wealth to overbalance popular majorities. Deeming the electoral exploitation of corporate wealth an unconstitutional elevation of a financial aristocracy, the partyists turned to democratic organization to rebalance the Constitution. Whigs, meanwhile, argued that executive patronage and the Subtreasury were tools for subordinating and manipulating individual conscience. Locating the main threat to the Constitution in partisan coercion of otherwise free, individual judgment, they resorted to political organization of the independent to free the individual and thus the Constitution from party and spoils. But only in the campaigns of 1840 did each party's constitutional theory and interpretation of American history emerge as fully coherent justifications of comprehensive party organization.

CHAPTER SEVEN

Ideological Origins of the Two-Party Constitution, 1839

The preceding chapters have argued that the political heritage of Illinois was one of vigorous political competition within an antipartyist and effectively partyless constitutional order. If a party system were to emerge from such a firmly ensconced order, it would have to arise from efforts to preserve essential characteristics of that order. Accordingly, previous chapters have shown that arguments for or against various kinds of party did, in fact, aim to preserve the partyless democracy that was the people's constitutional inheritance. As the partyist offensive developed across the 1830s, arguments about party and the constitutional order increasingly became the preoccupation of politicians on all sides. In particular, by 1839, Democrats and Whigs focused on controlling the public's understanding of the history of American constitutional politics within its international context, each side seeking to disseminate a kind of antiparty version of that history.

"The Democracy," as party members routinely called their party, esteemed itself the same "democracy" that classically had meant not a party or faction but the entire popular stratum of the polity,[1] the stratum that the Democrats routinely presumed to comprise "nineteen-twentieths" of the people. As the campaign of 1839–40 would show, Democrats understood their party as the avant-garde of an international historical movement toward democracy. They considered the party's purpose to be the institutionalization of the American democracy's suprapartisan, suprafactional primary assemblages, in which its sovereignty might regularly be asserted and exercised. Specifically, the American democracy would preserve its sovereignty by the device of binding (because majoritarian) nomination and by enforcement of that rule through the spoils system. In so institutionalizing popular sovereignty, the American democracy would counter the Old World's assumption that no "democracy" could ever be fit to rule.

The Whigs, on the other hand, drew on a tradition that condemned party organization of virtually any kind. For them, the old three-part categorization of constitutions was irrelevant, because there was only one constitutional stratum in the United States, preserved in its sovereignty by the ingenious institutional design of the Constitution[2]—certainly not by the device of party. The threat of the Old World lay not in its futile impugning of "the democracy" but in its principles of political patronage and dependence—including Walpolean "influence"—so contrary to the principle of independent judgment that lay at the foundation of the American Constitution. Their fear, in short, was not the resurgence of aristocracy but the creation of an overbearing officeholder interest, a network of executive patronage, that would use the convention system to control the popular will.[3]

Yet the Whigs too began to organize in the 1830s. They nevertheless refused to embrace explicitly the ethic of strict party loyalty, either with regard to convention nominations or in the distribution of patronage. Defined not by its organizational attributes but by its voluntarism, such a party was intended to wither away as soon as the partyist movement had been buried by a national reaffirmation of democratic antipartyism.[4]

These constitutional concerns of both parties necessarily intersected with policy questions like the Independent Treasury, but the constitutional issues were not mere by-products of such questions. Rather, one might almost say, in the interests of provocation, that the policy questions, or at least the particular shapes they took, were mere by-products of the parties' constitutional debate. Carried on in the midst of economic crisis, the campaign of 1840 was a struggle to control the historical interpretation of the founding and development of the American Constitution. The Independent Treasury was only the issue of the moment in the Van Burenite Democracy's climactic struggle to imbue democratic party organization with ultimate constitutional authority. Through issues of fiscal and monetary policy, the Democratic politicians might link their organization fundamentally, exclusively, and inseparably with the tradition of strict construction of the federal Constitution, with states' rights, and with majoritarianism. The depression that followed the Panic of 1837, like the one that followed the Panic of 1819, might have been addressed without the aid or obstacle of mass party organization. But the creation of the parties by constitutional conflict was already under way when the Panic struck. In the event, the urgency of the economic situation accelerated the entrenchment of the parties in 1840, but only because it increased the already sizable stakes in the war for control of American constitutionalism. In that war, Van Buren stocked the intellectual armory from which Democratic politicians drew their new-fangled weapons of historical interpretation. The Whig militia, meanwhile, dusted off the tried and true musketry of traditional antipartyism.

Martin Van Buren's History of the American Constitution

Illinois Democrats entered the presidential campaign season in a sober mood. Their state had given two-thirds majorities to Jackson in 1828 and 1832 and even a solid majority to Van Buren in the multiple-candidate race in 1836. But in 1838 it had yielded only 51 percent to the Democratic gubernatorial candidate in the first clear, statewide test of Whig and Democratic strength. Moreover, elections across the country had produced a sometimes shocking series of triumphs for the Whigs in 1837 and 1838.[5] In response, Democratic leaders concluded that party distinctions needed to be clarified as thoroughly as possible.

Chief among these leaders was Van Buren. His "Thoughts on the approaching election in N[ew] York"[6] was his outline of a model Democratic address, and its gist was retailed by Democratic politicians in Illinois and across the nation in 1840. It reveals a man genuinely stunned by Whig ascendancy and determined to show his party colleagues how to nip it in the bud. He meant to do so by coaching his compatriots in a proper interpretation of the history and nature of American constitutional politics. Coming from the pen of the Democrats' national leader and virtual creator, Van Buren's "Thoughts" is the indispensable introduction to the campaign by historical interpretation that was the Democratic strategy in 1840.

Van Buren began by attributing the Democrats' recent losses partly to newly intense Whig activity and organization but mostly to Whig election fraud. The American democracy now faced the characteristic and often fatal difficulty of all democracies. Disarmed by its unreflective antipathy to party organization, the democracy was at all times vulnerable to the aristocracy's pseudo-democratic pandering, covert organization, and outright election fraud. Democrats could survive this attack only by making the campaign rest clearly on constitutional principle. The election must be about the "purity of elections" and the necessity of universal organization. Whig corruption must motivate the democracy to liberate itself not only from election fraud but from the anti-democratic constitutionalism out of which election fraud grew.[7] A democracy that embraced its own organization as a constitutional principle would produce an electoral atmosphere in which the people would know that there was only one democratic party, which would see that the people's votes were counted as they were cast. In that event, there could be no doubt of a large Democratic majority.

To this end, Van Buren's "Thoughts" suggested the argument that he wanted the Democratic membership of New York's legislature to use in its address to the voters. This argument proved to be a history of American political parties from their origin. It sought to establish the constitutional character of all party division and the consequent necessity of the democracy's organization as a party.

According to Van Buren, Alexander Hamilton planted the first seeds of party division under the new government when he began his campaign to sap the Constitution by loose construction: "The establishment of the principles involved in the creation of a national Bank was the first great victory obtained over the spirit of the constitution + obtained too under the lead of one (Genl. H.) whose views had been more extensively thwarted in the convention than those of any other man, + has in its consequences been the cause of most of the dissentions . . . which have subsequently distracted the Republic + been well nigh instrumental in upsetting the Govt. as was foretold by Mr. Jefferson."[8] The subsequent break between Hamilton and Jefferson established the principles of party division that, according to Van Buren, still obtained in 1840. In this war, Jefferson stood for democracy and for the strict construction that was the only barrier to discretionary rule by a federal aristocracy. Hamilton, on the other hand, stood for aristocracy by way of loose construction.[9]

First acting under the name Federalist, but later using whatever names might best deceive the people, the consolidationists were distinguishable by a number of reliable characteristics: their distrust of popular self-governance; their hostility to public discussion, as evidenced by the Sedition Act; their antipathy to immigrants, illustrated by the old Alien Act as well as by new Whig efforts to obstruct naturalization of the hounded "friends of freedom"; their resistance to broad suffrage; their pursuit of "partial legislation"; their attachment to banking systems and a permanent public debt, both as means to "individual aggrandizement" and as "elements of political power which are by the law of their nature opposed to popular controul"; their passion for creating artificial distinctions on the model of monarchy; and their neo-Tory vindictiveness toward the democracy.[10]

In contrast, the Republican party arose only in response to the very "excesses and apostacies from the principles of the Revolution"[11] that were perpetrated by the Federalists. In every respect, they contrasted with the Federalists: They were composed entirely of Whigs of the Revolution, devoted to the democratic principles of the Declaration of Independence. Believing that republicanism rested on truth, they supported full and open discussion at all times and uncompromisingly opposed the Sedition Act. Believing that immigrants were entitled to the same freedoms as native citizens, they opposed the Alien Act's attempt to give the government a "tyrany over the minds of men."[12] Trusting the power of the vote to cure all abuses of power, they relentlessly sought its extension. Conceiving of government as the tool of the governed rather than a mechanism for "individual aggrandizement," they opposed all artificial distinctions, all special legislation, and especially Hamilton's funding and banking systems as "by their nature hostile to popular rights" and as "the great lever of Hamiltonian corruption."[13]

Van Buren then asked, "Who is there that can fail to recognize in this account of the first great parties which divided the country a faithful description also of those which now exist and which under various names have divided it from the administration of the elder Adams to the present day."[14] In particular, the Whigs' present-day resistance to suffrage extension, their preference for lifetime appointments to the judiciary from which they attempted to control the popularly elected branches of the government, their well-known nativism, and their continued advocacy of a public debt as a public "blessing," along with the other trappings and devices of a paper-money aristocracy, all confirmed their identity with Federalism.[15] If there remained any doubt as to the anti-democratic character of the opposition of 1840, one only needed to look at its nominee, William Henry Harrison, an unreconstructed Federalist of 1798 who favored the Bank of the United States, who was "latitudinarian in all his constitutional views," and whose nomination was made in such loose constructionist language as had not been heard in years.[16]

Van Buren often skated by without evidence in this outline, but Illinois Democrats could easily fill in their own experiences: In 1839, Alexander P. Field tried to retain indefinitely the office of secretary of state against the will of the new Democratic governor. In 1840, the Whig Supreme Court was reputedly prepared to strike down Illinois's traditional practice of allowing aliens to vote. And to Democrats the Whig elite of bankers and legislators—the paper-money aristocracy—appeared responsible for Illinois's devastation when the Panic of 1837 brought the banking and internal improvement systems crashing down around the taxpayers' ears.

The intensity of Van Buren's fears for the fate of democracy and his consequent anxiety to define the role of party correctly are best understood through the international perspective then so salient. Van Buren was acutely aware that, in the estate-conscious Old World, government by the democracy was an object of contempt. Specifically, he knew that the international enemies of democracy pointed to America's persistent party divisions as conclusive evidence of the futility—not the health—of democracy. Van Buren's task was to explain American party competition in such a way as to refute that position. But, far from developing a modern understanding of a "party system," he drew on nineteenth-century concerns about democratic, aristocratic, and monarchical constitutional orders to explain the structure of American politics.

Van Buren's analysis of the campaign of 1840 makes sense only if one understands Van Buren's unspoken, pre-modern premise: that party competition was not among democrats but between democrats and aristocrats (or "monocrats"). On that premise, if the outcome of the election actually remained uncertain, then the democracy's very commitment to its own sovereignty was in doubt. Thus to some it appeared that the people could not even unequivocally maintain their commitment to a self-governing constitutional order, let alone conduct a government within that order. Here is Van Buren's frank (if syntactically challenging) acknowledgment of the plausibility of this charge:

> That the choice of the people of the U. States between two parties so undeniably divided in [?] principles + objects, which are, with almost the single exception of the form of the Government[,] identical with those for which the Revolution itself was waged, should ever be doubtful has been a source of surprise + regret to many intelligent and well disposed observers of the workings of our system in all parts of the world, + a fruitful theme of derision to the enemies of free Government. They glory in the supposition as affording triumphant evidence of their favourite theory, that the mass of the people are every where too fickle in their opinions, too little informed in public affairs + too unstable in their views for the enjoyment of self Government.[17]

Van Buren argued here that everyone abroad recognized the American party division as a conflict between self-government and aristocracy, the opposing principles of the American Revolution. The only change since the Revolution was that the opposition no longer contended for the actual "form" of the British government, constitutional monarchy. Otherwise the contest continued as it always had. The fact that, to foreign eyes, this contest's outcome "should ever be doubtful," then, was sufficient reason for the world to question the people's capacity for self-government—the people's ability both to conduct their government and to sustain their commitment to the Constitution that gave them such responsibility.

Having acknowledged this indictment of democracy and party politics, Van Buren did not dispute the underlying constitutional theory with a modern theory of two-partyism. Instead, he actually seemed to agree that uncertainty in the outcome of a looming presidential contest might legitimately cast doubt on the people's capacity for democratic rule. But he refused to accept that any uncertainty actually existed in these races. Rather than argue that close, two-party competition reflected the healthy diversity and freedom of a democratic society, he argued that the competition between the democracy and the aristocrats was never really that close. Although a minority of the democracy might occasionally be misled by crypto-aristocratic deceptions, in fact, the nation had always sustained the democratic party by large majorities in every national election.[18]

According to Van Buren, the people had voted decisively to sustain democracy in every presidential election since the organization of parties in 1798. In the one case where an aristocratic president was elected, John Quincy Adams's election by the House in 1825, the choice had not been made by the people but in defiance of the people's clear preference for a democrat.[19] There was no reason to doubt that the people would continue to vote their own obvious and well understood constitutional convictions. Neither did Van Buren doubt that the "only issue" for the previous forty years had been and remained, "shall the will of the people be obeyed or shall it be defeated by sinister + unlawful means."[20]

Of course, it was true that the opposition regularly received votes beyond what the small aristocracy pictured by Van Buren could have produced by itself. But these extra votes were artificial, according to Van Buren. They were products of corporate power. Chief among corporations were banks, which were able to control naturally democratic voters and politicians by making men financially dependent on them. According to Van Buren, whenever labor and enterprise rendered the economy comparatively independent of banks, the latter were always able to reestablish some measure of dependency. Insufficiently wary citizens would repeatedly be ensnared by calculatedly excessive note issues on disarmingly easy terms. Similarly, politicians could be made directors and stockholders, positions that slowly made even men of the greatest integrity suspicious of and then prejudiced against the will of "the community."[21]

Primary though banks were in diverting citizens and leaders alike from devotion to the popular will, all corporations, even literary and benevolent societies, so consistently opposed the will of the people, in Van Buren's reckoning, as to make it appear a "law of their nature" to do so. It appeared that they would universally "ally themselves with the dynasty of associated wealth in attempts to defeat by their united efforts the end + aim of our free institutions by making the few masters over the many. Thus acquiring in this happy land by indirection + fraud, what is in monarchical Government secured by the principles upon which they are instituted."[22]

In understanding this last remark, it is important to remember the way monarchical societies worked. They consisted of innumerable, hierarchical networks of dependencies and approached their version of the public good by continual reinforcement of those ties.[23] Thus in Van Buren's view the principle of these corporations was perfectly appropriate to monarchical societies, where the people could not constitutionally hope for anything more than what was entitled to them from their superiors as part of their dependency. But Ameri-

can society had rejected the principle of dependence to embrace individual independence as the essential attribute of popular self-governance. Corporations
sought to reintroduce dependence, to substitute the interests of the elite for the
interests of the people by reducing the interests of the people to mere dependence
on the success of the elite. Therefore, the limited successes of the anti-democratic
opposition were attributable only to elitists' reintroducing such dynamics of
dependence into a polity otherwise dedicated to individual independence.

Although the people had not been able to root out this influence entirely,
they had retained popular dominance in the national administration. Thus
arose, according to Van Buren, the anti-democrats' many post-election efforts
to defraud the people of their chosen leaders. Examples ranged from the Federalist attempt to use Aaron Burr to defeat Jefferson in the House election in
1801[24] to the Whig scheme to unseat the Democratic representatives from
New Jersey elected in 1838.[25] In returning to the question of election fraud
here, Van Buren returned to his opening contention that Whig ascendancy in a
democratic polity, given the now well elaborated character of the parties, could
only come by illegal means. He concluded with the usual exhortations to organization by distribution of documents, raising of local meetings, and organization of Democratic Associations, "the leading object of [which] should be
to preserve + promote the purity + freedom of elections."[26]

The "leading object" he sought was not an end to corporations as such, although he made clear in the manuscript why he would hem them in, nor the
defense of the Independent Treasury, nor any other policy question. Rather, it
was the maintenance of the purity of elections so as to vindicate the democratic
nature of the American electorate and Constitution at the polls. If elections
were free and organized by constitutional parties, then the democracy would
forever be equipped to spy and defeat all attempts, corporate or otherwise, to
re-create a society of anti-democratic dependency. And every election would
yield an overwhelming Democratic majority.

The Democrats' History of
the Constitution in Illinois

Martin Van Buren was not an Illinoisan and did not take any direct part in the
campaign in Illinois. But he was without doubt the preeminent theorist of partyism in his day. Even before becoming president, he had had an enormous influence on popular political thought through his leadership of the Democratic
party in New York and through his influence on Jackson.[27] More particularly,
the Illinois press regularly reprinted political argument from New York papers. These reprints included in this campaign at least one long excerpt from

the address of the Democrats of the New York legislature, the address for which Van Buren's manuscript was intended as the model. The excerpt followed Van Buren's lead in arguing the identity of the Federalists, the Whigs, and the various other incarnations of "the anti-democratic party."[28] Still more important, Illinois Democrats themselves increasingly adopted full-blown, Van Burenesque historical arguments for the constitutional partyist view of politics.

The Democrats unofficially kicked off the campaigns of 1840 at their Eighth of January celebration at the state capital in 1839.[29] There, several prominent Democrats provided the keynote for the campaigns by invoking the historical crimes of the Federalists as the model and source of the behavior of the Whigs. To future senator Samuel McRoberts, as to Van Buren, the original parties of the 1790s had been organized for and against the principle of popular government—in other words, for and against the Constitution:

> It was reserved for the genius of Alexander Hamilton . . . to devise a plan by which the people would be gradually deprived of political power, and by which it would be imperceptibly placed in other hands. . . . Great corporations, commencing with a National Bank, were the instruments devised. The power of these *moneyed* and *political* institutions were necessarily placed in the hands of the *few*, and by their management the government [over] the many—the people—was to be achieved. . . . [This power] had been refused by the men who framed the Government. And its establishment afterwards in defiance of the constitution, shows you how illegitimate power may secretly steal into the world.
>
> It was with the power of Banks and chartered monopolies, that the advocates of an unlimited construction of the constitution sought to govern the country.

Thus did McRoberts unambiguously explain that the objection to banks and corporations was above all constitutional. "It is their strides for *political* power that is most remarkable. . . . Some of them appear determined up to this day, to connect Banks with the *political* power of the Government, peaceably if they can, or forcibly if they must," thus violating the principle of the "separation of bank and state" as the Democrats liked to say. McRoberts concluded with a concrete example of the inevitable consequences: the recent unseating of democratically elected state representatives in Pennsylvania, enforced by military power under the command of the Bank-controlled governor of that state. He concluded, "All the predictions of the Hero of New Orleans, and of Col. Benton, as to what might be apprehended from that dangerous institution are already realized."

John McClernand too described the current "tide of Bank influence" as a familiar phenomenon. "The same influences are now perpetually at work, which originated the alien and sedition laws; which during the late war denounced 'Democracy as a syren voice, sanctioned only by demagogues and traitors.'" While the Independent Treasury was manifestly sound, popular, and constitutional, he argued, "The Monopolists support the union of Bank and State, because its tendency is to render the Government and its revenues subsidiary to their ambition and cupidity. The question then becomes one between the Banks and the people—whether shall the people or the Banks govern; whether shall equal or exclusive rights prevail."

The same constitutional question which had originally distinguished Federalists from Republicans now distinguished Whigs from Democrats. And even in the middle of a depression, questions concerning banks and currency were elements of the constitutional conflict more than matters for economic debate, because politicians conceived of prosperity and opportunity as products of a proper constitution as much as a proper economic theory.

The party understood abolitionism, a secondary target of the speeches, in the same way. According to Orlando Ficklin, once the "consolidation party" failed in the constitutional convention to establish a government of unlimited power, it turned to "a latitudinous construction of the constitution of the United States, to break down the great barriers contained in that sacred charter of our rights." By such means were the anticonstitutional and anti-democratic Alien and Sedition Acts passed under John Adams, and by such means might modern abolitionism achieve its ends: "Gentlemen, in the latter days, the same party with the son of the elder Adams at its head, is lead on to a conflict more ruinous in its consequences than those emanating from the passage of the 'alien and sedition laws.' Need I say to you that Abolitionism finds no advocate except amongst the broad constructionists—those who believe that the Congress of the United States is omnipotent, and has no check but its own discretion."

Abolitionism and bankism might be bad enough in their own rights, but to the Democrats of 1839 their chief danger was that they threatened to establish the principles of loose constitutional construction and unchecked congressional rule at the expense of state sovereignty. Should either or both policies triumph, their principles would sanction not only a paper economy and the reckless liberation of the slaves but any similarly anticonstitutional measure that a federal, congressional elite might be induced to support by a corporate aristocracy. Such a consolidated constitution, substituted for the historical Constitution, would constitute a permanent triumph for the centralized, interlocking "aristocracy of wealth" over the democracies of the states.

Later in the year, Democrats held county meetings in preparation for the Democratic state convention in December. These meetings' resolutions were not quite the faithful outlines of constitutional partyist history that the Eighth of January addresses were. They were consistent with partyist history and often explicitly invoked it, but they also focused more on state affairs and current economic issues. Even here, though, the resolutions generally confirmed the constitutional character of the elections by connecting current events to partyist history or to the preservation of the democratic Constitution.

A convention might begin with a justification of public assembly as a popular right and continue with a brief but orthodox account of partyist history. Then, generally, it would present the Independent Treasury, the "Gag Bill" (which would restrict the political speech of officeholders), the Illinois secretary of state case, and other issues as constitutional questions. Finally, it might call for repeal of the duty on salt and for scaling back the state internal improvement system. These last two were usually argued in frankly economic terms, but they occasionally emerged as constitutional issues as well.

The Fayette County meeting[30] began with an address by W. L. D. Ewing, aimed at showing the "intimate connection of the Whigs of the present day with the Federalists of '98 and 1812." Its resolutions celebrated the Independent Treasury as "the only constitutional mode of keeping and disbursing the public revenue," while they condemned the creation of a National Bank as "a palpable violation of the spirit and intent of the Constitution." In addition, the "connection of Bank and State," now referring to the pet banks as much as to a national bank, had caused repeated, artificial fluctuations in the currency.

Moving to another constitutional issue, the meeting attacked the Illinois senate for denying Governor Carlin the right to name a secretary of state until the previous secretary, Alexander Field, had resigned. The Democrats saw this as an "encroach[ment] on the prerogative of a co-ordinate branch of Government." And they saw the state supreme court's upholding of Field's right to the office as "engrafting upon our institutions the principle of life-office," a Federalist principle contrary to the common sense and common practice of every state in the Union. Finally, the convention turned to the "Gag Bill," the Whig proposal in Congress to limit the political activities of officeholders: "*Resolved*, that the Gag Bill, depriving certain officers of the right of speech . . . is unjust, tyrannical, and unconstitutional . . . undermining the very foundation which sustains the glorious superstructure of our Democratic Government."

The meeting adopted these resolutions unanimously, as well as several others offered from the floor. Included were calls for repeal of the salt tax and for modification of the internal improvements system to relieve the economic burdens of the citizenry. The resolutions also advocated an investigation of the

State Bank for alleged charter violations and the limiting of judicial offices to a definite term. The resolutions of this convention, like those of most others, were a mixture of the uncomplicated policy preferences of the moment and an abiding concern for the vitality of the Constitution.

Madison County's Democratic resolutions were even more explicitly constitutional.[31] The preamble began with a declaration of the people's duty to gather in "public assemblies" to evaluate the performance of public servants, and the authors clung to the formulation that this convention was a meeting of the people, choosing not to use explicitly partisan language. They embraced the principles of the nine Democratic administrations since 1801 and contrasted them with the "principles and policy of the Federal party as set forth by the speeches and votes of its members in the convention that formed our excellent Constitution." Originating in the conflict between aristocracy and democracy in the Constitutional Convention itself, those principles also infused the administrations of the two Adamses and all of the activities of the anti-Democratic opposition since 1801.

Having established the constitutional partyist historical context in the preamble, the resolutions characterized the principles of the Van Buren administration as those that had been "repeatedly and triumphantly sanctioned by large majorities of the people." They endorsed the Independent Treasury on grounds of economic stability and the public's constitutional right to equality in receiving the favors of the federal government. They deemed a prospective national bank both unconstitutional and unwise for several reasons: because it would be owned by foreigners in large degree; because it would drain the nation's specie; because it would interfere in elections as the old Bank had; because its resources would render it beyond the control of law; and because it could destroy state banks, created by the people's representatives, and thus override democratic decisionmaking. Likewise, "incorporations for the public good," generally, were deemed beyond the effective control of law because the individuals involved were released from personal responsibility for the corporation's actions. In summing up, the authors compared their forefathers' flight from old world aristocracy with their own battle against "the aristocracy and despotism of incorporations . . . which are more soulless, more degrading and more injurious in their effects than that of hereditary birth."

Marshall County Democrats justified themselves by observing that the Whigs had already organized and thus left the Democrats no choice. Therefore, they would "support the constitution and laws with all the energy of freemen" against the attacks of "the federalists." Virtually all the resolutions brought the Constitution into the argument. The state supreme court's sustaining of Field in office, for example, was "in accordance with the principles of monarchists and aristocrats, who incessantly revile, and would destroy the constitutional government of our country." Even the salt tax resolution took on constitutional character in Marshall. The meeting resolved that the tax sustained a salt monopoly, which was "a violation of equal rights, and repugnant to the constitution."[32]

Clark County's resolutions consisted almost wholly in outlining constitutional partyism: "We entertain no doubt but that the great contest in 1840, will be characterised by the very same principles, and contested upon the same ground, which separated the republican from the federal party in the year 1798 and 1800." They identified the Whigs with "bank monopolies, exclusive privileges," nativism akin to the "*damned* but famous alien law of John Adams," a gag law "more odious than the sedition law of 1798," and a "latitudinarian construction of the constitution." "On the other hand the democratic Republican party are now as they were in 1798 and 1800, contending for the rights of the people and the States, for a strict construction of the constitution, and are opposed to the exercise of doubtful power." Under these principles, the Democrats were opposed to monopolies and especially a national bank, which had been "the principal author of the panics and disorganization" of the economy. And they favored the Independent Treasury because it would democratically entrust care of the public money "to those only, who are made directly responsible to the people." The meeting concluded by resolving that "we fully approve the holding of primary conventions among the people as the only effectual mode of organizing the Democratic Republican party."[33]

County after county held its Democratic convention,[34] and nearly all of them placed the issues generally in the frame of constitutional partyist history. Still, these local meetings did not attempt the relatively full historical analysis that Van Buren and the Illinois state convention would. In their brief resolutions, they stopped short of the full explication of the self-reinforcing process by which the elite's measures legitimated the elite's constitutionalism and vice versa. In the address of the December state convention, democrats would read the full story of how the aristocrats sought, in effect, to seduce them with legislative bribes until clouds of dependency obscured their view of the democratic Constitution altogether.

The top Democratic leadership understood that, to justify partyism to the electorate, party had to be convincingly separated from the idea of faction, with which the antipartyists naturally linked it. To that end, partyism had to make clear its own antipartyist origins in the original war against a federal, loose-constructionist, banking aristocracy.

The policy focus of the 1839 state convention's address was the Independent Treasury, because it was an excellent vehicle for party leaders' linking of immediate policy to abiding constitutionalism. It was the vehicle for training the viscerally antiparty electorate in a principled understanding of party. For Democrats its main virtue was that, constitutionally, it was the exact opposite of the Bank destroyed by Jackson. That is, it was the "expressly delegated"— strict-constructionist—means of managing the government's money and thus was a product of the democracy. A national bank, on the other hand, while being as risky for the economy as the Independent Treasury was safe, was dangerous mainly for the constitutional reason suggested above: its creation required loose construction of the Constitution and thus sanctioned an unchecked elitism, the assumption by Congress of authority to make whatever policy was deemed "necessary and proper," rather than strictly binding federal politicians to those powers expressly delegated to them.

The address began with the Van Burenite history of the origins of parties. Establishing first that the original parties were opposed on the most fundamental grounds, the address went on to make the case that, from that day to its own, the anti-democrats had sought to enact not just unconstitutional policies but anticonstitutional policies, measures whose main purpose was to institutionalize an aristocratic interpretation of the Constitution. In their constant promotion of "*political distinctions* among men," the "opponents of our republican institutions" repeatedly ran into the stout resistance of "the great body of our republican countrymen." Consequently, "the leaders of the federal party attempted to effect, by indirection, by a latitudinarian construction of the Constitution, that which they had failed in obtaining the power to do directly." The proof lay in Alexander Hamilton's most famous achievements— the funding system, the national bank, a protective tariff—as well as Federalist incorporation laws and the Alien and Sedition Acts. These were bad policy in themselves, but, more importantly, they were wholly illegitimate, because their very purpose was to destroy the nation's democratic political structure as outlined by the Constitution. They were intended to establish the discretionary power of an elite, resting on social dependency, rather than the discretely delegated power of the mass, resting on social equality:

The whole of this is contrary to the genius of a government of limited powers. If Congress may do whatever it deems expedient for the general welfare, and without reference to the express grants of power in the Constitution, then its powers are absolutely unlimited, and the Government a despotism. It is *these artificial systems* that were resorted to, for the purpose of creating the very distinctions in society, which federalism has ever been intent in establishing. They could not obtain a recognition in the Constitution to their creed, to wit: that *the few should be provided for at the expense of the many*, that the *few* were the *rich* and the *well-born*, and the *many consisted of the mass of the people*; that *Government should be founded upon property*, and that *offices should be created for life*, but they attempted to produce those distinctions, and inequalities in the relative condition of the community by the creation of monopolies, the most dangerous and oppressive of which, was the Bank of the United States.

It was by these means, that the great charter of American liberty was in danger of being annihilated by construction.

The now familiar class distinctions of market society are those "artificial distinctions" created by incorporation that the Democrats apprehended. These distinctions are today accepted or even celebrated by most people as normal or even indispensable characteristics of modern, capitalist democracies. Few now argue that Americans live in a literal aristocracy by the very fact of their embracing the special corporate privileges at the heart of the economy. But Democratic leaders of the 1830s saw in corporate organization an issue only incidentally economic. Incorporation, to them, was a political and constitutional problem. It was a device for re-creating a literally aristocratic polity by first creating "distinctions in society" every bit as stable, clear, and controlling as the hereditary lines which legitimated aristocratic power in traditional states. Democrats were not generally opposed to success in the market; they were opposed to a systematic, anticonstitutional partiality of the central government that, worse than making some persons undeservedly rich, tended to re-create an aristocratic polity of fixed social, economic, and political dependencies. Without such anticonstitutional government action, the society of independence would endure; with it, the counter-Revolutionary essentials of traditional aristocracy would be restored.[35]

To Democrats, strict construction of the Constitution and preservation of popular sovereignty through party organization were mutually reinforcing. The written Constitution was a carefully limited grant of power by the democracy to a potentially aristocratic engine amid the naturally democratic polities of the states. Popular sovereignty called for the majoritarian unity of independent white men, protected by their majoritarianism against the minoritarian attractions of aristocratic dependency, wealth, and power. And such a vision of self-government might be preserved as long as the written Constitution's protective devices, especially states' rights, remained intact. Consequently, the federal government's systematic overconstruction of the written Constitution in the enactment of policy, weakening the democratic states, was virtually the only way that the nascent aristocracy could roll back the triumph of popular sovereignty.

Begun in 1787, according to this Democratic address, the battle continued in the 1830s. Jackson's "war" on the Second Bank of the United States, according to the state convention, was a war on a "*political engine*" (only secondarily an economic institution), which had the power "to create artificial distinctions in society; to build up an aristocracy founded upon wealth; to control the public press; to influence elections, and to destroy the equilibrium and the whole theory of our democratic government."[36] A Congress-created central bank carried the self-reinforcing dangers of legitimating loose construction and creating an economic aristocracy well placed to exploit the newly unlimited powers of the national government.

The Independent Treasury, however, did neither. The arguments for this measure were more negative than positive. Effective aristocracy, after all, could only rise in America by positive action of the government. After the address deflected all the Whig, antispoils arguments against the measure, the convention resolved simply that the Independent Treasury was "the only safe and constitutional plan yet suggested for keeping and disbursing the public revenue." No one tried to glorify the measure but only to contrast it with the anticonstitutional Bank and its vassal state banks. Together, amid natural plenty, these corporations had wrecked the economy by the uncontrolled "contraction and expansion of their loans, which have been chiefly managed with a view to political effect."[37]

The line of argument established in 1839 was adhered to throughout the following year. The *Belleville Advocate*, for example, published a correspondent's long, Van Burenite campaign piece[38] that had little to say about candidate Van Buren but plenty about the origins of the parties:

> The first eight years of [the government's] practical existence it was administered by men who were guided . . . by the axiom, "that Republican Governments derive their just powers from the consent of the governed," and that, therefore, no powers should be exercised by those administering the Government, except such as are expressly delegated in the Constitution; . . . and those who took this view received the name, as politicians, of DEMOCRATS. The succeeding four years, the Government was administered by men who contended for *discretionary* powers; . . . and, in consequence of their claiming this sovereignty in the Federal Constitution, they received the name, as politicians, of FEDERALISTS. This has been the line of division ever since.

Van Buren men, according to the writer, now took the position of the original Democrats, while Harrison men took "the opposite and aristocratic view that was then taken by the Federalists." Thus, while the nation was in some ways divided into numerous factions, there really were "but *two* contending political parties" then and now, and these were defined by their attachments to two wholly different constitutions.

This history, then, made the bearer of a Democratic regular nomination the only constitutionally democratic candidate. And the authenticity of Van Buren's nomination as the voice of the democracy was proven by the "fact, that the Democrats have had their township meetings, their county meetings, their State conventions, and finally their convention of delegates from each State at Baltimore, which nominated him." A voter, then, had only two practical choices. First, he could support the Democratic regular nomination, because it was the regular nomination of the nation's democratic polity, systematically organized for that sole purpose. In so doing, he would sustain the nation's antipartisan Constitution by means of party organization. To vote Whig, on the other hand, was to vote for whatever the federal elite deemed expedient at any moment, heedless of constitutional restrictions, according to the author, and regardless, especially, of states' rights—the constitutional bulwark of democracy.

The Democrats believed that the federal government's overriding of a states'-rights Constitution was the source of, as well as the goal of, anti-democratic power, whereas the true home of democracy was in the organic polities of the states. The minuscule numbers of aristocrats in each state could create no base of continuing aristocratic power unless through institutions distant from the people and separate from their state institutions; that is, only in a national government. And even there they could do so only if the Constitution's strict democratic limits on federal power were circumvented. The federal government, therefore, was the present and historical source of the constitutional party division.

Moreover, although aristocrats infected each state polity, stout resistance to federal loose-constructionism would eliminate aristocratic power not only in the federal government but within the states as well. Aristocrats were relatively helpless within the democratic states without the powers afforded by broad construction of a national constitution. Such powers had included, according to "St. Clair," the enactment of the Alien and Sedition Acts of 1798 and the passage of a protective tariff in 1828, the central acts of the only two Federalist administrations the nation had known. No state would have enacted these measures, which were designed to bolster the aristocracy. And the federal government could not have enacted them either if it had respected its own constitutional limits. Both of these actions were unconstitutional, he argued, and so unjust as to bring the nation to the brink of disunion and thus to the brink of destroying the world's only hope for self-government. They provoked the two most radical defenses of states' rights known to American history and would have eventuated in disunion "had not the Democracy at those critical periods gained an ascendancy." The result of "the Democracy's" regained ascendancy was repeal of the offending measures and restoration of the proper constitutional separation between central and state governments, by which the proper constitutional balance of parties, an overwhelming democracy against an isolated aristocracy, was also restored.[39] Here, St. Clair echoed Van Buren's own view that enforcement of the basic structures of the Constitution always had been and always must be achieved by the organized democracy's reassertion of itself, especially in presidential elections, not by judicial construction.[40]

In sum, the Democratic leaders sought to guide the voters in 1840 by an explication of the world-historical position they occupied. They offered a picture of a precarious democracy in the avant-garde of a history dominated by aristocracy and monarchy. The democratic character of the American Constitution was salvageable only if the democracy recognized the new forms that traditional aristocratic constitutionalism assumed in a society of independent men. If the American Constitution rested on the sovereignty of the state democracies, and on individual independence, according to the partyists, then aristocratic restorationism rested on a corporate, loose-constructionist anticonstitutionalism that re-created systematic social dependency and overrode the power of the states. And it was no coincidence that the enemies of the Constitution consistently condemned party while the defenders of popular sovereignty and states' rights relied always on the Constitution's indispensable institution, the democratic political party.

The Whig History of the Constitution and the Campaign of 1840

The Whigs, although not relying on a standard party history to the same degree as the Democrats, did present explicit historical answers to the Democratic version of American political development. These answers could be somewhat different in different hands: some ignored the existence of the Federalists altogether and began with the election of 1828; others included the Federalists so as to paint the Democrats as the true modern home of Federalist consolidationism; and so-called Conservatives often began only with the start of Van Buren's administration. But always the thrust of the interpretation was that a partyless and prosperous political order had been corrupted by the partyists. The latter had abused the federal government's power over the economy to substitute party for popular sovereignty and the Constitution.

With St. Clair County's local elections just concluded in the late summer of 1839, the editor of the Belleville *Great Western* warmed up for the coming presidential election with a retrospective of the years since Jackson's first election.[41] The "PRESENT DOMINANT PARTY," wrote the editor, had come into power on a promise to purify a political system polluted by the supposedly executive-consolidationist administration of Adams the younger, but Jackson was scarcely "warm in his seat" before his organ declared "a *universal proscription for opinion's* sake." Where the Democrats claimed to preserve each citizen's independence by preserving political equality against the broad-constructionist elitism of Federalism, the Whigs countered with a picture of the Democrats in which dependency was all. This dependency radiated out from the executive through legislators and officeholders to the rank-and-file adherents of the party. It was a dependency, nominally democratic, that in fact mirrored the executive-centered political structure of dependency that was the essence of monarchy.

Appointing congressmen to office as no president before him and in direct violation of his previously broadcast convictions, Jackson proved the accuracy of his own prediction that such a practice would make "*corruption . . . the order of the day.*" "The effect was soon manifested in the pliant disposition of a very large portion of his partisans in" Congress. The test of this pliancy and dependency came in Jackson's arbitrary decision to destroy the Bank. Washington and Madison had sanctioned this Bank. It had provided a sound currency to a prosperous nation. But Jackson took it upon himself to declare it unconstitutional. The editor expressed no distress that Jackson had thereby challenged the Supreme Court's *McCulloch* decision, which had found the Bank constitutional,[42] but only that he had changed the rules of political struggle by which such constitutional issues were normally settled.[43] The editor did not seem to disagree with Jackson's suggestion that "the people and the states" might control mere judicial precedent,[44] but politics must be properly constituted for such a function. Up to that time, whatever constitutional heresies were propagated, the people and their representatives were left free to combat them. But now, while the currency was being destroyed, "many a man was compelled by the force of party discipline, reluctantly to sanction the act." Opposition to the Bank had been an unpopular and largely unagitated position until this whim of the president. Still, the Bank would have been safe but for executive invasion of congressional consciences by party devices; that is, by appointment of congressmen to office and by proscription on a scale unknown to American government.

The origin of modern parties, in this account, was not in the 1790s but in the schemes of the 1820s and 1830s that had resulted in national economic collapse. The party division was not the reflection of an eternal, natural battle between constitutions but an artificial imposition, under the mere name of "Democracy," on a once partyless people. From the day when politicians introduced party into the legislative process, claimed the editor, "may we date the commencement of the innumerable inconveniences and hazards to which we have of late years been subjected, from the unsound and unsettled condition of the currency." The partyists' economic promises had proven baseless, while their unspoken constitutional goal—"to establish upon the ruins of a FREE, UNTRAMMELLED, Representative Government, an immense colossal power utterly unknown to the constitution"—had nearly been achieved. To this end, every post office, land office, and other outlet of government activity had become an "electioneering bureau" of the executive. Meanwhile, and not coincidentally, the expenditures of the government had tripled, and the various keepers of the revenues had practically reduced embezzlement to an art. The list lengthened, and in almost every case, the editor indicted "the party who rules the country" not for bad policy but for attacks on the American antipartisan constitutional order. Bad policy was merely one category of evidence used to convict the Democrats of a conspiracy "to consolidate the Government, to trample upon the rights of the States, to destroy individual independence, to prostrate political morals, and to rally around [Van Buren] a party dependent solely upon himself, and ready to obey his will as the supreme law." Consequently, Whig principles for 1840, as listed by this editor, were almost entirely constitutional: the preservation of self-government by restraining the three branches of government within their constitutionally defined spheres; popular sovereignty; "elevation" of the people by education and the raising of moral standards; opposition to officers' interference in elections; retention of public money by Congress or its accountable designate; restoration of the country's former peace and moral condition; destruction of the "monster" that was "party" or at least a mitigation of "the violence of party spirit"; restoration of "mutual confidence and good feeling"; and an end to officeholders' embezzlements. In the presence of such a restored constitutional and moral order, good policy, which the editor left largely undefined, would presumably follow all but automatically.

Between this editor in the southern half of the state and a correspondent of the *Chicago American* in the north there was general agreement about the origins of parties, although the latter was more inclined to ignore Jackson's role. The self-styled "Seventy-Six" set out to rebut the central claim of the Democratic state convention, "that the Whig [party] is the federal bank party."[45] First, Seventy-Six noted the Democrats' charge of Federalist and Whig opposition to "the freedom of elections." He retorted that the Whigs now had a bill before Congress to restrict the campaign manipulations of federal officers but that the Van Burenites opposed it. In fact, "Executive officers are supported and encouraged by [Van Buren], in the commission of acts at elections, which would have been considered by Jefferson or Jackson as good cause for removal. By this test, let every candid man answer—which is the federalist?"

Similarly, the correspondent agreed that the founding of the government on property and the creation of artificial distinctions in society were Federalist notions. But it was Van Buren who had formerly advocated property qualifications for voting in New York, qualifications that would allegedly have disfranchised the likes of William Henry Harrison himself. And it was Van Buren whose aristocratic wealth and bearing so contrasted with the democratic plainness of Harrison's life.

The Democratic address charged Federalism above all with harboring the "principles of 'a strong executive government' and 'a broad construction of the constitution.'" Seventy-Six rebelled against the implication that such principles were now Whiggish rather than Democratic. If the test of a real democrat is resistance to consolidation,

> then what is Martin Van Buren, when he is endeavoring to place the whole control of the currency of the country not only in the hands of the General Government, but in those of the executive? We see, too, that the Tennessee Legislature, true to the principles of federalism, has had the audacity to instruct that State's U.S. Senators to bow in implicit obedience to the will of the National Executive—thus taking the honor and interests of that State from those men to whom she had intrusted them, and placing them entirely in the hands of the General Government—yes, of *Martin Van Buren!*

By the devices of party, then, Van Burenism consolidated the power of the federal government into the executive branch and simultaneously induced the states to yield their independence to that branch in the name of Democratic party unity. The ideology of partyism was nothing more than a justification for general dependency on a neo-Walpolean, consolidated executive, above checks and balances, above separation of powers, above states' rights.

If Seventy-Six had now satisfied himself that the Democratic party under Van Buren was constitutionally Federalist, it was a small matter to conclude his announced project of painting Democrats as bank men as well. He affirmed that Whigs were in favor of banks when chartered with proper restrictions, but he accused the Democrats of having created the vast majority of the nation's banks and of having sanctioned by legislative action nearly all of their abuses: "Now which is the federal party?"

"An Old Jackson Man," meanwhile, filled in the voters of the central part of the state through the *Sangamo Journal*. Where the *Great Western* had emphasized the continuous train of abuses under Jackson and Van Buren, and where Seventy-Six had skipped over Jackson's administration in identifying the Van Buren administration with old Federalism, this correspondent tried to vindicate Jackson and paint Van Buren as an anti-democratic mole in the Jackson administration. Among many revered Jacksonian principles, he specified the single presidential term as one on which "in my humble opinion, depends the permanency of our free government." He acknowledged that Jackson violated this principle but insisted he was moved to do so only "by the Van Buren faction by which he was entirely surrounded." The faction sought the additional four years to complete their buying up of the nation's newspaper editors and influential men with federal patronage, while they assured Jackson that his reelection was necessary to the internal peace of the nation.[46]

Where Jackson had sincerely condemned electioneering by officeholders, Van Buren was transparently hypocritical: "Look at the list of Van Buren Conventions held throughout the State[;] in all of them you find the Registers and Receivers of Land Offices the prominent members of all such conventions dictating to the people who they shall vote for." And where Jackson had had at least one public defaulter tried and convicted, Van Buren had regularly ignored defaulting officers rather than have his "partizans" exposed.[47]

The campaign of 1840 was a contest of histories. These Whig histories varied in some of their particulars, but, like the Democratic histories, they had a consistent constitutional focus. They detected a Democratic manipulation of economic policy and spoils to create an executive party. Such a party would permanently deprive both the sovereign states and the individual voters of the independence necessary for democracy. But persuasive historical interpretation was not enough to win the election. As the Democrats knew, so the Whigs learned that opponents of party required nothing so much as organization to defeat organization.

Whig Organization: The Antiparty
Party of the Independent

In yet another Whig twist on constitutional history, the editor of the *Journal* adopted an element of Democratic argument. Late in the campaign, he affirmed that amid all the windings of the post-Revolutionary generations, exactly two parties of principle had contested the constitutional terrain, although he characterized these parties very differently from the Democratic version. He no more accepted the constitutional legitimacy of his opponents than they acknowledged the Whigs'. But, when faced with a rigidly organized party opponent, the only way to defend the Constitution was to accept a measure of organization and vote a straight Whig ticket.[48]

The obvious paradox for the Whigs—the necessity of partyism to defeat partyism—would contribute mightily to the ultimate entrenchment of the party system, but it did not always seem a paradox to them. Like the Democrats, they conceived of their party as a polity[49] and the opposition's as a faction. Theirs was a polity committed to open-ended debate, in contrast to the Democrats' efforts to foreclose conscience-driven political action with conventions, spoils, and partyism. As of 1840, the Whigs' continuing aspiration was to integrate their own increasing use of conventions and patronage, the very stuff of partyist corruption, into a theory of political action that nevertheless rejected party in the sense of compromising individual conscience.

In 1839, the Whigs held their first national convention and their first Illinois state convention. Under fire from the Democrats for hypocrisy, the Whigs would distinguish their conventions and partyism from the Democratic versions by insisting that Whig organization left Whigs free to vote by their consciences rather than by party discipline.

A Whig meeting at the close of the General Assembly in March 1839 set the ball rolling. Predictably, it characterized itself not as a Whig meeting but as a gathering of the opponents of Van Buren, a more expansive designation that reflected the Whigs' self-image as "the people" mobilized in opposition to "the party." It indicted the Van Buren administration for incurring a new national debt to pay the salaries of officeholders and for absorbing, rather than investigating, the multitude of defalcations by spoilsmen. It therefore urged unity and expressed confidence in the ability of the "Great Whig and Conservative parties" to present a candidate behind which all opponents of executive corruption could unite. It mentioned no other issues and assumed no authority as a party agency but only "earnestly recommend[ed]" to sympathetic citizens that they "sacrifice upon the altar of their country's good, all prejudices and predilections for or against particular individuals—to come to the rescue of the nation—to do battle for principles and not men—and to unite with us in supporting for the presidency, the man who shall be presented as the opposing candidate to Martin Van Buren."[50]

The tone of the Whig campaign was set. It was to be a far more widely organized campaign than previously, but it was to remain preeminently an antipartyist movement. Its organization derived not from any positive theory of organization but, supposedly, from popular voluntarism. The Whigs relied on individual, independent consciences to recognize the exigencies of the campaign and sacrifice minor preferences for the sake of the great constitutional principle within which lesser desires might be pursued.

In June, the *American* expressed the Whigs' continuing reluctance to think of themselves as a party even as Whig county meetings organized to choose state convention delegates. The editor condemned the sentiment in Thomas Hart Benton's famous call, endlessly reprinted by Democratic papers, to sacrifice everything for the good of "the party" and nothing for men. Instead, said the editor, the patriot should be stirred by the refrain, "*Everything for the country, nothing for men.*" He presented this slogan as the true Whig sentiment that would unite all patriots behind either Clay or Harrison, whoever was nominated at the national convention: "As between either of these two candidates and Martin Van Buren, who that calls himself a friend to his country can for a moment hesitate?"

The editor's insistence that the Whigs looked not to party but to country was linked more than casually with his claim, common to all Illinois sources in 1839, that Clay and Harrison were the only possible nominees. The March meeting and the summer's county conventions, like this editor, all pledged themselves to support the national nominee before the fact. Such a pledge might seem an abandonment of traditional antipartyism since it was, on its face, a submission to party authority. But the pledge was easily justified under the immediate circumstances of 1839, since it was not taken blindly but on the assumption that the race was to be between Van Buren and either Harrison or Clay.[51] In that circumstance, a prior pledge of support was not a sacrifice of independence to party, not a blind commitment to others' judgments, but a fully informed, patriotic declaration that either man would be a true champion of Whig constitutionalism. Either man might be sacrificed for the other without loss of the pledger's individual independence or of the great antipartisan principle at stake in the election.

While most county meetings left this sentiment implicit in their promise of support for the nominee, the Tazewell County Whigs, at least, made the obvious explicit: "*Resolved.* That while we have our individual preferences in relation to the candidates already named . . . we feel willing to sacrifice those preferences for the sake of HARMONY, believing that the great principles for which we are contending would not be endangered in the event of an election of either of the whig candidates, and feeling that it is far more important to contend for principles than for men."[52] And the Whig state convention itself, rather than endorsing a nameless nominee-to-be, pledged itself explicitly to Clay or Harrison as the convention might choose.[53]

All the above themes and developments—the centrality of the Independent Treasury, its status as a constitutional rather than economic issue, the Whig understanding of their conventions as expediential and voluntaristic rather than impelled by an organizational ethic, the Whigs' explicit antipartyism even while forced to organize in a crisis, the crucial assumption that Harrison and Clay were the only possible presidential nominees, the Whig self-image as the embodiment of country rather than party—all of these, in varying combinations, were reflected in the resolutions of the county conventions that chose delegates to the state convention.

Warren County, for example, emphasized not the economic disutility but the unconstitutionality of executive policies:

> 4. Resolved, That the encroachments of the Federal Executive on the other powers and departments of the government, are such as justly to create alarm in the minds of those who are, and who profess to be, devoted to the federal constitution—First, in removing worthy men from office and appointing less worthy in their stead.—2d, In the abuse of the veto power, by which the manifest will of the representatives has been defeated.—3d, By removing the public money from the vaults of the Bank of the U.S. (where they were safely kept by the authority of Congress) and depositing them in pet banks of his own selection.—4th, In persisting, in defiance of the will of the people, in congress expressed, in the adoption of the sub-treasury scheme—thus placing the whole monies of the whole nation in his hands.[54]

Similarly, Marshall County justified Whig organization by explaining how partyists had manipulated public policy to vitiate the Constitution:

> 2. *Resolved* . . . that we firmly believe that [the administration has] introduced new and dangerous principles—that the constitution has been grossly violated, and the known and oft expressed opinions of the majority of the people disregarded and contemned—the great agricultural, mercantile and manufacturing interests of the country, trodden down—the currency and finances in a state of inextricable confusion and derangement, and the money of the people employed to reward unprincipled partizans or "Swartwouted" away by Locomotive Sub-Treasurers, from whom the only qualification sought or required, was servile submission to the dominant party.
>
> 3. *Resolved*, That the repeated and persevering efforts made by those now in power to unite the *purse* and the *sword*—to augment the executive power and patronage, and to reward or punish for "opinions sake," clearly demonstrates, that, in the hands of the present profligate and corrupt administration, our system of government is rapidly tending towards an elective monarchy.[55]

Monroe County reinforced the rhetoric of royal despotism in claiming that the Subtreasury would so extend the executive's "already immense patronage" that "the people might in vain endeavor to displace him—surrounded as he is by his myriads of retainers who are dependent alone upon him for their sustenance."[56] Clinton County called on "all opponents of the present dynasty" to unite on one man to oppose the "present party incumbent."[57]

The Sangamon County meeting, like so many others, believed that organization of a national convention resting on "primary meetings" would be "expedient and proper" under the circumstances.[58] The conventions were not manifestations of principle in themselves but merely devices for the more efficient enactment of principle. "Expedient" was the word used to self-describe convention after convention among the Whigs. Democrats understood loyalty to convention nominations as a central principle of democracy. Whig conventions only cited the practical lessons of recent experience in urging the ad hoc necessity of a convention nomination and the sacrifice of "caprices and minor differences of opinion" for the triumph of antipartyist constitutionalism.[59]

The St. Clair County anti–Van Buren convention, however, added to the usual resolutions a vow not to support anyone for state or national representative who was a supporter of Van Buren.[60] A number of other Whig conventions did the same, and Democrats seized on this resolution specially to indict the Whigs for the partyism they claimed to oppose. But the Whigs emphasized the difference between refusing to vote for Van Burenites and committing to vote for anyone else in particular. In Whig theory, Van Buren's purpose was to reduce legislatures, national and state, to mere tendrils of the executive branch by means of patronage. A Whig vow not to support those legislative candidates who would assist their own subsumption into the federal executive was not a vow of blind party loyalty but a declaration of independence from party slavery. In theory, Whig success would not mean the success of mere party candidates but of candidates who would defend the very constitutional independence of the legislatures.

Throughout the preparations for the first ever Whig state convention, the Whigs insisted that the whole point of their activity was opposition to party, opposition to the crypto-monarchical, patronage-driven constitution that Van Burenite measures proved was the true end of partyism. Urging peace between Clay men and Harrison men just before the state convention, the *Great Western* crammed almost all the central Whig contentions into just two sentences of concentrated, post-Walpolean, pre-modern, states'-rights, constitutional antipartyism: It advocated hostility only to "that great MAMMOTH POWER by which the President seeks to prostrate the rights of the states by destroying the independence of the people—against that *obedient* and *slavish* system of party tyranny which compels men to violate their consciences, and by which the President aims to establish a PRACTICAL MONARCHY through the instrumentality of *modern democracy*. . . . We care not who the Opposition may select as the instrument of bringing about a REFORM in the administration of our Government, so that the present corrupt and unfaithful dynasty be displaced, and our beloved country rescued from the hands of the spoilers."[61]

When the convention finally came off, the same editor celebrated it as the first "Democratic Whig" state convention in Illinois and eagerly differentiated it from Democratic conventions: "It was not a *packed* convention of *office-holders*, and expectants." Rather, it was a collection of patriots seeking "the perpetuation of our *original* system of Government."[62]

The first business of the convention was to name a state central committee, authorized to name subcommittees in every county for the general organization of the party. Next, five candidates for presidential elector were nominated to be "recommended to the voters of this state." Resolutions followed, which faithfully echoed those of the various county conventions: the convention supported either Clay or Harrison as the national convention might choose; it pictured the Van Buren administration, exemplified by the Subtreasury, as a spoils-driven machine for the establishment of an *"Elective Monarchy"*; it briefly addressed state affairs; and, finally, it claimed a latent anti–Van Buren majority, needing only organization to succeed, and urged that "to effect this desirable organization, the whig party in this State, and throughout the Union, must merge all personal predilections, all local questions and all minor differences of opinion, in consideration of the general weal."[63]

The Democrats, of course, did not let all this activity just slide by. As Whigs organized, the *State Register* repeatedly reminded them of their supposed opposition to party organization and refused to acknowledge that their partyism could somehow be antipartyist. In March the editor had indicted Whig legislators for participating in a "federal convention" after having been elected to represent Democratic counties on the strength of their *"no-party* professions."[64] In October, he ridiculed the state Whig party for holding "one of those much abused conventions."[65] When news of Harrison's selection arrived in December, he insisted that the candidate had been "regularly nominated" by the Whigs.[66] The following February, he announced his discovery of the Whig central committee's secret circular, hypocritically outlining a plan for an unprecedentedly thorough organization of the entire state.[67] Similarly, the Shawnee-town *Western Voice* asked,

> Who opposed Mr. Van Buren [in 1836] because he was the nominee of a convention? The Whigs.
>
> Who support General Harrison because he is the nominee of a convention? The Whigs. . . .

Who in 1837 denounced conventions as dangerous to the Republic, "conventions of craft and cunning"? Whigs!!

Who in 1839 obsequiously take the yoke imposed by a convention? Whigs!![68]

In the face of these accusations, the Whigs were able to press unhesitatingly forward because they had a well developed defense of their organization as qualitatively different from the Democrats'; it was a temporary, voluntaristic, antiparty party of last resort. Thus the party nominations of the national convention arrived soaked in antiparty rhetoric. For example, the *American* hoisted Harrison and Tyler with four principles attached that historians have often thought next to meaningless but which expressed for Whigs the all-important necessity of constitutional antipartyism.[69] These principles were the single presidential term, the integrity of the public servants, the safety of the public money, and the general good of the people. As vapid a collection of principles as any cynic might want to find, these planks nevertheless resonated with meaning for any Whig. They evoked the necessity of removing presidential temptations to party-building and returning to qualifications of merit alone for public appointees, the natural result of which would be the general welfare and the safety of public funds from partisan plunderers. For anyone to whom this was not obvious, the *American* printed the address of Philip Barbour on taking the presidential chair at the national convention, an address which saw not emptiness but constitutional crisis in the current battle of principles:

Truly we are in the midst of a revolution. . . . Those conservative walls erected by our forefathers to protect and restrain the different branches of the government, have been already trampled down by the foot of power, and we find the executive placing itself above the legislative and judicial branches, until the chief officer of the nation has become the mere head of a party, and places are conferred as rewards of party services, which formerly were given as rewards of merit.[70]

As the new year began, the *Journal* offered ten reasons to vote for Harrison, including seven that were essentially constitutional. Only one, a reminder that Harrison was the supposed father of the liberal public land system, touched a question of policy.[71] Amid all the antipartyism, the Whig papers felt perfectly comfortable and consistent in urging "the one thing essential to success— *organization*." They were comfortable because Whig organization would yield more than a "mere *party triumph*,"[72] because voluntarism was so unlike the Democratic organization's reliance on the new-fangled, pseudo-democratic ethic of party authority.

Conclusion

In *Political Parties and Constitutional Government*, Sidney Milkis writes, "By the 1830s, Jacksonians were defending political parties, indeed, a party *system*, as constitutional doctrine."[73] For reasons already indicated, I reject Milkis's use of "party *system*" to describe what the partyists were after. That term, with its implication that the partyists embraced a division of "the democracy" into parties, not only reads a modern model of party competition too far back in time, but obscures the precise "constitutional doctrine" that Van Buren and the partyists identified with party organization: the active sovereignty of the democracy as a whole. By this doctrine, the partyists meant not just party competition's facilitation or encouragement of broad popular participation. They meant the institutional embodiment of the sovereign people for active governance, something only the Democratic party could provide. That said, Milkis is right to paint Van Buren's project as an effort to correct the Madisonian Constitution's "inadequate regard for self-government" and vulnerability to "the centralizing ambitions" of men like Hamilton.[74] Understanding localism (states' rights) and a genuinely active people as mutually indispensable and as central to the Constitution itself, Van Buren and the partyists saw party as the institution, or the "constitutional doctrine," without which the Constitution's promise of true self-government lay unfulfilled.[75]

The campaign of 1840, however, did not entrench Van Buren's doctrine of party sovereignty. Rather, it institutionalized a continuing struggle over the meaning of popular sovereignty. In time, the *practice* of two-party competition would yield a *theory* that made two-party competition a defining element of popular sovereignty, but only after the founding theories of Whigs and Democrats had slowly self-destructed. To historians, the Second Party System has signified the institutionalization of legitimate opposition and thus the final eclipse of the Madisonian Constitution as a "constitution against parties."[76] To the participants, however, an opposition party represented not a legitimate, alternative policy direction but a structural threat to the people's rightful hold on power. Most Illinoisans had long since forgotten and abandoned the founders' elitism in favor of a frank egalitarianism and, for most, a commitment to states' rights reminiscent of the Anti-Federalists. Yet these democrats of both parties still embraced the original constitutional imperative of faction-free governance, even if the two parties had very different notions of how faction-free popular sovereignty was to be constructed as a practice.

The principles that drove the campaign of 1840 made that election the climax—but not the conclusion—of the great constitutional conflict that ultimately yielded what we call the party system. To its participants, and to their political heirs, it was arguably the gravest election since 1800. The Whig fear of a spoils-based, anticonstitutional government by executive party was matched by the Democratic fear of a corporation-based, anticonstitutional government by an unchecked federal aristocracy. Each party posed as a defender of the state's and the common citizen's independence against an anticonstitutional structure of dependency supposedly advocated by the other. But where Whigs found personal independence and liberation in political atomization, Democrats found it in mechanisms that would bind each individual to the majority will rather than allow the atomized conscience to drift into dependency on a neo-aristocracy.

In contrast to the modern model of democracy by "party system," these combatants saw themselves not as competitors within a democratic consensus but as champions of fundamentally different constitutions or, what was the same thing, fundamentally different constructions of the federal Constitution itself. Each party insisted that it stood for localist self-government, and each understood that the only way to establish the abiding *meaning* of popular sovereignty was through the actual *exercise* of popular sovereignty—certainly not by resort to the judiciary. For all this apparent agreement, however, the two sides' stark disagreement on the relationship between party and the Constitution made clear that they differed not just on public policy but on the very nature of constitutional self-government.

Four years of open warfare between these irreconcilable constitutionalisms had now forced unprecedented political organization on Illinois. The election would offer an undiluted, mass two-party contest between Van Buren and Harrison.[77] In retrospect, the greatest significance of that fact may lie in its de facto establishment of a two-party model of democratic politics. In prospect, however, the significance of 1840 was in providing the first clear test of strength between two sets of constitutional principles—two models of popular sovereignty, two histories of America's first half-century under the Constitution—that ultimately made the emergence of the "party system" possible. The right to interpret the American Constitution as well as the history of its construction and reconstruction was the chief prize of the campaign, and, in 1840, the interpretations offered by each side still read the other out of democratic, constitutional legitimacy.

CHAPTER EIGHT

The Elections of 1839–1840: Popular Sovereignty?

I

f the Madisonian Constitution was founded on popular sovereignty, yet premised on a generally "absent People,"[1] Jeffersonian and Jacksonian politics remade the Constitution on the premise of an active, sovereign "People." The necessity of an active sovereign was especially the doctrine of the partyists, but the ascendancy of egalitarian ideology, the readiness of politicians to identify threats to popular freedom,[2] and the great frequency of elections,[3] meant that even the relatively conservative Whigs could not be far behind.[4] The Democratic party was, then, self-consciously designed to activate the sovereign people permanently and constantly, ever watchful for the ever present threat of aristocracy. The Whigs, on the other hand, reacting to the Democratic threat, sought originally to activate the sovereign only in the rare moments of crisis when, as one Whig ideologue put it, the forces of "Prerogative" dared challenge the people's "Privilege."[5] But the organized competition between the two parties had the effect of keeping the people mobilized in unprecedented numbers year after year.[6] Observing the phenomenal activity of the people in the campaigns of 1840, Van Buren could believe that he had succeeded in using party to engage the sometimes absent sovereign in a reconstruction of the Constitution. And that was true even though, once the ballots of 1840 were counted, the process of constitutional reconstruction had brought with it his own electoral defeat.

Local elections in 1839 remained fairly traditional, but by 1840 presidential party affiliation controlled local races as never before. Both parties extended organization to the most local levels of elections. Although each party normally blamed the other for instigating any extension of organization or party behavior, the Democrats were generally the pioneers in this respect. In 1839 and 1840 Democrats widely argued that the same signs of aristocracy that had appeared in national politics were now increasingly detectable in state politics as well. Consequently, they easily satisfied themselves that Democratic organization must be extended as a matter of principle from presidential politics all the way down to municipal politics.

The Whigs responded with similar organization, pleading necessity all the way, and intensifying their need to distinguish the Whig brand of party organization from the Democratic. Where Democrats continued to use a radical majoritarianism to justify their party as the embodiment of the entire legitimate polity, the Whigs steadily refined their self-image as an all but spontaneous rising of the resolutely independent, not a party but the second coming of the Revolution itself.

The pervasive party organization of the campaign of 1840 marked a sea change in the terms of the unwritten constitution. It is easy, and in some ways accurate, to portray the Whigs as the party of the past in this transformation and the Democrats as the party of the future. It is also true, however, that the Whigs out-organized the Democrats in many areas. And the Democrats justified everything they did not as forward-looking innovation but as the ancient, antipartisan usages of the democracy. The campaign of 1840 forced Americans as never before to confront the practical questions entailed by an abstract, national commitment to "popular sovereignty" or "democracy." If the Constitution enshrined self-government by free and equal individuals, then how were those abstractions to be put into practice? If equality implied majority rule, if majority rule implied compromises of individual judgment, if an individual's freedom and equality were actually conditioned on his or her social, economic, and political resources, if political organization could enhance individual freedom and equality in some circumstances but fatally compromise it in others—if all these things were true, then how was self-government by free and equal individuals to be implemented? Was the Constitution's formal institutional design the whole answer? Or did the Constitution's basic principles necessarily imply a further institutionalization of the sovereign people? The ideologues of the Democratic and Whig parties of 1840 claimed to have the answers, and in the elections of 1839–40 the newly mobilized sovereign considered their claims.

Local Elections in 1839

Democrats in 1839 were eager to emphasize the party character of even local elections. The *Register*, for example, exulted that the Galena city election was contested "directly upon the question of Federal-Whiggery and Van Buren Democracy" and that, consequently, Democrats had reclaimed the city.[7] At the same time, newly created Du Page County, in the north, was graced with an immediate organization of the Democratic party. The convention nominated only local officers and took the occasion to advocate the county's embrace of constitutional partyism from birth. Its resolutions said nothing of policy, local or otherwise, but simply announced the rules by which every democrat, right down to the county surveyor, must be governed: "*Resolved*, That every democrat is bound to show his attachment to the principles he professes at the ballot box, by voting for men of sound democratic principles, and none others, as expressed by a majority of the party through their delegates in convention assembled."[8]

In the south as well Democrats worked to justify organization at the local level. A Democratic meeting in Fayette County aimed to prove that a real aristocratic threat existed, not only nationally but even within the state, and that regular nominations for state legislators were necessary to the defense of popular sovereignty.[9] The meeting's opening speaker argued that the state "Federal" party, like its national counterpart, had attempted in the assembly to establish "aristocratical" principles. The state senate, for instance, had "decree[d] that the present Secretary of State held his office *for life*," which echoed the U.S. Senate's obstruction of Jackson's cabinet removals during the Bank War. A further example of creeping aristocracy was the Whigs' support for a charter for Vandalia that would have restricted the municipal suffrage to property holders. Such a charter would have been the "*entering wedge* to the final establishment of a landed aristocracy in the State."

The meeting adopted resolutions in the spirit of this speech, declaring the people's right and duty "frequently to recur to first principles so as to prevent the introduction of aristocracy and king-craft into our republican government." It thus concluded that "many of the acts of the last Legislature admonish the democratic party, that they ought to support none but Democratic[10] Van Buren Republicans for Senators or Representatives to the Legislature." More specifically, it branded as a new "*sedition law*" a failed assembly resolution to limit the political activities and speech of Illinois officeholders. And it endorsed the Independent Treasury for reasons that emphasized the danger of "'an established dynasty of banks throughout our free and happy country'"; it even claimed, turning the tables on the Whigs, that the Independent Treasury would happily "limit Executive patronage." The climactic resolution justified regular nominations. Many of Illinois's Federalists, it declared, had hidden their now obviously aristocratic principles to get "elected by a confiding democratic people." In so doing, they had shown that they could not be "trusted with power," especially in the coming election of a United States senator. Consequently, the "Democratic Van Buren Republicans" of the district were urged to unite on assembly candidates by means of nominating conventions that rested on Democratic primary meetings.

While organized partyism made such strides in a southern county like Fayette, Cook County, the fountainhead of Illinois partyism, saw the Whigs nearly outdo the Democrats in their adherence to partyist theory. The Democrats held their usual convention for county offices but, to the delight of the Whigs, failed to unify themselves. They did elect their regular nominee for county recorder, but they barely overcame two Democratic bolters and a Whig in doing it.[11]

As the Democrats broke into factions, the Whig editor hopefully urged attendance at Whig ward meetings. He argued that no one could complain of improper nominations who did not attend "primary meetings."[12] The following day he warned the Whigs not to sacrifice their organization to ally with one of the Democratic factions.[13] And in the wake of the county and precinct Whig conventions, he sounded almost like a partyist ideologue: "In every instance the candidate who obtained the majority, was declared to be the unanimous choice of the Conventions. Respecting as the Whigs do, the democratic maxim that 'the majority shall govern' they reduced their principles to practice, and whatever their individual preferences might have been, they yielded them without hesitation to the will of the majority." In contrast, the "so styled 'democratic' convention" was suffused with "anarchy."[14]

By 1839, the Whigs of Cook County were no longer the same kinds of antipartyists that had dominated the state in the 1820s. But even in 1839, committed as they had become to organization and to party unity, they continued to argue that their unity came from voluntarism and individual integrity rather than from the constitutional obligation to a party organization that informed capital-"D" Democracy. Thus, for example, when a rumor appeared that a member of the unanimous Whig county convention had withdrawn his support from the Whig nominee, the editor refuted the rumor not by claiming, as a Democrat would, that a good party member must never bolt a regular nomination. Instead, he declared that the Whig ranks included no man who would break such a solemn pledge as all the members of the convention had, in fact, freely given to the nominee.[15] Whereas membership in the Democracy was a matter of constitutionally compelled organizational discipline, membership in the equally organized Whig party was a matter only of free choice and individual integrity.

Cook County, along with the other four counties in its senatorial district, saw one other election in 1839, a special election for state senator in November. The Democrats nominated a pioneer of the convention system, while the Whigs had trouble getting anyone to accept their nomination. The Whigs' positions on the issues were clear enough, however. Just as at the national level, the chief concern in the legislative elections was the Independent Treasury and all that it implied:

Resolved, That while the Administration party are now warring against all the banks of the country, as political in their objects and influence, and oppressive and ruinous in their operations, they are at the same time striving to erect upon their ruins a *Federal* SUB-TREASURY GOVERNMENT BANK—a MONSTER, with its head at Washington, and its Briarous arms in every State—connected, as a "part of one stupendous whole," with the CUSTOM HOUSE, with its revenue cutters, surveyors, collectors and gaugers—the LAND OFFICE, with its agents and receivers, and the POST OFFICE, with its 35000 agents!—forming a moneyed despotism in its most odious forms, under which the prosperity and liberties of our republic would be ground down together.[16]

Elections at all levels apparently bore on the national Constitution and therefore on the national prosperity. They were, therefore, party elections.

Another county with a history of political sophistication was St. Clair, the home of William Kinney, John Reynolds, Adam Snyder, Gustave Koerner, and other prominent Democrats. But in its county elections in 1839, it exhibited an essentially pre-partyist electoral culture. The county's only newspaper, the *Great Western*, was a fervent Whig publication. Like Chicago's *American* and Springfield's *Journal*, the *Western* increasingly advocated Whig organization, even as it worked to limit Whig concessions to partyism and to distinguish Whig organization from Democratic. At the level of county offices, however, it was fully pre-partyist, arguing that local offices were no legitimate object of party activity and that the various surreptitious efforts of partyists to influence the elections must be met not by organization but by individual attention to the public good.

Six weeks before the county election, the *Western* warned sarcastically that wire-pullers in Belleville, the principal town of the county, were busily determining nominations for the county offices and would only require that the people march up and vote as they were instructed: "To this the people certainly cannot object. *It is in accordance with the usages of the Democratic party*."[17] But, in spite of this and other alleged efforts to inject party into the elections,[18] only self-nominations appeared.[19] No conventions were held. If the Democratic party sought to influence the election in any significant degree, it was not advertising the fact. And the lone openly partyist candidate was trounced by the incumbent, while another supposed tool of the "junto" won decisively.[20] In short, party affiliation appears to have had little, if anything, to do with the election, even as the threat that it would was the only question that the editor thought necessary to address. All other local questions were left to the people to discuss on their own.

This sampling of some of 1839's more sophisticated counties suggests that party organization probably remained beyond the bounds of normal political competition in most of Illinois, even as it made notable strides here and there. Conventions for local offices remained rare outside the north of the state. Self-nomination, combined with either nonpartisanship or antipartyism, was the continuing norm, even for the offices of state representative or senator. Only in the far north does partyist ideology appear to have controlled the Democrats down to the lowest offices. And, correspondingly, only in the north do Whigs appear to have come close to matching the Democratic willingness to organize.

Local Elections in 1840

In 1840, the dam broke. Campaign activity and voter turnout boomed, and the presidential party division expanded its influence dramatically at all electoral levels. In St. Clair County, preparations for the legislative elections of 1840 began as early as the summer of 1839 when an anti–Van Buren presidential convention resolved to support no candidate for Congress or the state legislature the following year who supported Van Buren. As some Democrats eagerly pointed out, this resolution was remarkably "proscriptive" for an antipartyist meeting. But, while the resolution did proscribe avowed Van Burenites in local elections, it did not call for anti–Van Burenites to adhere to party nominations.[21] In the meeting's view, Van Burenites had tied themselves to the will of a virtual monarch by their openly avowed theory of party organization. The very purpose of Van Burenism was to eliminate individual political independence by means of partyism. Supporting a Van Burenite, therefore, could not be the act of an independent man. Whig voluntarism and independence meant that a Whig might support whoever he chose, since he was burdened by no theory of party obligation akin to the Democrats', but could not rationally support any candidate who had publicly discarded his independence altogether.

In any case, Democratic complaints about proscription functioned mainly as a much needed justification for organization. Led by Adam Snyder, the Democrats took the anti–Van Buren convention as an excuse to urge open Democratic organization for the first time in this county.[22] The *Western* responded immediately with a call for "Whigs and ALL OTHER INDEPENDENT REPUBLICANS" to hold a county meeting to repudiate Van Buren and to "show yourselves above *party*."[23] And so the campaign would go, each side justifying its organization by the charge that the other had organized first, each side calling on the electorate to adhere to a party and in the same breath condemning partyism.

In these preparations for 1840, the Whig response to Democratic conventionism was no longer to condemn party organization as such but to condemn the Democratic brand of party organization. At the beginning of the new year, the *Western* articulated the themes of 1840 by identifying the Whig party as the exclusive champions of the "CONSTITUTION" and of the "COUNTRY," who disdained a "mere *party triumph*." But when the Democrats were organizing there was only one practical, if ambivalent, response: "Let us imitate our opponents in the one thing essential to success—*organization*."[24]

As spring approached, the editor focused more particularly on the coming summer elections. Thus, when the Democrat Gustave Koerner insisted on the Independent Treasury as a test question of Democracy for 1840, the *Western* ridiculed him, since such a test would have been failed by virtually every Democrat before 1837. A *New York Times* reprint showed that the Independent Treasury had always been rejected, even by Van Buren, until it suddenly became a tool of "PARTY" under the new administration.[25] The following week it was discovered that the St. Clair Democrats, who had long told the locals that they were opposed to convention nominations, were about to bring out county candidates: "Although our opponents *profess* to be very much shocked at the bare mention of *Convention*, or *Caucus*, for the purpose of bringing out candidates for office, yet our town is to be honored to-day by one of those little county *Caucusses*," composed solely of the office-seekers themselves.[26]

In the wake of the Democratic meeting, the editor condemned the "Caucus" of the "'*Sub-Treasury Democracy*,'" who openly put "their Party, 'RIGHT or WRONG,'" above their country. He asserted that the nominations had been arranged before the meeting and that the "*Caucus System* has very justly and repeatedly been condemned by the clearly expressed voice of the Democracy of this country" exactly because it gives the power of dictation to the pre-concerting few. Consequently, "the spurious manner in which they have been brought before the public" was sufficient in itself to reject their candidacies. And from that point on the *Western* considered the race to be between "the Caucus Ticket" and an anticaucus ticket yet to be named by "the people generally." Such a ticket could be named "without the aid of a *Caucus*, and in a manner perfectly satisfactory to every Republican in the county," or so the *Western* asserted.[27]

To this end, the editor published a call for a general meeting of the citizens of the county, which invited those who supported Harrison and the single-term. Editorially expanding on the character of the meeting, he labeled it a "HARRISON and anti-Caucus meeting."[28] The following week he continued his efforts to distinguish this meeting from Democrat-style party organization. He claimed that the only objects of the meeting, which was called by men "purely

Democratic Republican" and which would be "emphatically *a meeting of the People*," would be to examine the issues of the day and, vaguely, to secure harmony of action. This was not a nominating convention or in any way caucus-like but an open meeting of the "Republican Whigs" to discover their collective will.[29]

At the end of this editorial, one could not be sure whether the meeting was intended for all citizens, or for Harrison supporters, or for Democratic Republicans, or for Republican Whigs. The day of the rally, the same paper settled on the label "Democratic Republican Whig."[30] But, however unclear the editor was about who was included, the only people excluded were the party of caucus, spoils, and Subtreasury.

The editor had originally suggested that the meeting was necessary to produce a ticket for the county elections, but it turned out to be a rally almost entirely devoted to the presidential question. Its resolutions were primarily constitutional as it promoted "*Harrison* and *Reform*."[31] And, even though the meeting made no nominations, it set the constitutional tone for local elections as well as national.

As soon as the rally was over, self-nominations began to appear in the *Western*. Just before the gathering, "A Farmer" had called for better candidates than the caucus "ponies" then on the track: "As to the present batch of candidates that are placed before the people, I would say, sir, let their talents be what they may, it is no doubt the true policy of every friend to his country to oppose their election, while they stand pledged to sustain the party whose motto is '*to the victors the spoils belong*.'" Rather, he suggested that the county's modest but pure Jeffersonian Democrats might be induced to offer themselves if there were sufficient expression of popular vigilance in the cause of reform.[32] Presumably, the Harrison meeting was just such an expression, since three men were immediately self-nominated for the three representative seats as were one senatorial candidate and one for county commissioner.[33]

A week later, "Lebanon" offered to fill out the "Independent Whig Ticket." He named a candidate for sheriff who was honest, an old resident, a farmer, a "legitimate son of the Democracy of Illinois," and "*no party bound and time serving politician*." He also offered a name for coroner and thought that, with those two names, the "opponents of political combinations, and of a presumptuous cabal, can safely take the field."[34] There was no officially sanctioned Whig party ticket nor a county Harrison ticket. The link between national and county elections was only implicit most of the time. The number of labels applied to the opponents of Van Buren was mind-boggling. But it was increasingly clear that the "opponents of the Administration, and of caucus nominations"[35] were essentially the same.

The Democratic response came from the newly founded *Belleville Advocate*. It opened its career with a brief justification of regular nominations, and it spoke the unrestrained majoritarianism of constitutional partyism in summing up its politics: "In a word we will act up to the established principles of the Democratic party; and have placed at the mast-head the regular nominations of a majority of the people, in whom is vested all rights, and the manner of expressing and asserting them." Its Democratic nominations were not merely the nominations of a party but of the popular majority that was the legitimate political embodiment of the people as a whole, the repository of "all rights."[36]

Observing the organizing of the great Whig rally, the *Advocate* began a campaign of discrediting Whig professions, which mirrored the ongoing Whig campaign against caucuses. It suggested that there was a Whig "secret committee" which had already determined a Whig ticket and now sought to legitimate it through the pomp and distraction of a public rally. Such deception contrasted starkly with "the open, the honest, the independent usages of the Democratic party."[37] Where the Whigs were "ready to blindly follow the dictation of their party leaders," a Democratic convention gave each voter a voice in the doings of the party. In particular, the editor cited the nominees of the March Democratic county convention as exemplary products of conventionism. They were unexceptionable men who had solicited no nominations but had been called out by the people. Therefore, they could "have no other pride in being elected than the honest one, that the cause which they support is supported by the majority of the people." And they had none of the temptations to make empty promises and build artificial coalitions that plagued candidates who relied on their individual popularity and exertions.[38]

There was even a tendency among writers in the *Advocate*, consistent with the locality's antipartyist traditions, to charge the Whigs with being more party-bound than the Democrats. "An Enemy to Judas-ites," for example, observed that two of the Whigs' legislative candidates had only recently turned traitor to the Democratic party. He hoped the Whigs would "not be so far governed by party enthusiasm, as to entrust their suffrages" to such self-seeking candidates as these.[39] The editor agreed: "We are aware that the contest is much to be decided on party grounds, but we cannot believe that the independent Whigs will, or can, support men for the Legislature whose only claim is, that they are of their party, two of whom have apostized to receive the votes of the Whigs."[40] This came from a Democrat whose own party creed was that a party nomination was always to be supported for the sufficient reason that it was a party nomination. But to Democrats a party nomination produced by a "majority of the people," by the suprapartisan democracy itself, carried a legitimate claim on each voter, while the nomination of a factional party, a group defined only by its one-time coincidence of self-interest, carried no such authority.

The two apostate Democrats in the race were not actually avowed Whigs. They were self-nominated without mention of party, and their announcements appeared in both newspapers. They were embraced by the Whigs as anticaucus candidates and shunned by the Democrats as accomplices in the internal improvements debacle and as political weathercocks.[41] Of course, they claimed that they remained the true Democrats in the race and that they had abandoned Van Buren only when the Van Burenites tried to tie them to party measures in the legislature and so compromise their independence.[42] Their claim to support, then, was not that they were of the Whig party but that they disdained party control of their actions at all.

On the Democratic side, the election address of senatorial candidate James A. James was that increasingly rare item, a simple list of policy positions, with little hint of constitutional thought.[43] His ticket-mate, Daniel Baldwin, however, drew tight connections between national and state affairs by injecting constitutional reasoning into his address. Taking the orthodox Democratic position on the Bank, he extended the reasoning to Illinois's own State Bank, which possessed extraordinary powers and commanded unconstitutional aid from the assembly when no longer able to sustain itself within the rules of its charter. He therefore called for tight restrictions on all banks and corporate charters, including repealability by any subsequent General Assembly.[44]

Such arguments were supplemented during the campaign by other writers' warnings that popular liberties were at stake. "St. Clair" argued that old Federalism survived in a new Bank-sponsored editorial campaign that glorified wealth rather than liberty. The Whig "gag-law," for example, would silence anti-Bank officeholders politically, and the people were encouraged to accept this restraint as the price of promised wealth, even though the real result of a Bank-controlled economy would be the creation of a "monied aristocracy," with the people both poor and politically dependent.[45] Complementarily, Democratic congressman John Reynolds argued the identity in principle between congressional Whig efforts to modify the naturalization laws and to restrict officeholders' political rights, on the one hand, and the Federalist Alien and Sedition Acts, on the other. He did not disrespect either the early Federalists or the current Whigs for being principled aristocrats, but he wanted it to be clear that that was what they were.[46]

The St. Clair campaign of 1840 was typical of many campaigns in the state. Where constitutional campaigns before 1840 had usually been clear contests between partyism and antipartyism, the anti-Democrats of 1840 adopted too many trappings of party to accommodate their older arguments about the inherent corruption of political organization. As they increasingly used party devices as electoral expedients and increasingly referred to themselves as a party, antipartyist argument remained pervasive but more narrowly aimed against the ethic of party obligation and toward an eventual withering away of organization. The anti-Democrats saw their relatively organized party of 1840 as qualitatively identical to the unorganized antipartyist movement of previous years. Their goal remained the preservation of the democratic power of the politically independent.

At the same time, elements of antiparty rhetoric also persisted among Democrats. Their radical majoritarianism, which called for collective defense of the individual independence of each democrat, tolerated no sustained division among democrats. To them, as well, the party division was not between equivalent kinds of parties. It was between a democratic constitutional party and an aristocratic factional party.

Compared to southern Illinois's St. Clair County, central Illinois's Sangamon County had been well integrated into the national party organizations before 1840. It had had no more party conventions for local office—none, that is—than had St. Clair. But it was newly the home of the state capital in Springfield, and it had had two party newspapers exerting pressure on the electorate to vote party tickets since 1836. By 1840, the *Sangamo Journal* and *Illinois State Register* were by common consent the state organs of the Whig and Democratic parties. As such, they both worked to impose the incipient national party division on Illinois. And they both found the county elections' importance almost exclusively in their local articulation of the national battle. Consequently, Sangamon's local elections, even more than those of St. Clair, became little more than local skirmishes in the national war.

The national war, however, did not yet look like a party system to them. One suggestive piece of evidence in this regard is that when the Sangamon Whigs held their precinct and county conventions in 1840 they usually labeled them Harrison conventions, not Whig conventions. They, like the St. Clair anti-Democrats, portrayed themselves as part of a focused movement, not as part of a political institution. The thoroughness with which the national Harrison and Van Buren movements dominated the local elections of 1840 did turn out to be a harbinger of the future. But to Illinoisans of 1840, the spontaneous sacrifice of the local character of local politics in the drive to permanently shape the national constitutional order seemed, rather, the climax of twelve years of revolution and counterrevolution.

Whig organization began with precinct conventions in late February. Most of these called themselves meetings of the "friends of Harrison and Tyler," even though their only explicit function was to choose delegates to the county nominating convention. Nominating county candidates had nothing inherently to do with the presidential campaign, but the county gathering too called itself a "Harrison" convention.[47]

The ten precinct meetings devoted their resolutions to the national campaign, not to state affairs. They made no mention of internal improvements or state banks. And they named delegates to the county nominating convention almost as afterthoughts to their Harrison resolutions. They did not bother to justify the novelty of a partisan county convention, perhaps because they did not think of themselves as partisans. In a significant but rare step for a Whig convention, however, they did pledge themselves in advance to support the convention's nominees, apparently because those nominees had been reduced to mere appendages of the Harrison movement, their ultimate roles as public employees having no immediate salience for these activists.

The resolutions were almost all constitutional in nature, and most argued an antipartyist line. The traditional triple condemnation of party, conventions, and spoils remained, although it was modified somewhat by a preoccupation with spoils. For example, the Richland precinct meeting of "the friends of General Harrison" made a very traditional antipartyist argument, "deplor-[ing] the extent to which party spirit is carried in our country," urging "the friends of Gen. Harrison . . . to abstain from all existing party questions," and declaring Harrison "less of a party man than any man of equal distinction in the Union" since he had "received the approbation and confidence of all, from Washington, Adams, Jefferson, Madison, Monroe and J. Q. Adams."[48]

Most other meetings made more specific arguments about the Subtreasury and its implications for the nature of American government. The current economic distress, however, was a distinctly secondary consideration, often not appearing at all in the resolutions. The Upper Lick Creek meeting resolved that "we look upon the sub-treasury scheme as a plan eminently calculated to perpetuate those evils tending to the consolidation of power in the general government and anti-republican in its influence."[49] In Bloomington, the conventioneers more thoroughly tied economic policy to the constitutional threat posed by Van Burenism:

> Resolved, That the enormous expenditures of the Government are not only in open contempt of the promises of the party in power; but are justly calculated to excite the most serious apprehensions on the part of the people. Resolved, further, that the odious doctrine . . . that "to the victors belong the spoils," is directly calculated to debase and corrupt the public morals, and to undermine and subvert our republican form of Government.

. . . Resolved. That the interference of Federal officers in the State and general elections tends directly to a concentration of all power in the hands of the office-holders, and unless speedily rebuked by the indignant voice of the people will be destructive of liberty.

. . . Resolved, That the Sub-Treasury is subversive of the whole practice of our Government from the origin to the time when it [the Subtreasury] came into practical operation, and is calculated to increase the power and patronage and expenditures of the Government, and to add ten-fold to the sufferings of the people.[50]

Fiscal profligacy, spoils, and Subtreasury hard-moneyism, in short, were all aspects of the same constitutional danger—officeholder aristocracy.

The county convention summed up the constitutionalism of the precinct meetings. It pledged support for the county nominees and for Harrison but emphasized the patriotic voluntarism involved in that support. It stipulated that "the friends of Constitutional Government . . . have reached a ground upon which they can meet—a ground on which all personal preferences . . . as well as all petty differences growing out of sectional interests, may be laid aside." These comrades had not been herded together by party leaders bearing spoils. Rather, they spoke spontaneously as individuals in a voice that had "come up, 'like the sound of many waters,' from all parts of our common country, declaring that misrule shall end,—that the Constitution shall be restored—that Executive power . . . shall be confined within its proper limits—and he who . . . is now seeking through the aid of his army of office-holders, to '[rear?] on the ruins of the Republic, the throne of his despotism,' shall give up the place." The succeeding resolutions pledged the delegates to support the county nominees and Harrison.[51] The language of this pledge, which obligated the delegates but did not pretend to obligate a party rank-and-file, was the language of voluntarism and independent sacrifice for the greater good, not the language of majoritarian authority characteristic of Democratic conventions.

The Democrats, for their part, denied that the Whig convention counted as a convention at all. A convention could only properly be a meeting of the democracy of the county. The Whig gathering, on the other hand, was "a packed meeting . . . , got up by the secret influence of the Junto and *called* a Convention." "It was well understood that no man could be nominated, unless by the permission of the Junto," the same "junto" that Democrats had for years charged with secretly controlling the anti-Democratic nominations of the county. The only novelty was that, whereas the junto used to deplore open conventions, now they adopted them in form while still manipulating their doings in secret. "THE TIME HAS COME, we think, when the *real* democracy of the county, the men who are resolved no longer tamely to submit to the misrule of the Junto, to meet in convention, form a ticket from among the honest and upright of the *real*, not the *sham* democracy of the county, and present it to the PEOPLE for *their* consideration."[52] The writer said little, however, to help a reader distinguish between a "real" meeting of the democracy and a "sham" one.

By July 1840, the *Journal*'s preoccupation with the national, constitutional campaign had led it not only to merge local elections into the presidential election but also to create almost a mirror-image constitutional partyism with which Whigs might control local elections. As the county convention had edged toward a Van Burenesque principle of party obligation, now the *Journal* edged toward a Van Burenesque acceptance of permanent party competition between one legitimately democratic party and one illegitimately anti-democratic party. The leading edge of the Whig movement now envisioned permanent, organized defense of democracy against the specific threat of an executive party: "There are two great parties in the United States, which date their existence as far back as our revolution, and which in all probability will continue to exist so long as we remain a nation. These parties are as opposite in their principles as the two antipodes. The federal party are now, and always have been, the advocates of Executive power, whether claimed by a King or President." Increasingly mirroring the Democrats' partyism, the Journal now demanded of the Whigs "a rigid adherence to their principles, and to the men who support and sustain them. Surely no reflecting man can ever suppose it possible to accomplish the overthrow of the President while his advocates and friends are permitted to fill all the offices in the Federal and State Governments." If the "federalist" Democrats sought to extend executive control by imposing party division in every locality, then the Whigs would have no choice but to extend their principles and organization to local elections where five years earlier such things would have been anathema.

The editor's remaining justifications for bringing party organization to local elections were concrete extensions of this logic. The next General Assembly was due to elect a senator and to reapportion the state's congressional districts. A Democratic majority would mean a Democratic delegation to Congress, with perhaps a Democratic president holding their leashes. Whig organization at every level, on the other hand, would prevent such an extension of executive-party control of Congress: "It is not sufficient that the Whigs elect Gen. Harrison to the Presidency, for Martin Van Buren does not embody in his little person the whole essence of loco focoism,—it exists in all his satellites; and we cannot hope to bring back the Government to its original purity, without purging the Halls of legislation in Congress, and in the States also."[53]

And the *Journal* carried the outline of American constitutional government in its supposed "original purity" on its masthead:

HARRISONIAN PRINCIPLES

Executive Power and Patronage confined within the limits prescribed by the Constitution.

Economy in Public Expenditures.

Rigid accountability of Public Officers.

The will of the People, expressed through their Constitutional Representatives, to be the Law of the land.

The Patronage of the General Government NOT to be brought into conflict with the freedom of Elections.

The General Government to abstain from interfering in the domestic affairs of the States.

No Conscription Law, or Standing Armies in time of Peace.

The same Currency for the Office-Holders and for the People.

The encouragement of Productive Industry, and the securing of FAIR WAGES to the laborer by the prudent use of a system of credit, and the restoring of confidence between man and man.[54]

Scattered evidence from other counties illustrates some diversity in attitudes but confirms the general truth of the points made so far. Some examples of Democratic argument will confirm that party's general, but not universal, application of Van Burenite theory to every level of politics.

The Fulton County Democratic convention warned of "a most powerful faction within our very vitals, who have conspired to . . . check the growth of free institutions, and warp our constitution to a British model."

This faction is composed of the rich who have nothing but wealth to found distinction on; of the learned, whose learning, unregulated by political virtue, has rendered them haughty; of the ambitious, who, in the language of the elder Adams, would overturn all governments . . . rather than remain in the station to which they naturally belong; of those who consider themselves well born . . . ; hungry, rapacious office-seekers—those whose extravagance and dissipation have plunged them in debt, want an artificial currency that can be had for nothing to extricate themselves; and finally, of those terrible fanatics [abolitionists] who . . . are willing to kindle the flame of civil war among the political divisions of this fair Republic.

These "enemies of free government" hoped to "misdirect" part of the democratic majority from its own interests, restore the Bank as servant of a "moneyed aristocracy," give the people no currency but "the circulating debts of that aristocracy," and thereby restore the British socio-constitutional order:

> The nation will be (as the elder Adams said it ought to be) divided into the gentlemen and the simple men; and we shall enjoy that kind of happiness which another distinguished Federalist of that time said we should enjoy, when the common people would be glad to work for a sheep's head and pluck a day, and sleep under a cart at night. Old England has a national bank. . . . Has that bank enriched the population? Let the millions of starving mechanics of her cities, and miserable operatives of her cotton manufactories answer.

Democratic majorities could prevent this replication of the British sociopolitical order of dependency in America. But the task required rigid adherence to the convention system, and it required "a majority so large, as to convince [the Federalists] that their power in this county is forever at an end." The convention briefly acknowledged that there were state affairs to be attended to by the next legislature. But it quickly connected these to the national campaign by reminding the people that the "complexion of the next Legislature" would probably determine the state's choice in the presidential election.[55]

While a Democratic meeting in Bond County refused "to apply the party test to local officers," who need only be "honest and capable" and to whom "no political trust is committed,"[56] the Clinton County address was almost entirely an orthodox constitutional partyist history of American politics, cast as a justification for tying local elections to the national party division. It began with an assertion of the permanence of parties: "Political parties have always existed in this country, and always will; . . . When founded on a difference in principles, the collisions they beget, enable the people to discover the truth, and awaken them to a sense of their rights and of their danger, and they will side with the one or the other party." From a twenty-first-century perspective, one could almost read this statement as a justification of pluralist multipartyism, but, in fact, its point was that when the parties clashed it was easier for the community to see the irreconcilability of their constitutional principles:

> The two great parties which have ever divided this country have been long known by the distinction of Democratic and Federal. . . . The Federal party . . . had John Adams and Alexander Hamilton for their leaders, who publicly proclaimed, that the British Government, with its [king?, lords], gentlemen and peasantry, was the [best on?] earth; that there were natural dis-

tinctions in society, of rich and poor; that the people were not capable of self-government; . . . and that no Government could long exist, where the people were permitted to exercise political power.

The Democrats, on the other hand, had always maintained the "entire capability of the people for self-government."

The address went through the familiar, Van Burenite history of American politics before returning to the question of partyism's extension to local elections. The authors implied that when such comprehensive principles were at stake as those separating Democrats from Federalists, they applied as much to county elections as to national ones. Just as was the case with a regularly nominated presidential candidate, so "in the candidates selected by the Democratic meeting of this county, we have every assurance that they will remain true to their principles, and never betray your interests for those of corporations, to which they are under no obligations; and that they will carry out, by their votes, Democratic measures—they will oppose gag laws, and all attempts to deprive our alien friends of any of their rights and privileges."

With its invocation of "corporations" and social "distinctions" here, the Clinton convention joined its counterpart in Fulton in evoking the constitutional order of dependency that awaited the country if it misread its political and constitutional history. At all levels of government, the stakes were "a Government of the PEOPLE" against "that of heartless *banking corporations*." Corporations were virtually a constitutional estate unto themselves, the American version of a fixed aristocracy calling in "obligations" until the democracy was rendered dependent and powerless. Amid such a constitutional struggle, legislative elections and presidential politics were of a piece. And no candidate for the legislature could be a democrat if he did not support Van Buren: "As the Democratic party throughout the Union, have nominated Martin Van Buren for re-election, . . . it cannot be possible, that the supporter of any other man, and especially of the Harrisburg Convention *nominee*, can be of the same party."[57] Martin Van Buren, local Democratic candidates, and the Democratic party were unified at the most fundamental level by a commitment to majoritarian constitutionalism as against corporate aristocracy. It was meaningless to support one candidate of "the majority of the people" without supporting the rest.

If there was one thing that Whigs and Democrats agreed on, then, it was that an unprecedented number of local elections in 1840 should be controlled by the national election. They had, in a sense, agreed that the year's politics ought to be controlled by a two-party division. This was not, however, a party division resting on a constitutional consensus nor one that should have been, in their minds, closely competitive. Most Democratic leaders and some Whig leaders even saw this party division as a permanent feature of American democracy. But both sides also saw the two parties as separated by a constitutional gulf. And it was the constitutional nature of the conflict that, in the event, provided a principled linkage between local elections and the presidential election. The linkage was made relatively easily because the stakes were constitutional, the maintenance of popular sovereignty, and thus applicable in principle to every last election conducted within the Constitution.

Analysis of a sample of Whig arguments confirms the power of constitutionalism to justify the new extension of the national party division into local elections. Early in the year, the editor of the *Chicago American* hoped to land the year's first blow for Harrison by electing a Whig in the Chicago mayoral contest. Mayors were generally thought of as mere administrators with little if any political role. But the *American* recognized that every election in 1840 had become political: "The locos have said that their success at the Charter Election will have a favorable bearing on the Presidential Election in November next. And so it will. Chicago will be pointed to as a locofoco city in favor of Martin Van Buren; and the fact of the Municipal power being in their hands, will operate materially against us in this City and County. Will the friends of HARRISON and REFORM consent to this?"[58] City officers had the power to affect the course of the November election both by managing the polls unfairly[59] and by wielding the political influence that inhered in every public office, no matter how small.[60] The argument was not that the Whigs sought the political influence of office for themselves but that they must deny it to the Democrats.

The nominating meeting of the first ward resolved that the city election was "vitally important" to the national election. Without mentioning any municipal issues, it ratified Harrison's nomination and condemned Van Buren. Finally, it resolved that "as the Whig nominations in this ward have been unanimous, we hereby pledge ourselves to abide by them, and use all honorable means to secure the election of the nominees, and of him who may be nominated by the Convention to be held to-morrow, as our candidate for the Mayoralty."[61]

The tying of the city nominations to the national party division and the pledging of support for nominees were important steps in making the Chicago Whigs a full-fledged party. But the pledge was conditioned on the fact that the ward nominees for assessors, alderman, and delegates to the city convention had been unanimous. It compromised no one's conscience. As always, the Whigs believed their unity did and should come from the voluntary adherence of individuals. They believed that the free judgments of sensible individuals

would tell them that scattering their votes was useless, that personal preferences were nothing compared to the necessity of electing constitutionally sound
candidates, and that no party elite was trying to appropriate their votes. As a
Third Ward meeting declared, "Resolved, That we will not support our party
in the wrong; but that we will by all honorable means support them in the
right."[62] Independence was all.

The Whigs were also quite capable of bringing the economic dimension of
dependence and independence into the constitutional argument. At the Whigs'
Washington's birthday rally, note was taken of the Van Burenite promise that
the Independent Treasury would bring down inflated wages and prices. According to the Whigs, however, the real meaning of such artificial deflation
would be the reduction of "the independent yeomen of our country to the condition of the serfs of Russia and China, from which was borrowed the subtreasury system, and set up the lordly office holders over them, to fatten upon
the fruits of their labor." The resolutions honored the mayoral candidate with
only a brief declaration of his sterling character as they reduced him to a local
prop of the national campaign against "dependence."[63]

As Chicago's mayoral campaign concluded, Whig meetings across the state
began to choose delegates to the grand Harrison meeting in Springfield in
June. These meetings served both the national campaign and many of the campaigns for local office. The St. Clair Harrison meeting discussed above was an
example. It did not nominate local candidates, but it was clearly part of the
local as well as the national campaign. Likewise, most other county or local
meetings, sometimes identifying themselves as Harrison meetings and sometimes as Whig meetings, emphasized the national election, while often taking
some steps regarding their local elections. Some Whig counties held actual
nominating conventions for local offices, while others did not. But in either
case the county Harrison meetings set the tone and designated the issues for
the August and November elections alike.

For example, the Bureau County meeting did name delegates to a district
convention to nominate a legislative candidate. Its resolutions argued that
since the county was blessed with fertile land and a healthy climate, the only
cause for its depressed economy was the government and its "anti-democratic
rule." The meeting offered no examples of how the government had destroyed
the economy but implied that the Independent Treasury was akin to the government's past efforts to "reduce the laborer to a level with the bondman and
the slave."[64]

A meeting in Winnebago County made no nominations but made similar arguments in more forceful terms. It urged the people, amid economic distress
and bankruptcy, to look to "causes which have only happened under this un-

toward party misrule." The resolutions described that misrule as the experiments of "*the* party" in reducing the economy to a hard-money basis, while reserving gold and silver for the pay of the officeholders.[65] Hardly a Whig meeting failed to portray Democratic hard-money policy as an enriching of officeholders, appointed for party purposes, and a reduction of the working population to dependence.

With a series of such meetings under their belts, the Whigs met in June in Springfield for their state rally. The *Journal* claimed an attendance of 5,000, representing seventy counties, and even the *Belleville Advocate* conceded that there were over 3,000 marchers.[66] The centrality of constitutionalism in the resolutions was predictable. The meeting "hail[ed] this Convention of the People, who have spontaneously come to the rescue, as a practical development of one of the most interesting features of our Constitution." Presumably, this was a reference to the Constitution's guarantee of the right of peaceable assembly. But more important, it was a celebration of Whig constitutionalism's emphasis on the independence and voluntarism of individual democrats in such a gathering, in contrast to Democratic conventionism's reduction of the Democratic individual to dependence. And the substantive resolutions recapitulated the issues and rhetoric so thoroughly worked over in the local campaigns: The enemy was the spoils-based hard-money experimentation that would effectively overturn the democratic Constitution, that would separate the government from the people until all power and prosperity emanated not from the will and labor of the democracy but from executive whim.[67]

The Conclusion of the Presidential Campaign

Presidential election years had a roughly consistent pattern in Illinois. Jockeying for national nominations began sometime in the year before the actual election. The focus shifted to the localities in the late winter and spring. As the local elections climaxed, attention returned to the national campaign in August. In 1840, however, the local activists turned the local elections into wholly derivative elements of the national campaign, and the presidential race effectively buried local politics by the late spring.

The remainder of that race was largely a reprise of themes analyzed above but with one newly critical element for the Democrats. Whigs continued to portray the Democrats as a pseudo-majoritarian executive party of spoilsmen. The Democrats continued to paint the Whigs as the latest incarnation of Federalist, pro-Bank, aristocratic constitutionalism. But, by the middle of 1840, the party of "nineteen-twentieths" of the people found itself reeling from unprecedented Whig mobilization. Increasingly, therefore, the Democracy had to explain why so many of the democracy seemed to be opposed to the party of popular sovereignty. Accordingly, Stephen Douglas and other leading Democrats attacked the Whig event in Springfield by arguing that the Whigs drew on tried and true devices of European aristocracy—pageantry, bribery, and deception—to separate democrats from their natural convictions.[68]

These Democrats published six resolutions and an address to the people of Illinois. To the usual litany they added resolutions that Whig substitution of pageantry for reasoning was "one step to the subversion of the Government of the United States" and that the Springfield rally's "silks and satins," its "gilt buttons . . . worn by the gentry," and especially its idolatrous, life-sized portrait of Harrison evoked the banners, emblems, and black cockades of Federalist days. The hauling of log cabins through the streets by "stockjobbers" and bankers disguised the true scorn with which such men treated the real inhabitants of such homes.[69]

The address suggested that such distractions were calculated to debase the citizenry: "The degradation of the intellect of man is, and always has been, one of the most efficient means of destroying free and representative Governments: and if ever the liberties of the people of this Republic are to be lost, and forever destroyed, it can, alone, be accomplished by such means as those now in progress, where reason and intellect are utterly disregarded, and nothing but the baser passions of our nature appealed to."[70] Appropriately, the despotic tumult of the Whig rally had occurred on the birthday of George III. These Democrats thus called on all members of the Democratic party to gather at their county seats on the Fourth of July. There they would reaffirm the principles of the Declaration of Independence and soberly swear to live and die as freemen, "uncontaminated, and unstained by political heresies. . . and spurn as freemen should, the corrupting influences of banking corporations and associated wealth."[71]

Four months later, on the eve of the election, the Sangamon Democratic Association Executive Committee condemned Whig pageantry in similar terms before announcing that it was the task of Democrats to restore reason and democracy to the polity. To that end, the committee disdained hoopla and outlined the facts of constitutional partyist history one last time: Hamilton's and Adams's explicit distrust of popular government; the Federalists' failed attempts in the 1787 Convention to give Congress the power to create corporations; the original Bank's role as the source of the loose-constructionism by which the Alien and Sedition Acts were justified; democracy's restoration in the election of 1800; the Federalists' congressional attempts in 1801 to treat that " 'election of the People as though it had not taken place' "; the Federalists' treachery in wartime; their slow and secret revival with the loose-constructionist chartering of the second Bank and passage of a protective tariff; and finally, in 1840, "[r]elying upon the powerful auxiliary force of the Abolitionists, and the potent power of Bank influence," their plan to carry the presidency "by storm" and not by reason.[72]

The Whigs' concluding efforts mirrored Democratic arguments in that they laid far less emphasis on the policies to be implemented by their leaders than on the need first to return to the pure constitutional order that had prevailed at the American founding. Certainly, they attacked the Subtreasury as an economic measure. But its economic effects were dangerous mostly because of their constitutional effect: the consolidation of all power in the federal executive. The defeat of Van Buren and the election of Harrison were necessary to restore the independence of Congress, the states, and the people from the executive and his favorites.

In a speech to the Whig "Young Men's National Convention" at Baltimore, Illinois's Joseph Duncan went beyond condemning Van Buren to insist that the work of the Whigs would not be done until a number of constitutional amendments were passed. Every one of his proposed amendments was an antiparty attempt to eliminate the executive's power to threaten independence. He called for a single presidential term, an end to executive appointments for congressmen, an end to executive spending except by specific congressional act, a transfer to the states of the executive's authority to choose printers of the laws, and Senate approval for removals from all high offices.[73]

Whigs argued the democratic pedigree of such amendments and of the Whig mission in general by repeated citations to Jefferson's own railings against party spirit and party mechanisms. The *Journal*, for example, anticipating Harrison's win and desiring a strong justification for the removals that it expected, urged the Whigs to keep records of Democratic officeholders' electioneering and quoted Jefferson's proscription of the practice. Jefferson, like the Whigs of 1840, emphasized the anticonstitutional violation of state autonomy that would result from local electioneering by the party dependents of the federal executive:

> Finding under his administration that some government officers were disposed to use their offices and patronage for party purposes, he issued a circular to them, embracing the following declarations:—
>
> "The President of the United States has seen *with dissatisfaction, officers of the General Government* taking, on various occasions active parts in the election of public functionaries, whether of the general or state governments. Freedom of election being essential to the mutual independence of

the governments, so vitally cherished by most of our constitutions, *it is deemed improper for officers depending on the Executive of the Union* to attempt to control or influence the free exercise of the elective right; and further it is expected that he (the officer) will not attempt to influence the votes of others, nor to take any part in the business of electioneering, that being deemed inconsistent with the constitution and his duties to it."—*Thomas Jefferson.*

The *Journal* then identified Harrison as "a true Jeffersonian Democrat" who would never deny any public officer the right to "[express] his opinions and [go] to the polls as an independent man," but who would not hesitate to remove an officer conclusively shown to have "use[d] his office for party purposes."[74] The chief political value of this party, then, was independence—the independence from party of both states and individuals. And the various threats to independence in 1840 were fused in the image of a national executive's commanding the "unlimited patronage" offered by the Subtreasury bill. By such patronage, in the supposed words of the British *St. James Chronicle*, Martin Van Buren was steadily reducing the people of the United States to a "rational system of . . . MONARCHICAL OBEDIENCE."[75]

In November, Harrison won the national election but lost Illinois. The *Journal* was convinced, however, that Illinois's conversion was only a matter of time. Harrison would redeem his pledge to serve only a single term; "government officers will now be taught that they have other duties to perform than electioneering"; and these principles in action "will have the most happy effect in alleviating that infuriated party spirit which has even interrupted the socialities of private life.—These principles which have been repudiated by the *spurious* democracy of the country, are those which will be sustained by the democrats of the Jeffersonian school, by which we mean always to be understood the *Whig* party."[76]

The Democrats' victory in Illinois, meanwhile, was bittersweet. The national election was lost, and their majority in the state fell far short of the predictions dictated by their constitutional theory. Martin Van Buren's "Thoughts" had articulated the conviction of many Illinois Democrats, that the only way the Whigs could beat the Democrats in a national election was by stupendous fraud. As the election approached, then, the *Register* had repeatedly warned the Democrats to beware of the election-day frauds that were the natural concomitants of Whig deception and secrecy throughout the campaign.[77] In the wake of the election, the editor took such consolation as he could in confirming that the frauds invented by "New York" Whigs had been imported to Illinois and that the supposedly antispoils Whigs were tripping over themselves in the pursuit of office only days after the national results were confirmed.[78] For a constitutional partyist Democrat, only fraud and deception could explain such a Whig triumph.

In these attacks on the Whigs and Harrison, Martin Van Buren was all but invisible. He was the long-tried and faithful public servant whose name only appeared at the end of Democratic addresses. As a self-avowed creature of the party, his virtues were not really personal to him; they were, instead, the virtues of the party—the virtues of the Independent Treasury and the democratic, states'-rights constitutionalism for which it stood.

Conclusion

"Jeffersonian democracy" remained in 1840, as it had become in 1800, the dominant political faith of the nation. The Revolution of 1800 had vindicated the Constitution's guarantees of popular sovereignty and states' rights against the constructions of aristocrats and monocrats, or so Americans in 1840 universally believed. But were any of the politicians of 1840 Jefferson's true heirs? The extension of rigid party voting down to the most local elections hardly conformed to the original Jeffersonian construction of popular sovereignty. For all their claims to conservatism, the parties of 1840 had created something new under the sun: mass parties in control of politics and governance at every level (if not in every locality).

Moreover, for the first time, one party had created and refined a positive theory of party authority and deployed that theory uniformly across the state and nation. It thereby assimilated a large part of the electorate to an ideology of permanent party organization. The consequence for the electorate of 1840 was not yet legitimation of the "party system" that developed from these efforts. It was, nevertheless, to initiate the American tradition of mass party competition that would come virtually to define "democracy." The subsequent history of the Second Party System, then, was a kind of golden age of popular sovereignty. That is not to insist that every citizen was obsessed with politics and the Constitution. Nor is it to forget those who were left out in an age when gender and racial distinctions denied the vote to the true majority of the population. It is only to recognize that by 1840 American politicians had developed for the first time devices that could mobilize and activate nearly all of the legally sovereign people, "virtually the whole population."[79] Women too, disfranchised though they were, participated widely and meaningfully in the campaign[80] and thus began to take the steps that would see them and other excluded groups eventually making use of those same devices of "popular sovereignty."

There is a big difference, however, between the existence of continuing, close competition between two democratic parties and the legitimation of such competition in the minds of the participants. The "two-party system" has, like any institution, changed importantly over time. In its first incarnation, one of its most important characteristics was that neither party accepted that the other's most basic ideas about democracy could be squared with the Constitution.

The Democrats believed the Whigs to be essentially minoritarian, seeking special legal privileges with which to build an aristocracy. National banks, protective tariffs, and the like were minoritarian because they benefited only special interests, and they were unconstitutional because, unsurprisingly, the democratic Constitution enumerated no such minoritarian powers for the federal government. Only loose construction could torture that document into the aristocratic charter of dependency that the Whigs would make of it. And only aristocratic obstruction of Democratic party organization could prevent the democracy from putting down that loose-constructionist minoritarianism.

The Whigs, on the other hand, thought Democratic party practice equally contrary to the Constitution. The Whigs themselves moved from a loose movement of antipartyists into an organized, antiparty party of the "independent," but they justified their activity by portraying the Democratic federal government as a neo-Walpolean, spoils-driven tool of an executive party. Through the convention system, the Van Burenites replaced constitutional elections with extra-constitutional "regular nominations." Through spoils, Van Buren abdicated his constitutional duty to take care that the laws be faithfully executed through his officers. Instead, he took care only that those officers' livelihoods depend on their toeing the party line and on their willingness to appropriate public resources to party purposes and to manipulation of the public will. Through the legitimation of party itself, the Democrats substituted government by officeholding aristocracy for the popular sovereignty contemplated by the Constitution.

For both parties, the overriding policy issues of the day, especially the question of the government's response to a deepening depression, were mainly aspects of a far more fundamental clash over the relationship between party organization and the democratic Constitution. That clash would eventually yield, among other things, a "party system" in the modern sense, although I hesitate to date its arrival. Some political activists had even begun to grow comfortable by the end of 1840 with a rough equality in party strength over time.[81] Their increasing acceptance of such competitive party politics across the 1840s, however, was inconsistent with the ideologies that had justified organization and mobilized the people in the first place. The Second Party System, consequently, was beset with instability from the start. Successfully activating the sovereign people, each party denied that the other had any legitimate part in that achievement. While the parties continued to clash on the most fundamental matters, each party internally faced the challenge of integrating its founding procedural principles and its developing substantive identity after 1840. The instability of the 1840s and the realignment of the 1850s would reflect, in important part, the failure of either party to meet that challenge.

The Rise and Fall of Constitutional Partyism: Illinois and the Nation, 1815–1854

The seven preceding chapters have constituted a case study of politicians reconstructing the Madisonian Constitution. In Jacksonian Illinois, they reinterpreted that antiparty document as a charter of mass party organization. In this final chapter, however, I want to look beyond any single state. Here, I want to suggest how the experience of Illinois in creating two-party competition might shed light on the states and nation more generally, both in the initial creation of a party-based Constitution and in the course of constitutional politics during the Second Party System.

The recent historiography of Jacksonian politics, prodded and influenced by an outpouring of social history, has focused on the social compositions of the parties' constituencies and the substantive coherence of the parties' ideologies. The result has been the development of a new synthesis of Jacksonian and antebellum politics rooted in the social history of religion, immigration, and economic development. While the so-called ethnocultural school has identified reliable lines of political division that placed some religious and ethnic groups consistently in the Whig party and others consistently in the Democratic party,[1] another group of historians has increasingly emphasized divergent reactions to an emergent market economy.[2] These two schools have had their historiographical skirmishes, but increasingly they are understood to reinforce each other. In this now ascendant synthesis,[3] party conflict reflected the real diversity of American responses to capitalism, sectarianism, and immigration. And the two parties proved to be more than cobbled-together coalitions of office seekers; they carried two internally consistent ideologies that spoke clearly to the people's experience of their social history.

This focus on the substantive issues of party conflict, however, has obscured the important question of why political conflict ultimately took the form of party conflict. Readers have been left to suppose that the party politician and his machinery were thrown up almost spontaneously by preexisting social divisions, despite the universal antipartyism that had always prevented the entrenchment of party-organized politics. Before the social history boom, of course, political historians produced some excellent accounts of self-conscious party-building by ambitious politicians,[4] but these too were limited by the assumption that a pluralist two-party system must inevitably follow from broad suffrage and social conflict. As the previous chapters indicate, I do not think that that supposition is an adequate explanation for the emergence of mass party politics. Social divisions do not simply create political organizations.[5] Politics has a large measure of autonomy, and the emergence of parties out of a partyless constitutional order cannot be explained by mere reference to social developments like the rise of the market amid democratic suffrage. Parties had been universally reviled for good reasons—not because they did not work but because they did and because, when they did, they revealed seriously antilibertarian and disorderly tendencies. If politicians were now to make them the guardians of the Constitution, then those politicians could not just state the obvious: that organization of a party was an effective way to advance an agenda. Everyone knew that; yet party organization remained out of bounds as ultimately inconsistent with popular sovereignty and confederated government. The only way to create an effective party in democratic America was to paint it as the defender of the Constitution against anticonstitutional attack and thus as the defender of traditional antipartisan values themselves.

Of course, a modern perspective might suggest that the proper defender of the Constitution is not primarily one or both political parties but the judiciary and, in particular, the Supreme Court.[6] In the nineteenth century, however, as the partyists worked to isolate the threat of aristocracy, they identified the courts, and especially the Supreme Court, as generally allied with that aristocratic threat, both in principle—because relatively independent of popular control and popular feeling[7]—and in historical fact. It is this attitude to the judiciary that most clearly highlights the constitutional quality of partyist theory—the quality that is necessary to recognize Jacksonian political development as more than epiphenomenal to Jacksonian social history. If, as partyist theory suggested, the Constitution lived preeminently in an active democracy's preemption of any important role for the courts in constitutional development, then the constitutional history of the period could be expected to lie mostly in popular politics and only marginally in the history of judicial review.

Even the original Federalist theorists of judicial review had little expectation or desire that that device would play more than a marginal role in giving meaning to the Constitution.[8] Van Buren himself, an accomplished lawyer[9] and no enemy of judicial review as such, noted that the jurisdiction of the federal judiciary was originally "of little consideration"[10] and insisted with Jefferson that ultimate constitutional meaning in the American system arose not from adjudication but from politics, the ultimate constitutional arbiter being not the Court but the sovereign people: " 'Each of the [federal branches] is the agent of the people, doing their business according to the powers conferred; and where there is a disagreement as to the extent of these powers, the people themselves, through the ballot-boxes, must settle it.' This is the true view of the Constitution. It is that which was taken by those who framed and adopted it, and by the founders of the Democratic party."[11]

In the cases of *Martin v. Hunter's Lessee* (1816)[12] and *McCulloch v. Maryland* (1819),[13] however, the Marshall Court threatened that state of affairs. It threatened to elevate the judiciary above the popular majority as arbiter of the Constitution. In *McCulloch* the Court read the Constitution's grant of all "necessary and proper" powers to the federal government as a grant of nearly unlimited congressional discretion. In *Martin*, the Court vindicated its own power to review the judgments of state courts when they interpreted federal law, including the law of the Constitution. It thereby eliminated the courts of the states as checks on the sort of consolidationism endorsed by *McCulloch*. To Van Buren, then, the Court seemed ready to undermine the essentials of popular sovereignty: state supremacy in all but the specifically enumerated spheres of federal authority; and subordination of the judicial branch, like the more obviously "political" branches, to majority will.[14]

But the grand threat did not come to fruition, at least not until the *Dred Scott* case.[15] In the wake of *McCulloch*, although in response to much other than *McCulloch*, Van Buren and the partyists inaugurated their campaign to restore control of the Constitution to the popular majorities of the states. As R. Kent Newmyer has suggested, the project of restoring states' rights through politics after *McCulloch* needed no selling in the South, where the prospect of an unconstrained northern majority in Congress "hit southern sensibilities like a firebomb."[16] In the North, the threat of consolidation after *McCulloch* was greeted with similar hostility, if not with quite the same degree of alarm. There, too, the states'-rights constitutional tradition remained a powerful force.[17] Neither in the North nor in the South, however, would it be easy to sell party organization as the proper device for advancing this constitutional politics.

By the early 1820s, then, the stage was set. The Court had made a bid to vindicate nearly any power that the federal Congress might seek to exercise, and it had sought to arrogate to itself the ultimate power to determine constitutional meaning, thus reducing the legislative arena to mere subconstitutional policymaking.[18] Meanwhile, the federal government under Monroe and then

Adams seemed poised to exploit fully the space given it by the Court. Here was the threat to states' rights and popular sovereignty that required and justified the organization of a political party as defender of the Constitution against a consolidationist faction. Although the partyists had to overcome an entrenched antipartyism to gain control of the anticonsolidationist movement, the Democratic party would ultimately succeed in drawing explicitly constitutional limits on federal power that were much narrower than the Court's. In so doing, they would vindicate "the majority of the people" and party politics, rather than the courts and adjudication, as the ultimate arbiters of constitutional meaning.[19]

The preceding chapters have shown how Illinois's politicians in the 1820s and 1830s created parties on just such a constitutional foundation. This concluding chapter discusses the experience of politics in the states generally from the earliest days of the Jacksonian period to the collapse of the Second Party System. This history can show, first, that Illinois's experience in the 1820s and 1830s probably tracked the experiences of many other states in the most important respects. Second, it suggests some ways in which the founding dynamics of the party system may illuminate the life, death, and constitutional character of the Whig-Democrat conflict. In particular, it suggests that the parties' roots in distinctive constitutionalisms continued, after the 1830s, to shape and make possible the party-organized conflicts on substantive questions that are the usual focus of historians of antebellum politics. Those constitutional roots are necessary to explain the climactic events of the Second Party System, in which the parties' procedurally oriented constitutionalisms confronted an increasing intransigence, from diverse quarters, on the substantive constitutional question of federal power over slavery in the territories. Neither the Democrats' founding principle of strict constitutional construction and states' rights, enforceable preeminently and indispensably through the properly organized Democracy, nor the Whigs' founding principle of congressional, state, and individual independence from executive party could supply the American "democracy" with a mechanism for resolving that ultimate constitutional question. Instead, the Court returned with a vengeance, ending this chapter of American constitutional history in the *Dred Scott* case by, in effect, declaring the partyists' theory of constitutional party organization defunct and opening the door to a new relationship among the parties, the courts, and the Constitution.

Creation of Mass Parties
in the States, 1815–1840

Although the two major parties ultimately produced coherent, substantive responses to the emerging market economy, I do not think that their substantive ideologies existed in anything like a fully formed state before the birth of the parties, much less that such ideologies required and spontaneously created political parties as their agents. Instead, as Illinois's experience suggests, the origins of the Second Party System indicate that the parties' substantive ideologies developed mostly after the organization of the parties, as a consequence of the parties' electoral need to advertise intelligible programs of governance.

It may seem counterintuitive that the substantive platforms came second, since both parties established substantive positions early in their careers and since those positions obviously addressed social issues that predated the mass parties. But any electoral organization must draw on preexisting controversies to advertise a substantive program of governance, as the Whigs and Democrats did, even if the party's reason for being is not that substantive program but the sort of constitutional reform identified here. And the very evidence, adduced below, that social conflict did not create durable party conflict before the 1830s, whereas the constitutional debate of the 1830s ultimately did, all suggests that the substantive ideologies were at least as much the products of the parties as they were the producers of the parties. Although sociopolitical conflict was a necessary condition for party conflict, constitutional reformism caused mass party organization, and mass party organization reduced the preexisting social conflicts to elements of just two party ideologies.

The Partyless Period in American Politics

Let me begin with the emergence of the parties' substantive ideologies from the pre-partisan politics of the 1820s. During the Second Party System, Democrats tended to oppose banks of any kind or at least advocate their stringent regulation. They also tended to oppose government funding of internal improvements and a protective tariff. And they generally advocated easy availability of public lands to settlers. Finally, the party's constituency comprised almost all the Catholics in the nation as well as many non-evangelical Protestants. The Whigs, in contrast, tended to favor banks in general and especially a national bank. They usually supported government funding of internal improvements and a protective tariff. And they tended to oppose hasty opening of the public lands to private buyers. While Whig membership and evangelicalism hardly matched up perfectly, the overlap was very great. In general, then, the Democrats exhibited a wariness of the market economy and a devotion to the individual's landed autonomy from debt, taxation, corporations, and any externally imposed morality. The Whigs, on the other hand, generally championed a capitalist morality of hard work and prudent investment, looking to maximize a general prosperity through the expansion of credit, the building of infrastructure, the fostering of domestic industries, the judicious use of communal resources, and the close management of the citizenry's moral life.

So goes the currently ascendant account of the Second Party System, and I would not want to argue with it as far as it goes. But the neat coherence across issues that historians have found in the debates of the 1840s has tended to obscure for the antebellum period a basic truth about political parties: each party contained a diversity of views on most issues but pressed its membership to speak, write, and think alike on the most important issues of the day. New York's early Van Burenite governor Enos Throop thus noted: "Those party divisions which are based upon conflicting opinions in regard to the constitution of the government, or the measures of the administration of it, . . . tend, inevitably, in the spirit of emulation and proselytism, to reduce the many shades of opinion into two opposing parties."[20] More concretely, it seems clear that any voter of any religious identity could have coherently concluded, for example, to oppose a national bank as the Democrats did but to support a protective tariff as the Whigs did, or vice versa. Or the voter could have supported government aid to internal improvements as the Whigs did while favoring rapid naturalization of new immigrants as the Democrats did. Any number of combinations of positions on the issues was plausible and sensible. And this observation suggests again that the development of two coherent, opposed modes of dealing with the market, immigration, and sectarianism was the product of the prior creation of two-party competition. And this point is not just a matter of common sense but is borne out by a look at American politics in the years before the emergence of the mass parties.

Already in the 1820s, the tariff, the Bank, internal improvements, and the public lands animated national politics, but they did not automatically create a polarized, party-organized politics. The tariff, for example, was the source of never-ending negotiations among the various economic interests in the land throughout the 1820s. With time, the so-called Tariff of Abominations provoked not a party division between pro- and anti-market types but a southern protest movement against the federal government's imposition of a partisan, numerical-majoritarian will on a minority. South Carolina's John Calhoun led the fight against the tariff in the late 1820s and early 1830s not as a self-avowed party leader, not as an ideologue of pre-market economics, but as a constitutional theorist of pre-partisan republicanism in a federal system. Calhoun spoke for a highly market-oriented class of large planters, which objected to the tariff not because it was a prop of some dreaded credit system, but because the particular structure of duties seemed to discriminate unconstitutionally against southern interests. Such misgovernment evidenced factional, antisouthern control of the national government and threatened minority interests generally, including the slaveholding interest as such. And Calhoun's response to the tariff was not to organize a political party but to develop the constitutional theory of the concurrent majority, a device meant—like the Madisonian Constitution itself—to prevent the formation of majority parties in the federal government.[21]

By Calhoun's reasoning, the numerical-majoritarian tariff proved that Madison's theory in Federalist no. 10, that a large federal republic would prevent the coalescence of majority interests, was, at best, obsolete.[22] Now, the only way to prevent party oppression of minorities through the federal government was to recognize each individual state's constitutional authority to veto legislation. Such an arrangement would compel federal legislators to look to the good of the whole at all times, since attempts to pass partial legislation would be "nullified."[23] In the subsequent Nullification Crisis, Jackson's quasi-consolidationist response proved to many southerners that the federal government was indeed a danger to the antipartisan constitutional order. Unsurprisingly, then, the states'-rights responses to Jackson often proved to be the founding acts of southern Whig parties.[24]

Thus the tariff controversy did not create two organized parties debating the merits and demerits of the market. Rather, it stimulated the coalescence of a party opposed to Jackson's consolidationist assertion of federal power. The tariff failed to create a party division of its own force as a matter of policy, but it did prove to many antiparty southerners, as other issues proved to many antiparty northerners, that the federal government was in the hands of an executive party, ambitious to impose its will and its discipline on the state polities. In that constitutional capacity, the tariff was crucial to the coalescence of the Whigs even as, in its capacity as a policy matter, the tariff actually divided those same Whigs.

Similarly, the Bank of the United States failed to stimulate party division as an economic measure, but it carried important constitutional meaning in the Van Burenite drive to re-create Republican organization in the states. The Bank had been a central point of contention in the so-called First Party System, a period of national party competition now recognized as constitutional and pre-partisan in its nature.[25] Originally a part of Hamilton's plan to strengthen the Constitution, the Bank was allowed to expire by the Republican Congress in 1811. After the War of 1812, however, most Republicans had concluded that the Bank's capacity for corrupting constitutional government paled in comparison to the nation's need for a well-regulated currency. With the Federalists dead or dying, a newly chartered Bank provoked no new party divisions, even when the Panic of 1819 and the *McCulloch* decision brought a new round of criticisms. The Bank never lacked enemies, who saw in it an excessive concentration of both economic and political power.[26] But those enemies did not immediately see themselves as a party. They did not think that they should also, for example, oppose protective tariffs and government funding of internal improvements just because of their position on the Bank. That development awaited the Jackson administration's partyist campaign to tie all democrats to the substantive positions of the party. When Jackson vetoed the recharter of the Bank in 1832, the partyist campaign was well under way, and many of those who would come to support the veto and, especially, Jackson's "removal" of the deposits had actually been supporters of the Bank before the party line was laid down.[27] Like the Nullification Crisis, the Bank War did not really divide the pro-market from the anti-market but those willing to concede the authority of the Democratic party from those who deemed it an agent of "executive usurpation."[28]

The question of how to dispose of the public lands further illustrates the pre-partisan nature of politics in the 1820s. Although the Democrats and Whigs would convert the public lands into a partisan issue by the late 1830s, the bitter battles over their disposition in the 1820s did not produce parties. In fact, the years of struggle over proposals for preemption, graduation, cession, and distribution had finally left the issue all but moribund when the creation of the parties gave it new life in the late 1830s. Across the 1820s, the Old South had generally opposed both cheap land and Henry Clay's American System of federally funded internal improvements and a high protective tariff. The Southwest had favored cheap land and opposed the tariff but had been divided on federal funding for internal improvements. The Northwest had favored cheap land and the entire American System. And the Northeast had tended to favor the American System but was divided on the question of cheap land. None of the sections had been perfectly united on any of these questions, of course, but all these responses had been alive in the national debate on economic policy after the panic and throughout the 1820s. None had been associated with a political party before the 1830s.[29]

Ongoing policy debate amid broad suffrage, then, was proving inadequate to produce mass parties in the states. Virtually every state continued to be dominated by antipartisan ideology, even those few states with substantial histories of party competition.[30] Policy questions abounded in a contentious but widely partyless politics. Yet this solid antipartyist consensus would presently face the challenge of Van Buren's democratic partyism in Washington and in the states. The story of the Van Burenite challenge and the anti–Van Burenites' response is the real story of the origins of the party system in Illinois and appears to have been so in other states as well.

The Partyist Revolution in Washington, D.C.

The Van Burenites' understanding of the imperatives of popular sovereignty grew out of their experience in the "First Party System," the misnamed period in which neither party accepted the other's legitimacy or its own permanence as an institution. A generation of this sort of party competition did not shake the antiparty convictions of the nation.[31] Rather, schoolchildren destined to be members of the Democratic party were taught democracy and antipartyism by the same textbooks.[32] And one of the chief theorists of the Van Burenite movement, historian and activist George Bancroft, chronicled the rise of popular government in work that anticipated a final triumph of partyless democracy over aristocracy.[33]

Bancroft may have gotten a little carried away in anticipating a political millennium. Van Buren himself believed that the battle against aristocracy was permanent. But his campaign for the presidency in 1836, like Bancroft's history, rested on the principle that only one party under a democratic constitution could stand for popular sovereignty and that in the United States the Democrats were it. His claim to the votes of all democrats, then, rested simply on his being the regular nominee of the democracy. One might even say that, just as Van Buren's campaign for Jackson in 1828 was designed more to reestablish the Jeffersonian party of the Constitution than to elect Jackson, the main point of his own presidential campaign was to establish party nominations by convention as "part of the living constitution."[34] In that campaign, the Democrats continued to embrace the language of strict construction and states' rights, of course, but they also elevated party organization itself as a chief principle of the national campaign, indispensably linked to those constitutional principles.[35] To Van Buren, Jackson had been the tribune of the democracy, protecting the people against the factions. But tribunes were temporary; the Democratic party must be as permanent as the Constitution.[36]

As soon as Van Buren took office, the Panic of 1837 presented him with a great opportunity to impress upon the nation the centrality of party organization to popular sovereignty. At the special session of Congress in 1837, Van Buren presented his proposal for an Independent Treasury and, more generally, for divorcing the federal government's fiscal operations from banks. In the most extreme form of "divorce," the federal government was to hold all its funds in its own hands, receiving and paying only hard money, not bank notes.

But when Van Buren presented this proposal, he did not beseech Congress to put aside party and all its evils in the interest of the public good. Instead, he presented the divorce proposal as party policy to which all good democrats must adhere. Quickly, it became clear that the Independent Treasury was not just a response to an economic crisis but a party test. It was a device for separating those who were prepared to accept the authority of the party—assertedly, the voice of the people—from those who would insist that their own private judgments were of greater authority for them than the majority's. By Van Buren's lights, the democracy's commitment to a hard-money policy was clear not only in the congressional democracy's majority support for divorce but also in the fact that the alternative to the Independent Treasury was an unconstitutional national bank. For Van Buren, then, the contrast between Democratic hostility to government dependence on banks and the opposition's incorrigible Bankism was less a reflection of differences in economic theory than in constitutional vision. He sought to ensure that the people saw clearly the division between the democracy and a financial aristocracy. Such had been the nature of the party division in Jefferson's time, and so it remained in Van Buren's, just as it was the natural division of any political nation.[37] If pressing the Independent Treasury meant the consolidation of an opposition party and the loss of that minority of his own party that could not go along with a measure "that [Van Buren] believed with all his mind and heart expressed the genius of democratic political institutions," then that was exactly the right price to pay to clarify the true, constitutional nature of the difference between the parties.[38]

The Whigs, meanwhile, agreed that the issue was more constitutional than economic. If the Democratic organizers' great fear was a connection between organized self-interest and government—the very definition of aristocracy—then the great fear of the Whigs was executive-party government, which by definition divided an otherwise unified polity into classes.[39] This fear had been the salient one at the founding of the Whig opposition to Jackson and would continue to be. To some historians, the later organization of the Whigs as a mass party rendered the movement's origins as an antiparty resistance to "executive usurpation" essentially irrelevant to its later development as a party of national economic reform.[40] But the opposition of Whigs and Conservative Democrats to Van Buren's economic measures actually helped to perpetuate the Whigs' original constitutional principles.

So-called Conservative Democrats like William Rives of Virginia and Nathaniel Tallmadge of New York (not to mention all three of Illinois's representatives in the House) resisted Van Buren's supposed attack on the credit system from the moment the Independent Treasury was introduced, but even more than that they resisted its use as a vehicle of party authority.[41] Waves of Jacksonians had abandoned the Democratic party in opposition to "executive usurpation" at any of several critical moments—the Maysville Road veto, the veto of the Bank recharter, nullification, deposit removal, the nomination of Van Buren. Now in the late 1830s, the last wave of dissident, original Jacksonians would leave the party in response to the Independent Treasury's deployment as a party test, some temporarily, others never to return. Rives himself equated party domination of the government with rule by the president alone.[42] When many Jacksonians chose to go with their party against their well-known individual preferences for a less radical policy, the hold-out Conservatives were confirmed in their antipartyism. They hardly needed to add that the Independent Treasury unconstitutionally consolidated the power of the purse in the executive.[43]

The election of 1840 brought the simple two-sided contest that Van Buren had longed for. Early in 1840, the Democrats had finally gotten the Independent Treasury through Congress, and Van Buren was convinced that with party lines sharply drawn between strict-constructionist democracy and loose-constructionist aristocracy, the result could not be in doubt. The one true democratic party must command a permanent majority in democratic America whenever party lines were clear.[44] Unfortunately for him, the Whig campaign turned out not to be a drive for a national bank and the American System behind Henry Clay but an antiparty crusade behind Harrison, true to the Whigs' origins in resistance to executive encroachment. The Whig campaign was not shy about defending the credit system as against the hard-money Independent Treasury, but it buried the specifics of any Whig economic program in its conviction that the fundamental source of the nation's troubles, economic and otherwise, was executive engrossment of power and government by spoils. Economic problems would not be difficult to solve, in the Whig vision of statecraft, once the Constitution was restored; that is, once candidates were freed from party platforms, party discipline, and the will of the executive.

The Partyist Revolution in the States

Against the failure of earlier substantive questions to create a party system, the successful creation of a mass party *by constitutional reform* stands out. And, as Illinois's experience suggests, the partyist president's campaign was not confined to Washington, D.C. Substantial evidence exists in secondary work that within the states the parties formed according to a logic quite similar to that of Illinois. That is, when politicians created parties they relied on constitutional justifications; parties did not simply emerge as by-products of social developments.

Thus, for example, even in New York, supposedly in the avant-garde of two-partyism at least since the 1820s,[45] the partyist struggle actually echoed Illinois's experience in the most important ways. The state's partyist vanguard, Van Buren's "Albany Regency," explicitly targeted the factionalism that had so often reigned in American politics, yet it publicly and expressly insisted on individual members' faithfulness to the decisions of a political organization, the Regency's party of the democracy. It took this unprecedented step not just as a tactical matter but as a moral imperative, as the constitutive principle of the party itself.[46] In fact, the party sometimes operated under the label "Friends of Regular Nominations," to emphasize that its fundamental commitment was to democratic procedure rather than to any substantive platform. Moreover, the Regency welcomed an organized opposition as a spur to its own organization, not because alternation in power was of the essence of democracy but because the opponents who appeared could be counted on to expose their aristocratic character by training their guns mainly on party organization itself, as Dewitt Clinton's "People's Men" of the 1820s predictably did.[47] Although important aspects of the party development of the 1830s were prefigured in New York's First Party System, mass parties in continuing conflict with each other emerged only in the 1830s in response to Van Burenism. As in other states, the Democrats subordinated all substantive policy questions to the question whether popular sovereignty could be preserved outside a tightly organized party,[48] and, as in other states, the Whig party coalesced around the principle that such Democratic organization was entirely subversive of democracy.[49]

Similarly, in Southampton County, Virginia, no party cohesion existed at the beginning of the 1830s.[50] The Whigs organized in 1834 in reaction to the executive high-handedness of Jackson in the nullification and deposit-removal episodes.[51] And when Van Buren pressed the Independent Treasury on Congress, economic arguments mattered, but "fears of 'an unnecessary enlargement of executive power and patronage' gave the issue ideological intensity."[52] Finally, this new politics of party became entrenched only by the "Conservative revolt" that "gained momentum in Virginia from such fears [of arbitrary executive power] at least as much as from the economic issues involved."[53]

In Ohio, the focus of politics from that state's founding was the locus of sovereignty. Jeffersonian localists during the First Party System accused the Federalist territorial elite of appropriating popular power by means of a court party fed by federal patronage.[54] Admission to statehood and the ascendancy of democratic ideology did little to settle the definition and mechanisms of democracy for Ohio, although it remained clear that candidates widely refused to admit to membership in a party.[55] Even the presence of a small, partyist avant-garde and a remarkably wide use of nominating conventions by the 1810s did little to erode the state's fundamental antipartyism.[56] It should come as little surprise, then, that the Panic of 1819 produced a populist movement that targeted both the Bank of the United States and caucus control of Ohio politics as mechanisms by which popular power was siphoned away to elite groups.[57] When the Bank War really began in the 1830s, in Ohio, as in Illinois, the debate had more to do with party organization and political practice than with economic policy. It was in this crisis that the Whigs coalesced, and even in the 1840s some Ohioans still made resistance to party more important than economic issues as such.[58] Meanwhile, as the Democrats came together, they spoke the pure language of Van Burenite constitutionalism. Like Van Buren, Ohio's Benjamin Tappan "interpreted all history as a Manichaean struggle . . . between two opposing armies: the democracy . . . and the aristocracy."[59] Believing that "the Democracy or, as they often put it, the True Democracy" was "not a party" but "the people themselves,"[60] Tappan and the Ohio Democrats publicly sought and expected " 'the complete and permanent ascendancy of the democratic party.' "[61]

In Michigan, admitted to statehood only in 1837, virtually the only issues debated by the emerging Democratic and Whig parties in the mid-1830s were the issue of party organization itself and the closely allied question of alien suffrage. The Democratic newspaper in Detroit made almost no political arguments in these early days except to advocate the Van Burenite theory of democratic party organization. The first Whig efforts at organization were directed only to those who would resist the imposition of party organization on the free electorate of Michigan, and the new movement bemoaned alien voting as a self-serving device of Democratic party manipulators.[62]

Well into the 1830s, Mississippi elections remained universally and pointedly antipartisan. The first hints of party division in Mississippi originated in protests against party division in the national government. First, Senator George Poindexter broke with the Jackson administration over its patronage policy and the Bank War, and then this solidly Jacksonian state endured an 1832 revolt against Van Buren's convention nomination as Jackson's running mate. When the Democrats began to organize in 1834, the Whigs followed suit. But where the Democrats got quickly to the business of making party nominations, the Whigs resolutely insisted that theirs was merely an antiparty organization of self-defense. They did not make nominations or distribute spoils but only resolved that the states were sovereign and that party was inconsistent with free government.[63] After 1834, the parties in Mississippi did not achieve even this level of organization again until 1839, and, according to the state's most recent historian, the lure of party quickly faded, never really taking hold before the Civil War.[64]

Georgia's factional politics did not much resemble party politics for the first decades of its political life. And when mass parties did emerge in reaction to the Democratic party's embrace of party authority, "the two parties differed most significantly in their attitudes toward the rise of political parties," not on questions of substantive policy.[65] In Tennessee, meanwhile, the origins of mass party competition lay in the 1836 presidential campaign. Hugh White's candidacy that year focused on the question whether Democratic party organization and party nomination were legitimate mechanisms of popular sovereignty.[66]

In the absence of state studies that focus specifically on the question of what moved the polities to create and accept party organization,[67] the generalizability of Illinois's experience remains uncertain. As the evidence above suggests, however, the apparent similarities in party development in many states suggest little reason to think that Illinois's experience was unique. If there were regional variations in particulars and timing,[68] the essentials appear similar. State and national political cultures that had continued roundly to reject party organization into the 1820s—even where organization had made the most progress in the First Party System and even amid controversies over internal improvements, the public lands, the Bank, and the tariff—finally began to yield comprehensive, mass party organization mostly in the 1830s. These new parties did not simply separate those of one economic ideology from those of another. Rather, they separated two groups of different constitutional ideologies: first, those who were willing to accept Jackson's lead into a Van Burenite organization, insisting on the construction of a single, dominant party of "the democracy" as the means of fulfilling the antiparty promise of the Constitution; and, second, those who, in several waves, rejected that leadership and that ideology. As the spoils of 1829, the Maysville Road veto, the veto of the recharter bill, the nullification crisis, the removal of the deposits, the anointing of Van Buren, the openly partyist presidential campaign of 1836, and the imposition of the Independent Treasury as a party test proved that the fundamental issue in American politics was the Van Burenite injection of party into the Constitution, traditional antipartyists determined that Van Buren could be met only by a mass antiparty crusade. They had to form a party of national unity for the 1840 presidential campaign. The two resulting organizations necessarily faced the challenge of substantive policy questions from the start, but their founding constitutionalisms were the indispensable prerequisites for the institutional development that was mass-party competition. So it was in Illinois, and so there is good reason to believe it was generally.

The Ascendancy of the Mass Party, 1840–1848

What, then, does this process of party formation say about the resultant constitutional structure? The Whig-Democrat conflict continued for another dozen years or more after 1840, managing the nation's emergence as an ethnoreligiously diverse country, headed down the road to a complex market and industrial economy, and repeatedly confronted by the crises that a union of slave and free states entailed. The roots of the party conflict in constitutional reformism suggest some constraints within which the system approached that task, some reasons why it produced certain answers to those social problems and not others, and some reasons why it finally collapsed in the early 1850s. In particular, the parties' procedurally oriented constitutionalisms played an important role in determining substantive policy results, but neither party's constitutionalism equipped it to deal with the single greatest challenge to popular sovereignty that the politicians of the Second Party System would identify: the constitutional question of federal power over slavery in the territories and the uncompromisable (as it turned out) substantive positions that so many Americans subsequently adopted on that issue.

The Whigs in the Second Party System

The course of the Whig party was determined at least as much by its founding antipartyism as by the substantive program and ideology that historians have identified with the party. It must be admitted, however, that Abe Lincoln's hero was not Bolingbroke but Henry Clay. The most basic political commitment of Lincoln and his like before, during, and after the organization of the Whig party was not antipartyism but the liberating effects of the market economy. Like Clay, he thought that a national bank, government-funded internal improvements, and a protective tariff would produce an economy of unlimited opportunity for those who sought to escape the bondage of poverty.[69]

In that substantive goal, he was joined by most Whigs (not to mention many Democrats), but the party was not all harmony on such issues. John Tyler, after all, was the Whig president who vetoed the 1841 national-bank bill as an unconstitutional expansion of federal power while aggressively sustaining the antipartyism that had motivated his Whiggism from the early 1830s.[70] There was a reason why the American System as such and especially the project of a national bank had been absent from the Whig campaign in much of the nation in 1840. The 1840 Whig movement was, by its own terms, an antiparty movement rather than a campaign for the American System, and for many of that movement's adherents a national bank was at best problematic.[71]

The old view that the Whigs were an incoherent agglomeration of ideologically disparate elements had a large germ of truth in it. States'-rights southern Whigs lived in some tension with protective-tariff, American System types.[72] Georgia's Whigs, for example, "struggled for four years to adapt their views to those of the national party on a national bank, the tariff, and Texas annexation, only to falter at the polls."[73] And the tensions within the Whig party on the questions of expansionism and slavery are also well known.[74] Finally, while nativists generally supported the Whigs, many Whigs opposed the nativist project of dramatically expanding the waiting periods for voting and citizenship for immigrants. The tensions between nativists and anti-nativists in the party hampered the Whigs in every presidential election.[75]

Nor was the Whig party perfectly united in its antipartyism. Still, if many Whigs like Lincoln and Clay were eager to drop all the touchiness about party organization, their movement owed its very capacity to organize its antipartisan constituency to its constitutional antipartyism. The Whig party as an organization had declared its character to be fundamentally different from the Democrats' by virtue of its antipartyism; and an indispensable part of its constituency—perhaps a great majority of the party—still harbored its original opposition to parties and especially to the ethic of party authority that would consolidate power in the federal executive.

The crucial role of antipartyism in sustaining a heterogeneous Whig party that had founded itself on that very principle can be seen throughout the party's life. In Illinois, for example, Lincoln wasted no time in trying to perpetuate the spirit of organization that had prevailed in the Harrison campaign by trying to get up a convention for the 1842 gubernatorial nomination. He failed, however, because of broad Whig resistance to the device.[76] He and his coadjutors tried again in 1843 for the congressional elections. But they did not dare justify the convention system in principle: "Whether the system is right in itself, we do not stop to enquire; contenting ourselves with trying to show, that while our opponents use it, it is madness in us not to defend ourselves with it."[77]

While the committee of 1843 succeeded in getting up some conventions and establishing some committees, it never was able to control the party. The old leader of the antipartyist movement that had founded the Whigs, Joseph Duncan, responded to Lincoln's urgings with an anticonvention, antiparty manifesto. He contrasted such ad hoc Whig gatherings as the Harrisburg convention, which had merely recommended Harrison to the nation in 1839, with the convention system. The latter was "nothing more nor less than a contrivance of government officers, of office seekers, and men who make politics a trade, to take the selection of all public agents from the people."[78] Through spoils and through ostracism of those who deviated from the demands of the convention system, party leaders were able to commit the rank and file against its own convictions of good policy and good candidates. He concluded with a catalogue of the "most important points at issue between the parties," a list of proper Whig commitments with a familiarly constitutional character as well as a pro-market bent. "Whenever these things can be effected, and the people shall once more prefer the success and prosperity of the whole country to the triumphs of party, our Government will be pure, our liberties safe, and the people united, prosperous and happy."[79]

Although the party again organized in impressive fashion for the 1844 presidential campaign, Whig resistance to party obligation and specifically to the convention system remained vital. The Whigs failed to organize in the 1846 gubernatorial campaign and barely ran a campaign at all behind their self-nominated candidate.[80] Lincoln's own letters reveal the persistence of an anti-convention-system wing of the party that obstructed Lincoln's and others' efforts to permanently organize the party.[81] And Lincoln himself joined vigorously in the Taylor campaign of 1848, when Whiggism amounted to little but an insistence on a "no party" presidency. Although historians have sometimes deemed this national "no party" campaign all but issueless,[82] Lincoln swallowed hard and threw himself into it. In the United States House of Representatives, he defended the fact that Taylor ran on an entirely constitutional platform with no legislative program. He contrasted the Democrats' vision of the president as a man who makes up the minds of his people and enforces his opinions on them by the devices of party with the Whig vision of the president as wholly the servant of the people's will.[83]

Nationally as well, the Whigs' constitutional vision of a citizenry of independent political thinkers, unbound by party or executive influence, continued to inform the party. When the ultra-antipartyist Tyler exercised his independent Whig judgment to veto Clay's cherished national bank, Clay deemed him a traitor to the Whigs. But Clay's next step was not to invoke the ethic of party obligation (much as he might have liked to). Rather, it was to return again to the Whigs' fundamental antipartyism and identify once again the rise of executive influence in Tyler's effort to create an independent presidential party.[84]

In the summer of 1842, Clay spoke to a crowd in Lexington, Kentucky, about the continuing depression.[85] He blamed the hard times on those Jacksonian policies that had been motivated solely by the imperatives of party. He did not condemn Jacksonian ignorance of economics. He insisted only that frugality and industry, a sound currency, and an adequate tariff had been sacrificed to the interests of party.[86] For Clay, the root cause of the panic was in three actions by Jackson: the veto of the recharter bill; the removal of the federal deposits from the Bank; and the pocket veto of the Land Bill.[87] According to

Clay, the central motive for destroying the Bank was that "it refused to make itself basely and servilely, instrumental to the promotion of political views and objects." The veto, therefore, was "necessary to sustain [Jackson's] party, which could only be done by sustaining him."[88] The effect of party organization was to take the interests of one man and his immediate political dependents and impose them on the rank and file. Had there been no party organization, it would follow, there would have been no sustained opposition to the Bank and ultimately no panic. Clay illustrated this phenomenon with the turnabout of the Democratic legislature of Pennsylvania, which had supported the Bank until the veto was issued and party discipline invoked. Further charging the Democratic party with responsibility for such events as nullification and the Dorr Rebellion, Clay nevertheless refused to suppose that all Democrats truly supported such attacks on republican rule. Rather, they had allowed themselves to be swayed by party ties. Under such influences, "not only individuals but whole communities abandon their long cherished interests and principles."[89]

John Pendleton Kennedy's *Defence of the Whigs*,[90] a Clay campaign text published in 1844, developed fully the antipartyist vision of the Second Party System. Kennedy, a novelist and member of the Twenty-seventh Congress, understood all politics under representative government to be episodes in the eternal contest against "Prerogative." Prerogative was always wielded by a single man at the head of a political organization—Walpole and Jackson, for example, and now Tyler. In contrast, the Whigs, being the people as a whole, became politically "embodied" only when party ascendancy prompted the people to defend their liberty. Such crises had occurred in 1688, 1776, and again in 1830 when a half century of secure liberty was threatened by the rise of the Jackson party. Jackson's executive abuses called forth the spontaneous rising of the Whigs against the usurpations of Prerogative and party,[91] a "universal revolt" that was headed off temporarily by "the artful engendering and skillful control of faction."[92] By 1840 Democratic trickery could no longer withstand the popular commitment to the principles of '76, and Harrison was elected.

At issue that year were not the passing issues of economics, important as those were, but the defense of free government against party domination. And so the principal rallying point for the Whigs was not advocacy of the Bank but of constitutional measures to thwart party. These included the single presidential term; the reduction of patronage; the non-interference of government officers in the elections; and the modification of the veto power, that central "instrument of Party Domination." Such measures, aimed against "the enlargement of Executive and the diminution of Legislative power" by means of party, comprised the "first, and immeasurably the greatest [aim]" of the Whigs in 1840.[93] And so they would again in 1844, Kennedy avowed. Whig dissatisfaction with Tyler resulted not so much from the importance of the Bank itself as from a fear that Tyler was using the Bank issue to destroy the Whigs. Since Tyler knew that the Whigs would never permit him a second term, Kennedy went on, he had to find a way to create a personal party as a vehicle for his ambition.[94] Whig preservation of republican politics would preserve forever the chance to fight for the Bank, but the perpetuation of party Prerogative, whether under Tyler or the "Locofocos," threatened to eliminate free government altogether.[95]

In the middle period of its brief life as a party, then, under the leadership of Henry Clay, abundant evidence suggests that the Whigs remained rooted in and limited by their founding, constitutional, antipartyist orientation.[96] And as they approached their old age, the 1848 Taylor campaign only reaffirmed the Whigs' dependence on their original constitutional principles. No doubt, Taylor's candidacy was for some Whigs (probably for Lincoln) an entirely tactical effort to manufacture a majority by running a military hero in place of the true embodiment of Whig principles, Henry Clay. But the no-party language of the Taylor campaign and its origins in the agitation of political independents outside the two parties were decisive attractions for many Whigs. As the candidate of the Whig party, Taylor's main message was that in fact he "would not be the mere President of a party" but of "the whole people."[97]

The Democrats in the Second Party System

Like the Whigs, the Democrats harbored serious internal divisions on substantive issues throughout the Second Party System, divisions that the party managed by frequent recurrence to its founding partyist principle. Although the dominant Democratic positions show that many antebellum Americans severely doubted the compatibility of democracy with capitalism,[98] it is also true that many Democrats decidedly favored banks,[99] government aid to internal improvements,[100] and other measures congenial to a dynamic, market economy.

From the late 1830s, the Democrats were divided between radical hard-money activists and soft-money men. The hard-money wing often went so far as to advocate the outlawing of banks altogether. The soft-money wing, on the other hand, was happy to augment regulation of banks after the Panic of 1837 but resisted antibank excess and even voted with the Whigs when the anticapitalist, hard-money men pushed too hard. In the Southwest, the hards were strong enough to repudiate the state's bank-bond debt in Mississippi and to abolish banks and domestic paper money in some states, even though a minority of Democrats tried to keep the movement from undertaking more than moderate reform. In the Northwest, Democratic hards were again the majority of the party and sought the same result as in the Southwest but were defeated in their main goals by periodic defections of soft Democrats to the Whigs. In fact, it would not be too much to say that, on the question of banks, the central division in the Northwest was not between the Democrats and the Whigs but between the hard-money Democrats, on the one hand, and the soft-money Democrats and the Whigs, on the other.[101] In the East, relatively stable banking systems blunted the opposition of the hards. There, too, the party was divided between authentic, hard-money radicals and soft-money Democrats, but truly radical antibank proposals never stood a chance in the East.[102]

The Democrats also included constituencies representing the full range of opinion on government funding of internal improvements and protective tariffs. When the Democratic Congress and President Polk substantially reduced tariff levels in the mid-1840s, protectionist Democrats felt betrayed.[103] So also, when Congress passed a rivers and harbors improvements bill, Polk's veto rebuffed pro-internal-improvement Democrats[104] as Franklin Pierce's similar veto would again in 1854.[105]

In principle, even persistent divisions on substantive questions such as banks, tariffs, and internal improvements should not have presented a problem for the Democrats, since their founding principle was not opposition to pro-market legislation or any other substantive policy position but commitment to the democratic principle of majority rule within a party of diverse substantive inclinations. Thus, when the party was unable to produce complete unity on any particular issue, the danger was not really that the party appeared to be divided on substantive policy and thus without a coherent, collective ideology. Rather, the problem was that it appeared to have forsaken the very principle that had justified its organization in the first place, individual subordination of all preferences to the overriding principle of majority rule within the democracy. Where the Whigs in principle could not apply the device of the party test, the Democrats' requirement of adherence to the positions of the party majority stood as the test of one's commitment to popular sovereignty.

Or so went the theory that had launched the party, the theory that was to make the party the true manifestation of democratic antipartyism itself. But, of course, as the Whigs lacked perfect unity in their founding antipartyism as much as in their substantive tendencies, so the Democrats lacked perfect unity in their constitutional partyism as much as in their policy inclinations. Illinois, for example, contained opposition to the convention system among Democrats throughout the 1840s. In the spring of 1843, one Democratic congressional candidate wrote to another that they must settle on who would run by some method other than a convention since "there is a very large portion of the Democratic party who are opposed to conventions from principle and will support no man who accepts a nomination from one."[106] Even in 1848, a potential candidate for a seat on Illinois's supreme court reported to a fellow Democrat, "There is great opposition to conventions in this [southwestern] part of the state to bring forward candidates for any office + I think there would be more opposition to conventions for judicial offices than others."[107] In Alabama, similarly, "the populace was always suspicious of conventions . . . because of their purported potential for oppression."[108] In fact, in counties where the Democratic majority was large enough to make the election of a Whig a rarity, the device of the convention never established itself and was regarded as anti-democratic by candidates and electorate alike. Perhaps a majority of Alabama counties disdained convention nomination of state legislators in the 1840s.[109] The party, therefore, lacked perfect unity with respect to at least this important aspect of its founding theory. Still, this resistance to a certain party device does not seem to have seriously undermined the Democrats' central principle—the principle of majoritarian party authority—except for certain small groups like the Calhounites who lived on the party fringes, in and out of the party as their substantive goals might dictate.

On the basis of both its constitutionalism and its substantive positions, the Democratic party built a small but fairly reliable majority that, unlike the membership of the Whig party, widely embraced the principle of party obligation. The result was that the Democrats could generally control politics in this period even though the Democratic party position on any particular issue might well be the minority position in the nation. On the Bank question, the tariff, and internal improvements, Democratic party control rested at least in part on the party's principled ability to obligate members to support party positions even against their prior preferences and to support party nominees for no other reason than that they were the nominees of the party.

Across the 1840s, then, even as the sectional crisis increasingly threatened to undermine everything the party stood for, the Democrats used the principle of party to achieve the very mission Van Buren had assigned to party back in the 1820s. The party dominated American governance for a generation after Jackson's retirement and, in that generation, it established the unconstitutionality of a national bank, a protective tariff, and federal funding for non-national internal improvements, each a vindication of strict construction and states' rights. And none of this was achieved by resort to the courts—even though the Supreme Court was now a Jacksonian Court substantially more sympathetic to states' rights than the Marshall Court had been[110]—but through the revived party of the sovereign people.

The party had succeeded in using antipartisan, democratic values to legitimate the very thing—party authority over each democrat and over the meaning of the states'-rights Constitution itself—that the Whigs foundationally rejected as anti-democratic. To be a Democrat was, above all, to identify popular sovereignty with party loyalty and party obligation, just as to be a Whig was, above all, to reject any such compromise of individual judgment as fundamentally inconsistent with democracy.[111]

The Challenge of Slavery in the Territories, 1844–1854

The real test of the parties' founding constitutionalisms, of course, came in the steady growth of sectional tension within the parties. The territorial slavery issue raises the question of what role these founding principles played in producing the major policy results of the sectional crisis—the Compromise of 1850 and the Kansas-Nebraska Act—and the ultimate collapse of the Second Party System.

Unlike most southern Democrats, John Calhoun had never accepted the founding theory of the Democratic party of which he was sometimes a member. Contrary to Van Buren's numerical-majoritarianism and ethic of party obligation, Calhoun believed that minorities might have fundamental substantive commitments, the disregard of which by a numerical majority—however fairly assembled—constituted majoritarian tyranny rather than principled democracy.[112] Although few Americans embraced Calhoun's theory of the concurrent majority, the sectional crisis would increasingly test southern Democrats' Van Burenite majoritarianism. That crisis steadily pressed to the fore the possibility that a national majority would reject a substantive position—southerners' "equal rights" to carry their property into the territories—that many southerners deemed indispensable to democracy. The crisis would similarly test northerners' majoritarianism, as they increasingly feared that a congressional majority would be mustered to legalize slavery in the territories, even against the wishes of the settlers. Although few in either section ever rejected majoritarian democracy as such, increasing numbers in each section began to find the basic procedural constitutionalisms of their parties no longer adequate to preserve democracy, because they proved unable to generate satisfying positions on the substantive question of slavery extension. Democratic constitutional theory had harbored from the start a potential clash between its majoritarianism, on the one hand, and its commitment to states' rights and strict construction of the Constitution, on the other. This danger had been assumed away by repeated observations of the historical link between localism and majoritarianism. But the sectional crisis would inescapably raise the specter of democratic majorities tempted to indulge in loose construction and centralization of power.

When Calhoun entered the cabinet of the partyless President Tyler, he set about securing southerners' substantive rights by pressing for the annexation of Texas and, ultimately, his own nomination for president by the Democrats. This episode was not the first exhibition of the tension between slaveholding and majoritarian democracy, nor, more generally, between substantive convictions and procedural theories of democracy.[113] But it is a fair place to begin the story of the antebellum period's ultimate encounter with that tension.

Following what Van Buren and the Democratic party regulars thought of as the aberrant (and illegally achieved) Whig victory in 1840, Van Buren was the Democrats' presumptive candidate for 1844.[114] But the Calhounites looked to 1844 as an opportunity to vindicate southern rights in particular and minority rights in general—instead of Van Buren's majoritarian proceduralism—as fundamental to republican government.[115] At the 1844 convention, a nearly solid southern wing of the party, joined by a significant minority of northern delegates, pushed through the same two-thirds rule that had obtained at the Democrats' two previous presidential conventions.[116] But unlike the situation at those first two conventions, here a candidate (Van Buren) actually received a majority of the votes only to be denied the nomination by minority resistance. From the core Van Burenites' perspective, a minority had imposed a substantive party test—annexation of Texas (on which Van Buren was lukewarm)—on the majority.

Ultimately, the party united behind a southern Democrat, James K. Polk, who was also a tried and true party regular. The Van Burenites could live with the nominee even if they believed that his elevation was the product, in part, of an essentially "aristocratic" disruption of Democratic party organization. The question was whether the new president and the party would vindicate the party's basic principle during the next four years.

That question was answered in the negative in 1846 for increasing numbers of Van Burenites. Texas had been annexed under Tyler in 1845, but Polk failed the northern wing of the party on the Oregon question—the conflict with England over the Oregon boundary—thus exacerbating northern fears that a southern minority was in control of the party. The Independent Treasury was again made law after having been repealed by the Whigs in 1841, but a serious reduction in tariff rates and Polk's veto of the rivers and harbors bill again enhanced the feeling of some regular Democrats that the party had been captured by a southern-rights minority. When Polk contrived a war with Mexico, holding out the possibility of more territorial gains, the Democrats were again united behind him. But many regular northern Democrats had concluded that the democratic quality of party decisionmaking must be tested.

The northern free-soil Democrat, David Wilmot, therefore offered a mea-

sure that would have preemptively barred slavery from any territory to be ac-
quired from Mexico in the war. But Wilmot was not the sort of fringe Democrat whose political polestar was substantive opposition to slavery. As is well
known, he was among the most regular of Democrats. He did not offer the
Proviso as a northern party test but as an expression of many northern Democrats' perception that the party had become enthralled to the southern-rights
Democrats, whose own willingness to impose substantive tests had diverted
much of the party from its bedrock majoritarianism. The point of the Proviso
was not to announce a substantive condition on which free-soil Democrats'
cooperation with the party would depend, but to insist that "northern sentiments deserved a full and fair hearing" in the party.[117] Two could play at the
game of substantive tests, but the result of that game could only be the destruction of the nation's fundamental democratic institution, the majoritarian
Democratic party organization. The constitutional crisis provoked by the war
and the Proviso within the Democracy persisted into the next presidential election year, and the enormous accession of territory accomplished in the peace
treaty only exacerbated the situation.

Meanwhile, Van Buren's New York Democratic party had split into two factions on the sectional question. Van Buren's Barnburners traced their roots to
the hard-money, ultra-partyist faction of the New York Democrats of the late
1830s and now generally supported the Proviso as a constitutional message to
the party. Meanwhile, the Hunkers, traceable to the soft-money side of the
party in the 1830s, generally opposed the Proviso. Consequently, they received
preferential patronage treatment from the Polk administration, despite their
status, at least in Van Buren's eyes, as a rebellious minority within the New
York Democracy. To the Barnburners, the southern-rights minority of the
party seemed in control of the one party whose fundamental principle was majoritarianism. And that minority had extended the project even into the New
York state party by imposing opposition to the Proviso as a party test for purposes of patronage and admission to the national convention.

In 1848, the Barnburners sent a delegation to the national convention just
as the Hunkers did, but the Barnburners did not arrive as the party of the Proviso. They claimed admission simply as the properly chosen representatives of
the majority of the regular Democratic party of New York. They disavowed
any attempt to impose substantive tests on any of their fellow Democrats and
equally denied the convention's right to put any substantive conditions on
their admission to the party's national deliberations.

When the convention refused to do more than offer a compromise on admission to the Barnburners and Hunkers, both groups declined to participate
and the Barnburners disavowed any obligation to support the decisions of the

convention. The convention decisions from which they thus maintained their distance included the nomination of Lewis Cass and adoption of a platform of "popular sovereignty." Such convention decisions hardly constituted ringing victories for southern-rights Democrats, but neither were they a full vindication of partyist principle. Consequently, the Barnburners, deprived of their national party, drifted into an alliance with "Conscience Whigs" and political abolitionists in the Free Soil Party. Much to his dismay, Van Buren found himself nominated for president by this constitutionally motley crew. Reluctantly accepting the nomination, Van Buren insisted that he was the candidate solely of the regular New York Democracy and conducted the campaign as a "salutary admonition to the southern Democracy";[118] that is, as a defense of party organization and regularity against the attempts of minorities, both North and South, to impose their substantive desires in the face of majority disapproval.

Van Buren had to strain to interpret his bolt and his subsequent nomination by the Free Soil Party as true evidence of party regularity, and the Hunkers let him know it. But this sort of paradox was nothing new to Van Buren. After all, it was Van Buren who had first articulated the notion that permanent organization of the Democratic party was the only way to preserve the essence of antiparty democracy. Van Buren was learning all the contortions that his theory must drive him to in the real world of politics, where one's notions of majoritarian procedure are not always that easy to distinguish from one's preferred substantive result. Still, he worked to render his every political action an advertisement for the indispensability of single-party majoritarianism to the defense of democratic politics.[119]

Of course, many of Van Buren's allies in the Free Soil Party of 1848 held to a fundamentally different constitutionalism. And his efforts to distance himself from them—old partyists like Van Buren often preferred to identify themselves as "the Free Democracy"[120]—evinced his commitment to the theory of majoritarian, constitutional partyism more than any substantive preference for free soil. The theory of party espoused by the political abolitionists in the Free Soil Party, on the other hand, was that party was justified only on the basis of the membership's prior unity on substantive policy questions. Former members of the abolitionist Liberty Party, in particular, brought with them the ultimate commitment to the ethic of the "redemptive" party,[121] refusing to be disciplined by any talk of proceduralism, rejecting any sacrifice of individual conscience to the cause, and failing completely to see the high principle and salvation that partyists saw in such values. Instead, they hoped to build the cause only out of uncompromised, antislavery consciences. These political abolitionists believed not only in the moral wrongness of slavery but also that the very principle of party loyalty was a central bulwark of slavery (tying otherwise antislavery citizens to the will of the slaveholding class) and that only a movement free from the principle of party obligation could convert the benighted, break down party loyalties, and, thus, restore principle to government generally.[122] In this sense, the party was no party at all—at least for the likes of Van Buren—because it had no special authority over any individual member. Party nomination wholly lacked the "infallible cachet"[123] and constitutional authority that it had for Democratic believers in party as such. Rather, every nomination was legitimately subject to scrutiny by each and every member after the fact.

This description applies in part to the Whigs as well, with their antiparty roots and their celebration of the independence of their members. The constitutive Whig theory of party, however, was that party took its legitimacy solely from its temporary mission to eliminate the ethic of party obligation from the Constitution—not from prior substantive commonalities among Whigs. The Free Soil Party, on the other hand,[124] served its non–Van Burenite members mainly as a redemptive party, whose foundation in a prior policy commitment rendered it permanently and inherently innocent of the crimes against individual conscience that the Democratic organization avowed as its purpose, and that the Whig organization committed in spite of itself, as it drifted ever further from its anti-organizational origins.

When the Conscience Whigs bolted the nomination of Taylor and his no-party campaign, justifying the bolt by declaring that a convention might issue only "recommendation, not law,"[125] the rest of the Whigs could hardly deny the force of the argument. They might point to the realities and say that a Whig of good judgment ought to support the no-party constitutional campaign of Taylor. But they could not easily accuse the bolters of constitutional defectiveness.

When Taylor was elected in 1848, the question of federal authority over slavery's place in the territories stood as a great unresolved issue of substantive constitutional law, but it also stood as the great test of the procedures—the unwritten constitution—of democratic politics. The method by which the question was to be resolved was as much at issue as was the substantive result—both questions going equally to the heart of popular sovereignty under the Constitution—as the constellation of procedural and substantive constitutionalisms in the 1848 election had attested.

The resolution of the slavery question for several territories came in the so-called Compromise of 1850. Antiparty militants on the slavery question, both North and South,[126] pressed for an unambiguous legislative declaration of the rights of slaveholders and free-soilers while deeply doubting the capacity of political parties to facilitate such principled action. Their doubts were confirmed when Stephen Douglas maneuvered a series of bills through Congress that technically settled nearly all of the outstanding questions regarding slavery. Admitting California as a free state, allowing New Mexico and Utah to legislate as they saw fit regarding slavery, restricting the slave trade in the District of Columbia, and passing a stronger Fugitive Slave Law, among other matters, the Compromise was actually several separate bills passed by very different majorities, with only a minority of Congress openly supporting the entire package.[127] It embodied neither a principled statement by either party on the status of slavery in the territories nor a statesmanlike compromise of principled positions in order to preserve the higher principle of Union. Instead, with advocates of rigid principle looking on disapprovingly from both sections, it simply disposed of troublesome issues in the arbitrary way of clever politicians, more skilled in parliamentary maneuver than in principled representation.

However, it is also true that the four main congressional blocs in 1850 approached the crisis in ways consistent with their constitutional histories to that point. This Compromise that was not a compromise thus represented well the chaotic state of American constitutionalism at mid-century. It was enacted not by the same sort of party-line voting that controlled most important legislative business in the 1840s but, roughly, by coalitions of the four sectional half-parties. As John Ashworth and others have pointed out, the core moderates who got the Compromise through were mainly the northern Democrats, led by the partyist Douglas, and the southern Whigs, while the northern Whigs and southern Democrats tended to take relatively extreme positions.[128] Thus as the national parties began to split sectionally they nevertheless retained an important degree of their identity as parties within the sections.

Let me begin with the northern parties' attitudes toward compromise. Northern Whigs and northern Democrats shared a desire never to see slavery in the territories, but in 1850 they decidedly did not share a vision of slavery's future and its developing relationship to American democracy. They consequently voted differently in the Compromise Congress. And the roots of these differences, I would suggest, lay at least partly in their constitutionalisms. Given their basic assumptions about American politics, the northern Whigs had good reason to be scared. The southern members of their so-called party held strong proslavery convictions—although southern Whigs did tend to be moderate on slavery extension—and evinced a characteristically Whiggish disinclination to have their independent judgments bound by the national Whig majority's antislavery disposition. This group could hardly be counted on to draw a firm line on slavery extension. The northern Whigs also saw a northern Democracy composed overwhelmingly of citizens who opposed slavery as a substantive matter but who had tied themselves by the principle of party obligation to the positions of the Democratic party oligarchy, as they had on every issue since the veto of the Maysville Road. And these northern Whigs did not have to think too hard to identify that oligarchy. It was composed of southern-rights Democrats and northern Democratic leaders, preeminently the arch-partyist Douglas, who controlled much of the northern electorate for what many northerners were coming to call "the slaveocracy." Seen in this constitutional light, the prospect of slavery in the territories seemed to the northern Whigs not just bad policy in itself, a position that would hardly distinguish them from the great majority of northern Democrats. It also seemed increasingly imminent and pregnant with the triumph of party authority and executive consolidation over democracy. I do not want to discount the fact that victory over slavery in 1850 would have meant, in part, a victory for a substantive principle, a substantive antislavery constitutionalism toward which many northern Whigs and free-soilers were moving. But I do want to emphasize that it would also have constituted a victory over party mechanisms and the ethic of party obligation. For the Whig party as such, these were the fundamental, long-term threats to the Constitution and the very devices that made the minority South's domestic institution an issue for northerners.

The Compromise of 1850 looked very different, of course, to most (although not all) northern Democrats. A few northern Democrats had permanently bolted the party in 1848 after concluding that southern slaveholders had taken control of the party. Most, however, like Van Buren, had returned after the election of 1848, rejoining the party that had always billed itself as the only possible vehicle of American democracy, now and forever.[129] The crisis of 1850, then, presented a major test of that party's fundamental self-identification with majoritarianism. It was a test that, in significant degree, the party would fail, since it failed to produce national party unity behind any single majoritarian solution in 1850. But, following Douglas's lead, the northern Democrats did seek that national unity of the Democracy above all other goals. Although they generally dreaded the day that slaves might appear in real numbers in the territories, Democrats' ultimate commitment lay not in opposition to slavery but in the capacity of majoritarian partyism, as could be embodied only in the Democratic party, to vindicate the democratic will and to unite every voter of democratic principle behind that will. Moreover, residing in the majority section, they had little reason to fear that any "majority" would or could ever force a substantive, proslavery test on them. Not until the mid-1850s would a significant segment of the northern Democracy conclude that the party of majoritarianism par excellence had become a minoritarian party of pro-slavery constitutionalism. And, even then, most of the northern wing of the party declined to go over to the Republicans, the latest neo-Federalist party of substantive—in this case, antislavery—constitutionalism. Instead, Douglas and most northern Democrats compromised as best they could in 1850, while continuing to fight within the Democratic party to salvage its true meaning, its true constitutionalism, and its unity on that partyist basis. They saw no other place to go, in good times or bad.

Among the southern Democrats, who balanced the northern Whigs at opposite extremes in 1850, there were pronounced traditions of both Van Burenite constitutionalism and substantive southern-rights constitutionalism, with the latter waxing slowly as the sectional crisis intensified.[130] Although "southern rights" was a watchword for the few avowed anti-democrats in the South, both of these traditions were employed generally in the name of democracy. In the minority South, however, the commitments to the two traditions—to Van Buren's procedural, partyist majoritarianism, on the one hand, and to the security of slavery and "equal rights," on the other—had been in some increasing tension over the course of the Second Party System. Thus, just as many northern opponents of slavery would have denied that slavery could consist with democracy even where supported by a majority, so Ashworth notes that by 1848 many southern Democrats, fearing a tyrannical emancipation of the slaves by a northern majority, had begun to reevaluate their formerly doctrinaire majoritarianism.[131] Similarly, William Freehling comprehensively discusses the persistent dilemmas of antebellum southerners, caught between their constitutional commitment to majoritarian democracy, on the one hand, and their equally constitutional commitment to their substantive right to slavery, regardless of the national majority's opinion, on the other.[132] By 1850, doctrinally obligated to support any majority decision of the party but increasingly aware of antislavery agitation as a significant force within that party, southern Democrats might rightly fear the unthinkable—being committed against slavery by the northern majority of their party. So they sidled toward a substantive pro-slavery party test, a substantive "states' rights" constitutionalism that threatened to eclipse the procedural majoritarianism with which the Democracy had always fused states' rights. And they moved away from a Compromise that had the potential not only to slowly destroy their way of life and their constitutional "equal rights" but to prove that the basic constitutional doctrine of their party—party obligation—had had the potential all along to deprive them of the very means to fight for those rights. That recognition meant that many southern Democrats were no longer willing to trust in Douglas's majoritarian proceduralism but were ready increasingly to insist on a substantive party test, guaranteeing slaveholders' "equal rights" in the territories, regardless of the sentiments of any Douglas-defined "majority" of the party. This was a challenge that Douglas would finesse for years as he fought tire-

lessly to sustain the intersectional party on its original Van Burenite principles[133] and to convince those Democrats who were moving to substantive constitutionalisms, North and South, that the only democratic model for American politics remained Van Buren's section-neutral proceduralism.

I do not want to exaggerate the level of southern Democrats' fears in 1850.
Only a small minority of southerners, even among the Democrats, feared such
an imminent destruction of democracy and slavery as southern-rights radicals
had been predicting. The Nashville Convention of that year, after all, was a
great bust. Most southern Democrats had hardly given up on their party or on
their hope for the North's basic commitment to equal rights. Still, they were
confronted with newly stark evidence of the potential for conflict between what
they had always taken to be equally and compatibly fundamental principles
of the Constitution. And this point suggests why the southern Whigs would
have approached the crisis of 1850 somewhat differently from the southern
Democrats.

The southern Whigs, while condemning Douglas's theory of American politics, joined his northern Democrats in 1850 as the core supporters of the Compromise, which was early championed by one of their own, Henry Clay. Why
did these southern Whigs not harbor the same terror of a northern antislavery
majority that drove their Democratic fellow-southerners to oppose compromise? Again, much of the answer may lie in contrasting constitutionalisms.
Never confronted with the southern Democrats' prospect that their own constitutionalism could require them to turn against slave-state interests, never
facing the confounding of their most basic notions of democracy, the southern Whigs were much better able to look to the North with some equanimity.
There they could see a section as devoted to peace and democracy as they were
themselves, at least for the time being. That is not to say that they saw no crisis. But politics and compromise as usual seemed as available and as effective
to them as ever. On the question of slavery, a solid South and a large part of the
North were committed to the South's equal rights. The southern Whigs did not
have to fear, as southern Democrats did, that a willingness to compromise now
would deprive them of an intellectually consistent way to stand on southern-
rights principle later. Their judgments were their own, not the property of some
party to whom they had rashly conceded sole possession of democracy; and
they judged that as of 1850 the North wanted peace and that the abiding danger to democracy—the partyism of the Democratic party—was no danger to
southern equality in the here and now. The southern Democrats in 1850 increasingly feared the northern wing of their own party for its potential to turn
majoritarian obligation against them at any time. But the southern Whigs actually feared those northern Democrats no more in 1850 than they always

had; that is, they were willing, as always, to vote with the Democrats for good measures like the Compromise, while remaining free to oppose them whenever, inevitably, partyism turned them against the national interest.

For many, the Compromise of 1850 was cause for great rejoicing. But for many others, it simply failed to settle any important issues in acceptable fashion. As the above account indicates, the meaning of the slavery question in politics, for most Americans, was not the moral question of whether slavery was a good or bad institution in itself. Rather, it was a constitutional question: the question whether the national government had any power to restrict or protect slavery in the territories; or, perhaps even more important, the question whether the people, through their party-politician representatives, were adequately governing themselves. On the slavery question, Americans increasingly detected schemes in their opponents to manipulate the practice of popular sovereignty, to appropriate the people's power through some anti-democratic constitutional structure. Never did any significant number of northerners oppose by political means slaveholding itself; but many opposed the Slave Power that had so corrupted the Democratic party and thus the northern electorate.[134] Or, as Freehling puts it, they increasingly believed that "the Slavepower [had] enslaved the Democratic Party and thus the not-so-democratic republic."[135] And mirror-image suspicions of a northern abolitionist conspiracy grew in the South. With no ambitions to take slavery north, increasing numbers of southerners did fervently desire to thwart a northern threat to strip them of their constitutional rights as well as the tools of political self-defense.[136] In this atmosphere, the parliamentarily manufactured Compromise offered no reassurance that democratic procedures were in place in the parties or, what was the same thing, in the government. Issues had been disposed of, but the abiding meaning of popular sovereignty under the Constitution had been more muddled than settled.

For these skeptics, perhaps only a minority of the people but one sufficiently large to control the electoral fates of the parties, the situation was only exacerbated when both national party leaderships included endorsement of the Compromise in the national platforms for the 1852 presidential race. In so doing both leaderships tried to cut off debate on the issues that were the most important of the day for at least a large minority of each party. Even if the leaderships were right that such debate would undermine national party unity, they ignored the possibility that such debate—within the states, at least—might be indispensable to the electorate's confidence in one party or the other as an active defender of the people's Constitution. The danger in removing a vital issue from public debate was only exacerbated by the fact that most of the other defining issues of the Second Party System had become obsolete. The

Whig dream of a national bank had long since been given up, and state banking questions had been widely resolved with the passage of free banking laws. The tariff was low and not about to budge amid a general prosperity. Tired of being shut out of a large and rapidly growing immigrant vote, the Whigs in many states had increasingly abandoned their nativism and joined the Democrats in welcoming the immigrant vote. A party system whose roots were in both parties' claims to be the defenders of a true, democratic antipartyism, but whose practice looked more like the institutionalization of a system that was useful only to party politicians, now found the chickens coming home to roost.[137]

The lesson of the 1852 election for many in both sections and both parties was that the parties had departed from their founding, constitutional principles—the Democrats now controlled by one minority faction or another and the Whigs having evolved into something more like a self-perpetuating party than an antiparty movement. And the legacy of the election was a resurgence of self-conscious constitutional reformism reminiscent of the 1830s.

The Democrats, to begin with, had not yet found a strategy to reconcile the party's fundamental majoritarianism with the diversity of its membership's substantive positions on slavery extension. But in the 1852 campaign they had begun to try. The Democratic leadership, including Douglas, had begun to interpret the Compromise not as a feat of political juggling that had staved off disaster but as a natural, practically inevitable, manifestation of the Democracy's constitutional principles.[138]

This increasingly vigorous reinterpretation of the party's recent struggles would soon animate the last great act of the Democratic party in the Second Party System, Douglas's effort to revivify the party of majoritarianism, and thus American constitutional politics in general, by pushing a new measure of majoritarian expansionism before the nation. In so doing, Douglas would again make the Democrats the party of the majoritarian Constitution and force the opposition again to reveal its aristocratic, antimajoritarian colors. The bill to organize the Nebraska territory would unify the party behind its chief substantive policy in the 1850s, westward expansionism, and declare the resolve of the majority to pursue its will without regard to minority obstruction. Rather than allowing the inevitable slavery controversy to sidetrack the Democracy's expansionism, the party would present "popular sovereignty" as the established democratic solution to the territorial problem and announce it explicitly as the test of Democratic constitutional principle in the age of sectionalism. For Douglas, there was ultimately no need to view slavery as an intractable question, manageable only by parliamentary maneuvering. Rather, it was an issue like any other, best managed by a bold recurrence to the essentially interchangeable first principles of the Democracy—majoritarianism, strict construction, and states' rights, now rolled up in the distinctively Democratic slogan of "popular sovereignty." In the face of such democratic principles, aristocratic insistence on one substantive interest or another must yield. That was the principle that made the Compromise of 1850, in retrospect at least, not a compromise at all but a true Democratic party measure. And that was the principle that made the Kansas-Nebraska Act not a dangerous reopening of the slavery controversy but a fearless reassertion in the normal course of governance of the most basic constitutional principle of American democracy, majoritarian popular sovereignty.

In this respect, the party leadership's ruthless demand for regularity on the Kansas-Nebraska Act recalled Van Buren's original consolidation of the party in the Independent Treasury campaign. That the new measure was meant to reassert the Democracy's timeless understanding of the Constitution was made clear by the act's original sponsor in the House, Augustus Dodge: "I cannot but regard [those who attack the Kansas-Nebraska bill] as federalists or monarchists at heart. . . . Never was there a question which revived more thoroughly the distinctive differences between federalism and democracy, State rights and consolidation, than does the 'Nebraska-Kansas' bill."[139] The Democratic proponents of Kansas-Nebraska in 1854 were as eager to organize the territories as the Van Burenite corps of the 1830s had been eager to minimize the evil that was paper money. Bills advancing those positions, therefore, were inevitable projects of the party. But the special importance of each bill to its sponsors was simply that, at a moment when the world's only party of majoritarianism was at risk, the bill stood as a Democratic party measure. The test of democracy itself lay in such tests of the public authority of the Democratic party as the preeminent institution of popular governance and thus of the Constitution itself. The Kansas-Nebraska bill was asserted to be both the will of the Democratic party majority—because the party had endorsed the bill's principle of popular sovereignty in the 1848 and 1852 elections—and the only resolution of the great national issue that was consistent with that majority's retention of its ability to discover and enact its will. By one's stand on a Kansas-Nebraska Act so freighted, one's ultimate commitment to a democratic Constitution, or lack thereof, could be known.[140]

Of course, Douglas's constitutional cure for the disease afflicting American politics ultimately failed. His attempt to control the great substantive question of slavery extension by reassertion of an essentially procedural principle—that deference must always be paid to the majority will—failed to discipline that large minority of northern Democrats that soon went over to the Republicans. And it similarly failed to reconcile enough southern-rights Democrats to Douglas's procedural vision of the party. Maybe the alienated Democrats ultimately forsook Douglas's tortuous effort on behalf of "popular sovereignty" because they simply preferred antislavery or proslavery to any procedural principle. Or maybe they abandoned him because they could not agree on what procedures added up to genuine expressions of majority will. Either way, the campaign for popular sovereignty across the 1850s was the last, failed effort of the constitutional partyist Democrats to reduce substantive conflict to majoritarian proceduralism.

For the Whigs, the Kansas-Nebraska Act was a superfluous nail in the party's coffin. The party never was able to revitalize itself after 1850. It lacked its old economic issues, since, as many historians have observed, those issues did not meaningfully distinguish the parties any more. And it abandoned its old nativism in pursuit of the growing immigrant vote. The live issue was slavery, and the party was seriously divided on that question, as 1850 had shown. To invigorate itself, therefore, the party needed a position on that issue, and it had to be a position consistent with the party's self-image as a counterforce and alternative to the Democrats' partyism.

But the Whigs found no such position. Declaring the finality of the Compromise of 1850 to keep the southern half of the party on board, but nominating Winfield Scott to keep the northern half on board, the 1852 convention alienated enough of the membership in both sections to leave it a shadow of its former self. And the convention's declaration of the finality of the Compromise, thus disrespecting widespread Whig dissent in the North, seemed to forsake the fundamental principle of the Whig party, the freedom of each voter's independent judgment.

Of course, most of the Whigs still voted Whig in 1852, judging presumably that such compromises of principle were unavoidable and seeing no more effective option. But the Whigs' fundamental character had been compromised and, as soon became clear, its back broken. Throughout the 1840s, the Whigs had suffered from some measure of internal diversity on many substantive questions, but the party had never before imposed a substantive party test in quite the way it did in 1852. Its general positions on the issues of the day were always known, and the membership was reasonably well aligned. The party's very existence as an institution meant, in addition, that the membership always felt some pressure to conform. However, the party had never announced a substantive test of Whig party membership in the way the Democrats often did, because a basic principle of the Whig party was, in fact, opposition to any such party obligation, any such party control of the voter's independent judgment. That changed in 1852, when the southern Whigs, like the southern Democrats, required assurances from their ostensible political allies regarding the main substantive condition—African slavery—for the only brand of democracy they had ever lived. When the national convention complied by compromising on platform and candidate, the party itself was compromised. The Whigs could hobble through the 1852 campaign, but, despite the best efforts of pragmatists like Lincoln, always more interested in policy than antipartyism, they could go little further.

Instead, the Whigs were put out of their misery in rather short order after 1852 by the rise of the Know-Nothing movement, a close replica of the original Whig movement in its core antipartyism and nativism.[141] The Know-Nothings, like many of the original Whigs, generally opposed the rights of new immigrants to vote. They preferred a long waiting period during which the immigrant might grow out of the party-fostering, truckling habits of old-world aristocracy and learn the independent habits of democracy. Many Know-Nothings, though, opposed only the political power of the Catholic Church and did not really care about non-Catholic immigrants at all. This position was just another variation of the same antipartyist impulse. The Catholic Church, after all, was, in Know-Nothing ideology, an anti-democratic political force, both because, like degenerate political parties, it controlled the consciences of its members, and because, not coincidentally, it delivered its members to a single political party, the Democrats. Just as many old Whigs would have endorsed Horace Bushnell's declaration that the tyranny of parties over the independent judgments of their members was "the worst form of papacy ever invented,"[142] so the Know-Nothings integrated fears of papal and partisan control of the electorate into a single ideology.[143] Moreover, in the South, where nativism had never been an important part of Whiggery, the Know-Nothings' movement of political purification was, similarly, defined less by its nativism than by its antipartyist unionism, complementing the fire-eaters' antipartyist secessionism.[144]

Had the Know-Nothings never emerged, the Whigs just might have been able to soldier on as the best available alternative to Democratic partyism. But the Know-Nothings were a practically inevitable response when the Whig party opted for a pragmatic, substantive partyism over its principled antipartyism in the sectional crisis. The Know-Nothings constituted, initially, a wildly popular rejection of the idea that either the slavery question or American politics in general was best given over to party politicians.[145] The ascendancy of the party politician was, in fact, the very reason why sectional feeling had become so exacerbated as to threaten the future of the Union, thought the Know-Nothings. And the movement was aimed at such a purification of politics as would permit the slavery question to be settled rationally and peaceably.[146] In these convictions, the Know-Nothings proved themselves true heirs of recent American constitutionalism by rejecting as merely factional any party except their own, the only one necessary to purify American politics and restore control to the real democracy.

The Know-Nothing movement, however, rose and fell in a moment because, in the end, it offered little that the Whigs had not already tried. A strongly antipartyist segment of the electorate still believed that a pure people's movement could regenerate American democracy by being truer to Whiggery than the Whig party had proved to be. But when the party met at its national convention in Philadelphia in 1855, it too discovered the intractability of the territorial slavery problem and the impossibility of settling it by recourse to an antipartyist, nativist constitutionalism. The party could find no satisfying basis for unity if antipartyism could not yield an accommodation on the substantive issue of slavery in the territories. The Know-Nothings thus followed the Whigs into political impotence.[147]

In their failure, the Know-Nothings helped to clarify the nature of the Democratic and Whig failures as well. All three of these parties were created to ensure that no organization or party of merely substantive principle—no faction—could succeed in American politics. The result was that all questions of substance in the Second Party System were handled by parties whose histories required that they justify themselves only in the procedural, constitutional, antiparty terms that had defined the original conflict of mass parties. Any other justification would be an attempt to legitimate mere faction.

Conclusion

Before the 1830s, antipathy to party organization remained dominant in America's quickly democratizing constitutional culture. Inherited from the founding generation (and from generations before that), this commitment survived the profound warfare between Federalists and Republicans that kept the nation's constitutional character in doubt through the War of 1812. In fact, very few Americans then could even imagine a permanent politics of mass parties. Only in reaction to the "amalgamation" of the older parties of "magnates and notables" after the War of 1812 and the consequent resurgence of "consolidationism" in America's constitutional politics—both judicial and electoral—did Van Buren and his cohorts begin the partyist campaign. And only under pressure from that campaign did American constitutional culture come to accommodate parties.

Drawing on the inherited, Old World notion that polities were composed of "estates"—"the democracy," "the aristocracy," and "the monarchy"—Van Buren hoped to restore the ascendancy of the democracy in the American constitutional scheme. His device for doing so was the political party, given life by the convention system and committed to no principle but the constitutional equality that required both strict majoritarianism and confederated government. Because the party embodied the entire democracy—at least in principle and, in fact, more nearly than any other available institution—the party was to speak for, if not actually become, the only sovereign body in the constitutional scheme. Each of the lawmaking institutions explicitly created by the Constitution was just one of several coordinate, subsovereign institutions, supreme in nothing, but charged only with doing some aspect of the sovereign people's work. The Supreme Court, especially, had no higher role with respect to the Constitution than did the other federal branches and the states themselves. Only the people, who could not speak but through a party of the democracy, possessed that genuine constitutional supremacy to which the irresponsible Court made pretense in cases like *McCulloch v. Maryland*.

The vision that animated the partyist reformers generally in the 1830s, then, had nothing to do with a "two-party system" and everything to do with the "exclusive and towering supremacy"[148] or "complete and permanent ascendancy of the democratic party."[149] Understanding all politics as the elaboration and defense of a constitutional order, the Democratic partyists organized their institution not simply to represent a coalition of non-evangelical Protestants and Catholics or the yeoman victims of market dependency. They organized it and deployed it successfully to restore strict construction and states' rights in the name of "the majority of the people," the landmarks of this success being their thorough marginalizing of the American System that had seemed ready to take the country by storm in the post-*McCulloch* 1820s.

The successes of the partyists, however, never matched the predictions of their theory. Every step of the way, the Democrats faced spirited competition from mass parties that condemned the partyist revolution. As of the time of his final writings in the 1850s, Van Buren continued to understand the history of American presidential elections as reflecting the permanent dominance of the single party of the democracy over the minoritarian, antiparty, corporate aristocracy and its most reliable ally, the federal judiciary. The Whig victories of 1840 and 1848 he explained away as products of passing crises, the Democratic victories of other years as reflecting the settled constitutional principles, the "sober second thought," of the people.[150] But the fact is that the partyist reforms did not in the end produce a party of "complete and permanent ascendancy." Instead, the effort to do so provoked a sustained politics of competitive parties that only gradually evolved into an accepted, permanent way of conducting a democracy.

From a modern perspective, the party competition of Van Buren's last years looks like the beginnings of our regularized two-party competition. It has been a very long time since any party has held itself out as the embodiment of the democracy rather than as a more or less coherent collection of interests and social groups. As of the 1850s, however, this sort of regularized competition between parties of substantive commitment was only beginning to emerge. In Van Buren's view, the sectional crisis over slavery in the territories was tearing the democracy apart, moving erstwhile genuine democrats to fall in with the merely factional movements of the southern-rights Democrats and the free-labor Republicans—neither party now resting on the democracy as a whole but only on the partisans of its substantive policy preferences.[151] This difference was a fundamental one to Van Buren, because the rise of two-partyism or, as he would have seen it, the rise of a politics of faction rather than constitutional principle, left the Constitution without its legitimate interpreter—the embodied people. It therefore ceded control of the Constitution to the worst possible institution: the federal judiciary, unelected, life-tenured, and irresponsible. And such an antipopular politics tended inevitably to consolidation.

For Van Buren, the most dramatic and damning result of this development was *Dred Scott*.[152] It is not that Van Buren was particularly progressive on racial matters. He actually endorsed, although with reservations, Taney's holding that African-Americans could not be citizens within the meaning of Article III of the Constitution.[153] Rather, Van Buren complained that this Jacksonian Court[154] had reached beyond that holding to settle a question not before the Court. In the true Federalist fashion that even the most democratically pedigreed judges ultimately found irresistible,[155] Taney claimed judicial supremacy over the nation's constitutional politics. Not satisfied with merely disposing of cases, he and his majority asserted the Court's authority over the constitutionality of the Missouri Compromise, even though that question was now unnecessary to disposition of the case.[156] For Van Buren, this question, like all constitutional questions, belonged preeminently in politics where the sovereign majority might authoritatively dispose of it. Among the party's grand achievements had been the scotching of the notion, trumpeted in the days of the Alien and Sedition Acts and *McCulloch v. Maryland*, that "it belongs to the judicial power to decide upon [the] constitutionality" of laws while only "their expediency" lay with Congress.[157] But *Scott* had revived that doctrine. Delivered by a Democratic Court and held out as the last word on the Constitution by a Democratic president, the case represented the dreaded triumph of Federalist consolidationism within the Democratic party itself.[158]

Moreover, this ruling was not the temporary lapse that Van Buren insisted it must be.[159] Rather, *Scott* signalled the end of any operative role for Van Burenite constitutionalism. Van Buren understood, of course, that the old Democratic party had been thoroughly disrupted by the sectional crisis. He did not, however, understand that the reconstruction of party politics as a "party system"—the demise of "the democracy" before a politics of special interests in party coalitions—was permanent. Nor could he have foreseen *Scott*'s ultimately successful implanting of "substantive due process" into the federal judicial system as the natural, anti-democratic complement to the rise of merely factional parties. Today, *Dred Scott* is universally condemned, but it is also remembered as the first federal example of that doctrine of broad judicial review,[160] warmly embraced by many who otherwise revile the case. Modern Americans thus often see *Scott* as an aberrational start to an otherwise salutary doctrinal line.[161] Had Van Buren lived to see a later Supreme Court invalidating state laws on the basis of the Due Process Clause, however, he would have seen those Court offensives as the legitimate heirs of *Scott*'s own consolidationism. And he would have seen federal judicial ascendancy over state legislative power as the natural complement to a politics now dominated by a persistent two-party competition—maybe he would have called it the "two-faction system"—in which his Democrats actually became for a time the minority party before the consolidationist Republicans. The ironies would have been painful. Using the constitutional theory of popular sovereignty, he had built a magnificent new institution, the party of the sovereign democracy that had restored the confederated Constitution after *McCulloch*. Yet the party politics yielded by that reform only brought a fundamentally different institution and a contrary constitutional theory—the "two-party system" of mere interest-group management and subconstitutional policy negotiation, linked to judicial supremacy in constitutional interpretation.

In the climax of the sectional crisis, the Democratic party was decisively stripped of its original justification as its organized opposition parties were stripped of theirs. A single party could not embody democracy in itself, yet no retreat was possible from a politics of organized mass parties. As succeeding generations of Americans would discover, a system of mass parties in routinized competition on substantive questions could embody a sort of unwritten constitution that most Americans would come to call "democracy." If the 1850s hardly marked the end of antipartyism in America, then, it is nevertheless true that little remained of James Madison's "Constitution against parties" in the wake of Martin Van Buren's constitutional reform and its legacy.

Abbreviations

CHS   Chicago Historical Society, Chicago, Illinois
ISHL   Illinois State Historical Library, Springfield, Illinois

Introduction

1. Hofstadter, *Idea of a Party System*, 40.

2. In this definition, I follow, among others, Hofstadter, *Idea of a Party System*. He expands on these ideas usefully at pp. 4–5. See also the discussion in chapter 7 of Chambers, *Political Parties in a New Nation*.

3. On this latter point, see Maurice Duverger, *Political Parties*, which argues for something like a sociological law that such a structure must yield a two-party system.

4. Hurst, *Growth of American Law*, 437. For a concise celebration of Hurst's formulation of legal history as the history of governance (with special emphasis on the historical role of federalism), see Scheiber, "Federalism and the Processes of Governance in Hurst's Legal History." Also see Novak's appreciation of Hurst's sophisticated redefinition of legal history in "Law, Capitalism, and the Liberal State," 113–14. Novak points to Hurst's list of lawmaking institutions—which included political parties, lobbyists, and the bar—and his description of his legal history as the history of "all formal and informal aspects of politically organized power." Hurst, *Law and Social Order*, 25.

5. Hurst, *Growth of American Law*, 56–62, quotations on 56.

6. Skowronek, *Building a New American State*, 24–31; William E. Nelson, *Roots of American Bureaucracy*, 17–30.

7. For a full description of the mass parties' dominance of American politics in these decades, see Silbey, *American Political Nation*.

8. Even so, it is not hard to find work on the relatively weak parties of modern America that treats them, in important respects, as arms of the government. See, e.g., Persily and Cain, "Legal Status of Political Parties," 785; Lowenstein, "Associational Rights of Major Political Parties," 1754–59. For some of the early history of this idea, see Winkler, "Voters' Rights and Parties' Wrongs," 877–78.

9. McCormick, *Party Period and Public Policy*. For a modification of this view, see Formisano, "'Party Period' Revisited."

10. Ronald P. Formisano can claim much of the credit both for establishing the pre-partyist character of the First Party System and for describing the continuing presence of antipartyism even during the development and dominance of mass party politics. See his *Transformation of Political Culture*; *Birth of Mass Political Parties*; "Deferential-Participant Politics"; "Federalists and Republicans"; "Political Character, Antipartyism and the Second Party System"; "'Party Period' Revisited." Others who have helped to establish the persistence of antipartyism after the demise of the First Party System include Shade, "Political Pluralism and Party Development"; McCormick, *Party Period and Public Policy*; Kruman, "Second American Party System"; Vos-Hubbard, "'Third Party Tradition' Reconsidered"; Friedman, *Revolt of the Conservative Democrats*; Thomas Brown, *Politics*

and Statesmanship; Heale, *Making of American Politics*; Ethington, *Public City*; Kleppner, *Third Electoral System*; Ranney, *Curing the Mischiefs of Faction*.

11. Van Buren, *Inquiry*, 180.

12. Hofstadter, *Idea of a Party System*; Wallace, "Ideologies of Party," and "Changing Concepts of Party." More recently, see Jaenicke, "Jacksonian Integration of Parties into the Constitutional System." These works represent an enormous advance beyond prior studies that barely recognized an American tradition of antipartyism in their eagerness to identify an inevitable party system as early as the 1790s. See, e.g., Charles, *Origins of the American Party System*; Chambers, *Political Parties in a New Nation*; Goodman, "First American Party System." A more comprehensive narrative of the slow emergence of mass parties well into the nineteenth century appears in Nichols, *Invention of the American Political Parties*, but he too pays little attention to the theory of antipartyism and to the persistent power of the antiparty tradition.

13. See, e.g., Schattschneider, *Party Government*; Binkley and Moos, *Grammar of American Politics*, chap. 10; Duverger, *Political Parties*.

14. The durability of the pluralist account is illustrated in the recent effort by political scientist John Aldrich to explain the emergence of parties. Aldrich added a "social choice" dimension to the Hofstadter-Wallace interpretation but did not consider the continuing problem of antipartyism after the eclipse of the First Party System. Aldrich, *Why Parties?* See also A. James Reichley's recent account, *Life of the Parties*, 88–92, which follows Hofstadter's model.

15. The ascendant interpretation of antebellum politics constitutes an increasingly harmonious synthesis of the so-called "ethnocultural" school (see, e.g., Formisano's work cited above) and another school of thought that emphasizes conflicts over economic ideology. All of the following (among many others) have contributed to the construction of the new synthesis: Thornton, *Politics and Power in a Slave Society*; Watson, *Liberty and Power* and *Jacksonian Politics and Community Conflict*; Feller, *Jacksonian Promise*; Wilson, *Space, Time, and Freedom*; Silbey, *American Political Nation* and *Partisan Imperative*; Shade, *Banks or No Banks* and *Democratizing the Old Dominion*; Ashworth, *"Agrarians" and "Aristocrats"* and *Slavery, Capitalism, and Politics in the Antebellum Republic*; Sharp, *Jacksonians versus the Banks*; Cayton and Onuf, *Midwest and the Nation*; Bridges, *City in the Republic*; Feller, "Politics and Society"; Howe, "Evangelical Movement and Political Culture in the North" and *Political Culture of the American Whigs*; Kohl, *Politics of Individualism*; Sellers, *Market Revolution*; Levine, *Behavior of State Legislative Parties*; Kruman, *Parties and Politics in North Carolina*; Atkins, *Parties, Politics, and the Sectional Conflict*; Carey, *Parties, Slavery, and the Union*; Egnal, "Beards Were Right."

16. Wilson, "Republicanism and the Idea of Party in the Jacksonian Period"; Baker, *Affairs of Party*, chap. 3.

17. John, "Governmental Institutions as Agents of Change."

18. Hurst, *Law and the Conditions of Freedom*.

19. Novak, *People's Welfare*.

20. See Scheiber, "Private Rights and Public Power," 847–61.

21. See, e.g., Snowiss, *Judicial Review and the Law of the Constitution* on the early history of judicial review. Needless to say, citations to the literature on this subject could fill many pages.

22. Cook, *American Codification Movement*.

23. See, e.g., Hall, "Judiciary on Trial"; Nelson, "Re-Evaluation of Scholarly Explanations."

24. For the ostensibly nonsubstantive quality of debates about judicial authority, see,

e.g., chap. 5 of Cook's *American Codification Movement*. Other examinations of the ways in which substantive policy goals interacted with nineteenth-century efforts to work out theories of legal institutions include, e.g., chap. 8 of Cover, *Justice Accused*, which discusses antebellum notions of formal and precedential limits on judicial authority in the context of the antislavery movement; Ellis, *Jeffersonian Crisis*, which discusses struggles in the early nation among radical Republicans, moderate Republicans, and Federalists to define the proper relationships among governmental branches after the Jeffersonian "Revolution of 1800"; and Horwitz, *Transformation of American Law*, which argues that instrumentalist and formalist theories of proper judicial authority rose and fell with the economic-distributive results that the judges desired.

25. See Hofstadter, *Idea of a Party System*, which discusses Federalist no. 10 at 64–73; Wallace, "Ideologies of Party in the Ante-Bellum Republic" and "Changing Concepts of Party." The general assumption that Federalist no. 10 was influential in its day is contested by Kramer, "Madison's Audience," but I do not think that Kramer's argument undermines the value of Federalist no. 10 as an emblem of the elitist antipartyism that undergirded the Constitution.

26. The general history of Illinois in this period can be gleaned from James E. Davis, *Frontier Illinois*; Doyle, *Social Order of a Frontier Community*; Pease, *Frontier State*; Simeone, *Democracy and Slavery in Frontier Illinois*; Jensen, *Illinois*; Faragher, *Sugar Creek*; Stroble, *High on the Okaw's Western Bank*.

27. Ackerman, *We the People*, 59. Ackerman follows Skowronek in enumerating the political parties (along with Court, Congress, Presidency, states, and voters) among the important institutions of governance. See also Whittington, *Constitutional Construction*, in which the distinction between "construction" (usually the elaboration of institutional roles by political actors) and "interpretation" (usually the elaboration of specific constitutional texts by the judiciary) closely parallels my distinction between the unwritten constitution and the written Constitution.

28. Hurst, *Law and the Conditions of Freedom* and *Legitimacy of the Business Corporation*; Novak, "Law, Capitalism, and the Liberal State," 132–35; Freyer, *Producers Versus Capitalists*.

29. Freyer, *Producers Versus Capitalists*, 14.

30. Hurst, *Legitimacy of the Business Corporation*, 41–47.

31. The centrality of these ideas in the years before the development of partyist theory is established in, e.g., Cornell, *Other Founders*; Ellis, "Persistence of Antifederalism after 1789" and *Union at Risk*; Storing, *What the Anti-Federalists Were For*.

32. I do not mean to imply that the adoption of these provisions was unproblematic, only that their virtues were thought to include the usual virtues of federal representation, centrally the delivery of crucial decisions into the hands of representatives of national vision. Although some, including Madison himself, might have preferred election by the people rather than permitting the president to become dependent on the Congress, the prevailing principle at the convention remained government by elitist "filtration," not direct democracy. See Rakove, *Original Meanings*, 89–90, 214–27, 259–60, 264–68; Nedelsky, *Private Property*, 58.

33. See, e.g., Wood, "Interests and Disinterestedness in the Making of the Constitution."

34. Here I share Whittington's reluctance to endorse Ackerman's notion of discrete "constitutional moments" (see Whittington, *Constitutional Construction*, 217 and fn. 8), believing instead that "normal" politics crosses the boundary into constitutional politics fluidly and frequently, although with varying levels of intensity or importance. See Ackerman, *We the People*, which distinguishes between periods of "normal politics" and pe-

riods of "constitutional politics" or "higher lawmaking." Ackerman emphasizes only three "constitutional moments" where I would emphasize the constitutional quality of almost all the most prominent political issues of the early republic. But this may only be a matter of emphasis, since Ackerman, p. 196, certainly recognizes examples of constitutional politics outside his three leading moments.

35. The Whigs were not as consistently and explicitly preoccupied as the Democrats with principles of constitutional interpretation, but when the occasion demanded it, they made clear that they placed their hopes in the positive action of a Congress equipped with broad constitutional powers. See, e.g., Whittington's discussion of the constitutional nationalism embodied by the great Whigs Henry Clay and Daniel Webster in the Nullification Crisis. Whittington, *Constitutional Construction*, 74–93. The implied-powers jurisprudence that supported that vision was articulated most famously by Marshall in *McCulloch*, of course, and also by Supreme Court Justice Joseph Story, who bridged the gap between Marshall and the emergence of the Whig party. See Newmyer, "Harvard Law School," 829–31; Newmyer, *Supreme Court Justice Joseph Story*, 95, 109–13, 126–27, 313.

36. One pointed example of this scholarly rediscovery is Whittington, *Constitutional Construction*, although Whittington would insist on a sharper distinction between construction and interpretation than seems necessary to me. Whittington argues that much of the development of "constitutional meaning" in America has gone unobserved because it happens outside the courts in the course of apparently normal policy debates. Such debate can truly be constitutional insofar as it successfully establishes "authoritative norms of political behavior" (p. 8) and thus "constrain[s] future political debate" (p. 6). Among the many constitutional issues that are often dealt with by "political" rather than judicial actors are the "structures of political participation" (p. 9), which certainly include the place of political parties in American governance. Whittington concludes that the "meaning of the Constitution is . . . a very real prize of political struggle" (p. 18), as Van Buren and all of the politicians of his generation would certainly have affirmed.

With respect to federalism in particular, see (in addition to Whittington) Larry Kramer's argument that, historically, American courts have almost never enforced constitutional federalism (states' rights) as a legal principle but have left its vindication to the political process. Effective defense of that constitutional principle was, of course, exactly the function that the partyists expected democratic party organization preeminently to serve, in the face of "aristocratic" efforts to consolidate power in the federal government and especially the federal courts. See Kramer, "But When Exactly Was Judicially Enforced Federalism 'Born' in the First Place?"; Kramer, "Putting the Politics Back into the Political Safeguards of Federalism"; Kramer, "We the Court."

A further selection of work on the political branches as constitutional interpreters might include Fisher, *Constitutional Dialogues*; Ackerman, *We the People*; Devins, "How Constitutional Law Casebooks Perpetuate the Myth of Judicial Supremacy"; Fisher and Devins, *Political Dynamics of Constitutional Law*; Killenbeck, "Pursuing the Great Experiment"; William E. Nelson, *Fourteenth Amendment*, esp. 27–34 regarding antebellum federalism; Newmyer, "John Marshall and the Southern Constitutional Tradition," 116; Hyman and Wiecek, *Equal Justice under Law*, 115–46, 203; Graber, "Federalist or Friends of Adams"; Scheiber, "Federalism and the American Economic Order," 72–86; and Peabody, "Coordinate Construction," fn. 4, which cites further sources.

37. This phrase I borrow from Jaenicke's insightful article, "Jacksonian Integration of Parties."

38. *Dred Scott v. Sandford*, 60 U.S. 393 (1857). See Fehrenbacher, *Dred Scott Case*.

39. 17 U.S. 316 (1819).

40. For a nice account of some of the continuing thrusts and parries in the struggle to define the scope of party authority even after the Civil War and to build institutions and theories that might limit the scope of that authority, see William E. Nelson, *Roots of American Bureaucracy*.

Chapter One

1. See, e.g., Rakove, *Original Meanings*.

2. Gordon, *Controlling the State*, chap. 8.

3. See Ackerman, *We the People*, 186, 260, and chaps. 7 and 9 more generally.

4. See Amar, *Bill of Rights*; Cornell, *Other Founders*, chaps. 3–4.

5. Here I follow the terminology of Whittington, *Constitutional Construction*, describing constitutional meanings that develop outside the courts and relatively independent of specific constitutional text as "constructions."

6. This is a central theme of Huston, *Securing the Fruits of Labor*.

7. This is the argument of the first half of Kishlansky, *Parliamentary Selection*.

8. For England, see the second half of Kishlansky, *Parliamentary Selection*, and O'Gorman, *Voters, Patrons, and Parties*. For America, see McCormick, *Second American Party System* and Watson, *Jacksonian Politics and Community Conflict*.

9. Hofstadter, *Idea of a Party System*, 12.

10. Clark, *English Society*.

11. O'Gorman, *Voters, Patrons, and Parties*, 106–41; Kishlansky, *Parliamentary Selection*, Conclusion and chap. 1, esp. p. 20.

12. Wood, *Radicalism*; Bushman, *King and People in Provincial Massachusetts*; Marston, *King and Congress*.

13. Division of a community was not only a sign of challenge to hierarchy and constitution but a sign of ungodliness. Still on board the Arbella, John Winthrop told the Puritans, "God Almightie in his most holy and wise providence hath soe disposed of the Condicion of mankinde, as in all times some must be rich some poore, some highe and eminent in power and dignitie; others meane and in subieccion." This hierarchy created opportunities for persons to express God's wisdom and love and to build the Puritan community as an indivisible, mutually dependent "body." John Winthrop, "A Modell of Cristian Charity," 10, 16, 20. In the communities that the Puritans founded in Massachusetts and Connecticut, the covenants that created the several towns embodied this ideal. No town remained utterly free from conflict. Some were, in fact, riven with it. And most towns, possessing abundant land and lacking the clear social differentiations among the gentle and the simple that characterized English society, looked much more like democracies than most English were used to. As economic change and religious division developed, traditional ideals came under increasing stress. Still, it seems clear that, at least for a time, reasonably stable hierarchies developed and that these little polities pursued, above all else, the unity of their communities as mandated by their covenant-constitutions. Lockridge, *New England Town*; Zuckerman, *Peaceable Kingdoms* and "Social Context of Democracy in Massachusetts"; Bushman, *From Puritan to Yankee*, esp. chap. 1. Of course, in some towns division was not so well forestalled. But when it was not, the sense of failure and even catastrophe that resulted only dramatized how deeply held the commitment to unity was. The detection of witchcraft in Salem appears to have been the result of that town's notoriously long-standing and un-Christian divisions. See, e.g., Boyer and Nissenbaum, *Salem Possessed*. The less deadly but equally dramatic events of the Great Awak-

ening also highlight the desire for unity. That event was, on the one hand, an anticonstitutional plague of divisiveness and a model for resistance to authority. But, on the other hand, the separating movements did not look to institutionalized division but to a truer unity in new covenanted communities that rejected division as squarely as the old communities had. Bonomi, "'Just Opposition.'"

14. Zuckerman, *Peaceable Kingdoms*, chap. 5.

15. Bailyn, *Origins of American Politics*.

16. Bailyn, "Politics and Social Structure in Virginia" and *Origins of American Politics*; Ekirch, *"Poor Carolina"*; Kammen, *Colonial New York*; Bushman, *From Puritan to Yankee*, esp. the summary in chap. 16. Even in the middle colonies of New York and Pennsylvania, where historians have located the most contentious and most nearly modern politics before the nineteenth century, public embrace and justifications of party competition were few, far between, and quite rudimentary. Leisler's Rebellion in New York and the relationship between Quaker activists and William Penn in Pennsylvania were among the factors that tended to give politics in these colonies a surprising degree of acrimony with a surprisingly durable shape. Historians have thus been able to find statistical correlations in voting from one election to the next, some private acknowledgments of "party" membership among political elites, and the rare individual's embrace of "party" as an aspect of colonial politics. Tully, *Forming American Politics*. See also Newcomb, *Political Partisanship*. But even in these most advanced of all colonies no one had developed a theory to justify permanent party organization, and antiparty language remained pervasive. Moreover, even those rare souls who edged toward a frank embrace of party had hardly even begun to imagine the public institutionalization of convention nominations, partisan patronage, and party authority that would be central to the rise of mass party competition in the next century. In the colonies, then, while the old order was under some strain and new forms of politics were emerging in some places, the inherited antiparty consensus arrived and survived almost completely intact into the nineteenth century. See Hofstadter, *Idea of a Party System*, 35–39.

17. See, e.g., Gunn, "Influence, Parties and the Constitution" and *Factions No More*; Hill, "Executive Monarchy and the Challenge of Parties"; Mansfield, *Statesmanship and Party Government*; O'Gorman, *Voters, Patrons, and Parties*; Plumb, *Origins of Political Stability*; Clark, "General Theory of Party, Opposition and Government" and *English Society*.

18. Kramnick, *Bolingbroke and His Circle*, chaps. 2–3, 127–36.

19. Ibid., 111–27.

20. Ibid., chaps. 2, 3.

21. Bolingbroke saw the estates as the operative units of politics and thus put them roughly in the place that parties would occupy, but he does not seem to have referred to them explicitly as parties. His allies and admirers, however, occasionally did use that label for them while rejecting the legitimacy of party within an estate. See Gunn, *Factions No More*, 12–15. Hofstadter traces this identification of "party" with a sociopolitical "estate" back through Machiavelli to Aristotle as well. Hofstadter, *Idea of a Party System*, 51 n. 11.

22. Kramnick, *Bolingbroke and His Circle*.

23. Hofstadter, *Idea of a Party System*, 16–23.

24. Kramnick, *Bolingbroke and His Circle*, 76–83.

25. Ibid., 121–22.

26. Ibid., 24.

27. Kemp, *Sir Robert Walpole*, 84–94.

28. Bailyn, *Origins of American Politics*, 14–23, 36–38; Hofstadter, *Idea of a Party System*, 16–23.

29. Bailyn, *Origins of American Politics*, chap. 3. See also Wood, *Radicalism*, chaps. 7–9.

30. Bailyn, *Origins of American Politics*, 59–124. For a somewhat different version, see Wood, *Radicalism*, 112–44.

31. Bushman, *King and People*, 111–20.

32. Ibid., 59–99.

33. Ibid., 55–63.

34. Ibid., 111–20.

35. Ibid., 122–32, 95.

36. With the resolution of the constitutional issues by 1740, the colonists settled for a generation into an existence sufficiently secured from official avarice. They retained control over the governor's salary. They also continued a pattern of smuggling and other circumventions of those imperial economic regulations that would have enriched imperial drones at the expense of the colonial economy. Ibid., 139–49. The constitutional tension in colonial politics remained latent until the imperial crisis of the 1760s and 1770s.

37. Ibid., 176–229. See also Liddle, " 'Patriot King or None,' " and Marston, *King and Congress*.

38. Hofstadter, *Idea of a Party System*, 40.

39. Bailyn, *Ideological Origins of the American Revolution*; Tully's *Forming American Politics* presents an account of Pennsylvania's politics that suggests that its peculiar circumstances—e.g., proprietary government, a unicameral legislature, a dominant Quaker ideology that was radically egalitarian for its time—made its political development unique among the colonies, perhaps including a unique degree of acceptance of party organization. But Tully's evidence suggests to me that such acceptance most likely extended, again, only to organization of a constitutional party, charged only with defense of the consensus-based "ideology of civil Quakerism" against forces external to the community.

40. Among historians the idea is so well known as not to be worth citing particular writers. The same might be said of legal scholars, but a seminal article is Sunstein, "Interest Groups in American Public Law."

41. Wood, *Creation of the American Republic*, chap. 11; Rakove, *Original Meanings*, 30–31; Hofstadter, *Idea of a Party System*, 40; Patterson, *Political Parties in Revolutionary Massachusetts*, 220–26; Dargo, "Parties and the Transformation of the Constitutional Idea," 99–100.

42. See, among many others, Main, *Political Parties before the Constitution*.

43. Rakove, *Original Meanings*, 30.

44. Hofstadter, *Idea of a Party System*, 53.

45. Rakove, *Original Meanings*, 214–27; Nedelsky, *Private Property*, 49–52.

46. Rakove, *Original Meanings*, 46–56.

47. See Kramer, "Madison's Audience," 612–15.

48. Federalist no. 10, 132–33, in *Federalist*.

49. See Sunstein, "Interest Groups," 38–45.

50. Madison, Federalist no. 10, 130.

51. Ibid., 134; Nedelsky, *Private Property*, 46–66.

52. Nedelsky, *Private Property*, 52–55.

53. Ibid., 55–57.

54. Ibid., 57–61. As Nedelsky notes, Madison had little faith in judicial review as a practical obstacle to congressional action, preferring instead a Council of Revision, but he certainly accepted it as better than nothing.

55. Wood, *Creation of the American Republic*, chap. 12.

56. Ibid., 503–18, esp. 513; Hofstadter, "A Constitution Against Parties" (chap. 2), in *Idea of a Party System*.

57. Quoted in Hofstadter, *Idea of a Party System*, 17.

58. Stourzh, *Alexander Hamilton*, 81–85; Wood, *Creation of the American Republic*, 551.

59. Stourzh, *Alexander Hamilton*, 81–85, 95–106.

60. Banning, *Jeffersonian Persuasion*, 135–40.

61. Cornell, *Other Founders*, 187–94.

62. See Hofstadter, *Idea of a Party System*, 123–28; Dunbar, "Study of Monarchical Tendencies"; Banning, *Jeffersonian Persuasion*, 110–13, 119–20, 265–66.

63. Ketcham, *Presidents above Party*, 100–113; Hofstadter, *Idea of a Party System*, 123–28; Pasley, "'A Journeyman Either in Law or in Politics.'"

64. On the use of aristocrat and democrat, see Palmer, "Notes on the Use of the Word 'Democracy,'" 205–6.

65. Banning, *Jeffersonian Persuasion*, 194–200; Storing, *What the Anti-Federalists Were For*, chaps. 6, 7.

66. Quoted in Banning, *Jeffersonian Persuasion*, 194–95, from Taylor's *An Examination of the Late Proceedings in Congress Respecting the Official Conduct of the Secretary of the Treasury* ([Richmond, Va.]: [Samuel Pleasants and Co.], 1793).

67. David Hume, "Of Parties in General," 58; Burke, *Thoughts on the Cause of the Present Discontents*; Hofstadter, *Idea of a Party System*, 29–33; Mansfield, *Statesmanship and Party Government*; Tully, *Forming American Politics*, 405–6; Ketcham, *Presidents above Party*, 119.

68. Quoted in Mansfield, "Thomas Jefferson," 44.

69. Ibid., 44–45.

70. Ibid., 45–49.

71. Onuf, *Jefferson's Empire*.

72. Quoted in Onuf, *Jefferson's Empire*, 120.

73. Ibid., 8–10, 64–79, 120–21.

74. Mansfield, "Thomas Jefferson," 49.

75. Ketcham, *Presidents above Party*, 100–113; Hofstadter, *Idea of a Party System*, 150–82.

76. The anti-Hamiltonian John Taylor of Caroline defined aristocracy as "the transfer of property by law"; see Ashworth, *Slavery, Capitalism, and Politics*, 24. See also Huston's discussion of the "political economy of aristocracy" in *Securing the Fruits of Labor*.

77. Banning, *Jeffersonian Persuasion*, chap. 6, esp. 163, 168; Hofstadter, *Idea of a Party System*, 125–27; Ketcham, *Presidents above Party*, 102.

78. Banning, *Jeffersonian Persuasion*, 212–19, 233–38, 251–64.

79. Cornell, *Other Founders*, 230–62.

80. Hofstadter, *Idea of a Party System*, 150–55; Ketcham, *Presidents above Party*, 104–6; Mansfield, "Thomas Jefferson," 46–47.

81. Hofstadter, *Idea of a Party System*, 155–58; Cunningham, *Jeffersonian Republicans in Power*, esp. chaps. 2–3.

82. Brown, *Republic in Peril*; Ketcham, *Presidents above Party*, 100–123, esp. 119–22; Hofstadter, *Idea of a Party System*, 182–83.

83. David Hackett Fischer, *Revolution of American Conservatism*; Prince, *Federalists*.

84. For Van Buren's boundless worship of Jefferson, see Van Buren, *Inquiry*, 424, and "Autobiography," 188. And for other Jeffersonians, see Hofstadter, *Idea of a Party System*, 241–42.

85. Van Buren, "Autobiography," 303.

86. See Ketcham's *Presidents above Party*, drawing on Bolingbroke's *Idea of a Patriot King*.

87. Cf. Ward, *Andrew Jackson*.

88. Cole, *Van Buren and the American Political System*, 53–57.

89. Ceaser, *Presidential Selection*, 131–32.

90. Hofstadter, *Idea of a Party System*, chap. 6; Cole, *Van Buren and the American Political System*; Ketcham, *Presidents above Party*, chap. 8; Niven, *Martin Van Buren*; Remini, *Van Buren and the Making of the Democratic Party*; Wallace, "Ideologies of Party" and "Changing Concepts of Party." Modifications of the standard view appear in Wilson, "Republicanism and the Idea of Party"; Ceaser, *Presidential Selection*, chap. 3; Baker, *Affairs of Party*, chap. 3.

91. See Wallace, "Changing Concepts of Party," 469–71, and "Ideologies of Party," chap. 3. The preceding paragraphs are taken largely from Niven, *Martin Van Buren*, chaps. 1–6, from Cole, *Van Buren and the American Political System*, chaps. 1–3, and from Van Buren's own "Autobiography."

92. Hofstadter, *Idea of a Party System*, 188–200, 226–31; Remini, *Van Buren and the Making of the Democratic Party*, chaps. 2–3; Ketcham, *Presidents above Party*, 124–30.

93. Remini, *Van Buren and the Making of the Democratic Party*, chaps. 4–7.

94. Hofstadter, *Idea of a Party System*, 195; Chase, *Emergence of the Presidential Nominating Convention*, 110–11.

95. Hofstadter, *Idea of a Party System*, 233–37.

96. Remini, *Van Buren and the Making of the Democratic Party*, 130–33, quotation on 130.

97. On the election of 1828, see, especially, Remini, *Van Buren and the Making of the Democratic Party* and *Election of Andrew Jackson*. On Jackson's gradual conversion to a kind of partyism, see Latner, *Presidency of Andrew Jackson*, 126–29.

98. A valuable, though brief, survey of the evolution of the two-party constitution is in Milkis, *Political Parties and Constitutional Government*.

99. Van Buren wrote his *Inquiry* and his autobiography in his retirement in the 1850s.

100. Van Buren, *Inquiry*, 11–12.

101. Ibid., 38–39.

102. Ibid., 50–56.

103. Ibid., 261–62.

104. See Amar, *Bill of Rights*; Cornell, *Other Founders*.

105. Van Buren, *Inquiry*, 271.

106. Ibid., 32, 74–80.

107. Ibid., 161.

108. Ibid., 180.

109. Ibid., 160–66.

110. Ibid., 121–60.

111. Ibid., 413–22.

112. Ibid., 212; see also 223–26.

113. Ibid., 238.

114. See, e.g., ibid., 247–58.

115. Ibid., 246–47.

116. Ibid., 259.

117. Ibid., 263–67.

118. Ibid., 268.

119. Ibid., 5. Van Buren acknowledged that there had been one exception to this pattern, presumably his own defeat in 1840, but insisted that that isolated instance was "susceptible of easy explanation." He did not go on to offer the easy explanation in full, but he had in mind the terrible depression the country faced during his administration, produced by the banks but plausibly blamed on him. The people then went on to vindicate him and his party by their "sober second thought" in the 1844 election of James K. Polk. See Ibid., 228–29, 231.

120. Stourzh, *Alexander Hamilton*, 111.

121. See Wilson, "Republicanism and the Idea of Party."

122. Van Buren, *Inquiry*, 226.

123. Ibid., 3–5.

124. Van Buren, "Autobiography," 234.

125. Ibid., 303.

126. Ibid.

127. Ibid.

128. Ibid., 193–95, 199, quotation on 195.

129. Ibid., 196.

130. When Monroe won the presidency nearly by acclamation in 1816, Jackson wrote the new president, urging him to disregard political affiliations when making appointments so as to put down the "monster" that was party, a position that Van Buren, of course, could not endorse. See, e.g., ibid., 233–38.

131. Ibid., 198.

132. Ketcham, *Presidents above Party*.

133. Hofstadter, *Idea of a Party System*, 188–203; Ketcham, *Presidents above Party*, 124–26, quotation from Monroe on 126.

134. Monroe's first inaugural address in Richardson, *Compilation* 2:579.

135. Monroe's second inaugural address in ibid., 2:655.

136. Ibid., 2:662.

137. Ketcham, *Presidents above Party*, 133–35.

138. Richardson, *Compilation* 2:862–63.

139. Ibid., 2:863.

140. Ibid., 2:863–65.

141. 17 U.S. 316 (1819).

142. See, e.g., McDonald, *States' Rights and Union*, 80–86.

143. 14 U.S. 304 (1816).

144. For concise discussion of the case, see Currie, *Constitution in the Supreme Court*, 91–96.

145. Knupfer, *Union as It Is*, 130–45.

Chapter Two

1. Sellers, *Market Revolution*, 32.

2. See Freyer, *Producers versus Capitalists*, 10–12, 14, 35, 41–42.

3. See Whittington, *Constitutional Construction*.

4. There are a number of studies that suggest the continuing strength of antipartyism as

a democratic, constitutional conviction in most of the states in the 1820s. Examples include the following: Olsen, *Political Culture and Secession in Mississippi*; Ratcliffe, *Party Spirit in a Frontier Republic*; Watson, *Jacksonian Politics and Community Conflict*; Formisano, *Transformation of Political Culture*; Cayton and Onuf, *Midwest and the Nation*; Shade, *Democratizing the Old Dominion*; Forderhase, "Jacksonianism in Missouri"; Krueger, "Party Development in Indiana."

5. See "Constitution of Illinois—1818," in Thorpe, *Federal and State Constitutions* 2:972–85.

6. On the process of democratization in this period, see, e.g., Wood, *Radicalism*, chaps. 14–19; Formisano, *Transformation of Political Culture*; Williamson, *American Suffrage*; Hatch, *Democratization of American Christianity*.

7. This summary of the state of the territory is drawn mainly from Alvord, *Illinois Country*, 420–33.

8. *Western Intelligencer*, May 8, 1816.

9. Ibid., May 29, 1816.

10. Ibid., November 27, 1817.

11. Ibid., December 11, 1817.

12. *Illinois Intelligencer*, April 14, 1819.

13. *Illinois Gazette*, April 20, 1820.

14. See Thompson, "Elections and Election Machinery in Illinois," for a full description of the workings of self-nomination.

15. *Illinois Gazette*, June 3, 1820.

16. Ibid., July 22, 1820.

17. See "Randolph" in *Illinois Intelligencer*, July 22, 1820.

18. Cook received 65 percent of the vote. Pease, *Illinois Election Returns*, 4.

19. See "Randolph" and "One of the People" in *Illinois Intelligencer*, July 22, 1820.

20. See Leichtle, "Rise of Jacksonian Politics in Illinois." Also helpful on this election and other Illinois politics in the 1820s is Stroble, *High on the Okaw's Western Bank*, chap. 6.

21. *Illinois Intelligencer*, February 20, 1821.

22. Leichtle, "Rise of Jacksonian Politics in Illinois," 94–95.

23. Ibid., 95–96.

24. Ibid., 97–98.

25. Ibid., 97.

26. Nathaniel Buckmaster to John Buckmaster, April 14, 1822, Buckmaster-Curran Papers, ISHL.

27. *Edwardsville Spectator*, May 9, 1820. See also Isom Gillham's piece, *Edwardsville Spectator*, June 13, 1820, addressing the same issue in nearly the same way.

28. *Illinois Intelligencer*, March 10, 1819, March 17, 1819; "For the Good of the Public," *Illinois Intelligencer*, March 17, 1819.

29. *Edwardsville Spectator*, May 29, 1819.

30. See, e.g., Ratcliffe, *Party Spirit in a Frontier Republic*, which describes use of conventions in Ohio before this date.

31. *Edwardsville Spectator*, June 5, 1819.

32. *Illinois Intelligencer*, June 9, 1819. There was one last entry in this debate, a suggestion by "One of the People" for electoral run-offs. He argued, "Virtue, talents, and patriotism, are essential requisites to office; of these the people, not the pretender, should be the judge." The author condemned self-nominations, but he also rejected caucus nominations as well as the provision in Illinois that a mere plurality was sufficient for election to

any office. Instead, all elections should end in a run-off between the two highest vote-getters, a proposal that never had any perceptible impact in the state (*Edwardsville Spectator*, June 19, 1819).

33. See, e.g., Sellers, *Market Revolution*; Thornton, *Politics and Power in a Slave Society*; Watson, *Liberty and Power* and *Jacksonian Politics and Community Conflict*; Feller, "Politics and Society"; Ashworth, *"Agrarians" and "Aristocrats"*; Shade, *Democratizing the Old Dominion*.

34. Contrast Huntington, *Political Order in Changing Societies*, 130–31.

35. Leichtle, "Rise of Jacksonian Politics in Illinois," 97–98, quotation on 98.

36. The legislative scheming is thoroughly described in Pease, *Frontier State*, 77–79.

37. *Edwardsville Spectator*, March 1, 1823.

38. Birkbeck, "Appeal to the People of Illinois," 148.

39. Ibid., 149.

40. Ibid., 149. See also Birkbeck to Edward Coles, March 1, 1823, in Washburne, *Sketch of Edward Coles*.

41. Birkbeck, "An Appeal to the People of Illinois," 152–53. Cf. Freehling, *Road to Disunion*, which argues similarly that the cultures of slaveholding and white man's democracy in the South proved deeply incompatible.

42. Huston, *Securing the Fruits of Labor*, 309–17.

43. Birkbeck, "An Appeal to the People of Illinois," 159.

44. See "One of Many," *Illinois Intelligencer*, May 14, 1824, and "One of the People," *Edwardsville Spectator*, July 6, 1824, as well as the next two notes below.

45. See "A Plain Citizen" and "Convention" in *Illinois Intelligencer*, March 15, 1823. Also see "A Plain Citizen," *Illinois Intelligencer*, March 22, 1823, and the report of a proconvention public meeting in the *Edwardsville Spectator*, March 1, 1823.

46. *Edwardsville Spectator*, May 31, 1823.

47. Ibid., January 20, 1824.

48. Ibid., February 24, 1824.

49. Ibid., January 27, 1824, February 10, 1824.

50. See chapter 1 above for a discussion of this tradition.

51. Coles to Morris Birkbeck, January 29, 1824, in Washburne, *Sketch of Edward Coles*, 183.

52. *Illinois Intelligencer*, February 13, 1824.

53. Ibid., February 13, 1824.

54. Ibid., March 5, 1824.

55. Ibid., February 20, 1824.

56. *Edwardsville Spectator*, April 13, 1824.

57. There is no thorough study of political committee systems as such in the states, but this conclusion is suggested by McCormick, *Second American Party System*, and Cunningham, *Jeffersonian Republicans in Power*, both of which survey early political organization in the states and find relatively little of it, especially in the South and West.

58. *Edwardsville Spectator*, April 13, 1824.

59. Ibid., July 6, 1824.

60. *Illinois Gazette*, June 12, 1824.

61. Ibid., June 24, 1824.

62. Jacob Harlan to Archibald Williams, July 29, 1824, Harlan-Sargent Papers, ISHL.

63. *Illinois Intelligencer*, August 20, 1824.

64. *Illinois Gazette*, July 17, 1824.

65. "Convention" in *Illinois Intelligencer*, July 16, 1824 .

66. The convention was defeated by a vote of 57 percent to 43 percent. Cook won by a vote of 63 percent to 37 percent. Pease, *Illinois Election Returns*, 27, 24.

67. *Illinois Gazette*, August 7, 1824, cited in Kurt E. Leichtle, "Edward Coles."

68. See, e.g., John Reynolds to Elias Kent Kane, April 29, 1824, Kane Papers, CHS; Theophilus W. Smith to Kane, June 28, 1824, Kane Papers, CHS; William Brown's memoir of Cook in Edwards, *History of Illinois*, esp. 260–63; Leichtle, "Rise of Jacksonian Politics in Illinois," 102; Leichtle, "Edward Coles," 190.

69. *Edwardsville Spectator*, February 1, 1823.

70. Ibid., April 20, 1824.

71. *Illinois Gazette*, January 31, 1824.

72. Ibid., May 22, 1824.

73. Ibid., March 1, 1823.

74. Ibid., March 8, 1823, March 22, 1823.

75. *Edwardsville Spectator*, August 17, 1824.

76. See *Illinois Gazette*, April 17, 1824; April 24, 1824; September 18, 1824; September 25, 1824.

77. Ibid., October 2, 1824.

78. Ibid., October 9, 1824.

79. Ibid., September 25, 1824; *Edwardsville Spectator*, September 14, 1824.

80. *Illinois Intelligencer*, September 24, 1824.

81. Ibid., September 24, 1824.

82. *Illinois Gazette*, October 30, 1824.

83. Kane to Jesse B. Thomas, January 8, 1824, Jesse B. Thomas Papers, ISHL.

84. Crawford received less than 5 percent of the vote in Illinois. The returns are in Pease, *Illinois Election Returns*, 30–35.

85. See, e.g., Congressman Daniel P. Cook's letter to Henry Eddy, April 24, 1824, Eddy Manuscripts, ISHL.

86. Thompson, "Genesis of the Whig Party in Illinois," 88; Pease, *Frontier State*, 90. See also William B. Archer to Jacob Harlan, December 7, 1824, Harlan-Sargent Papers, ISHL.

87. Reynolds, *My Own Times*, 241.

88. Pease, *Frontier State*, 111–13; Leichtle, "Rise of Jacksonian Politics in Illinois," 105. See also "No Partisan" in the *Illinois Gazette* of April 29, 1826, and Thomas Reynolds to Elias Kent Kane, December 1, 1825, Kane Papers, CHS.

89. Mering, *Whig Party in Missouri*, 10.

90. Remini, *Election of Andrew Jackson*, 20.

91. Pease, *Illinois Election Returns*, 24, 36.

92. See "No Partisan" in the *Illinois Gazette*, April 29, 1826; "Tyro" in the *Illinois Intelligencer*, July 6, 1826; and an Edwards campaign speech reprinted in Edwards, *History of Illinois*, 198–216.

93. Amar, *Bill of Rights*; Cornell, *Other Founders*.

Chapter Three

1. See, among many others, McCormick, *Second American Party System*; Thornton, *Politics and Power in a Slave Society*; Watson, *Liberty and Power* and *Jacksonian Politics and Community Conflict*; Formisano, *Birth of Mass Political Parties* and *Transformation of Political Culture*; Cayton and Onuf, *Midwest and the Nation*.

2. See Hofstadter, *Idea of a Party System*, 4–5.

3. See, e.g., Hofstadter, *Idea of a Party System*; Schattschneider, *Party Government*; Duverger, *Political Parties*.

4. Ackerman, *We the People*, 186, 260.

5. Remini, *Van Buren and the Making of the Democratic Party*, 130–33, quotation on 130.

6. *Illinois Intelligencer*, January 5, 1828.

7. Ibid., March 1, 1828.

8. Judging by the election returns in November, which included only three serious candidates for the three positions of Jackson elector, and by a brief reference in the proceedings of the Kaskaskia convention, the organization of a convention for the eastern district was probably accomplished, but I have no descriptions of the event. It is quite possible, however, that the eastern convention was not held and that the third elector was nominated in the same way as the Adams electors—that is, by consultation among political leaders.

9. Pease, *Illinois Election Returns*, 60.

10. See Ackerman, *We the People*, 174.

11. *Illinois Gazette*, May 31, 1828, June 28, 1828.

12. Ibid., February 16, 1828.

13. Ibid., March 1, 1828.

14. Ibid., September 13, 1828.

15. *Illinois Intelligencer*, February 16, 1828.

16. George Forquer to Henry Eddy, December 15, 1827, Eddy Manuscripts, ISHL.

17. *Illinois Gazette*, February 9, 1828.

18. Ibid., February 16, 1828.

19. Ibid., May 24, 1828.

20. Ibid., April 26, 1828, May 17, 1828.

21. Ibid., January 10, 1829; also November 15, 1828.

22. Ibid., April 19, 1828.

23. *Illinois Intelligencer*, April 5, 1828.

24. *Galena Miner's Journal*, July 22, 1828, quotation from August 9, 1828.

25. See, e.g., Sproat, *"Best Men"*; Hoogenboom, *Outlawing the Spoils*.

26. Quoted in Milkis, *Political Parties and Constitutional Government*, 41.

27. See, e.g., Hofstadter, *Idea of a Party System*, 156–58.

28. See John, *Spreading the News*, 227–32.

29. A summary of the salience of the Walpole story in America from the start of American politics is in Elkins and McKitrick, *Age of Federalism*, 13–21.

30. Illinois's constitution excepted the offices of justice of the peace, militia officer, and postmaster. See Article II, Section 25, of the Illinois Constitution of 1818 in Thorpe, *Federal and State Constitutions* 2:972–85.

31. Illinois General Assembly, *Journal of the Senate*, Third General Assembly, First Session, January 14, 1823, 143–44.

32. Ibid., 149, 159.

33. *Illinois Intelligencer*, August 20, 1824.

34. Edwards to Henry Eddy, November 22, 1822, Eddy Manuscripts, ISHL.

35. *Illinois Intelligencer*, January 4, 1823.

36. Edwards to President James Monroe, December 22, 1820, in Washburne, *Edwards Papers*, 166–76.

37. Wirt to Edwards, January 15, 1821, in Washburne, *Edwards Papers*, 185–89.

38. Edwards, *History of Illinois*, 263.

39. This reconstruction would remain in place until Reconstruction's reconstruction of the appointing power. In addition to Sproat, *Best Men*, and Hoogenboom, *Outlawing the Spoils*, on the civil service reform movement, see Whittington, *Constitutional Construction*, 117–32, on the impeachment of Andrew Johnson as a reconstruction of the president-Congress relationship with respect to partisan use of the patronage.

40. See, e.g., Samuel D. Lockwood to Mary Lockwood, December 6, 1828, Lockwood Papers, ISHL.

41. *Illinois Gazette*, January 17, 1829.

42. Richardson, *Compilation* 3:1001.

43. Pascal P. Enos to [Ninian Edwards], June 2, 1829, Pascal P. Enos Papers, ISHL.

44. See John, *Spreading the News*, 227–32.

45. Pascal P. Enos to "General" [John P. Van Ness], November 20, 1829; also rough drafts of same letter, Pascal P. Enos Papers, ISHL.

46. Ninian Edwards to Pascal P. Enos and Dr. Todd, [fall 1829]; Edwards to Enos, December 2, 1829, in Edwards, "Two Letters from Governor Ninian Edwards."

47. Pascal P. Enos to [Senator John McLean], December 5, 1829, Pascal P. Enos Papers, ISHL.

48. Duncan's diary is printed in Putnam, "Life and Services of Joseph Duncan." These quotations come from pp. 181–87.

49. *Illinois Gazette*, June 20, 1829.

50. Ellis, "Persistence of Antifederalism after 1789," 299.

51. On states'-rights thought in the period, see Ellis, *Union at Risk*, and McDonald, *States' Rights and the Union.*

52. Simeone, *Democracy and Slavery in Frontier Illinois*, chap. 1.

53. Illinois General Assembly, *Journal of the Senate*, Fifth General Assembly, First Session, December 20, 1826, 71.

54. *Illinois Intelligencer*, July 5, 1828.

55. Ibid.

56. Ninian Edwards to John McLean, June 24, 1828, in Washburne, *Edwards Papers*, 352.

57. Illinois General Assembly, *Journal of the Senate*, Sixth General Assembly, First Session, December 2, 1828; quotations, 20, 38.

58. Duff Green to Ninian Edwards, May 26, 1829; Ninian Edwards to John Reynolds, August 14, 1829, in Washburne, *Edwards Papers.*

59. S. D. Ingham to Stephen H. Kimmel, August 1, 1829, Eddy Manuscripts, ISHL.

60. Stephen H. Kimmel to Alexander F. Grant, December 20, 1829, October 29, 1829, Eddy Manuscripts, ISHL.

61. Reynolds, *My Own Times*, 286–99.

62. *Galena Advertiser*, December 14, 1829.

63. *Edwardsville Crisis*, extra edition, July 15, 1830.

64. *Illinois Gazette*, December 5, 1829.

65. Ibid., December 26, 1829.

66. Ibid., April 17, 1830.

67. Ibid., April 24, 1830.

68. Thus Reynolds's supporters repeatedly condemned Kinney and Kane both for their conservative position on the public lands—opposition to cession but advocacy of reduction in land prices—and for their partyist manipulation of the patronage—"proscription," although they did not link the issues further than that. "A Voter of Union," for ex-

ample, emphasized the importance of three issues: cession of the public lands; winding up the affairs of the State Bank; and adoption of general systems of education and internal improvements. Each of these, he asserted, had been thwarted in the past by "the *proscribing party*." Implicitly, this voter understood Kinney and his cohorts to look to party, not independent judgment, as the source of their policy convictions, including a public lands position that was contrary to the interests of their own communities and consistent with the interests of officeholders or of other communities. Ibid., July 3, 1830.

69. Ninian Edwards to the People of Illinois, May 21, 1830, in Washburne, *Edwards Papers*, 504. On the Jacksonians' use of land-office patronage as a central resource for party-building, see Rohrbough, *Land Office Business*, 273–83.

70. Ninian Edwards to the People of Illinois, May 21, 1830, in Washburne, *Edwards Papers*, 504–5.

71. *Illinois Gazette*, September 4, 1830.

72. Ibid., September 4, 1830.

73. Ibid., November 27, 1830.

74. Ibid., December 18, 1830. For another example of Kane's being associated all at once with proscription, loyalty to Van Buren, and opposition to cession of the public lands, see Sidney Breese to Thomas C. Browne, September 14, 1830, Eddy Manuscripts.

75. Ninian Edwards to the People of Illinois, May 21, 1830, in Washburne, *Edwards Papers*, 500–501.

76. Illinois General Assembly, *Journal of the House of Representatives*, Seventh General Assembly, First Session, December 7, 1830, quotations on 16, 50.

77. See, e.g., Currie, "Choosing the Pilot."

78. Ackerman, *We the People*.

79. Illinois General Assembly, *Journal of the House of Representatives*, Seventh General Assembly, First Session, December 8, 1830, 61–62.

80. Ibid., January 25, 1831, 347.

81. Ibid., January 18, 1831, 304–7.

82. For an explicit connection between the two, see George Churchill to Senator Kane, February 2, 1831, Kane Papers, CHS.

83. Illinois General Assembly, *Journal of the House of Representatives*, Seventh General Assembly, First Session, December 8, 1830, 63–64.

84. Henry Eddy to Alexander F. Grant, December 10, 1830, Eddy Manuscripts.

Chapter Four

1. *Sangamon Journal*, March 8, 1832.

2. Ibid., April 12, 1832.

3. Ibid., May 17, 1832.

4. Pease, *Illinois Election Returns*, 262.

5. *Illinois Advocate*, July 10, 1832.

6. Pease, *Illinois Election Returns*, 78.

7. Ibid., 76.

8. The eventual second-place candidate never appeared on the list, but this seems to have been an oversight and nothing more.

9. The campaign addresses of four of the candidates appeared in the *Illinois Advocate* on the following dates: Henry Webb, May 8, 1832; Charles Slade, June 5, 1832; and Ninian Edwards and Sidney Breese, July 17, 1832.

10. *Illinois Advocate*, January 6, 1832.

11. Ibid., January 6, 1832.

12. *Sangamon Journal*, January 26, 1832.

13. "Baldwin" in *Sangamon Journal*, February 16, 1832.

14. *Sangamon Journal*, March 1, 1832.

15. David M'Gahey to Senator Elias Kent Kane, February 16, 1832, Kane Papers, CHS.

16. Charles Prentice to Kane, May 10, 1832, Kane Papers, CHS.

17. *Illinois Advocate*, March 23, 1832.

18. Proceedings of the meetings, including the district conventions, appear in issues of the *Illinois Advocate* dated between March 23, 1832, and June 12, 1832.

19. *Illinois Advocate*, April 6, 1832.

20. Ibid., May 1, 1832. Illinois did, in fact, choose delegates to the Baltimore convention, but they were delegates named by the irregular meeting at Vandalia the previous December. Presumably this statement was meant to suggest that such a delegation was not sent by the Jacksonians of Illinois but only by a self-constituted clique of lawyers at Vandalia.

21. *Sangamon Journal*, December 1, 1831.

22. Ibid., December 8, 1831.

23. Ibid., January 12, 1832.

24. Ibid., July 26, 1832.

25. Ibid., March 8, 1832.

26. Ibid., October 20, 1832.

27. Ibid., January 12, 1832.

28. *Illinois Advocate*, January 13, 1832.

29. *Sangamon Journal*, August 18, 1832.

30. Ibid., August 18, 1832.

31. See the proceedings of the Fayette County meeting, ibid., September 15, 1832.

32. The proceedings of the state convention are in ibid., September 29, 1832.

33. *Illinois Advocate*, September 4, 1832.

34. *Sangamon Journal*, September 22, 1832.

35. Ibid., October 20, 1832.

36. *Illinois Advocate*, October 23, 1832.

37. Richard P. McCormick's *Second American Party System* concisely describes anti–Van Buren revolts in several states. For the Barbour movement, see pp. 192, 205, 241–43.

38. A. F. Grant to J. M. Robinson, January 14, 1834, Eddy Manuscripts, ISHL.

39. A. F. Grant to J. M. Robinson, January 29, 1834, Eddy Manuscripts, ISHL.

40. Robinson to Grant, February 21, 1834, Eddy Manuscripts, ISHL.

41. A. F. Grant to J. M. Robinson, March 10, 1834, Eddy Manuscripts, ISHL.

42. *Sangamon Journal*, January 11, 1834.

43. *Illinois Advocate*, April 5, 1834.

44. Ibid., March 22, 1834. Reynolds to Henry Eddy and R. W. Clark, July 6, 1834, Eddy Manuscripts, ISHL.

45. *Illinois Advocate*, April 12, 1834.

46. Ibid., April 26, 1834. For similar statements by other candidates, see Zadok Casey, ibid., July 26, 1834, and Robert K. Fleming, ibid., September 10, 1834.

47. Ibid., May 31, 1834.

48. Illinois General Assembly, *Journal of the House of Representatives*, Ninth General Assembly, First Session, December 2, 1834, p. 14.

49. Cf. Fox, "Bank Wars."

Chapter Five

1. See McCormick, *Second American Party System*; Silbey, *American Political Nation*.

2. *Illinois Advocate*, December 28, 1833; *Sangamon Journal*, June 21, 1834.

3. *Illinois Advocate*, December 28, 1833.

4. I am not aware of any full accounts of the idea of the "primary assemblage" as opposed to the party convention or to other kinds of popular action "out-of-doors." However, it is clear that the idea had its roots in the kind of ideology of public political action described by Pauline Maier in *From Resistance to Revolution* for the pre-Revolutionary era and by Gordon Wood in *Creation of the American Republic* for the immediate post-Revolutionary era. Wood's chapter 8, in particular, connects popular action out-of-doors, the ideological origins of American constitutional conventions, the development of the American commitment to popular sovereignty, and the general desire for a harmonious politics. The result is a picture of an American political ideology that was a close forerunner of the populist antipartyism articulated by Illinois's justifiers of "primary assemblages" in the 1830s.

5. *Chicago Democrat*, January 21, 1834.

6. For example, a Hillsboro meeting that assembled to pass anti-Bank resolutions understood itself as a primary assemblage called into being by the manifest emergency of the Bank's attempts to control elections. But the meeting went on to resolve that "the object of this meeting is of a more patriotic and elevated character, than to nominate, or aid in nominating or electing any candidate for any office whatever.—The object is to express the free and unbought opinion of American freemen" (*Illinois Advocate*, May 31, 1834). The implication of this language and of nearly all local practice in Illinois to that date was that to nominate a candidate would suggest that a meeting was under that candidate's influence rather than "free and unbought."

7. Pease, *Illinois Election Returns*, 86–87.

8. Meeting of Lick Creek and Island Grove, *Illinois Advocate*, February 22, 1834.

9. Sangamon County meeting, *Sangamon Journal*, March 15, 1834; see also the Sugar Creek Meeting, ibid., March 8, 1834.

10. New Salem meeting, ibid., March 15, 1834.

11. Sangamon County meeting, ibid., March 15, 1834.

12. *Sangamon Journal*, March 1, 1834.

13. Ibid., March 22, 1834.

14. Ibid., April 25, 1834.

15. See ibid., March 22, 1834, April 25, 1834, July 26, 1834; Pease, *Illinois Election Returns*, 275.

16. *Sangamon Journal*, April 25, 1834.

17. Address of the Ottawa Convention, ibid., March 29, 1834.

18. *Chicago Democrat*, March 18, 1834.

19. Ibid., March 25, 1834.

20. Ibid., April 1, 1834.

21. Ibid., April 8, 1834.

22. Ibid., May 28, 1834.

23. Ibid., June 25, 1834.

24. Ibid., July 2, 1834, July 9, 1834.

25. *Galenian*, February 7, 1834.

26. See Campbell's letter declining the Ottawa nomination, addressed to Stephenson et al., May 20, 1834, James W. Stephenson Papers, ISHL.

27. *Chicago Democrat*, May 28, 1834.

28. Pease, *Illinois Election Returns*, 267, reports returns from three of the six counties. Stephenson led Langworthy by 875 to 22. The other three counties are lost but include Stephenson's home county, where one might imagine he did just as well.

29. *Chicago Democrat*, August 6, 1834.

30. John Hamlin, *Galenian*, June 16, 1834.

31. Pease, *Illinois Election Returns*, 277.

32. *Illinois Advocate*, March 18, 1835.

33. Ibid., April 22, 1835.

34. Edgar County meeting, *Illinois Advocate*, April 22, 1835; Jacksonville meeting, *Sangamo Journal*, April 4, 1835; Sangamon County meeting, *Sangamo Journal*, April 18, 1835.

35. *Chicago Democrat*, May 20, 1835; see also the very similar La Salle County meeting proceedings in the same issue of the paper as well as the resolutions of other meetings advocating minute organization and conventions in the *Illinois Advocate*, June 3, 1835.

36. *Illinois Advocate*, May 6, 1835.

37. Ibid.; *Chicago Democrat*, May 20, 1835, May 27, 1835.

38. *Chicago Democrat*, June 10, 1835.

39. It hardly needs to be said, at this point, that Van Buren's acceptance letter confirmed that the campaign was about the preservation through party organization of republican government itself, which was endangered not by bad policies urged by another democratic party but by the advocates of "monarchical systems." Ibid., July 1, 1835.

40. *Sangamo Journal*, April 4, 1835.

41. Ibid., April 4, 1835.

42. Ibid., April 18, 1835.

43. Ibid., May 2, 1835.

44. "A true and steadfast friend of General Jackson" in *Sangamo Journal*, May 2, 1835.

45. Reprint from *Shawneetown Journal* in *Sangamo Journal*, May 2, 1835.

46. *Sangamo Journal*, June 13, 1835.

47. *Chicago American*, June 20, 1835.

48. *Chicago Democrat*, July 8, 1835.

49. Ibid., July 8, 1835.

50. Ibid., July 15, 1835.

51. *Chicago American*, July 11, 1835.

52. "A Citizen of Cook County," in the *Chicago American*, August 1, 1835.

53. *Chicago American*, August 1, 1835.

54. Ibid., July 18, 1835.

55. Ibid., July 18, 1835.

56. *Chicago Democrat*, July 29, 1835.

57. Ibid., July 22, 1835.

58. Ibid., August 5, 1835.

59. "Address to the Democratic Republicans of the United States," *Chicago Democrat*, September 9, 1835, and September 16, 1835; reprinted from the *Washington Globe* of August 6, 1835. This is the same address that is often known as "Statement of the Democratic Republicans of the United States," available in abridged form in Schlesinger, *History of American Presidential Elections* 1:616–38.

60. Schlesinger, *History of American Presidential Elections*, 1:618–19.

61. Ibid., 1:617.

62. Cf. Jaenicke, "American Ideas of Political Party."

63. The beginning of this quotation is in Schlesinger, *History of American Presidential Elections*, 1:620–21. The balance is omitted in that version.

64. Schlesinger, *History of American Presidential Elections*, 1:621–22.

65. Ibid., 1:634.

66. *Chicago Democrat*, December 2, 1835.

67. Proceedings of meetings appear in the *Chicago Democrat*, of September 23, 1835, October 14, 1835, October 21, 1835, and others, as well as in the *Illinois Advocate* of November 25, 1835, and December 9, 1835.

68. The proceedings are in the *Illinois Advocate*, December 16, 1835.

69. *Illinois Advocate*, December 16, 1835. See also Douglas, *Letters of Stephen A. Douglas*, 24–31, where the editor, Robert W. Johannsen, publishes the entire address as the work of Douglas.

70. Douglas, *Letters of Stephen A. Douglas*, 24–25.

71. *Chicago Democrat*, December 23, 1835. That the convention system was controversial among Democrats as well as anti-Democrats is further suggested by the passage of anticonvention resolutions by the state senate while the House voted similar resolutions down. See the *Chicago Democrat*, December 23, 1835, and December 30, 1835.

72. *Sangamo Journal*, December 12, 1835.

73. The account of this second night's debate was published in three parts in the *Sangamo Journal* editions of February 6, 1836, February 13, 1836, and February 20, 1836.

74. Ibid., February 13, 1836.

75. Ibid., February 6, 1836.

76. This charge echoed an earlier contention by "One What Seen," in the *Sangamo Journal* of November 28, 1835, that the Lewistown Democratic meeting had consisted of a total of three men who named themselves delegates to the state convention.

77. *Sangamo Journal*, February 20, 1836.

78. *Chicago Democrat*, January 20, 1836.

79. Ibid., January 27, 1836.

80. *Chicago American*, November 28, 1835, January 23, 1836.

81. Reprinted in *Chicago Democrat*, February 17, 1836.

82. *Sangamo Journal*, February 20, 1836.

83. Ibid., March 26, 1836, April 16, 1836.

84. *Illinois Advocate*, April 22, 1836.

85. Reprinted in *Chicago Democrat*, April 20, 1836.

86. *Illinois Advocate*, July 8, 1836.

87. Reprinted in *Chicago American*, June 18, 1836. See also Cyrus Edwards to Henry Eddy, June 2, 1836, Eddy Manuscripts, ISHL, confirming the importance of the convention system and the land bill as issues.

88. Some generically pre-partisan campaign letters can be found in the *Illinois Advocate*, May 6, 1836, and July 22, 1836.

89. Pease, *Illinois Election Returns*, 102.

90. May's letter, which was written to the *Jacksonville News*, appeared in the *Sangamo Journal*, April 23, 1836.

91. See, e.g., the *Sangamo Journal*, April 16, 1836.

92. May won 54 percent of the vote to John T. Stuart's 46 percent; Pease, *Illinois Election Returns*, 103.

93. *Chicago Democrat*, May 11, 1836.

94. See Hébert, "Emergence of the Democratic Party," 91–92, 98, 133, for accounts of the consistently small representation at conventions at least through 1838.

95. *Sangamo Journal*, July 2, 1836.

96. *Chicago American*, July 2, 1836.

97. These quotations are in two separate editorial articles in the *Chicago American*, July 16, 1836.

98. *Chicago Democrat*, June 29, 1836, July 20, 1836.

99. Ibid., July 20, 1836.

100. Ibid., July 20, 1836.

101. Ibid., July 20, 1836.

102. Quotations from excerpts from Pruyne's handbill as published in the *Chicago American*, July 30, 1836.

103. *Chicago American*, July 2, 1836.

104. Ibid., July 16, 1836.

105. Ibid., July 23, 1836. Giles Spring was nominated by his "numerous and intelligent friends" in the *Chicago American*, July 30, 1836. Harry Boardman's nomination by subscription letter appeared July 23, as did a similar subscription nomination for sheriff.

106. *Chicago American*, July 23, 1836.

107. Ibid., July 30, 1836.

108. In the congressional race, May received 78 percent of the vote in Cook, 72 percent in Will, and 59 percent in Lasalle; Pease, *Illinois Election Returns*, 103. In Pruyne's race, only 29 percent voted for the antipartyist Spring, and a negligible 3 percent went for the candidate of the Democratic bolters, Woodworth; Pease, *Illinois Election Returns*, 287. The two nominees who were not bolted received overwhelming majorities, probably on the order of 75 percent to 80 percent of those voting. Precise percentages are impossible because there were three positions to be filled by a single election, each voter voting three times and the top three vote-getters being elected. Thus, while the total number of votes is known, the total number of voters can only be estimated as marginally greater than one-third of the votes cast, or roughly equal to the number cast in the senatorial election; Pease, *Illinois Election Returns*, 302. The county convention's nominees for sheriff and county commissioners also appear to have received support roughly in the range of 70 percent to 100 percent of the voters; *Chicago American*, August 13, 1836.

109. See the reprint from the *Jacksonville News* in the *Sangamo Journal*, May 7, 1836.

110. *Sangamo Journal*, May 7, 1836.

111. Ibid., March 26, 1836.

112. Ibid., May 28, 1836.

113. Ibid., July 23, 1836.

114. Ibid., August 6, 1836.

115. *Illinois Advocate*, July 1, 1836. This argument was common outside of Illinois as well. See McCormick, "Was There a 'Whig Strategy' in 1836?"

116. *Illinois Advocate*, July 1, 1836; June 17, 1836.

117. *Sangamo Journal*, January 9, 1836.

118. Ibid., April 16, 1836.

119. The slow acceptance of a "Union Ticket" can be followed in the *Illinois Advocate*, August 19, 1836; September 2, 1836; September 16, 1836; September 23, 1836; October 7, 1836; October 14, 1836; October 21, 1836; in the *Chicago American*, September 10, 1836; October 8, 1836; October 22, 1836; October 29, 1836; in the *Sangamo Journal*, January 9, 1836, October 15, 1836.

120. *Chicago American*, October 22, 1836, October 29, 1836.

121. *Illinois Advocate*, October 7, 1836.

122. Ibid., October 14, 1836.

123. Ibid., October 21, 1836.

124. Ibid., October 28, 1836.

125. *Sangamo Journal*, October 29, 1836.

126. Pease, *Illinois Election Returns*, 104, 80.

127. *Sangamo Journal*, December 3, 1836.

128. See, e.g., Amar, *Bill of Rights*, for a textual argument for a populist reading of the Constitution.

Chapter Six

1. *Elrod v. Burns*, 427 U.S. 347 (1976); *Branti v. Finkel*, 445 U.S. 507 (1980); *Rutan v. Republican Party of Illinois*, 497 U.S. 62 (1990).

2. This is Justice Scalia dissenting in *Rutan*, 497 U.S. 62, 95.

3. See John, *Spreading the News*, 227–32.

4. See *Field v. McClernand*, 3 Ill. 79 (1839).

5. See, e.g., Van Buren, *Inquiry*, 325–52.

6. See, e.g., Reynolds, *My Own Times*, 292–99.

7. See, e.g., Winkle, "Second Party System in Lincoln's Springfield," 275–77; Rodney Owen Davis, "Illinois Legislators and Jacksonian Democracy," "Partisanship in Jacksonian State Politics," " 'People in Miniature.' "

8. Henry, "Memoirs," quotations on 73. For a similar account, see John T. Stuart to Julia D. Kirby (Duncan's daughter) in the Duncan Papers, ISHL. This letter is undated but was probably written well after the Civil War as an aid to Kirby's writing of a biography of Duncan.

9. Illinois General Assembly, *Journal of the Senate*, Tenth General Assembly, First Session, December 9, 1836, 23–24.

10. Ibid., 26–28.

11. For an account of the economic history of these events, see Temin, *Jacksonian Economy*.

12. Illinois General Assembly, *Journal of the Senate*, Tenth General Assembly, Second Session, July 11, 1837, quotation on 11.

13. Ibid., July 22, 1837, quotation on 179.

14. Silbey, *American Political Nation*, 28–32.

15. Illinois General Assembly, *Journal of the House of Representatives*, Eleventh General Assembly, First Session, December 4, 1838, 10–11.

16. Ibid., 12–13.

17. Ibid., December 7, 1838, 28–30.

18. Ibid., 30.

19. Sellers, *Market Revolution*, 32.

20. Freyer, *Producers versus Capitalists*, 14.

21. Cf. Huston, *Securing the Fruits of Labor*.

22. May seems to have lost an internal power struggle and thereby earned the lasting enmity of Douglas and others. See Johannsen, *Stephen A. Douglas*, 61–62, and Pease, *Frontier State*, 246–48. Also see Adam W. Snyder to James Semple, August 8, 1837, in John F. Snyder, *Adam W. Snyder and His Period*, 236.

23. Proceedings in *Washington Globe*, December 12, 1837.

24. For a parallel argument, see Freyer, *Producers Versus Capitalists*, which, in turn, draws on J. Willard Hurst's notion of the "balance of power." As elaborated in, e.g., *Law and the Conditions of Freedom*, the "balance of power" represents the American concern

in the nineteenth century to protect the individual political and economic actor from the concentrated power of wealth.

25. Letter from May to the editors of the *Washington Globe*, published in the *Madisonian* and reprinted in the *Sangamo Journal*, January 13, 1838.

26. See Lamborn to Jesse B. Thomas (son of the former Senator), December 1, 1837, Hardin Papers, CHS.

27. Davis to John T. Stuart, December 23, 1837, Stuart-Hay Papers, ISHL.

28. Browning to Hardin, January 4, 1838, Hardin Papers, CHS.

29. *Sangamo Journal*, December 30, 1837.

30. Ibid., December 23, 1837, February 17, 1838.

31. See Johannsen, *Stephen A. Douglas*, 66–67.

32. *Sangamo Journal*, July 7, 1838; Henry, "Memoirs," 68.

33. Wilson, *Presidency of Martin Van Buren*, 61–78 and esp. 63–64.

34. *Sangamo Journal*, May 26, 1838.

35. *Illinois State Register*, November 4, 1837.

36. Ibid., December 22, 1837.

37. Ibid., May 25, 1838.

38. Ibid., June 1, 1838.

39. Ibid., July 13, 1838, July 27, 1838.

40. Ibid., July 27, 1838; see also *Sangamo Journal*, July 14, 1838.

41. Pease, *Illinois Election Returns*, 108.

42. See *Sangamo Journal*, March 3, 1838, and reprint from the *Madisonian* in *Sangamo Journal*, May 5, 1838.

43. Snyder to [?], March 21, 1837, Snyder Papers, ISHL.

44. Snyder to [?], June 3, 1837, July 22, 1837, Snyder Papers, ISHL. Compare with Van Buren, *Inquiry*, 226, discussed in chapter 1, above.

45. Snyder to Gustave Koerner, October 18, 1837, in "Letters to Gustave Koerner, 1837–1863."

46. Ibid.

47. Snyder to Gustave Koerner, January 22, 1838, Snyder Papers, ISHL.

48. See the series of letters written by Snyder from Washington to unnamed Illinoisans, probably Koerner and James Semple mostly, between March 27, 1838, and June 29, 1838, especially the letter of June 26, 1838, in which he reports his decision to vote for the Subtreasury. All letters are in the Snyder Papers, ISHL.

49. *Illinois State Register*, July 27, 1838.

50. Snyder to [Koerner?], January 17, 1839, Snyder Papers, ISHL.

51. See Reynolds's campaign speech, tracking the soon-to-be standard Van Burenite history of American politics in the *Illinois State Register*, August 3, 1838.

52. The two bare exceptions were James Henry and William Kinney, each of whom received the nominations of small, nonparty, local meetings in 1834.

53. *Illinois State Register*, May 13, 1837.

54. Ibid., July 22, 1837.

55. Ibid., July 22, 1837.

56. Reprinted in *Illinois State Register*, September 15, 1837.

57. The address appeared in the November 4, 1837, issue of the *Illinois State Register*. It is also reprinted in Douglas, *Letters of Stephen A. Douglas*, 42–50.

58. Douglas, *Letters of Stephen A. Douglas*, 43.

59. Ibid., 44–45.

60. Ibid., 45.

61. Ibid., 47.

62. Ibid., 48.

63. Ibid., 48.

64. Hébert, "Emergence of the Democratic Party," 133.

65. *Sangamo Journal*, December 30, 1837.

66. Ibid., December 30, 1837.

67. Ibid., December 23, 1837.

68. Ibid., February 17, 1838.

69. Ibid., February 17, 1838.

70. *Illinois State Register*, January 5, 1838.

71. Ibid., March 2, 1838.

72. Adam W. Snyder to Gustave Koerner, January 22, 1838, Snyder Papers, ISHL.

73. Snyder to [Koerner?], April 15, 1838, Snyder Papers, ISHL.

74. See, e.g., Snyder to [Koerner?], March 27, 1838, and Snyder to [?], May 7, 1838, Snyder Papers, ISHL.

75. Snyder to [?], May 18, 1838, Snyder Papers, ISHL.

76. Snyder to [?], May 22, 1838, Snyder Papers, ISHL.

77. *Sangamo Journal*, March 31, 1838.

78. Ibid., May 26, 1838.

79. Editorial, correspondent's report, and reprint from *Free Press* in *Sangamo Journal*, June 16, 1838.

80. *Sangamo Journal*, July 21, 1838.

81. *Illinois State Register*, June 8, 1838.

82. Ibid., August 3, 1838.

83. Pease, *Illinois Election Returns*, 111–13.

Chapter Seven

1. See, e.g., Isaac Kramnick's discussion of theories of the British constitution in *Bolingbroke and His Circle*, 137–52.

2. See Bellamy, "Political Form of the Constitution." Bellamy discusses the origins of separation of powers in the American constitutional design as a product of the obsolescence of constitutional estates.

3. On this subject generally, see chapter 1, above.

4. Cf. Hofstadter, *Idea of a Party System*, 16–18.

5. Wilson, *Presidency of Martin Van Buren*, 124–25.

6. Van Buren, "Thoughts on the approaching election in N. York," [March, 1840], Martin Van Buren Papers, microfilm edition of the collection in the Library of Congress, Washington, D.C. See the brief but interesting discussion of this document in Wilson, *Presidency of Martin Van Buren*, 205–6.

7. Van Buren, "Thoughts," 1–3.

8. Ibid., 10.

9. Ibid., 10–11, 14–15.

10. Ibid., 15–18.

11. Ibid., 19.

12. Ibid., 21.

13. Ibid., 19–22, quotations on 22. Also note that "corruption" here is probably best taken in the sense in which Hamilton himself would have meant it; that is, as those devices

by which the executive (or "the government") could secure a continuing legislative majority.

14. Ibid., 23.

15. Ibid., 23–28.

16. Ibid., 29–32.

17. Ibid., 33.

18. Ibid., 34–39.

19. According to Van Buren, all three of the other candidates that year, Jackson, Crawford, and Clay (who later turned out to be a constitutional aristocrat), were then generally acknowledged to be old republicans. Jackson won a national plurality in the election, and together the three "democratic" candidates polled a large majority for, as Van Buren saw it, democracy.

20. Ibid., 34–39, quotation on 39.

21. Ibid., 41–43.

22. Ibid., 44.

23. See Bushman, *King and People*, and Wood, *Radicalism of the American Revolution*.

24. Van Buren, "Thoughts," 46–49.

25. Ibid., 53–55.

26. Ibid., 74.

27. See, e.g., Hofstadter, *Idea of a Party System*; Remini, *Van Buren and the Making of the Democratic Party*; Cole, *Van Buren and the American Political System*; Wilson, *Presidency of Martin Van Buren* and "Republicanism and the Idea of Party."

28. *Belleville Advocate*, October 24, 1840.

29. The following paragraphs are drawn from the *Illinois State Register*, January 29, 1839.

30. Proceedings in ibid., November 9, 1839.

31. Proceedings in ibid., November 23, 1839.

32. Proceedings in ibid., November 23, 1839.

33. Proceedings in ibid., November 23, 1839.

34. See, e.g., the proceedings printed in ibid., November 23, 1839.

35. For elaboration of these themes and this picture of the Democrats, see, e.g., Huston, *Securing the Fruits of Labor*; Thornton, *Politics and Power in a Slave Society*; Ashworth, *"Agrarians" and "Aristocrats"*; Sellers, *Market Revolution*.

36. All quotations from *Illinois State Register*, December 18, 1839.

37. Ibid., December 21, 1839.

38. The piece, written as a letter from Caspar Thiell to Mahlon Green and explicitly intended for publication, appeared in two parts in the *Belleville Advocate*, August 29, 1840, September 19, 1840.

39. *Belleville Advocate*, October 24, 1840.

40. See Van Buren, *Inquiry*, 330, 348–49. On the Founders' original expectation of this mode of enforcement, see Kramer, "Putting the Politics Back," 234–68, and Kramer, "We the Court." For emphasis on the people of the states severally, rather than the states as such or the American people as a whole, as the enforcers of federalism, see Fritz, "A Constitutional Middle Ground."

41. The following paragraphs are drawn from the *Great Western* of August 24, 1839.

42. 17 U.S. 316 (1819).

43. On the Bank veto generally as part of ongoing constitutional struggle in politics, see Magliocca, "Veto."

44. See Fisher, *Constitutional Dialogues*, 240.

45. *Chicago American*, February 5, 1840.

46. *Sangamo Journal*, March 6, 1840.

47. Ibid., March 13, 1840.

48. Ibid., July 3, 1840.

49. See Jaenicke, "American Ideas of Political Party."

50. *Sangamo Journal*, March 16, 1839.

51. The possibility of Winfield Scott's being nominated appears never to have been entertained in Illinois.

52. *Sangamo Journal*, October 4, 1839.

53. *Chicago American*, October 14, 1839.

54. *Sangamo Journal*, August 30, 1839.

55. Ibid., September 6, 1839.

56. Ibid., September 6, 1839.

57. Ibid., October 4, 1839.

58. Ibid., September 20, 1839.

59. *Chicago American*, September 17, 1839.

60. *Great Western*, August 3, 1839.

61. Ibid., September 14, 1839.

62. Ibid., October 12, 1839.

63. Convention proceedings were printed in the *Chicago American*, October 14, 1839, and the *Sangamo Journal*, October 11, 1839.

64. *Illinois State Register*, March 15, 1839.

65. Ibid., October 12, 1839.

66. Ibid., December 21, 1839.

67. Ibid., February 14, 1840.

68. *Shawneetown Western Voice*, May 16, 1840.

69. *Chicago American*, December 20, 1839. Pease, *Frontier State*, 265–70, and Gunderson, *Log-Cabin Campaign*, are examples of historians who have seen the pomp of the Whig campaign as obscuring any principles that might have been involved. More recently, historians have seen crucial ethnocultural and economic dynamics at work in the election of 1840 but have still tended to see the constitutional principles espoused by the Whigs as mere cover for those more important dynamics. For a more or less balanced view that still seems to me to shortchange the constitutional issues, see Holt, *Rise and Fall*, 105–11.

70. *Chicago American*, December 20, 1839.

71. *Sangamo Journal*, January 14, 1840.

72. *Great Western*, January 11, 1840.

73. Milkis, *Political Parties and Constitutional Government*, 25.

74. Ibid., 192–93 n. 59.

75. Ibid., 25–34.

76. Hofstadter, *Idea of a Party System*, esp. chap. 6; Silbey, *American Political Nation*, esp. chap. 2.

77. James G. Birney did run as the Liberty party candidate but received no attention in the press and less than one vote in every 500.

Chapter Eight

1. Ackerman, *We the People*, 186, 260.

2. See Thornton, *Politics and Power in a Slave Society*, xviii.

3. See, e.g., Silbey, *American Political Nation*, 46–48.

4. However, Glenn C. Altschuler and Stuart M. Blumin argue in *Rude Republic* that, whatever the strength of the new egalitarianism as ideology, actual popular engagement with politics in this period has been dramatically overstated.

5. Kennedy, *Defence of the Whigs*, part I, chap. 6. Kennedy's notion that the people would rise up in a body only in relatively rare moments of constitutional crisis is exactly the idea Bruce Ackerman attributes to the Framers, who marginalized the otherwise sovereign people in the original constitutional design. See Ackerman, *We the People*, 167–95.

6. For discussion of the high voter turnouts of these years, see Silbey, *American Political Nation*, 144–51; and, for another perspective, Altschuler and Blumin, *Rude Republic*, 18, 69.

7. *Illinois State Register*, April 19, 1839.

8. *Chicago Democrat*, April 24, 1839.

9. *Illinois State Register*, April 26, 1839.

10. Note the capitalization of "Democratic" here compared to the lack of capitalization of "democratic party" earlier in the sentence. I have tried not to overinterpret contemporaries' capitalizations or lack thereof, but it does seem to me that this is an instance where a plausible interpretation can be offered. If "democratic party" meant, traditionally, all those of the democratic stratum of the polity or all those of democratic constitutional convictions, whereas "Democratic party" meant the organization or institution that sought to be the expression of the "democratic party," then, by distinguishing upper- from lower-case in spelling D/democratic, this meeting argues that anyone looking to sustain his democratic constitutional convictions must vote Democratic. The choice of capitalizations here may reinforce the notion, which the meeting argues explicitly anyway, that the difference between the parties was above all constitutional. Of course, it could be nothing more than a printing error, but Joel Silbey too has noticed the use of capitalization as possible evidence of the institutionalization of the parties. See Silbey, *American Political Nation*, 39.

11. *Chicago American*, August 12, 1839.

12. Ibid., July 30, 1839.

13. Ibid., July 31, 1839.

14. Ibid., August 2, 1839.

15. Ibid., August 3, 1839.

16. Proceedings of Whig district convention, *Chicago American*, November 21, 1839.

17. *Great Western*, June 22, 1839.

18. See ibid., June 29, 1839, July 27, 1839, August 3, 1839.

19. Ibid., July 20, 1839.

20. Ibid., August 10, 1839. The latter was James Reynolds, son of John Reynolds. He was the alleged replacement for a candidate said to have been read out of the party. See ibid., June 29, 1839.

21. Ibid., August 3, 1839.

22. Ibid., October 26, 1839.

23. Ibid., November 2, 1839.

24. Ibid., January 11, 1840.

25. Ibid., February 29, 1840, March 7, 1840.

26. Ibid., March 7, 1840.

27. Ibid., March 14, 1840.

28. Ibid., March 28, 1840.

29. Ibid., April 4, 1840.

30. Ibid., April 11, 1840.

31. Proceedings of the "Great Meeting of the People" in ibid., April 18, 1840.

32. *Great Western*, April 4, 1840.

33. Ibid., April 18, 1840.

34. Ibid., April 25, 1840.

35. Ibid., May 2, 1840.

36. *Belleville Advocate*, April 4, 1840.

37. Ibid., April 11, 1840.

38. Ibid., April 25, 1840.

39. Ibid., July 25, 1840.

40. Ibid., August 1, 1840.

41. See, e.g., ibid., editorial, August 1, 1840.

42. See "A Voice from Ridge Prairie" in ibid., August 1, 1840. Also *Belleville Advocate*, editorial and communication from "A Farmer," July 18, 1840.

43. *Belleville Advocate*, June 13, 1840.

44. Ibid., July 4, 1840.

45. Ibid., June 27, 1840.

46. Ibid., July 25, 1840, August 1, 1840.

47. Proceedings of the precinct conventions are in the *Sangamo Journal*, March 6, 1840, March 13, 1840. Proceedings of the county convention are in the *Sangamo Journal*, March 20, 1840.

48. *Sangamo Journal*, March 6, 1840.

49. Ibid., March 6, 1840.

50. Ibid., March 6, 1840.

51. Ibid., March 20, 1840.

52. *Illinois State Register*, March 27, 1840.

53. *Sangamo Journal*, July 3, 1840.

54. Ibid., July 24, 1840.

55. *Illinois State Register*, May 29, 1840.

56. Ibid., May 29, 1840.

57. *Belleville Advocate*, July 4, 1840.

58. *Chicago American*, February 6, 1840.

59. A day earlier the *American* had made a point of noting that the current Whig city government had appointed such good and "independent" judges of election and established such sensible polling places as to ensure the fairness of the municipal election, something implicitly not to be expected of Democrats. Ibid., February 5, 1840.

60. See ibid., March 30, 1840.

61. Ibid., February 14, 1840.

62. Ibid., March 2, 1840.

63. Ibid., February 24, 1840.

64. Ibid., April 6, 1840.

65. Ibid., April 6, 1840.

66. *Belleville Advocate*, June 13, 1840.

67. *Sangamo Journal*, June 5, 1840.

68. S. A. Douglas et al. to the Democratic Party of Illinois, May 13, 1840, in Douglas, *Letters of Stephen A. Douglas*, 83–92.

69. Douglas, *Letters of Stephen A. Douglas*, 84–86

70. Ibid., 87.

71. Ibid., 91.

72. *Illinois State Register*, October 23, 1840. See also the report of Sidney Breese's campaign speech, articulating a similar version of constitutional partyist history, in the *Belleville Advocate*, October 17, 1840.

73. *Sangamo Journal*, May 22, 1840.

74. Ibid., September 11, 1840.

75. "An Original Jackson Man," number 2, *Sangamo Journal*, October 16, 1840.

76. *Sangamo Journal*, November 20, 1840.

77. *Illinois State Register*, September 18, 1840, October 16, 1840.

78. Ibid., November 13, 1840, November 27, 1840, December 4, 1840.

79. McCormick, *Second American Party System*, 276.

80. See, e.g., Varon, "Tippecanoe and the Ladies, Too" and *We Mean to Be Counted*; McCormick, *Second American Party System*, 276.

81. Rare persons may even have had a fully modern desire to see regular alternation between two equally legitimate parties. See, e.g., William Brock's citation of the Whig Calvin Colton and, more tentatively, a writer in the *Democratic Review*. Brock, *Parties and Political Conscience*, 22.

Chapter Nine

1. The classics of ethnoculturalism for the Second Party System include Benson, *Concept of Jacksonian Democracy*, and Formisano, *Birth of Mass Political Parties*.

2. Major works in this vein include Thornton, *Politics and Power in a Slave Society*; Watson, *Jacksonian Politics and Community Conflict*; Sellers, *Market Revolution*.

3. See Howe, "Evangelical Movement and Political Culture in the North"; Formisano, "New Political History and the Election of 1840"; Watson, *Liberty and Power*; Gerring, "Party Ideology in America" and "Chapter in the History of American Party Ideology."

4. See, e.g., McCormick, *Second American Party System*; Remini, *Van Buren and the Making of the Democratic Party*; Hofstadter, *Idea of a Party System*.

5. See John, "Governmental Institutions as Agents of Change."

6. For an account of the rise of such "judicial exclusivity," see Kramer, "We the Court."

7. Van Buren, *Inquiry*, 365–66.

8. See, e.g., Kramer, "Putting the Politics Back," 234–52; Kramer, "We the Court"; Killenbeck, "Pursuing the Great Experiment," 84.

9. See Mushkat and Rayback, *Martin Van Buren*.

10. Van Buren, *Inquiry*, 293.

11. Ibid., 330 (quoting Hugh Lawson White). Cf. Amar, "Consent of the Governed."

12. 14 U.S. 304 (1816).

13. 17 U.S. 316 (1819).

14. Van Buren, *Inquiry*, 281–352.

15. On *Dred Scott* as a neo-Federalist revival of *McCulloch*, see Van Buren, *Inquiry*, 358–76; Whittington, "Road Not Taken."

16. Newmyer, "John Marshall and the Southern Constitutional Tradition," 108–12.

17. See Cornell, *Other Founders*, esp. 278–88, which describes reaction to *McCulloch*.

18. See Whittington, "Road Not Taken," esp. 371–72.

19. See ibid., 372–77.

20. Quoted in Wallace, "Changing Concepts of Party," 488.

21. See Freehling, "Spoilsmen and Interests"; and Freehling, *Prelude to Civil War*.

22. Ford, "Inventing the Concurrent Majority." If Larry Kramer is right, then this aspect of Federalist no. 10 never had an audience even in its own day. See Kramer, "Madison's Audience."

23. Freehling, "Spoilsmen and Interests."

24. See, e.g., Carey, *Parties, Slavery, and the Union in Antebellum Georgia*, 24–31, 59; Thornton, *Politics and Power in a Slave Society*, 21–39; Lucas, "Development of the Second Party System in Mississippi, 1817–1846," chap. 7.

25. Formisano, *Transformation of Political Culture*, "Deferential-Participant Politics," and "Federalists and Republicans"; Hofstadter, *Idea of a Party System*. For a modification of this view, see Ratcliffe, *Party Spirit in a Frontier Republic*.

26. Whittington, "Road Not Taken," 369.

27. See, e.g., Latner, *Presidency of Andrew Jackson*, 119–21; Remini, *Andrew Jackson and the Bank War*.

28. See Remini, "Election of 1832," 509–12.

29. Feller, *Public Lands in Jacksonian Politics*.

30. See, e.g., Ratcliffe, *Party Spirit in a Frontier Republic*, for an account of a state (Ohio) that had been in the vanguard of party organization in the First Party System but that quickly reverted to an antipartyist consensus after the War of 1812.

31. See, e.g., Hofstadter, *Idea of a Party System*; Ketcham, *Presidents above Party*.

32. Baker, *Affairs of Party*, 85.

33. See ibid., 119–25, discussing Bancroft's *History of the United States from the Discovery of the Continent*.

34. Ceaser, *Presidential Selection*, 127.

35. See, e.g., Cole, *Van Buren and the American Political System*, 267–68.

36. Wilson, "Republicanism and the Idea of Party," 429–42.

37. See Wilson, *Presidency of Martin Van Buren*, 61–98.

38. Niven, *Martin Van Buren*, 448.

39. Wilson, *Presidency of Martin Van Buren*, 94.

40. Marshall, "Strange Stillbirth of the Whig Party." Holt seems to take a softer version of this position; *Rise and Fall*, 105–11.

41. Wilson, *Presidency of Martin Van Buren*, 63–64.

42. Friedman, *Revolt of the Conservative Democrats*, 16.

43. Ibid., 55–78.

44. Wilson, *Presidency of Martin Van Buren*, 202–8; Feller, "Brother in Arms," 64.

45. Hofstadter, *Idea of a Party System*; Wallace, "Changing Concepts of Party."

46. Wallace, "Changing Concepts of Party," 469–70.

47. Wallace, "Ideologies of Party in the Ante-Bellum Republic," chaps. 3 and 5, and "Changing Concepts of Party," 476–81; Hanyan, *De Witt Clinton and the Rise of the People's Men*.

48. Wallace, "Changing Concepts of Party," 469–71.

49. See chapters 5 and 6 of Wallace's "Ideologies of Party in the Ante-Bellum Republic."

50. Crofts, *Old Southampton*, 108.

51. Ibid., 111–12. See also Shade, *Democratizing the Old Dominion*, 165–67, 244–45.

52. Crofts, *Old Southampton*, 121.

53. Ibid., 138.

54. Cayton, *Frontier Republic*, 68–76.

55. See Pocock, "'A Candidate I'll Surely Be.'"

56. Ratcliffe, *Party Spirit in a Frontier Republic*. Ratcliffe argues convincingly that

democracy and party devices were more advanced and more important in early Ohio than has normally been supposed, but he does not deny that the antipartyist faith remained dominant at least until the emergence of the Second Party System.

57. Cayton, *Frontier Republic*, 129–37.

58. Fox, "Bank Wars"; Etcheson, "Private Interest and the Public Good," 90–98.

59. Feller, "Brother in Arms," 56.

60. Ibid., 57.

61. Ibid., 64 (quoting the 1836 state party platform).

62. See Formisano, *Birth of Mass Political Parties*; Leonard, "Antiparty Origins of the Party System." Also compare Wallace, "Changing Concepts of Party," 469–71, which observes that the original New York Van Burenites characteristically campaigned solely by way of calls to organization, without even the barest mention of substantive issues.

63. This account is taken from chapters 3–7 of Lucas, "Development of the Second Party System in Mississippi."

64. Olsen, *Political Culture and Secession in Mississippi*.

65. Carey, *Parties, Slavery, and the Union in Antebellum Georgia*, 38.

66. Atkins, *Parties, Politics, and the Sectional Conflict in Tennessee*, 40–54.

67. Ratcliffe's *Party Spirit in a Frontier Republic* is a step in the right direction here.

68. See McCormick, *Second American Party System*.

69. Boritt, *Lincoln and the Economics of the American Dream*.

70. Friedman, *Revolt of the Conservative Democrats*, 105–11.

71. See, e.g., Holt, *Rise and Fall*, 108.

72. See, e.g., Gunderson, *Log-Cabin Campaign*; Chambers, "Election of 1840"; Carey, *Parties, Slavery, and the Union in Antebellum Georgia*, 59–61; Holt, *Rise and Fall*, 108.

73. Carey, *Parties, Slavery, and the Union in Antebellum Georgia*, 78.

74. Brauer, *Cotton versus Conscience*; Michael Morrison, *Slavery and the American West*, 88–93; Carey, *Parties, Slavery, and the Union in Antebellum Georgia*, 71–76.

75. Carwardine, *Evangelicals and Politics in Antebellum America*, 66–68, 84–88, 92–94, 207–9.

76. Thompson, "Attitude of the Western Whigs toward the Convention System," 173.

77. Lincoln, *Collected Works* 1:314.

78. Duncan's response is reprinted in Thompson, "Attitude of the Western Whigs toward the Convention System," 181.

79. Thompson, "Attitude of the Western Whigs toward the Convention System," 186–88.

80. See Pease, *Frontier State*, chap. 15.

81. See, e.g., Lincoln to John Bennett, Mar. 7, 1843, in *Collected Works* 1:318–19; Lincoln to Benjamin F. James, Jan. 14, 1846, in *Collected Works* 2:353.

82. See Holt, *Rise and Fall*, 332. Holt notes and revises the traditional picture of the Whig campaigns of 1840 and 1848 as issueless manipulation.

83. Lincoln, "Speech in United States House of Representatives on the Presidential Question," July 27, 1848, in *Collected Works* 1:501–16.

84. The fact that Tyler did indeed attempt to build a presidential party for himself stands as perhaps the starkest illustration of the capacity of an apparently sincere and rigid devotion to the ideal of antipartyism to serve as the wellspring of highly partisan conduct. Tyler's party building is documented in Lambert, *Presidential Politics in the United States*.

85. Clay, "On Returning to Kentucky."

86. Ibid., 579–82.

87. Ibid., 572.

88. Ibid., 575.

89. Ibid., 582–90.

90. Kennedy, *Defence of the Whigs*.

91. Ibid., part 1, chaps. 4–6.

92. Ibid., 48.

93. Ibid., 48–49, 55.

94. Ibid., part 2, chap. 3.

95. Ibid., 120–22.

96. See also, e.g., Thomas Brown, *Politics and Statesmanship*, which argues the centrality of an antipartisan model of statesmanship throughout the life of the Whig party (esp. chap. 6 on the southern Whigs and Clay in the period before the election of 1844); Carwardine, *Evangelicals and Politics in Antebellum America*, which discusses (usually Whig) evangelicals' moral absolutism and accompanying wariness of parties (e.g., pp. 7–9); and Formisano, *Birth of Mass Political Parties*, *Transformation of Political Culture*, and "Political Character, Antipartyism and the Second Party System," which also detect the persistence of antipartyism as a strong current in Whig thought during the Second Party System.

97. Carwardine, *Evangelicals and Politics in Antebellum America*, 94, quoting Taylor's correspondence.

98. See Ashworth, *"Agrarians" and "Aristocrats"*; Sellers, *Market Revolution*; Thornton, *Politics and Power in a Slave Society*.

99. See Shade, *Banks or No Banks*; Sharp, *Jacksonians versus the Banks*.

100. See, e.g., Michael Morrison, *Slavery and the American West*, 141; Fehrenbacher, *Chicago Giant*, 45–47, 65–68, 76–78; Ashworth, *Slavery, Capitalism, and Politics*, 388–90, 431.

101. Shade, *Banks or No Banks*.

102. This paragraph derives mainly from Sharp, *Jacksonians versus the Banks*.

103. Potter, *Impending Crisis*, 26–27.

104. Ibid., 19–20; Brock, *Parties and Political Conscience*, 174–75; Ashworth, *Slavery, Capitalism, and Politics*, 431; Fehrenbacher, *Chicago Giant*, 45–47, 65–68.

105. Gara, *Presidency of Franklin Pierce*, 87–88; Fehrenbacher, *Chicago Giant*, 131.

106. John M. Palmer to LaFayette McCrillis, Mar. 27, 1843, Palmer Papers, ISHL.

107. Lyman Trumbull to Augustus French, April 2, 1848, French Papers, ISHL.

108. Thornton, *Politics and Power in a Slave Society*, 143.

109. Ibid., 143–45.

110. See Whittington, *Constitutional Construction*, 90–93.

111. Even those Whigs who ranked particular substantive goals as more important than the party's constitutionalism (and perhaps even rejected antipartyism outright) would have rejected, at least publicly, the idea that democracy depended on party obligation as such, on each Whig's willingness to subordinate his own substantive principles to some oxymoronic principle of Whig party obligation.

112. See, e.g., Freehling, *Road to Disunion*, 258.

113. Freehling's *Road to Disunion* describes at great length the specifics of the tension between majoritarianism and slaveholding in the antebellum South, but, of course, a similar tension existed, as I will suggest below, for those antislavery northerners who ultimately identified democracy with the absence of a slave system as much as with numerical majoritarianism. See William E. Nelson, *Roots of Bureaucracy*.

114. Feller, "Brother in Arms," 64–65.

115. Freehling, *Road to Disunion*, 411–18.

116. Ibid., 429. See also chapter 29 of Niven, *Martin Van Buren*, which describes in some detail the largely (although by no means exclusively) southern and even Calhounite impetus behind the adoption of the two-thirds rule.

117. Brock, *Parties and Political Conscience*, 181.

118. Niven, *Martin Van Buren*, 604. The quotation is Niven's characterization of Van Buren's recollections as of 1856.

119. The previous paragraphs have been derived mainly from my reading of chapter 31 of Niven, *Martin Van Buren*; also Cole, *Van Buren and the American Political System*, Brock, *Parties and Political Conscience*, Jaenicke, "American Ideas of Political Party," Chaplain Morrison, *Democratic Politics and Sectionalism*, and Silbey, "Democratic Party and Antislavery Politics."

120. Feller, "Brother in Arms," 71.

121. This is Jaenicke's term. See Jaenicke, "American Ideas of Political Party."

122. Ibid., chap. 14. Note a similar contrast in the divergent approaches to democracy and antislavery taken by Democrat Benjamin Tappan and abolitionist Lewis Tappan, discussed in Feller, "Brother in Arms."

123. Jaenicke, "American Ideas of Political Party," 257.

124. The FSP may also have served as a carrier for the Whig theory of party for some who were disillusioned with the evolution of the Whig organization. Carwardine actually suggests that the FSP was as much an antiparty movement for Whig evangelicals disillusioned with the deterioration of Whig political morality as it was a specifically, substantively antislavery movement. See *Evangelicals and Politics in Antebellum America*, 213–14.

125. Jaenicke, "American Ideas of Political Party," 431–32.

126. The antiparty character of many northern free-soilers has just been discussed. That of the southern fire-eaters constitutes an important theme of Thornton's *Politics and Power in a Slave Society*. See, e.g., pp. 138–39, 184, 194, 383–84. Also see Olsen, *Political Culture and Secession in Mississippi*.

127. Potter, *Impending Crisis*, 112–13.

128. Ashworth, *Slavery, Capitalism, and Politics*, 476–77, points out this alignment. Although this four-part alignment was hardly without exception, it was strong enough to support the contentions of Ashworth, *"Agrarians" and "Aristocrats,"* and Holt, *Political Crisis of the 1850s*, 87–88, that party dynamics remained strong even in the face of the heightened atmosphere of sectional conflict at this time.

129. See also the similar account of the Ohio Van Burenite leader, Benjamin Tappan, in Feller, "Brother in Arms," 71–74.

130. Although in 1850 it did not approach the level that the instigators of the Nashville Convention, for example, would have liked.

131. Ashworth, *Slavery, Capitalism, and Politics*, 448, 489.

132. See Freehling, *Road to Disunion*. Freehling's book actually emphasizes the South's own ambivalence about slavery itself as the source of much of its troubled relationship with the idea of democracy, but the South's consciousness of its status as the minority section in the Union on the slavery question is a major element of Freehling's argument as well.

133. In significant part, this was a repetition, as the chickens came home to roost, of Van Buren's own reconciliation of southern minority interests with majoritarian proceduralism in the original coalescence of the party. See Shade, "'Most Delicate and Exciting Topics.'"

134. Holt, *Political Crisis of the 1850s*, 52, 191.

135. Freehling, *Road to Disunion*, 410; see also 442, 558, 561–62.

136. Thornton, *Politics and Power in a Slave Society*, esp. 458–59.

137. Holt, *Political Crisis of the 1850s*, 101–38.

138. Michael Morrison, *Slavery and the American West*, 136–38.

139. Quoted in Michael Morrison, *Slavery and the American West*, 143. Cf. James L. Huston's characterization of Douglas's view of the Kansas-Nebraska Act as part of a tradition of "democracy by process," in contrast to a tradition in which democracy is defined by particular substantive positions, such as opposition to slavery. Huston, "Democracy by Scripture versus Democracy by Process."

140. This section has relied heavily on Michael Morrison, *Slavery and the American West*, esp. 136–38, 142–43, 146–48.

141. Formisano, *Birth of Mass Political Parties*; Bridges, *City*, 29–32; Anbinder, *Nativism and Slavery*, 103–26.

142. Quoted in Carwardine, *Evangelicals and Politics in Antebellum America*, 11.

143. Holt, *Political Crisis of the 1850s*, 163–69; Anbinder, *Nativism and Slavery*, 115–26.

144. Thornton, *Politics and Power in a Slave Society*, 354; Anbinder, *Nativism and Slavery*, 103, 167–68; Holt, *Political Crisis of the 1850s*, 165–67; Carey, *Parties, Slavery, and the Union in Antebellum Georgia*, 187–89; Olsen, *Political Culture and Secession in Mississippi*, chap. 7.

145. See Anbinder, *Nativism and Slavery*, 52–94, for an account of their early successes.

146. Carey, *Parties, Slavery, and the Union in Antebellum Georgia*, 188–89.

147. See Anbinder, *Nativism and Slavery*, 165–74, for an account of the Philadelphia convention.

148. Van Buren, "Autobiography," 303.

149. Feller, "Brother in Arms," 64 (quoting the 1836 state party platform).

150. Van Buren, *Inquiry*, 348–49; Van Buren, "Thoughts on the approaching election in N. York," Martin Van Buren Papers, Library of Congress.

151. For Van Buren's view that the slavery controversy was distorting the proper constitutional structure of American politics, see, e.g., Van Buren, *Inquiry*, 223, 369–76; Mintz, "Political Ideas of Martin Van Buren," 443–44; Niven, *Martin Van Buren*, 604–7.

152. *Dred Scott v. Sandford*, 60 U.S. 393 (1857).

153. Van Buren, *Inquiry*, 356–58.

154. Ibid., 353.

155. Van Buren, "Autobiography," 184–85, 219; Van Buren, *Inquiry*, 363–66.

156. Van Buren, *Inquiry*, 358–66.

157. Ibid., 374. See also Whittington, "Road Not Taken," for an argument that Justice Curtis, in dissent, had a view of constitutional decisionmaking much like the one I attribute to Van Buren. Whittington, too, sees *Dred Scott* as a kind of revival of *McCulloch*.

158. Van Buren, *Inquiry*, 366–76.

159. Ibid., 375.

160. Currie, *Constitution in the Supreme Court*, 271.

161. See, e.g., Wiecek, *Lost World of Classical Legal Thought*, 124–25.

Ackerman, Bruce. *We the People: Foundations*. Cambridge: Harvard University Press, Belknap Press, 1991.

Aldrich, John H. *Why Parties? The Origins and Transformation of Political Parties in America*. Chicago: University of Chicago Press, 1995.

Altschuler, Glenn C., and Stuart M. Blumin. *Rude Republic: Americans and Their Politics in the Nineteenth Century*. Princeton: Princeton University Press, 2000.

Alvord, Clarence Walworth. *The Illinois Country, 1673–1818*. Chicago: A. C. McClurg, 1922.

Amar, Akhil Reed. *The Bill of Rights: Creation and Reconstruction*. New Haven: Yale University Press, 1998.

———. "The Consent of the Governed: Constitutional Amendment Outside Article V." *Columbia Law Review* 94, no. 2 (1994): 457–508.

Anbinder, Tyler. *Nativism and Slavery: The Northern Know Nothings and the Politics of the 1850's*. New York: Oxford University Press, 1992.

Ashworth, John. *"Agrarians" and "Aristocrats": Party Political Ideology in the United States, 1837–1846*. London: Royal Historical Society, 1983.

———. *Slavery, Capitalism, and Politics in the Antebellum Republic*. Vol. 1, *Commerce and Compromise, 1820–1850*. Cambridge: Cambridge University Press, 1995.

Atkins, Jonathan M. *Parties, Politics, and the Sectional Conflict in Tennessee, 1832–1861*. Knoxville: University of Tennessee Press, 1997.

Bailyn, Bernard. *Ideological Origins of the American Revolution*. Cambridge: Harvard University Press, 1967.

———. *The Origins of American Politics*. New York: Alfred A. Knopf, 1968.

———. "Politics and Social Structure in Virginia." In *Colonial America: Essays in Politics and Social Development*, edited by Stanley N. Katz and John M. Murrin, 207–30. 3rd ed. New York: Alfred A. Knopf, 1983.

Baker, Jean H. *Affairs of Party: The Political Culture of Northern Democrats in the Mid-Nineteenth Century*. Ithaca: Cornell University Press, 1983.

Banning, Lance. *The Jeffersonian Persuasion: Evolution of a Party Ideology*. Ithaca: Cornell University Press, 1978.

Bellamy, Richard. "The Political Form of the Constitution: The Separation of Powers, Rights and Representative Democracy." *Political Studies* 44 (1996): 436–56.

Benson, Lee. *The Concept of Jacksonian Democracy: New York as a Test Case*. Princeton: Princeton University Press, 1961.

Binkley, Wilfred E., and Malcolm C. Moos. *A Grammar of American Politics: The National, State, and Local Governments*. 2nd ed. New York: Alfred A. Knopf, 1952.

Birkbeck, Morris. "An Appeal to the People of Illinois on the Question of a Convention." *Transactions of the Illinois State Historical Society* 10 (1905): 147–63.

Bolingbroke, Henry. *The Idea of a Patriot King* [1749]. Edited by Sydney W. Jackman. Indianapolis: Bobbs-Merrill, 1965.

Bonomi, Patricia U. "'A Just Opposition': The Great Awakening as a Radical Model." In *The Origins of Anglo-American Radicalism*, edited by Margaret Jacob and James Jacob, 243–56. London: George, Allen, and Unwin, 1984.

Boritt, Gabor S. *Lincoln and the Economics of the American Dream*. Memphis: Memphis State University Press, 1978.

Boyer, Paul, and Stephen Nissenbaum. *Salem Possessed: The Social Origins of Witchcraft*. Cambridge: Harvard University Press, 1974.

Brauer, Kinley Jack. *Cotton versus Conscience: Massachusetts Whig Politics and Southwestern Expansion, 1843–1848*. Lexington: University of Kentucky Press, 1967.

Bridges, Amy. *A City in the Republic: Antebellum New York and the Origins of Machine Politics*. New York: Cambridge University Press, 1984.

Brock, William R. *Parties and Political Conscience: American Dilemmas, 1840–1850*. Millwood, N.Y.: KTO Press, 1979.

Brown, Roger. *The Republic in Peril: 1812*. New York: Columbia University Press, 1964.

Brown, Thomas. *Politics and Statesmanship: Essays on the American Whig Party*. New York: Columbia University Press, 1985.

Burke, Edmund. *Thoughts on the Cause of the Present Discontents*. Dublin: M. H. Gill and Son, 1882.

Bushman, Richard L. *From Puritan to Yankee: Character and Social Order in Connecticut, 1690–1765*. Cambridge: Harvard University Press, 1967.

———. *King and People in Provincial Massachusetts*. Chapel Hill: University of North Carolina Press, 1985.

Carey, Anthony Gene. *Parties, Slavery, and the Union in Antebellum Georgia*. Athens: University of Georgia Press, 1997.

Carwardine, Richard J. *Evangelicals and Politics in Antebellum America*. New Haven: Yale University Press, 1993.

Cayton, Andrew R. L. *The Frontier Republic: Ideology and Politics in the Ohio Country, 1780–1825*. Kent, Ohio: Kent State University Press, 1986.

Cayton, Andrew R. L., and Peter S. Onuf. *The Midwest and the Nation*. Bloomington: Indiana University Press, 1990.

Ceaser, James W. *Presidential Selection: Theory and Development*. Princeton: Princeton University Press, 1979.

Chambers, William Nisbet. "The Election of 1840." In *History of American Presidential Elections, 1789–1968*, edited by Arthur Schlesinger, Jr., 643–90. New York: Chelsea House, 1971.

———. *Political Parties in a New Nation*. New York: Oxford University Press, 1963.

Charles, Joseph. *The Origins of the American Party System*. Williamsburg, Va.: Institute of Early American History and Culture, 1956.

Chase, James S. *Emergence of the Presidential Nominating Convention, 1789–1832*. Urbana: University of Illinois Press, 1973.

Clark, J. C. D. *English Society, 1688–1832: Ideology, Social Structure, and Political Practice during the Ancien Regime*. Cambridge: Cambridge University Press, 1985.

———. "A General Theory of Party, Opposition and Government, 1688–1832." *Historical Journal* 23, no. 2 (June 1980): 295–325.

Clay, Henry. "On Returning to Kentucky." In *The Life and Speeches of Henry Clay*, edited by James B. Swain, 2:560–90. New York: Greeley and McElrath, 1844.

Cole, Donald B. *Martin Van Buren and the American Political System*. Princeton: Princeton University Press, 1984.

Cook, Charles. *The American Codification Movement: A Study of Antebellum Legal Reform*. Westport, Conn.: Greenwood Press, 1981.

Cornell, Saul. *The Other Founders: Anti-Federalism and the Dissenting Tradition in America, 1788–1828.* Chapel Hill: University of North Carolina Press, 1999.

Cover, Robert M. *Justice Accused: Antislavery and the Judicial Process.* New Haven: Yale University Press, 1975.

Crofts, Daniel W. *Old Southampton: Politics and Society in a Virginia County, 1834–1869.* Charlottesville: University Press of Virginia, 1992.

Cunningham, Noble E., Jr. *The Jeffersonian Republicans in Power: Party Operations, 1801–1809.* Chapel Hill: University of North Carolina Press, 1963.

Currie, David P. "Choosing the Pilot: Proposed Amendments to the Presidential Election Process, 1809–1829." *Green Bag 2d* 4 (2001): 141–46.

————. *The Constitution in the Supreme Court: The First Hundred Years, 1789–1888.* Chicago: University of Chicago Press, 1985.

Dargo, George. "Parties and the Transformation of the Constitutional Idea in Revolutionary Pennsylvania." In *Party and Political Opposition in Revolutionary America,* edited by Patricia U. Bonomi, 98–114. Tarrytown, N.Y.: Sleepy Hollow Press, 1980.

Davis, James E. *Frontier Illinois.* Bloomington: Indiana University Press, 1998.

Davis, Rodney Owen. "Illinois Legislators and Jacksonian Democracy, 1834–1841." Ph.D. diss., University of Iowa, 1966.

————. "Partisanship in Jacksonian State Politics: Party Divisions in the Illinois State Legislature, 1834–1841." In *Quantification in American History,* edited by Robert P. Swierenga, 149–62. New York: Atheneum, 1970.

————. "'The People in Miniature': The Illinois General Assembly, 1818–1848." *Illinois Historical Journal* 81, no. 2 (Summer 1988): 95–108.

Devins, Neal. "How Constitutional Law Casebooks Perpetuate the Myth of Judicial Supremacy." *Green Bag 2d* 3 (Spring 2000): 259–65.

Douglas, Stephen A. *The Letters of Stephen A. Douglas.* Edited by Robert Johannsen. Urbana: University of Illinois Press, 1961.

Doyle, Don Harrison. *The Social Order of a Frontier Community: Jacksonville, Illinois, 1825–1870.* Urbana: University of Illinois Press, 1978.

Dunbar, Louise Burnham. "A Study of Monarchical Tendencies in the United States from 1776 to 1801." In *University of Illinois Studies in Social Sciences* 10, no. 1 (March 1922).

Duverger, Maurice. *Political Parties: Their Organization and Activity in the Modern State.* 3rd ed. New York: John Wiley and Sons, 1963.

Edwards, Ninian W. *History of Illinois, from 1778–1833; and Life and Times of Ninian Edwards.* Springfield: Illinois State Journal Co., 1870.

————. "Two Letters from Governor Ninian Edwards." *Journal of the Illinois State Historical Society* 2 (July 1909): 51–54.

Egnal, Marc. "The Beards Were Right: Parties in the North, 1840–1860." *Civil War History* 47, no. 1 (March 2001): 30–56.

Ekirch, A. Roger. *"Poor Carolina": Politics and Society in Colonial North Carolina, 1729–1776.* Chapel Hill: University of North Carolina Press, 1981.

Elkins, Stanley, and Eric McKitrick. *The Age of Federalism.* New York: Oxford University Press, 1993.

Ellis, Richard E. *The Jeffersonian Crisis: Courts and Politics in the Young Republic.* New York: Oxford University Press, 1971.

————. "The Persistence of Antifederalism after 1789." In *Beyond Confederation: Origins of the Constitution and American National Identity,* edited by Richard Beeman,

Stephen Botein, and Edward C. Carter III, 295–314. Chapel Hill: University of North Carolina Press, 1987.

———. *The Union at Risk: Jacksonian Democracy, States' Rights, and the Nullification Crisis.* New York: Oxford University Press, 1987.

Ely, James W., Jr. "The Oxymoron Reconsidered: Myth and Reality in the Origins of Substantive Due Process." *Constitutional Commentary* 16 (Summer 1999): 315–45.

Etcheson, Nicole. "Private Interest and the Public Good: Upland Southerners and Antebellum Midwestern Political Culture." In *The Pursuit of Public Power: Political Culture in Ohio,* edited by Jeffrey P. Brown and Andrew R. L. Cayton, 83–98. Kent, Ohio: Kent State University Press, 1994.

Ethington, Philip J. *The Public City: The Political Construction of Urban Life in San Francisco, 1850–1900.* New York: Cambridge University Press, 1994.

Faragher, John Mack. *Sugar Creek: Life on the Illinois Prairie.* New Haven: Yale University Press, 1986.

The Federalist. Edited by Benjamin Fletcher Wright. Cambridge: Harvard University Press, 1961.

Fehrenbacher, Don E. *Chicago Giant: A Biography of "Long John" Wentworth.* Madison, Wisc.: American History Research Center, 1957.

———. *The Dred Scott Case: Its Significance in American Law and Politics.* New York: Oxford University Press, 1978.

Feller, Daniel. "A Brother in Arms: Benjamin Tappan and the Antislavery Democracy." *Journal of American History* 88 (June 2001): 48–74.

———. *The Jacksonian Promise: America, 1815–1840.* Baltimore: Johns Hopkins University Press, 1995.

———. "Politics and Society: Toward a Jacksonian Synthesis." *Journal of the Early Republic* 10, no. 2 (Summer 1990): 131–61.

———. *The Public Lands in Jacksonian Politics.* Madison: University of Wisconsin Press, 1984.

Fischer, David Hackett. *The Revolution of American Conservatism: The Federalist Party in the Era of Jeffersonian Democracy.* New York: Harper and Row, 1965.

Fisher, Louis. *Constitutional Dialogues: Interpretation as Political Process.* Princeton: Princeton University Press, 1988.

Fisher, Louis, and Neal Devins. *Political Dynamics of Constitutional Law.* St. Paul, Minn.: West Publishing Co., 1992.

Ford, Lacy K. "Inventing the Concurrent Majority: Madison, Calhoun, and the Problem of Majoritarianism in American Political Thought." *Journal of Southern History* 60 (February 1994): 19–58.

Forderhase, Rudolph Eugene. "Jacksonianism in Missouri: From Predilection to Party, 1820–1836." Ph.D. diss., University of Missouri, 1968.

Formisano, Ronald P. *The Birth of Mass Political Parties, Michigan, 1827–1861.* Princeton: Princeton University Press, 1971.

———. "Deferential-Participant Politics: The Early Republic's Political Culture, 1789–1840." *American Political Science Review* 68, no. 2 (June 1974): 473–87.

———. "Federalists and Republicans: Parties, Yes—System, No." In *The Evolution of American Electoral Systems,* edited by Paul Kleppner, 33–76. Westport, Conn.: Greenwood, 1981.

———. "The New Political History and the Election of 1840." *Journal of Interdisciplinary History* 23, no. 4 (Spring 1993): 661–82.

———. "The 'Party Period' Revisited." *Journal of American History* 86, no. 1 (June 1999): 93–120.

———. "Political Character, Antipartyism and the Second Party System." *American Quarterly* 26 (Winter 1969): 683–709.

———. *The Transformation of Political Culture: Massachusetts Parties, 1790s–1840s.* New York: Oxford University Press, 1983.

Fox, Stephen C. "The Bank Wars, the Idea of 'Party,' and the Division of the Electorate in Jacksonian Ohio." *Ohio History* 88 (Summer 1979): 253–76.

Freehling, William W. *Prelude to Civil War: The Nullification Controversy in South Carolina, 1816–1836.* New York: Harper and Row, 1966.

———. *The Road to Disunion.* New York: Oxford University Press, 1990.

———. "Spoilsmen and Interests in the Thought and Career of John C. Calhoun." *Journal of American History* 52 (June 1965): 25–42.

Freyer, Tony A. *Producers versus Capitalists: Constitutional Conflict in Antebellum America.* Charlottesville: University Press of Virginia, 1994.

Friedman, Jean E. *The Revolt of the Conservative Democrats: An Essay on American Political Culture and Political Development, 1837–1844.* Ann Arbor: UMI Research Press, 1979.

Fritz, Christian G. "A Constitutional Middle Ground between Revision and Revolution: A Reevaluation of the Nullification Crisis and the Virginia and Kentucky Resolutions through the Lens of Popular Sovereignty." In *Law as Culture and Culture as Law: Essays in Honor of John Philip Reid*, edited by Hendrik Hartog and William E. Nelson, 158–226. Madison, Wisc.: Madison House, 2000.

Gara, Larry. *The Presidency of Franklin Pierce.* Lawrence: University Press of Kansas, 1991.

Gerring, John. "A Chapter in the History of American Party Ideology: The Nineteenth-Century Democratic Party (1828–1892)." *Polity* 26, no. 4 (Summer 1994): 729–68.

———. "Party Ideology in America: The National-Republican Chapter, 1828–1924." *Studies in American Political Development* 11 (Spring 1997): 44–108.

Goodman, Paul. "The First American Party System." In *The American Party Systems: Stages of Political Development*, edited by William Nisbet Chambers and Walter Dean Burnham, 56–89. 2nd ed. New York: Oxford University Press, 1975.

Gordon, Scott. *Controlling the State: Constitutionalism from Ancient Athens to Today.* Cambridge: Harvard University Press, 1999.

Graber, Mark A. "Federalist or Friends of Adams: The Marshall Court and Party Politics." *Studies in American Political Development* 12 (Fall 1998): 229–66.

Gunderson, Robert Gray. *The Log-Cabin Campaign.* Lexington: University of Kentucky Press, 1957.

Gunn, J. A. W. *Factions No More: Attitudes to Party in Government and Opposition in Eighteenth-Century England.* London: F. Cass, 1972.

———. "Influence, Parties and the Constitution: Changing Attitudes, 1783–1832." *Historical Journal* 17, no. 2 (June 1974): 301–46.

Hall, Kermit L. "The Judiciary on Trial: State Constitutional Reform and the Rise of an Elected Judiciary, 1846–1860." *The Historian* 45, no. 3 (1983): 337–54.

Hanyan, Craig, with Mary L. Hanyan. *De Witt Clinton and the Rise of the People's Men.* Montreal: McGill-Queen's University Press, 1996.

Hatch, Nathan O. *The Democratization of American Christianity.* New Haven: Yale University Press, 1989.

Heale, M. J. *The Making of American Politics, 1750–1850*. London: Longman, 1977.

Hébert, Paul David. "The Emergence of the Democratic Party in Illinois, 1828–1838." M.A. thesis, University of Illinois, 1963.

Henry, John. "The Memoirs of John Henry." Edited by C. H. Rammelkamp. *Journal of the Illinois State Historical Society* 18 (April 1925): 39–75.

Hill, B. W. "Executive Monarchy and the Challenge of Parties, 1689–1832: Two Concepts of Government and Two Historiographical Interpretations." *Historical Journal* 13, no. 3 (September 1970): 379–401.

Hofstadter, Richard. *The Idea of a Party System: The Rise of Legitimate Opposition in the United States, 1780–1840*. Berkeley: University of California Press, 1969.

Holt, Michael F. *Political Crisis of the 1850's*. New York: Wiley, 1978.

———. *The Rise and Fall of the American Whig Party: Jacksonian Politics and the Onset of the Civil War*. New York: Oxford University Press, 1999.

Hoogenboom, Ari. *Outlawing the Spoils: A History of the Civil Service Reform Movement, 1865–1883*. Urbana: University of Illinois Press, 1968.

Horwitz, Morton J. *The Transformation of American Law, 1780–1860*. Cambridge: Harvard University Press, 1977.

Howe, Daniel Walker. "The Evangelical Movement and Political Culture in the North during the Second Party System." *Journal of American History* 77, no. 4 (March 1991): 1216–39.

———. *The Political Culture of the American Whigs*. Chicago: University of Chicago Press, 1979.

Hume, David. "Of Parties in General." In *Essays: Moral, Political and Literary*, edited by Eugene F. Miller, 54–63. Indianapolis: Liberty Classics, 1987.

Huntington, Samuel P. *Political Order in Changing Societies*. New Haven: Yale University Press, 1968.

Hurst, James Willard. *The Growth of American Law: The Law Makers*. Boston: Little, Brown, 1950.

———. *Law and Social Order in the United States*. Ithaca: Cornell University Press, 1977.

———. *Law and the Conditions of Freedom in the Nineteenth-Century United States*. Madison: University of Wisconsin Press, 1956.

———. *The Legitimacy of the Business Corporation in the Law of the United States, 1780–1970*. Charlottesville: University Press of Virginia, 1970.

Huston, James L. "Democracy by Scripture versus Democracy by Process: A Reflection on Stephen A. Douglas and Popular Sovereignty." *Civil War History* 43, no. 3 (1997): 189–200.

———. *Securing the Fruits of Labor: The American Concept of Wealth Distribution, 1765–1900*. Baton Rouge: Louisiana State University Press, 1998.

Hyman, Harold M., and William M. Wiecek. *Equal Justice under Law: Constitutional Development, 1835–1875*. New York: Harper and Row, 1982.

Jaenicke, Douglas W. "American Ideas of Political Party as Theories of Politics: Competing Theories of Liberty and Community." Ph.D. diss., Cornell University, 1981.

———. "The Jacksonian Integration of Parties into the Constitutional System." *Political Science Quarterly* 101, no. 1 (1986): 85–107.

Jay, Stewart. *Most Humble Servants: The Advisory Role of Early Judges*. New Haven: Yale University Press, 1997.

Jensen, Richard J. *Illinois: A Bicentennial History*. New York: Norton, 1978.

Johannsen, Robert W. *Stephen A. Douglas*. New York: Oxford University Press, 1973.

John, Richard R. "Governmental Institutions as Agents of Change: Rethinking American Political Development in the Early Republic, 1787–1835." *Studies in American Political Development* 11 (Fall 1997): 347–80.

———. *Spreading the News: The American Postal System from Franklin to Morse.* Cambridge: Harvard University Press, 1995.

Kammen, Michael. *Colonial New York: A History.* New York: Scribners, 1975.

Kemp, Betty. *Sir Robert Walpole.* London: Weidenfeld and Nicholson, 1976.

[Kennedy, John Pendleton.] *Defence of the Whigs.* New York: Harper and Brothers, 1844.

Ketcham, Ralph. *Presidents above Party: The First American Presidency, 1789–1829.* Chapel Hill: University of North Carolina Press, 1984.

Killenbeck, Mark R. "Pursuing the Great Experiment: Reserved Powers in a Post-Ratification, Compound Republic." *Supreme Court Review* 1999, no. 2: 81–140.

Kishlansky, Mark A. *Parliamentary Selection: Social and Political Choice in Early Modern England.* Cambridge: Cambridge University Press, 1986.

Kleppner, Paul. *The Third Electoral System, 1853–1892: Parties, Voters, and Political Cultures.* Chapel Hill: University of North Carolina Press, 1979.

Knupfer, Peter B. *The Union as It Is: Constitutional Union and Sectional Compromise, 1787–1861.* Chapel Hill: University of North Carolina Press, 1991.

Kohl, Lawrence Frederick. *The Politics of Individualism: Parties and the American Character in the Jacksonian Era.* New York: Oxford University Press, 1989.

Kramer, Larry. "But When Exactly Was Judicially Enforced Federalism 'Born' in the First Place?" *Harvard Journal of Law and Public Policy* 22 (Fall 1998): 215–93.

———. "Madison's Audience." *Harvard Law Review* 112 (January 1999): 611–79.

———. "Putting the Politics Back into the Political Safeguards of Federalism." *Columbia Law Review* 100, no. 1 (January 2000): 215–93.

———. "We the Court." *Harvard Law Review* 115 (November 2001): 4–169.

Kramnick, Isaac. *Bolingbroke and His Circle: The Politics of Nostalgia in the Age of Walpole.* Cambridge: Harvard University Press, 1968.

Krueger, David Walter. "Party Development in Indiana, 1800–1832." Ph.D. diss., University of Kentucky, 1974.

Kruman, Marc W. *Parties and Politics in North Carolina, 1836–1865.* Baton Rouge: Louisiana State University Press, 1983.

———. "The Second American Party System and the Transformation of Revolutionary Republicanism." *Journal of the Early Republic* 12, no. 4 (Winter 1992): 509–37.

Lambert, Oscar Doane. *Presidential Politics in the United States, 1841–1844.* Durham, N.C.: Duke University Press, 1936.

Latner, Richard B. *The Presidency of Andrew Jackson: White House Politics, 1829–1837.* Athens: University of Georgia Press, 1979.

Leichtle, Kurt E. "Edward Coles, An Agrarian on the Frontier." Ph.D. diss., University of Illinois–Chicago Circle, 1982.

———. "The Rise of Jacksonian Politics in Illinois." *Illinois Historical Journal* 82, no. 2 (Summer 1989): 93–107.

Leonard, Gerald. "Antiparty Origins of the Party System: Michigan and the Nation." Unpublished manuscript.

"Letters to Gustave Koerner, 1837–1863." *Transactions of the Illinois State Historical Society* 12 (1907).

Levine, Peter D. *The Behavior of State Legislative Parties in the Jacksonian Era: New Jersey, 1829–1844.* Rutherford, N.J.: Fairleigh Dickinson University Press, 1977.

Liddle, William D. "'A Patriot King or None': Lord Bolingbroke and the American Renunciation of George III." *Journal of American History* 65, no. 4 (March 1979): 951–70.

Lincoln, Abraham. *The Collected Works of Abraham Lincoln.* Edited by Roy P. Basler. New Brunswick: Rutgers University Press, 1953.

Lockridge, Kenneth. *A New England Town. The First Hundred Years: Dedham, Massachusetts, 1636–1736.* New York: Norton, 1970.

Lowenstein, Daniel Hays. "Associational Rights of Major Political Parties: A Skeptical Inquiry." *Texas Law Review* 71 (June 1993): 1741–92.

Lucas, Melvin Philip. "The Development of the Second Party System in Mississippi, 1817–1846." Ph.D. diss., Cornell University, 1983.

Magliocca, Gerard N. "Veto: The Jacksonian Revolution in Constitutional Law." *Nebraska Law Review* 78 (1999): 205–62.

Maier, Pauline. *From Resistance to Revolution: Colonial Radicals and the Development of American Opposition to Britain, 1765–1776.* New York: Alfred A. Knopf, 1972.

Main, Jackson Turner. *Political Parties before the Constitution.* Chapel Hill: University of North Carolina Press, 1973.

Mansfield, Harvey C., Jr. *Statesmanship and Party Government: A Study of Burke and Bolingbroke.* Chicago: University of Chicago Press, 1965.

———. "Thomas Jefferson." In *American Political Thought: The Philosophic Dimension of American Statesmanship*, edited by Morton J. Frisch and Richard G. Stevens, 23–50. Chicago: Scribner's Sons, 1971.

Marshall, Lynn L. "The Strange Stillbirth of the Whig Party." *American Historical Review* 72 (January 1967): 445–68.

Marston, Jerrilyn Greene. *King and Congress: The Transfer of Political Legitimacy, 1774–1776.* Princeton: Princeton University Press, 1987.

McCormick, Richard L. *The Party Period and Public Policy: American Politics from the Age of Jackson to the Progressive Era.* New York: Oxford University Press, 1986.

McCormick, Richard P. *The Second American Party System: Party Formation in the Jacksonian Era.* Chapel Hill: University of North Carolina Press, 1966.

———. "Was There a 'Whig Strategy' in 1836?" *Journal of the Early Republic* 4 (Spring 1984): 47–70.

McDonald, Forrest. *States' Rights and the Union: Imperio in Imperio, 1776–1876.* Lawrence: University Press of Kansas, 2000.

Mering, John Vollmer. *The Whig Party in Missouri.* Columbia: University of Missouri Press, 1967.

Milkis, Sidney M. *Political Parties and Constitutional Government: Remaking American Democracy.* Baltimore: Johns Hopkins University Press, 1999.

Mintz, Max M. "The Political Ideas of Martin Van Buren." *New York History* 30 (1949): 422–48.

Morrison, Chaplain. *Democratic Politics and Sectionalism: The Wilmot Proviso Controversy.* Chapel Hill: University of North Carolina Press, 1967.

Morrison, Michael A. *Slavery and the American West: The Eclipse of Manifest Destiny and the Coming of the Civil War.* Chapel Hill: University of North Carolina Press, 1997.

Mushkat, Jerome, and Joseph G. Rayback. *Martin Van Buren: Law, Politics, and the Shaping of Republican Ideology.* DeKalb: Northern Illinois University Press, 1997.

Nedelsky, Jennifer. *Private Property and the Limits of American Constitutionalism: The Madisonian Framework and Its Legacy.* Chicago: University of Chicago Press, 1990.

Nelson, Caleb. "A Re-Evaluation of Scholarly Explanations for the Rise of the Elective Judiciary in Antebellum America." *American Journal of Legal History* 37 (1993): 190–224.

Nelson, William E. *The Fourteenth Amendment: From Political Principle to Judicial Doctrine.* Cambridge: Harvard University Press, 1988.

———. *The Roots of American Bureaucracy, 1830–1900.* Cambridge: Harvard University Press, 1982.

Newcomb, Benjamin H. *Political Partisanship in the American Middle Colonies, 1700–1776.* Baton Rouge: Louisiana State University Press, 1995.

Newmyer, R. Kent. "Harvard Law School, New England Legal Culture, and the Antebellum Origins of American Jurisprudence." *Journal of American History* 74, no. 3 (December 1987): 814–35.

———. "John Marshall and the Southern Constitutional Tradition." In *An Uncertain Tradition: Constitutionalism and the History of the South*, edited by Kermit L. Hall and James W. Ely, 105–24. Athens: University of Georgia Press, 1989.

———. *Supreme Court Justice Joseph Story: Statesman of the Old Republic.* Chapel Hill: University of North Carolina Press, 1985.

Nichols, Roy F. *The Invention of the American Political Parties.* New York: Macmillan, 1967.

Niven, John. *Martin Van Buren: The Romantic Age of American Politics.* New York: Oxford University Press, 1983.

Novak, William J. "Law, Capitalism, and the Liberal State: The Historical Sociology of James Willard Hurst." *Law and History Review* 18, no. 1 (Spring 2000): 97–145.

———. *The People's Welfare: Law and Regulation in Nineteenth-Century America.* Chapel Hill: University of North Carolina Press, 1996.

O'Gorman, Frank. *Voters, Patrons, and Parties: The Unreformed Electoral System of Hanoverian England, 1734–1832.* New York: Oxford University Press, 1989.

Olsen, Christopher J. *Political Culture and Secession in Mississippi: Masculinity, Honor, and the Antiparty Tradition, 1830–1860.* New York: Oxford University Press, 2000.

Onuf, Peter S. *Jefferson's Empire: The Language of American Nationhood.* Charlottesville: University Press of Virginia, 2000.

Palmer, R. R. "Notes on the Use of the Word 'Democracy,' 1789–1799." *Political Science Quarterly* 68, no. 2 (June 1953): 203–26.

Pasley, Jeffrey L. "'A Journeyman Either in Law or in Politics': John Beckley and the Social Origins of Political Campaigning." *Journal of the Early Republic* 16, no. 4 (Winter 1996): 531–69.

Patterson, Stephen E. *Political Parties in Revolutionary Massachusetts.* Madison: University of Wisconsin Press, 1973.

Peabody, Bruce G. "Coordinate Construction, Constitutional Thickness, and Remembering the Lyre of Orpheus." *University of Pennsylvania Journal of Constitutional Law* 2, no. 3 (April 2000): 662–75.

Pease, Theodore Calvin. *The Frontier State, 1818–1848.* Springfield: Illinois Centennial Commission, 1918.

———, ed. *Illinois Election Returns, 1818–1848.* Carbondale: Southern Illinois University Press, 1923.

Persily, Nathaniel, and Bruce E. Cain. "The Legal Status of Political Parties: A Reassessment of Competing Paradigms." *Columbia Law Review* 100 (April 2000): 775–812.

Plumb, J. H. *The Origins of Political Stability: The Growth of Political Stability in England, 1675–1725.* London: Macmillan, 1967.

Pocock, Emil. "'A Candidate I'll Surely Be': Election Practices in Early Ohio, 1798–1825." In *The Pursuit of Public Power: Political Culture in Ohio, 1787–1861*, edited by Jeffrey Brown and Andrew R. L. Cayton, 49–68. Kent, Ohio: Kent State University Press, 1994.

Potter, David Morris. *The Impending Crisis, 1848–1861*. New York: Harper and Row, 1976.

Prince, Carl. *The Federalists and the Origins of the United States Civil Service*. New York: New York University Press, 1977.

Putnam, Elizabeth Duncan. "The Life and Services of Joseph Duncan, Governor of Illinois, 1834–1838." *Transactions of the Illinois State Historical Society* 26 (1919): 107–87.

Rakove, Jack N. *Original Meanings: Politics and Ideas in the Making of the Constitution*. New York: Alfred A. Knopf, 1996.

Ranney, Austin. *Curing the Mischiefs of Faction: Party Reform in America*. Berkeley: University of California Press, 1975.

Ratcliffe, Donald J. *Party Spirit in a Frontier Republic: Democratic Politics in Ohio, 1793–1821*. Columbus: Ohio State University Press, 1998.

Reichley, A. James. *The Life of the Parties: A History of American Political Parties*. New York: Free Press, 1992.

Remini, Robert V. *Andrew Jackson and the Bank War: A Study in the Growth of Presidential Power*. New York: Norton, 1967.

———. *The Election of Andrew Jackson*. Westport, Conn.: Greenwood Press, 1980.

———. "The Election of 1832." In *The History of American Presidential Elections, 1789–1968*, edited by Arthur M. Schlesinger, Jr., 495–516. New York: Chelsea House, 1971.

———. *Martin Van Buren and the Making of the Democratic Party*. New York: Columbia University Press, 1959.

Reynolds, John. *My Own Times: Embracing also the History of My Life*. Belleville, Ill.: [printed by B. H. Perryman and H. L. Davison], 1855.

Richardson, James D., ed. *A Compilation of the Messages and Papers of the Presidents*. New York: Bureau of National Literature, 1897–1916.

Rohrbough, Malcolm J. *The Land Office Business: The Settlement and Administration of American Public Lands, 1789–1837*. New York: Oxford University Press, 1968.

Schattschneider, E. E. *Party Government*. New York: Holt, Rinehart and Winston, 1942.

Scheiber, Harry N. "Federalism and the American Economic Order, 1789–1910." *Law and Society Review* 10, nos. 1–2 (Fall 1975–Winter 1976): 57–118.

———. "Federalism and the Processes of Governance in Hurst's Legal History." *Law and History Review* 18, no. 1 (Spring 2000): 205–14.

———. "Private Rights and Public Power: American Law, Capitalism, and the Republican Polity in Nineteenth-Century America." *Yale Law Journal* 107 (December 1997): 847–61.

Schlesinger, Arthur M., Jr., ed. *History of American Presidential Elections, 1789–1968*. Vol. 1. New York: Chelsea House, 1971.

Sellers, Charles. *The Market Revolution: Jacksonian America, 1815–1846*. New York: Oxford University Press, 1991.

Shade, William G. *Banks or No Banks: The Money Issue in Western Politics, 1832–1865*. Detroit: Wayne State University Press, 1972.

———. *Democratizing the Old Dominion: Virginia and the Second Party System, 1824–1861*. Charlottesville: University Press of Virginia, 1996.

———. "'The Most Delicate and Exciting Topics': Martin Van Buren, Slavery, and the Election of 1836." *Journal of the Early Republic* 18, no. 3 (Fall 1998): 459–84.

———. "Political Pluralism and Party Development: The Creation of a Modern Party System, 1815–1852." In *The Evolution of American Electoral Systems*, edited by Paul Kleppner et al., 77–111. Westport, Conn.: Greenwood Press, 1981.

Sharp, James Roger. *The Jacksonians versus the Banks: Politics in the States after the Panic of 1837*. New York: Columbia University Press, 1970.

Silbey, Joel H. *The American Political Nation, 1838–1893*. Stanford: Stanford University Press, 1991.

———. *The Partisan Imperative: The Dynamics of American Politics before the Civil War*. New York: Oxford University Press, 1985.

———. "'There Are Other Questions Beside That of Slavery Merely': The Democratic Party and Antislavery Politics." In *The Partisan Imperative: The Dynamics of American Politics before the Civil War*, 87–115. New York: Oxford University Press, 1985.

Simeone, James. *Democracy and Slavery in Frontier Illinois: The Bottomland Republic*. DeKalb: Northern Illinois University Press, 2000.

Skowronek, Stephen. *Building a New American State: The Expansion of National Administrative Capacities, 1877–1920*. Cambridge: Cambridge University Press, 1982.

Snowiss, Sylvia. *Judicial Review and the Law of the Constitution*. New Haven: Yale University Press, 1990.

Snyder, John F. *Adam W. Snyder and His Period in Illinois History, 1817–1842* [1906]. Ann Arbor: University Microfilms, 1968.

Sproat, John G. *"The Best Men": Liberal Reformers in the Gilded Age*. New York: Oxford University Press, 1968.

Storing, Herbert J. *What the Anti-Federalists Were For*. Chicago: University of Chicago Press, 1981.

Stourzh, Gerald. *Alexander Hamilton and the Idea of Republican Government*. Stanford: Stanford University Press, 1970.

Stroble, Paul E., Jr. *High on the Okaw's Western Bank: Vandalia, Illinois, 1819–39*. Urbana: University of Illinois Press, 1992.

Sunstein, Cass R. "Interest Groups in American Public Law." *Stanford Law Review* 38, no. 1 (1985): 29–87.

Temin, Peter. *The Jacksonian Economy*. New York: Norton, 1969.

Thompson, C. M. "Attitude of the Western Whigs toward the Convention System." *Proceedings of the Mississippi Valley Historical Association* 5 (1911–12): 167–89.

———. "Elections and Election Machinery in Illinois, 1818–1848." *Journal of the Illinois State Historical Society* 7, no. 4 (January 1915): 379–88.

———. "Genesis of the Whig Party in Illinois." *Transactions of the Illinois State Historical Society* 17 (1912): 86–92.

Thornton, J. Mills, III. *Politics and Power in a Slave Society: Alabama, 1800–1860*. Baton Rouge: Louisiana State University Press, 1978.

Thorpe, Francis Newton, ed. *The Federal and State Constitutions, Colonial Charters, and Other Organic Laws of the States, Territories, and Colonies Now or Heretofore Forming the United States of America*. Vol. 2. Washington, D.C.: Government Printing Office, 1909.

Tully, Alan. *Forming American Politics: Ideals, Interests, and Institutions in Colonial New York and Pennsylvania*. Baltimore: Johns Hopkins University Press, 1994.

Van Buren, Martin. "The Autobiography of Martin Van Buren." In *Annual Report of the American Historical Association for the Year 1918*, edited by John C. Fitzpatrick, vol. 2. Washington, D.C.: Government Printing Office, 1920.

———. *Inquiry into the Origin and Course of Political Parties in the United States*. New York: Hurd and Houghton, 1867.

Varon, Elizabeth R. "Tippecanoe and the Ladies, Too: White Women and Party Politics in Antebellum Virginia." *Journal of American History* 82 (September 1995): 494–521.

———. *We Mean to Be Counted: White Women and Politics in Antebellum Virginia*. Chapel Hill: University of North Carolina Press, 1998.

Vos-Hubbard, Mark. "The 'Third Party Tradition' Reconsidered: Third Parties and American Public Life, 1830–1900." *Journal of American History* 86, no. 1 (June 1999): 121–50.

Wallace, Michael L. "Changing Concepts of Party in the United States: New York, 1815–1828." *American Historical Review* 74 (December 1968): 453–91.

———. "Ideologies of Party in the Ante-Bellum Republic." Ph.D. diss., Columbia University, 1973.

Ward, John William. *Andrew Jackson: Symbol for an Age*. New York: Oxford University Press, 1955.

Washburne, E. B. *Edwards Papers*. Chicago: Fergus Printing Co., 1884.

———. *Sketch of Edward Coles: Second Governor of Illinois, and of the Slavery Struggle of 1823–4*. Chicago: Jansen, McClurg & Co., 1882.

Watson, Harry L. *Jacksonian Politics and Community Conflict: The Emergence of the Second American Party System in Cumberland County, North Carolina*. Baton Rouge: Louisiana State University Press, 1981.

———. *Liberty and Power: The Politics of Jacksonian America*. New York: Hill and Wang, 1990.

Whittington, Keith. *Constitutional Construction: Divided Powers and Constitutional Meaning*. Cambridge: Harvard University Press, 1999.

———. "The Road Not Taken: *Dred Scott*, Judicial Authority, and Political Questions." *Journal of Politics* 63 (2001): 365–91.

Wiecek, William W. *The Lost World of Classical Legal Thought*. New York: Oxford University Press, 1998.

Williamson, Chilton. *American Suffrage: From Property to Democracy, 1760–1860*. Princeton: Princeton University Press, 1960.

Wilson, Major L. *The Presidency of Martin Van Buren*. Lawrence: University Press of Kansas, 1984.

———. "Republicanism and the Idea of Party in the Jacksonian Period." *Journal of the Early Republic* 8, no. 4 (Winter 1988): 419–42.

———. *Space, Time, and Freedom: The Quest for Nationality and the Irrepressible Conflict, 1815–1861*. Westport, Conn.: Greenwood Press, 1973.

Winkle, Kenneth J. "The Second Party System in Lincoln's Springfield." *Civil War History* 44 (December 1998): 267–84.

Winkler, Adam. "Voters' Rights and Parties' Wrongs: Early Political Party Regulation in the State Courts, 1886–1915." *Columbia Law Review* 100 (April 2000): 873–99.

Winthrop, John. "A Modell of Christian Charity." In *An American Primer*, edited by Daniel J. Boorstin, 1:8–25. Chicago: University of Chicago Press, 1966.

Wood, Gordon S. *The Creation of the American Republic: 1776–1787*. Chapel Hill: University of North Carolina Press, 1969.

———. "Interests and Disinterestedness in the Making of the Constitution." In *Beyond*

Confederation: Origins of the Constitution and American National Identity, edited by Richard Beeman et al., 69–109. Chapel Hill: University of North Carolina Press, 1987.

———. *The Radicalism of the American Revolution*. New York: Alfred A. Knopf, 1992.

Zuckerman, Michael. *Peaceable Kingdoms: New England Towns in the Eighteenth Century*. New York: Alfred A. Knopf, 1970.

———. "The Social Context of Democracy in Massachusetts." In *Colonial America: Essays in Politics and Social Development*, edited by Stanley N. Katz and John M. Murrin, 375–93. 3rd ed. New York: Alfred A. Knopf, 1983.